Esotericism & Narrative
The Occult Fiction of Charles Williams

Aren Roukema

APOCRYPHILE
PRESS

Apocryphile Press
PO Box 255
Hannacroix, NY 12087
www.apocryphilepress.com

Copyright © 2018, 2025 by Aren Roukema
Printed in the United States of America
ISBN 978-1-965646-21-2 | paperback

First published in 2008 by Koninklijke Brill NV, Leiden, The Netherlands.

Chapters 2-4 of this book contain elements published as part of Aren Roukema, "A Veil that Reveals: Charles Williams and the Fellowship of the Rosy Cross," *Journal of Inklings Studies* 5, no. 1 (April 2015): 22–71.

No part of this book may be reproduced, stored in a retrieval system, or transmitted in any form or by any means—electronic, mechanical, photocopy, recording, or otherwise —without written permission of the author and publisher, except for brief quotations in printed reviews.

Please join our mailing list at www.apocryphilepress.com/free. We'll keep you up-to-date on all our new releases, and we'll also send you a FREE BOOK. Visit us today!

For Deborah

"Is your work a romance?"

"It is a romance, and it is not a romance.
It is a truth for those who can comprehend it,
and an extravagance for those who cannot."

—Edward Bulwer-Lytton, *Zanoni* (1842)

CONTENTS

Abbreviations	ix
Acknowledgments	xi
Introduction: Through the Portal	1
1. Life and Times	34
Christian Occultism in Modern England	
2. The Fellowship of the Rosy Cross	93
A Modern Occult Experience	
3. Fiction and Experience	129
4. Kabbalah	185
Charles Williams and the Middle Pillar	
5. The High-Priestess	223
Charles Williams and Modern Magic	
6. A Magical Life in Fiction	252
7. The Transmutation of Charles Williams	291
Spiritual and Literary Alchemy	
Epilogue: The Coagulation of Belief	336
Bibliography	353
About the Author	372

ABBREVIATIONS

CWSA—Charles Williams Society Archive, Middlebury

College—Centre for Medieval and Renaissance Studies, St Michael's Hall, Oxford

Bodleian MS Res—Bodleian, Weston Library, Oxford (restricted manuscript)

CWA—Charles Williams Archive, King's College, London

ACKNOWLEDGMENTS

Like most projects of this kind, this book would still be but an embryo (if conceived at all) without the help and encouragement of colleagues, friends and family. I wish to thank Wouter Hanegraaff and Marco Pasi of the Center for the History of Hermetic Philosophy and Related Currents (HHP) at the University of Amsterdam for supervising my initial research into Charles Williams's esoteric associations, and subsequently encouraging me to expand that smaller project into a monograph. I am very grateful to Peter Forshaw and Ulrike Popp-Baier for their help with aspects of the initial research, and to all my colleagues at the University of Amsterdam for the long hours in cafes discussing matters cultural and historic. Thanks also to Bruce Shelvey and Lynn Szabo for helping me get to Amsterdam in the first place. Accolades for improvements on earlier drafts go to Roger Luckhurst, Egil Asprem for advice on the history of magic, Boaz Huss for feedback on Waite and the kabbalah, and Mike Zuber for help grappling with the history and philosophy of alchemy. All remaining errors are mine alone. Thank you to David Dodds and Sørina Higgins for helpful discussions on a number of aspects of Williams criticism, and to Brian Horne for facilitating access to the Charles Williams Society archive at Oxford. Many other friends and colleagues provided both emotional and intellectual support in the process of writing, editing and publishing this book. To attempt to name each one would be an exercise in futility (and accidental exclusion), but I am particularly thankful to Jimmy Elwing, Erica Gillingham, Francis Gene-Rowe, Rhodri Davies, and Aafke Beukema toe Water.

This book also would not have been possible without the unique collection of esoteric texts gathered at the Bibliotheca Philosophica Hermetica in Amsterdam, particularly the library's collection of both published and unpublished materials from A.E. Waite. I am grateful to the Ritman family for giving me access to their comprehensive collection and particularly thankful to Esther Ritman and Cis van Heertum for their enthusiastic assistance with navigating the collection. Thanks also to Bob Gilbert for his advice on aspects of this collection. Paul Monod and Kate Sykes, at Middlebury College's Centre for Medieval and Renaissance Studies at St Michael's Hall in Oxford, were equally helpful with access the Charles Williams Society (CWS) Archive. Thanks also to the staff at the King's College Archive, the Bodleian, and the British Library. I much appreciate permission from the CWS to quote material from its collection, from the Charles Williams estate to document notes from Williams's "Commonplace Book," and from the *Journal of Inklings Studies* to reproduce portions of "A Veil that Reveals: Charles Williams and the Fellowship of the Rosy Cross" (2015).

Last, but first, an attempt to represent in words my inexpressible gratitude to my family for their unflagging love and support, particularly to Cynthia and John Nyboer and most of all to my parents, Mabel and Peter Roukema, who nurtured my love of symbol and story from the cradle and pretended not to notice when I read at the dinner table. The *sine qua non* of this book, and, indeed, everything that orbits or bisects my life, is my wonderful wife Deborah. Thank you, Two, for your unflagging support, motivation, and understanding.

INTRODUCTION: THROUGH THE PORTAL

The inimitable fiction of Charles Williams is a category unto itself; a genre of theological, poetic, occult fantasy that exploits the surreal to bring the supernatural into the world. The unique character of Williams's seven novels is derived from the eclectic life and personality of the author himself. Williams, as much an accomplished poet, literary critic, amateur playwright, biographer, and theologian as a novelist, liberally imbued his fiction with material derived from engagement with a wide gamut of intellectual traditions—particularly esoteric philosophy and heterodox Christian theology—and emotional experiences, including several passionate though unrequited extramarital affairs and the magical excitation of altered states of consciousness through repression of libido and occult ritual activity. The quality and freshness of his work drew a number of significant admirers among the literary elite of his time, including T.S. Eliot, Dorothy L. Sayers, and W.H. Auden, and led to his involvement, along with C.S. Lewis and J.R.R. Tolkien, in Oxford's Inklings literary circle. Williams's novels are still current today but his work has never achieved the status and popularity of his fellow Inklings. Yet, he remains an important figure, particularly for those interested in esoteric movements and their cultural manifestations. As a fantasist, theologian, and literary critic Williams had a significant influence on the work of Lewis,[1] while his occult poetry and fiction ranks with that of Algernon Blackwood and Arthur Machen in quality and impact, though its influence has not been as marked as that of another of Williams's acquaintances—W.B. Yeats, still the most well-known literary figure involved with modern occultism. Despite his impact in the period, however, much of the credit for the continued currency of his work rests with his association with figures like Eliot and the Inklings.[2] This affiliation has centrally defined the study, categorization, and promotion of Williams's published work,[3] but it could not have played a significant role in most of its actual production as he did not take up with the Inklings until 1936, after much of his oeuvre, including five novels and most of the sixth, was already complete.[4]

Williams's earlier influences were diverse and can be difficult to trace, but one of the most significant was the result of a relationship formed much earlier in his life with Arthur Edward Waite, a leading

---

1. See Humphrey Carpenter, *The Inklings: C.S. Lewis, J.R.R. Tolkien, Charles Williams, and Their Friends* (London: Allen and Unwin, 1978), 160.
2. See Jan Curtis, "Charles Williams: His Reputation in the English-Speaking World from 1917 to 1985," *Inklings-Jahrbuch* 9 (1991): 145–47, on the influence of an "Anglican literati" including Eliot, Lewis and Sayers in promoting Williams's work following his death.
3. See, e.g., Gunnar Urang, *Shadows of Heaven: Religion and Fantasy in the Writing of C.S. Lewis, Charles Williams, and J.R.R. Tolkien* (Philadelphia: Pilgrim Press, 1971); Mark Robert Hillegas, ed. *Shadows of Imagination: The Fantasies of C.S. Lewis, J.R.R. Tolkien, and Charles Williams* (Carbondale, IL: Southern Illinois University Press, 1979); Robert James Reilly, *Romantic Religion: A Study of Owen Barfield, C.S. Lewis, Charles Williams and J.R.R. Tolkien* (Athens, GA: University of Georgia Press, 1971); Carpenter, *The Inklings*; Candice Frederick and Sam McBride, *Women among the Inklings: Gender, C.S. Lewis, J.R.R. Tolkien, and Charles Williams* (London: Greenwood Press, 2001); Colin Duriez and David Porter, *The Inklings Handbook: A Comprehensive Guide to the Lives, Thought and Writings of C.S. Lewis, J.R.R. Tolkien, Charles Williams, Owen Barfield and Their Friends* (London: Azure, 2001); Phillip Zaleski and Carol Zaleski, *The Fellowship: The Literary Lives of the Inklings* (New York: Farrar, Straus and Giroux, 2015).
4. On the lack of Inklings influence on Williams see Carpenter, *The Inklings*, 117, 60; Grevel Lindop, "Charles Williams and His Contemporaries," in *Charles Williams and His Contemporaries*, ed. Suzanne Bray and Richard Sturch (Newcastle upon Tyne: Cambridge Scholars, 2009), 7. Lindop's article is an excellent resource on what we know (which is usually not enough) of Williams's personal and literary influences.

INTRODUCTION: THROUGH THE PORTAL

social and intellectual figure in the Anglo-American context of what is often known as the "occult revival" of interest in magical and mystical currents,[5] beginning roughly about the middle of the nineteenth century and extending its temporal tendrils, in various peaks and troughs of popular interest, to the present day. At his friend's invitation, Williams became an active member of Waite's masonic Rosicrucian secret society: the Fellowship of the Rosy Cross (F.R.C.). He participated in the rituals and social life of this order from 1917 to 1927, a period of personal experience with ecstatic mystical and magical practices that enriched the author's perspective of the world as a unified, seamless blend of matter and spirit and provided him with the esoteric materials which saturate his novels.

Much of the unique flavour of the novels derives from this blend of occult experience and literary expression. This book explores the blurred lines between Williams's life and fiction, particularly in light of his intellectual and experiential interactions with occult ideas and practices. For a man who held a full-time editorship with the Oxford University Press for most of his adult life, Williams produced an astonishing amount of work in an array of genres, but it was primarily in his fiction that he felt best able to explore and reveal esoteric concepts in an arena of play and symbol that granted both a certain freedom and a certain anonymity. Each of Williams's novels penetrates a different terra incognita of occult symbolism and practice. *Shadows of Ecstasy* (1925–1932, published 1933) presents a powerful occultist who has perfected the alchemical transmutation of the self; *Many Dimensions* (1931) returns to alchemy, combining the fabled Philosophers' Stone with the kabbalistic stone of Scethiya in its depiction of the "stone of Suleiman," a magical object that offers

---

5. As discussed below, I use the terms "occult" and "occultism" in this book to refer to a loosely related network of esoteric traditions, figures and concepts, extending from this mid-nineteenth century surge of interest until the present day, rather than a particular philosophy. Without intending to infer any sort of historical paradigm, I use the term "modern occultism" to limit my era of reference to a period roughly synchronous with Williams's own historical context—from (roughly) the last few decades of the nineteenth century to the onset of WWII.

power, wealth and success, or, alternatively, mystical comprehension of the divine to those who wield it. *War in Heaven* (1930) contains several rituals drawn from both white and black magic and reflects the occult fascination with Arthurian mysticism, while *The Greater Trumps* (1932) does the same with the trumps of the tarot, given new significance and symbolic depth by modern occultists, particularly A.E. Waite, whose deck, designed with Pamela Colman Smith and released in 1910, has been very influential in occult circles.[6] *The Place of the Lion* (1931) relies the least on occult symbolism, but even here it is the leader of an occultist society who enables manifestations of supernal principles such as strength, intellect and beauty to intrude into the material world in animal form. The novel's hero, Anthony Durrant, sends these forms back into the supernatural, empowered by an adeptship gained via direct experience of the divine. *Descent into Hell* (1937) and *All Hallows' Eve* (1943) return Williams's attention to the occult, but in a different manner than in the earlier novels. Here Williams is less focused on mystical experience and the potentialities it unlocks within the mind and soul, and more on his unique formulation of "coinherence," the substitution of the self for another in order to heal and protect from spiritual, mental, and physical harm.[7] Elements of occult influence remain in this shift to a more coinherent context, however, as the practice has a number of magical properties and remains informed by the narrative and praxis of interior alchemical transformation explored in the earlier novels.[8] Other occult elements less related to personal experience appear in these last two

---

6. See Juliette Wood, "The Celtic Tarot and the Secret Tradition: A Study in Modern Legend Making," *Folklore* 109 (1998): 16.
7. See Charles Williams, *The Descent of the Dove: A Short History of the Holy Spirit in the Church* (London: Collins, 1963), 234–46. Cf. *Outlines of Romantic Theology* (Grand Rapids, MI: W.B. Eerdmans, 1990), 15–24; Barbara Newman, "Charles Williams and the Companions of the Co-Inherence," *Spiritus: A Journal of Christian Spirituality* 9, no. 1 (Spring 2009): 6–13; Susan Wendling, "'Flesh Knows What Spirit Knows': Mystical Substitution in Charles Williams' Vision of Co-Inherence," *Inklings Forever* 6 (2008).
8. As observed by several critics. See Edward Gauntlett, "Charles Williams, Love & Shekinah," *Charles Williams Quarterly*, no. 126 (Spring 2008); Newman, "Companions of the Co-Inherence," 12–13; Gareth Knight, *The Magical World of Charles Williams* (Oceanside, CA: Sun Chalice Books, 2002), 63.

INTRODUCTION: THROUGH THE PORTAL

novels as well, particularly at the hands of the two hundred year-old magus antagonist of *All Hallows' Eve*, Simon Leclerc, who seeks political power over the worlds of both the living and the dead via magical techniques learned from nineteenth-century occultists in Paris.

WILLIAMS AND THE OCCULT: SOME DISCURSIVE COMPLICATIONS

Imagine interpreting Dickens without thought for the social issues of the nineteenth century; Wilde without care for queer theory; Hemingway without concern for machismo or existentialism (or tapas and grappa). While such approaches are more than plausible, if taken over an entire field of study they would effect lapses that would significantly obscure understanding of these authors and their works. These scenarios may seem (and are) ridiculous, but this is precisely what has happened with analysis of Charles Williams in relation to occult concepts and practices. Early critics identified Williams's interest in magic and other esoteric phenomena as the most striking aspect of his fiction. The *Saturday Review* felt that his deployment of this material made for "a very successful book" and placed him in the literary heritage of "the fiction of mysticism from [Edward Bulwer] Lytton on," while the *Bookman* took this association one further, noting that though most novelists writing of "magic and the supernatural" had trouble avoiding the pitfalls of "farcical comedy," Williams was able to treat esoteric phenomena "in a serious vein demand[ing] a sincerity and clearness of thought that few novelists possess."[9] Similarly, a literary scholar at the University of London placed Williams side-by-side with Arthur Machen, alone among modern fiction writers in their ability to seriously explore "the full mysteries of the black art, which in them is raised above question and presented as an exact science."[10]

---

9. Review of *War in Heaven*, by Charles Williams, *Saturday Review*, 16 August 1930, 212; Review of *Many Dimensions*, by Charles Williams, *Bookman*, February 1931, 331.
10. F.E. Budd, "English Literature and the Occult," in *A Survey of the Occult*, ed. Julian Franklyn, 84–95 (London: Arthur Barker, 1935), 93–94.

Following this early period, however, there emerged a marked tendency in Williams criticism to brush by the prevalence of occult symbolism in his fiction, and overlook the influence of esoteric concepts in his life and work. This reluctance seems to have resulted from three central problems: difficult access to sources, discursive confusion over just what is meant by "occult" and "esoteric," and reliance upon negative assumptions about the traditions indicated by these terms, driven by polemics that have been present in Western culture, in varying forms, for centuries.[11]

Regarding the matter of sources, there are two pressing difficulties, both related to Williams's time in the F.R.C. One obstacle that cannot be overcome is his secrecy about his involvement with the order. As we will see in Chapters Two and Three, he seems to have shared more about his F.R.C. involvement via his novels than in conversation with friends and acquaintances. Fortunately, copies of the unpublished rituals of the F.R.C. can still be found, but a second problem has been accessibility. These days a number of rituals, mostly from the first three of the society's four orders, are freely available on the web; their hidden nature can now be revealed via a not-so-esoteric Boolean search. Before the web era, however, scholars were only able to access information about the F.R.C. through the publications of R.A. Gilbert, who included brief surveys of Williams's time in the order in his biography of A.E. Waite, *A Magician of Many Parts* (1987), and *Twilight of the Magicians* (1983), a history of the Hermetic Order of the Golden Dawn, a genetic ancestor of the F.R.C. and the most impactful occult secret society of the modern era.[12] Gilbert based his accounts on a collection of rituals and meeting

---

11. For a general history of Williams scholarship until 1991, see Curtis, "Charles Williams", and until 2008 see David Llewellyn Dodds, "Review Essay: Gavin Ashenden's *Charles Williams: Alchemy and Integration*," *Charles Williams Quarterly*, no. 126 (Spring 2008): 30–32.

12. Another potential source has long been available, but has gone entirely untapped. The rituals relevant to the grades of Neophyte, Adeptus Minor, and Adeptus Major are included in Israel Regardie, *The Complete Golden Dawn System of Magic* (Phoenix: Falcon Press, 1984), along with a complete set of the rituals of the Golden Dawn, from which Waite drew in writing the rituals of the F.R.C. Though Regardie's collection has

minutes in his possession, now held in the Waite Collection of the Bibliotheca Philosophica Hermetica in Amsterdam, to which I have been fortunate to gain access with the gracious permission of Joost Ritman and family. This is a rare opportunity, as Waite's rituals continue to hold sacred value for Rosicrucian and Christian mystical groups, who thus tend to be understandably reluctant to share their contents publicly. While I have great respect for this sentiment, I discuss a variety of different aspects of the F.R.C.'s ritual activity in detail in this book,[13] as awareness of the order's philosophy and practice is essential to understanding the relationship between Williams's fiction and his occult experiences.

A further difficulty that confronts critics attempting to analyze Williams's occult influences stems from the discursive flux surrounding terms such as "esoteric" and "occult," which has resulted in much confusion for scholars not aware of the permutations such terms have encountered in different times and cultures. Roma A. King, for example, has contributed valuable analysis of Williams's poetry in light of the symbolism of the kabbalistic Tree of Life, but is prevented from historically or culturally situating this imagery by his loose understanding of the occult as "generally associated with the esoteric and the bizarre."[14] Bernadette Bosky makes a game attempt to understand the impact of the Golden Dawn and the F.R.C. on Williams's work in a 1986 article,[15] but is waylaid by her misunderstanding of the nature of occultism, becoming stuck on the question of how Williams's personal involvement with "such an Order" could "coexist with his frequent, staunch denunciation of occult practice, not only in his novels, but argued at length, *in propria persona*, in his

---

been in publication for over thirty years, no previous Williams research seems to have taken advantage of this important resource.

13. However, out of respect I have limited direct quotation from any rituals not already freely available online.

14. Roma A. King Jr., "The Occult as Rhetoric in the Poetry of Charles Williams," in *The Rhetoric of Vision: Essays on Charles Williams*, ed. Charles Adolph Huttar and Peter J. Schakel (Lewisburg: Bucknell University Press, 1996), 165.

15. Bernadette Bosky, "Even an Adept: Charles Williams and the Order of the Golden Dawn," *Mythlore* 13, no. 2 (Winter 1986).

non-fiction study *Witchcraft*."[16] Bosky is to be admired for asking such a question at all, given that she evidently regards it as paradoxical, but the question is impossible to answer from a perspective wherein occultism is seen as directly equivalent to the European tradition of "goetic" or black magic that Williams denounces in *Witchcraft*. While this understanding of the occult certainly maintains a strong presence in Western culture, the late Victorian and modern occultism represented by the Golden Dawn and the F.R.C. had little in common with the (often fantastical) medieval phenomena analyzed in *Witchcraft*.

Adjectives such as "occult" and "esoteric" are often understood, even today, in the pejorative sense exhibited by Bosky. Wouter J. Hanegraaff argues convincingly that negative understandings of these terms stem from a "Grand Polemical Narrative" by which Western culture has defined its identity over the centuries in relation to a constructed other—a group of traditions such as alchemy, magic, kabbalah, witchcraft, and astrology—not always otherwise related but collected in an intellectual "wastebasket" within Western culture.[17] This process began, in Hanegraaff's conception, with the construction of a "pagan other" by Christianity as it gained sway in late antique cultures.[18] Pagan elements were incorporated into Christianity early on, and continued to exert influence in Western culture via the continued popularity of pagan practices and an interest in ancient wisdom found in ancient gnostic, Hermetic and neo-Platonic texts, particularly in the Renaissance and afterwards. These vestigial pagan remnants have been obscured however, by various Christian and, later, scientific rationalist polemics, deployed to purify their own identities from pagan attachments. By the eighteenth century, working from this dichotomy of pagan vs. Christian, Western culture began to acknowledge a relation between the traditions now under-

---

16. Ibid, 25.
17. Wouter J. Hanegraaff, "The Trouble with Images: Anti-Image Polemics and Western Esotericism," in *Polemical Encounters: Esoteric Discourse and Its Others*, ed. Olav Hammer and Kocku von Stuckrad (Leiden: Brill, 2007), 108.
18. Ibid.

stood as "esoteric" and to individuate them from other intellectual and cultural domains in which they had formerly been more seamlessly included. Alchemy proved perhaps the most dramatic example of this process. Where early modern alchemists like Paracelsus were respected as "natural philosophers," the scientific rationalism of the Enlightenment eventually pushed alchemy to an esoteric fringe through a complex web of legitimate empirical rejection and more ideologically based polemics.[19] Though the term "esotericism" was not actually used until the nineteenth century, it describes the formation of a "reservoir of what modernity rejects,"[20] specifically referring to the formation of Western culture around the central pillars of monotheism, which rejected esoteric knowledge as pagan, and Enlightenment rationalism, which rejected it as irrational and superstitious.[21]

An important aspect of Hanegraaff's argument is that this intellectual and cultural category of "esotericism" must be seen as the result of a series of specific historical developments, many of these the product of polemical cultural and social discourses, rather than as a single monolithic tradition of secret knowledge passed down from antiquity.[22] This latter conception is, as we will see, largely how Williams (and Waite) understood esoteric knowledge. However, this book approaches esotericism as it is understood by most contemporary analytical researchers—not as a hegemonic historical

---

19. On the historical development of alchemy's post-Enlightenment marginalization, see Lawrence M. Principe, *The Secrets of Alchemy* (London: The University of Chicago Press, 2013), 89–92; Mark S. Morrisson, *Modern Alchemy: Occultism and the Emergence of Atomic Theory* (Oxford: Oxford University Press, 2007), 4.
20. Hanegraaff, "The Trouble with Images," 110.
21. See *Esotericism and the Academy: Rejected Knowledge in Western Culture* (Cambridge: Cambridge University Press, 2012) for Hanegraaff's analysis of the historiography behind the development of Western esotericism. For shorter summations see Hanegraaff, "Forbidden Knowledge: Anti-Esoteric Polemics and Academic Research," *Aries* 5, no. 2 (2005): 230–46; "The Power of Ideas: Esotericism, Historicism, and the Limits of Discourse," *Religion* 43, no. 2 (2013): 256; Kennet Granholm, *Dark Enlightenment: The Historical, Sociological, and Discursive Contexts of Contemporary Esoteric Magic* (Leiden: Brill, 2014), 25–26.
22. Hanegraaff, *Esotericism and the Academy*, 368–74. Cf. Granholm, *Dark Enlightenment*, 25.

phenomenon, but as the manifestation of long-standing, often antagonistic discourses in Western culture. In this conception, esotericism is, as Andreas Kilcher describes it, "The sociologies, politics, techniques, cultures, and poetics of knowledge by means of which epistemological formations such as magic, kabbalah, occultism etc. are founded, transmitted, transformed, defended, or degraded."[23] Just as it should be understood that there is no specific "esotericism" that can be studied as a phenomenon in its own right, the individual movements grouped together in the wastebasket category of Western esotericism should also be seen as fluctuating traditions in Hans-Georg Gadamer's sense of a tradition as an ongoing dialectical conversation, in which it is assumed that a reified encapsulation of a particular tradition can never be authentically achieved.[24] Seen in the light of this understanding of tradition, every magician, every alchemist, every kabbalist in every period has found themselves exploring a particular tradition of knowledge from within their own subjective sphere of understanding, influenced by their own particular cultural context. Within these contexts they have added to already existing, *longue durée* traditions of esoteric knowledge, but also adjusted, defended and attacked these same traditions so that each is subject to a continuous process of transmutation, to the point where they can only be said to exist as "traditions" at all because of the necessity of categorization for the ordering of human thought.[25]

---

23. Andreas Kilcher, "7 Epistemological Theses," in *Hermes in the Academy: Ten Years' Study of Western Esotericism at the University of Amsterdam*, ed. Wouter J. Hanegraaff and Joyce Pijnenburg (Amsterdam: Amsterdam University Press, 2009), 145.
24. Hans-Georg Gadamer, *Truth and Method*, trans. Joel Weinsheimer and Donald G. Marshall (London: Sheed and Ward, 1999), 358–60.
25. Because each player in the discursive game coincidental to a particular esoteric tradition forms their own individual discourse within that tradition, Kennet Granholm has proposed that we describe particular esoteric currents as "discursive complexes": "The various individual discourses that constitute a complex—a current—are interdependent and modify each other. Each individual discourse assumes a unique form due to its dependences on the other discourses constituting the complex...a particular discourse can be a constituting element of more than one distinct complex, but...will assume different, though mutually recognizable and related, forms, functions, and rationales" (Granholm, *Dark Enlightenment*, 36).

INTRODUCTION: THROUGH THE PORTAL

My references to esotericism and specific esoteric traditions such as modern occultism are made in light of this view of "esotericism" as a term which represents the formation of a category that many have felt necessary, a term continuously redefined by on-going cultural and historical permutations.[26]

Before the term esotericism came into wide use, the same body of affiliated traditions was united under terms such as the "occult sciences," generally referring to more practical esoteric knowledge found in traditions such as magic and alchemy, and the "occult philosophy," a more encompassing notion used to describe an ancient wisdom passed down from fabled Near-Eastern sages such as Moses, Hermes Trismegistus and Zoroaster and reintroduced in the Christian context of the Renaissance.[27] This same tradition, or at least varying collections of its central elements, has also commonly been referred to as "Hermeticism," stemming from the centrality of the *Corpus Hermeticum* and *Asclepius* pseudonymously attributed to Hermes Trismegistus. These texts were written over several centuries in the late antique period, but viewed as a much older source of ancient wisdom in the Renaissance, so much so that attempts to synthesize magical, alchemical, kabbalistic and astrological phenomena with Christian theology, pursued by philosophers such as Pico della Mirandola, Marsilio Ficino, and Cornelius Agrippa, are often known as Renaissance Hermeticism.[28] In the modern era, Hermeticism was understood as a Western esoteric tradition connected to this Renaissance and late antique heritage, as opposed

---

26. There is a diverse range of opinions on the historical boundaries and theoretical definitions of "esotericism" or "Western esotericism." For some of the most authoritative see Wouter J. Hanegraaff, *Western Esotericism: A Guide for the Perplexed* (New York: Continuum International, 2013), particularly 2–17; Kocku von Stuckrad, *Western Esotericism: A Brief History of Secret Knowledge* (London: Equinox, 2005), 1–11; Henrik Bogdan, *Western Esotericism and Rituals of Initiation* (Albany, NY: State University of New York Press, 2007), 6–20; Kilcher, "7 Epistemological Theses," 143–48; Antoine Faivre, *Access to Western Esotericism* (Albany, NY: State University of New York Press, 1994), 10–15.
27. Wouter J. Hanegraaff, "The Notion of 'Occult Sciences' in the Wake of the Enlightenment," in *Aufklärung und Esoterik: Wege in die Moderne*, ed. Monika Neugebauer-Wolk et al. (Berlin: De Gruyter, 2013), 77–82.
28. See Hanegraaff, *A Guide for the Perplexed*, 23, 30–34.

to esoteric symbols and concepts with more Eastern origins.[29] "Magic" is another term that has been used for centuries to encompass both the practical and speculative aspects of the pursuit of esoteric knowledge and thus has a bewilderingly vast potential for signification. In the process of identity construction described by Hanegraaff, "magic" and "occult" were appropriated as polemical terms used to dismiss all knowledge branded with these labels as demonic (Christian polemics) or irrational (scientific rationalist polemics).[30] However, the virulent Enlightenment rejection of these terms also allowed for their sublimation by anti-Enlightenment elements in society. In the nineteenth century a number of individuals and movements began to specifically identify themselves as "occultists" and their activities as magical, and returned to esoteric currents of the Renaissance and early modern periods to further their knowledge of Hermeticism and the occult sciences.[31] In the early nineteenth century the term "occultism" began to make its way into Western culture, first in France and then quickly picking up favour in England as a result of the writings of the French magician Éliphas Lévi.[32] Like esotericism, the term acquired a wide scope; central referents included the ancient wisdom tradition, the applied arts of practical magic, and the means of achieving mystical illumination.[33]

This is the occultism that Williams engaged with, and it must be seen as a specific historical permutation of esoteric thought rather than a vaguely defined category of concepts having to do with hidden knowledge or ancient wisdom, the magical or the demonic. This specifically modern occultism began in the early to mid-nineteenth century, gained traction with Lévi's influential synthesis of the Jewish

---

29. Morrisson, *Modern Alchemy*, 18.
30. Hanegraaff, "The Trouble with Images," 110; "The Notion of 'Occult Sciences'," 83–87. On the history of the terms "magic" and "occult," see *Esotericism and the Academy*, 164–90.
31. Hanegraaff, "Forbidden Knowledge," 247.
32. Morrisson, *Modern Alchemy*, 12–13.
33. Alex Owen, *The Place of Enchantment: British Occultism and the Culture of the Modern* (London: University of Chicago Press, 2004), 47.

mystical tradition of kabbalah with magical praxis and the symbols of the tarot, and came of age in the late nineteenth century with the growing popularity of groups such as the Theosophical Society (1875/1879)—co-founded by the charismatic medium Helena Petrovna Blavatsky—and the Golden Dawn, launched in 1888 by three Freemasons, William Robert Woodman, William Wynn Westcott and Samuel MacGregor Mathers, the latter two of whom would prove to be very influential in the modern esoteric network. Occult adaptations of previous esoteric thought and practice included a greater synthesis of non-Christian (particularly Eastern) religions, the incorporation of new views on social hierarchy and gender inclusion, a quest for enchantment in the face of the disenchantment perceived to be perpetuated by Enlightenment rationalism and scientific materialism, and an incorporation, despite this quest, of Enlightenment values such as scientific advancement and biological evolutionism. Occultism thus offered not "a resistance to modernity, but...another modernity," not necessarily seeking to undermine recent scientific discoveries, but insisting that they were simply an affirmation, on another plane, of wisdom already found in ancient wisdom.[34] This embrace of scientific legitimation required, paradoxically, a movement away from material explanations for occult phenomena that could not be substantiated with empirical methods.[35] Thus, occultists often saw "magic" as an effect of imagination that produced psycho-

---

34. Robert Stockhammer, "Rosicrucian Radioactivity: Alchemy around 1900," in *The Golden Egg: Alchemy in Art and Literature*, ed. Alexandra Lembert and Elmar Schenkel (Cambridge, MA: Galda and Wilch, 2002), 134.

35. On the boundaries and characteristics of modern occultism see Wouter J. Hanegraaff, *New Age Religion and Western Culture: Esotericism in the Mirror of Secular Thought* (Albany, NY: State University of New York Press, 1998), 421–22; Olav Hammer, *Claiming Knowledge: Strategies of Epistemology from Theosophy to the New Age* (Leiden: Brill, 2001), 7; Marco Pasi, "Occultism," in *The Brill Dictionary of Religion*, ed. Kocku von Stuckrad (Leiden: Brill, 2006); Robert Galbreath, "Explaining Modern Occultism," in *The Occult in America: New Historical Perspectives*, ed. Howard Kerr and Charles L. Crow (Chicago: University of Illinois Press, 1983), 15–32; R. A. Gilbert, *The Golden Dawn: Twilight of the Magicians* (Wellingborough: Aquarian Press, 1983), 20–23. Faivre, *Access to Western Esotericism*, 86–90; Egil Asprem, *Arguing with Angels: Enochian Magic and Modern Occulture* (Albany: State University of New York Press, 2012), 45–77; Kennet Granholm, "Locating the West: Problematizing the Western in Western Esotericism and

logical effects within the self so that magicians themselves, rather than their surroundings, were affected.[36] A similar example is the development of a specifically spiritual form of alchemy that sought the transmutation of the self but rejected the traditional alchemical focus on the transmutation of metals.[37] In addition to these adaptations of earlier forms of esoteric practice, occultists were also more likely to embrace universal interpretations of the perennial ancient wisdom believed to have been passed down from antiquity.[38] Where their esoteric forebears looked for proof of the truth of Christianity in this ancient wisdom, occultists tended to synthesize a variety of systems on a more pluralistic playing field, with a love for bricolage which Egil Asprem calls "programmatic syncretism." With this term, which I will return to often, Asprem refers to the occultist tendency to systematically organize a wide range of symbolism from a variety of different traditions to develop "a pragmatically better and more refined esoteric system," one that could better communicate the universal esoteric knowledge available to all but found by few.[39]

With the exception of the turn to scientific legitimation, the esoteric material that emerges in Williams's novels and poetry is very much in line with these modern occult trends, as were the experiences he encountered in the F.R.C. and the doctrines he discovered in Waite's voluminous tomes of esoteric scholarship, particularly the *Secret Doctrine in Israel* (1913), a history cum personal interpretation of

---

Occultism," in *Occultism in a Global Perspective*, ed. Henrik Bogdan and Gordan Djurdjevic (London: Acumen, 2013): 18; *Dark Enlightenment*, 43–46.

36. Hammer, *Claiming Knowledge*, 49–52; Wouter J. Hanegraaff, "How Magic Survived the Disenchantment of the World," *Religion* 33, no. 4 (2003): 365–71.

37. See Lawrence M. Principe, and William R. Newman, "Some Problems with the Historiography of Alchemy," in *Secrets of Nature: Astrology and Alchemy in Early Modern Europe*, ed. William R. Newman and Anthony Grafton (Cambridge, MA: MIT Press, 2006), 388–95. Mike A. Zuber's excellent doctoral thesis on spiritual alchemy takes a wider perspective on the subject, tracing its roots back to the early modern period. See *Spiritual Alchemy from the Age of Jacob Boehme to Mary Anne Atwood, 1600–1900* (PhD diss., Universiteit of Amsterdam, 2017). Developments in modern magic and alchemy are further discussed in Chapters Five through Seven.

38. Pasi, "Occultism," 1367.

39. Egil Asprem, "Kabbalah Recreata," *Pomegranate: The International Journal of Pagan Studies* 9, no. 2 (2007): 135–36. Cf. Bogdan, *Western Esotericism*, 121.

kabbalah.[40] However, scholars have been prevented from realizing the congruities between Williams and other moderns invested in the occult by a "dark and tulgey wood of witchcraft" that most seem to envision when they hear the term.[41] This polemical understanding of occultism is the third obstacle that has hampered research into Williams's place in the occult network. Breathing in the residue of the centuries of discursive attacks described by Hanegraaff's Grand Polemical Narrative, scholars of Charles Williams generally approach esoteric materials from the premise that they are not, and never have been, compatible with orthodox Christianity. Some critics, such as F.R. Leavis and R.T. Davies, have expressed doubt about the value of his work as a result of its occult elements. Davies feels that episodes of black magic in *War in Heaven* and *All Hallows' Eve* "are described with such seductive relish, one is inclined occasionally to feel one would, if one had it at all, prefer one's pornography honest."[42] Leavis argues that Williams's interest in the occult cannot be missed if "you approach as a literary critic, unstiffened by the determination to 'discriminate Christianly,'" and rejects the possibility that his writings might be "spiritually edifying" as a result.[43]

Most critics, however, have downplayed the significance of occultism to Williams's oeuvre. Three central patterns have evolved. In the first, scholars admit the presence of occult material in Williams's poetry and fiction, but deny the possibility of an active, personal involvement on the author's part. Critics such as Thomas Howard, Alice Mary Hadfield, and Dorothy L. Sayers, all from an early generation of scholars,[44] have concluded, in Howard's words,

---

40. On Williams's attachment to this text see Anne Ridler, "Introduction to *The Image of the City* by Charles Williams," in *The Image of the City*, ed. Anne Ridler (Berkley, CA: Apocryphile, 1958), xxv.
41. George P. Winship Jr., "The Novels of Charles Williams," in *Shadows of Imagination: The Fantasies of C S. Lewis, J.R.R. Tolkien, and Charles Williams*, ed. Mark Robert Hillegas (Carbondale, IL: Southern Illinois University Press, 1979), 115.
42. R.T. Davies, "Charles Williams and Romantic Experience," *Etudes Anglaises* 8, no. 4 (Oct–Dec 1955): 298.
43. F.R. Leavis, *The Common Pursuit* (London: Hogarth, 1952), 253.
44. Early Williams scholarship was often undertaken by researchers who knew

that "no matter how bizarre and apparently occult Williams' tales may appear to be, he is never writing about anything other than the plain stuff acknowledged by all Christians."[45] Richard McLaughlin, reviewing *War in Heaven* for the *Saturday Review*, assumed that Williams had simply borrowed the novel's "black-magic apparatus" from occult fiction and that his intentions were little more than sardonic: "We could attend a Black Mass with Charles Williams and come away with him laughing through our bewitchment."[46]

A second popular approach is to theorize that Williams was interested in occultism at a younger age but matured, in the words of Glen Cavaliero, "from being a secret hermeticist into a humorous and companionable spiritual exemplar."[47] There is certainly a clear evolution in how and why Williams incorporated occult themes and symbols into his work over the course of his life, but this judgment relies on the analytically dubious assumptions that Christian concepts are more valuable and/or legitimate than those of occultism, and that an author's later opinions present the most accurate framework with which to understand the intentions behind their published works *in toto*. The maturation thesis is also belied by the

---

Williams personally or were able to gather sources from his friends and associates. Hadfield was particularly active in collecting letters and other resources and as such performed an invaluable service to future scholars. Her published work, however, is particularly affected by problematic (mis)understandings of occultism. See Scott McLaren, "A Problem of Morality: Sacramentalism in the Early Novels of Charles Williams," *Renascence* 56, no. 2 (Winter 2004): 14; Lindop, "Charles Williams and His Contemporaries," 15.

45. Thomas Howard, *The Novels of Charles Williams* (New York: Oxford University Press, 1983), 233–34. Cf. Alice Mary Hadfield, *Charles Williams: An Exploration of His Life and Work* (Oxford: Oxford University Press, 1983), 29–30. Winship, "Novels of Charles Williams," 114–15. Dorothy L. Sayers, "Introduction to *James I* by Charles Williams" (London: Morrison and Gibb, 1951), ix. David N. Samuelson, "Charles Williams," in *Supernatural Fiction Writers*, ed. E.F. Bleiler (New York: Charles Scribner's Sons, 1985), 632.

46. Richard McLaughlin, "Chasing the Grail in England," review of *War in Heaven*, by Charles Williams, *Saturday Review*, 1 Oct. 1949, 16.

47. Glen Cavaliero, review of *Alchemy and Integration* by Gavin Ashenden, *The C.S. Lewis Chronicle* 5, no. 5 (2008): 51. Cf. *Charles Williams: Poet of Theology* (London: Macmillan, 1983), 4–5; Gavin Ashenden, *Charles Williams: Alchemy and Integration* (Kent, OH: Kent State University Press, 2008), 72, 79.

fact that Williams's later novels and poetry are still in significant dialogue with occult symbolism and practice,[48] and must be interpreted as such.

A third common approach to the perceived tension between Christian faith and occultism has been to suggest that Williams encountered esoteric subject matter only on an imaginative, mythopoeic level that did not affect his actual intellectual or spiritual commitments. Ashenden argues that Williams employed occult phenomena in his poetry in its "cultural sense,"[49] while Roma A. King places his reliance on kabbalistic symbolism "within the larger Christian framework in which, [Williams] maintained, it found fulfillment." The contribution of occultism to Williams's poetry, according to King, "Was psychological and rhetorical, a stimulant for the imagination."[50] Verlyn Flieger identifies Williams's reliance on occult symbolism as an aesthetic strategy, arguing that the tension between "his avowed Christian impulse and his focus on the occult and the demonic" allowed him to communicate his philosophy of immanence—of the unity of matter and spirit in the world—by making a "virtue of disjunction" so that these apparently discordant elements work in support of one another.[51] This is an attractive concept, and, as I describe further in Chapter Three, Williams was indeed fond of contrasting multivalent perspectives in service of a greater philosophical whole. In this case, however, Flieger's argument only works if we can ascertain that Williams shared a dichotomous

---

48. See Urang, *Shadows of Heaven*, 62 for commentary on occult elements in the last two novels; King, "The Occult as Rhetoric" for occultism in Williams's later poetry.
49. Ashenden, *Charles Williams*, 177.
50. King, "The Occult as Rhetoric," 178. Cf. Howard, *The Novels of Charles Williams*, 233–45; Huw Mordecai, "Charles Williams and the Occult," in *Charles Williams: A Celebration*, ed. Brian Horne (Leominster, Herefordshire: Fowler Wright, 1995), 268; Charles Moorman, *Arthurian Triptych: Mythic Materials in Charles Williams, C.S. Lewis, and T.S. Eliot* (Berkeley: University of California Press, 1960), 89; Cavaliero, *Poet of Theology*, 161.
51. Verlyn Flieger, "Time in the Stone of Suleiman," in *The Rhetoric of Vision: Essays on Charles Williams*, ed. Charles Adolph Huttar and Peter J. Schakel (Lewisburg: Bucknell University Press, 1996), 75, 77.

view of Christianity and occultism, which, as I will illustrate throughout this book, he did not.

Occult imagery, themes, symbols, and practices certainly provide extensive enrichment to Williams's novels and poetry, but significant problems arise when we delimit his occult involvement to an imaginative realm of mythopoeia, hermetically sealed from his actual belief structure. Such simplifications commit a frequent error of scholarship identified by Kennet Granholm, who points out, speaking generally of analysis of esoteric currents in cultural products, that scholars tend to separate "real" esotericism from "simulacrum" forms found in popular culture. Granholm notes the near impossibility of separating actual from artificial forms of esoteric expression and advises that it is best to do away with assumptions that a cultural product may not reflect serious esoteric expression because it is an artistic creation.[52] In the case of Charles Williams it is particularly advisable to avoid such a separation, as it is clear when reading his fiction, as John Heath-Stubbs notes, that he held the ideas he employed for the purposes of entertainment "with profound seriousness."[53] Unless we approach his fiction with equal earnestness, we risk glossing over the deep meaning Williams extracted from the esoteric cultural milieu of his time, as well as the continuities that exist between his own life and the occult themes, symbolism, and characterization in his work.

These three approaches are, I am quite sure, largely unconscious patterns rather than conscious strategies; they do not represent some sort of conspiracy to represent Williams in a false light. Rather, the under-appreciation of the occult aspects of Williams's work is part of a much wider lack of attention to esoteric phenomena in literature which has resulted, as Hanegraaff argues, "simply because specialists were unfamiliar or uncomfortable with it, and because they found it difficult (understandably enough) to find reliable scholarship that

---

52. Kennet Granholm, "Ritual Black Metal: Popular Music as Occult Mediation and Practice," *Correspondences* 1, no. 1 (2013): 8.
53. John Heath-Stubbs, *Charles Williams* (London: Longmans, 1955), 8.

could help them interpret literary references to esoteric ideas or symbolism."⁵⁴ Unwitting or not, however, the assumption that Williams simply could not be involved with occultism on a meaningful level of practice or application has resulted, as Gavin Ashenden suggests, in the drawing of a *cordon sanitaire* around Williams and his work. Ashenden, speaking specifically of Williams and alchemy, observes that Christian academics have been leery about his interest in the subject because it incorporates "pre-Christian" elements, leading them to a cordon sanitaire approach that distances Williams from alchemy, ignoring his clear interest in the tradition. This criticism can be extended much further than the domain of alchemy. Ironically, Ashenden himself sets up a similar barrier around occultism. Speaking of the F.R.C. for example, the significant occultist nature of which I explore in Chapter Two, Ashenden uses a cordon sanitaire argument to reassure his readers that the order did not cause Williams to speak "from a position outside the boundaries of Christian orthodoxy."⁵⁵

There is little evidence that Williams shared the insistence on orthodoxy exhibited by this cordon sanitaire. Indeed, if Williams displayed unease it was with dogmatic attachments to codified doctrine. "Dunces do, and Romantics are apt to, fall into the serious error [wherein] everything must depend on their own gospel, and their gospel is nightly unwilling to be but a Part."⁵⁶ Occultism is not merely a path along which Williams has his readers travel in order to achieve a higher Christian or mystical spiritual goal—it is, by virtue of its inextricable entanglement with the central mystical and coinherent philosophies communicated in the novels, a central wing of the waiting room before the gates of the inexpressible. Modern occult belief structures were formed in tandem with competing thought

---

54. Hanegraaff, *A Guide for the Perplexed*, 156.
55. Ashenden, *Charles Williams*, viii.
56. Charles Williams, "Alexander Pope," in *The Image of the City*, ed. Anne Ridler (Berkeley: Apocryphile, 2007), 44. Williams refers to Pope's "An Essay on Criticism": "Most Critics, fond of some subservient Art,/ Still make the Whole depend upon a Part:/ They talk of Principles, but Notions prize,/ And all to one loved Folly sacrifice."

systems, particularly Christianity and scientific rationalism. As this book will frequently show, for every modern occultist who proposed esoteric ideas in order to purposefully oppose the claims of the dominant thought systems of the day, there was at least one more who engaged with occultism not to reject contrasting claims, but to join them together in holy intellectual matrimony. Such was Williams's approach. Cordon sanitaire arguments, while understandable given the fabric of polemical assumptions woven into Western culture, obscure the very real possibility that his thought was concurrently Christian and occult.[57] In Williams's view, the incorporation of esoteric currents and Christian theology did not demean his work—it enriched it.

This conclusion has begun to be reached with more frequency in recent years, as scholars such as Barbara Newman, Gareth Knight, David L. Dodds, and Edward Gauntlett have published research that indicates that Williams exhibited an active, personal engagement with the occult, one that may have shifted in nature but was maintained throughout his life.[58] Grevel Lindop's recent biography, *Charles Williams: The Third Inkling* (2015), provides us with a particularly valuable resource on this front and will hopefully dispel many of the problematic approaches seen in previous criticism. For the moment, despite these more recent voices calling for a reinterpretation of

---

57. As proposed by Gareth Knight (*Magical World of Charles Williams*, 11). Knight, a former member of Dion Fortune's Society of Inner Light, has himself synthesized occult and Christian worldviews (Francis King, *Ritual Magic in England: 1887 to the Present Day* (London: Neville Spearman, 1970), 158). Cf. Reilly, *Romantic Religion*, 10 on Williams's Coleridgian taste for synthesis.

58. See Newman, "Companions of the Co-Inherence"; Knight, *Magical World of Charles Williams*; Lindop, "Charles Williams and His Contemporaries"; Gauntlett, "Charles Williams, Love & Shekinah"; Thomas Willard, "Acts of the Companions: A.E. Waite's Fellowship and the Novels of Charles Williams," in *Secret Texts: The Literature of Secret Societies*, ed. Marie Mulvey Roberts and Hugh Ormsby-Lennon (New York: AMS Press, 1995); McLaren, "A Problem of Morality"; Joyce Goggin, "*The Greater Trumps*: Charles Williams and the Metaphysics of Otherness," in *Tarot in Culture*, ed. Emily E. Auger, 411–38 (Clifford, ON: Valleyhome, 2014). While he does not examine Williams's esoteric interests in detail and lacks awareness of the historical particulars of occultism, Humphrey Carpenter, like Bosky, is an early example of a researcher not afraid to allow for a valid, experiential interest in the occult. See Carpenter, *The Inklings*, 83.

INTRODUCTION: THROUGH THE PORTAL

Williams's work in relation to his occult involvement, David L. Dodds's 2008 observation that we are "still closer to the beginning... than very far advanced" toward considering Williams as an "occult writer" still haunts the field;[59] it echoes more widely into the greater realm of occult literature, a complex generic body which still receives less than the appropriate amount of research attention, resulting in a contextual gap in which interpretation is performed with little care for the esoteric aspects of particular texts.[60]

ENCOUNTERING THE OCCULT IN WILLIAMS'S FICTION: A LITERARY/HISTORICAL METHOD

In order to advance our understanding of the relation between Williams, modern esotericism and occultist literature in general, his life and fiction must be reevaluated in light of recent historical research on modern occultism, which has added significant flesh to the occult bones that have so long been unjustifiably feared and

---

59. Dodds, "Gavin Ashenden's *Charles Williams*," 46.
60. This is by no means a universal problem, however. Literary critics, in fact, have been more likely than most to take esoteric knowledge into consideration. The best examples are in W.B. Yeats research, which has long been connected to his involvement in the Golden Dawn (See, e.g., Richard Ellmann, *Yeats: The Man and the Masks* (New York: Norton, 1979); Joseph Ronsley, *Yeats's Autobiography: Life as a Symbolic Pattern* (Cambridge, MA: Harvard University Press, 1968); Kathleen Raine, *Yeats, the Tarot and the Golden Dawn* (Dublin: Dolmen Press, 1972). More recently a number of important publications have been released, including, but certainly not limited to: Andrew McCann, *Popular Literature, Authorship and the Occult in Late Victorian Britain* (New York: Cambridge University Press, 2014); Leon Surette, *The Birth of Modernism: Ezra Pound, T.S. Eliot, W.B. Yeats, and the Occult* (Montreal: McGill-Queen's University Press, 1993); Michael Saler, "Rethinking Secularism: Modernity, Enchantment, and Fictionalism," (2013), http://blogs.ssrc.org/tif/2013/12/20/modernity-enchantment-and-fictionalism/; Jeffrey J. Kripal, *Mutants and Mystics: Science Fiction, Superhero Comics, and the Paranormal* (Chicago: University of Chicago Press, 2011) and, in German, the collection of essays in *Erfahrung und System: Mystik und Esoterik in der Literatur der Moderne*, ed. Bettina Gruber (Opladen: Verlag für Sozialwissenschaften, 1997), as well as Andreas Kilcher's examination of relationships between kabbalah and German language and literature (*Die Sprachtheorie der Kabbala als ästhetisches Paradigma: Die Konstruktion einer ästhetischen Kabbala seit der frühen Neuzeit* (Stuttgart: J. B. Metzler, 1998). Much remains to be done, however, in connecting authors like Williams to relevant esoteric contexts, thus restoring texts that were important in their time to the historical picture.

despised. My first project, then, is historical. I will discuss pertinent aspects of Williams's life and thought within the context of other figures, groups, and belief systems that have been connected to the modern occult milieu, particularly focusing on his mystical experiences in the F.R.C. My aim in doing so is to establish Williams as, to some degree, a modern "occultist," but I want to emphasize that I do not intend this term to brand him with a particular identity or match him exclusively with a specific reified tradition, for this is precisely the cordon sanitaire methodology that has obscured the rich heterodoxy of his life and fiction. Rather, I wish to situate Williams within an assemblage of interacting cultural and intellectual currents, as a contributor to the dialectical conversation suggested by Gadamer's concept of tradition. Williams's place in the occult tradition is helpfully illustrated by the relativist view of social currents proposed by Actor-Network Theory (ANT), an approach to the formation of social networks first developed by sociologists Michael Callon, Bruno Latour and John Law in the 1980s.[61] ANT has since produced a diverse collection of theories and concepts, but I am currently interested in its view of how movements such as modern occultism are constructed and maintained. Rather than assuming the existence of a fabric of static groups and forces that perpetuate particular predictable human actions, ANT views what Latour calls "the social" as a web of both human *and* nonhuman actors, continuously engaged in the formation of particular social groups, patterns and movements.[62] This concept of group formation, among many other possible applications, reinforces the view that esoteric cultural movements are typified by a fluid, continuous process of discursive innova-

---

61. I encountered ANT through Latour, particularly *Reassembling the Social: An Introduction to Actor-Network-Theory* (Oxford: Oxford University Press, 2005). A useful guide is Mike Michael, *Actor-Network Theory: Trials, Trails and Translations* (London: Sage, 2017). Sharon Jackson provides a shorter summary, with discussion of possible applications, in "Toward an Analytical and Methodological Understanding of Actor-Network Theory," *Journal of Arts and Humanities* 4, no. 2 (2015).

62. Latour, *Reassembling the Social*, 33. For a good summary of the distinction between ANT and conventional approaches to sociology see ibid, 64–65. Cf. Michael, *Actor-Network Theory*, 5.

INTRODUCTION: THROUGH THE PORTAL

tion and renovation. I will not be systemically applying any sort of theoretical structure or set of analytical tools derived from ANT (it famously lacks these anyway),[63] but its use of the "actor-network" concept to reframe our understanding of social relations will be helpful in resituating Charles Williams in the modern occult context. In this view of the social, Williams was one actor among many in what Sharon Jackson calls "a heterogeneous network of aligned interests,"[64] rather than a figure who can be judged to be either inside or outside of some sort of clearly demarcated group, as occurs in cordon sanitaire thinking. As an "actor," Williams should not be seen as a simple source of an action—e.g. the writing of a text or the expression of a concept—but as "the moving target of a vast array of entities swarming toward" him.[65] Like an actor on a stage, the individual in an actor-network never acts alone, but is part of an incomprehensible array of influences and ideas. "Action is borrowed, distributed, suggested, influenced, dominated, betrayed, translated."[66] As an author of occult fiction and a member of a Rosicrucian secret society, Williams was a "moving target" in continuous, fluid relation to the concepts, individuals, discourses, texts, groups and practices that continuously informed the modern occult network.[67] This network (and the large amount of subnetworks continuously under formation within it) is only one of a number of religious, political, intellectual and personal networks in which Williams can be situated, and he was not a principal actor in the way of Aleister Crowley, H.P. Blavatsky or the Golden Dawn. Still, Williams played a consequential role in mediating and translating "actions" made by previous occultists and occult texts, working from deep personal experience to transcribe his encounters with occult thought and practice into fiction.

By far the most targeted object of my project of historical comparison is A.E. Waite, the node through whom many of Williams's occult

---

63. Jackson, "Toward an Analytical and Methodological Understanding," 30.
64. Ibid.
65. Latour, *Reassembling the Social*, 46.
66. Ibid.
67. Ibid.

network connections were translated. Waite's influence on Williams is widely recognized, but this association with a leading figure in modern occultism has not, as might be expected, resulted in a matching acknowledgement of the influence of occultism on Williams. This is largely because Waite has also been disassociated from the modern occult network, despite his active engagement in a number of masonic, Rosicrucian and Theosophical secret societies, as well as the enormous influence of his books on a wide variety of subjects close to the occultist heart. As discussed further in Chapter One, Waite distanced himself, his work, and the F.R.C. from occultism, based on a dichotomy between the occult and his own mystical philosophy that is more discursive than based in actual difference. Waite's biographer, R.A. Gilbert, provides us with an extremely well-researched picture of this previously overlooked figure, but he develops a picture of Waite's relationship to occultism that too faithfully represents the picture that the occultist developed for himself, rather than questioning his motives or attempting to contextualize his claims in comparison with other occultists or mystics.[68] Historical and discursive analysis, however, reveals that Waite frequently incorporated occult elements into his mystical philosophy with one hand, even while polemicizing against artificially reified traditions of "magic" and "the occult" with the other.

The view of Waite as mystic rather than occultist has been taken up largely without question by Williams scholars and applied to Williams himself, resulting in a fourth obstacle to an accurate appraisal of his heterodox philosophy. In order to achieve the advancement called for by Dodds, I have analysed aspects of Waite's life and work that may have been influential for Williams. Rather

---

68. Gilbert himself seems to hold some of the same polemical views of occultism that Waite frequently expressed, as he refers to masonic groups not focused on inward spirituality as "falling into the follies of occultism" (R.A. Gilbert, "The Masonic Career of Arthur Edward Waite," *Ars Quatuor Coronatorum* 99 (1986): 31), and says that those who prioritize Waite's studies of occultism over his mystical writings represent "the folly of an age that exalts the irrational" (*A.E. Waite: Magician of Many Parts* (Wellingborough: Crucible, 1987), 13).

than rely solely on Waite's disavowals of occultism as if they were made in a vacuum, with no personal motivations or social factors to influence them—no issues of temporal translation to dilute or obfuscate their meaning—this book evaluates numerous close relations between the modern occult network and Waite's philosophy and actual practice. These connections are tempered by an awareness that Waite constantly sought to define his own network, arranged around the Rosicrucian initiatory mysticism of the F.R.C., but his attempt to define his own brand of modern esotericism does not remove him from the general occultist milieu. I have undertaken this much needed reevaluation of Waite's occultist dimensions as a necessary precursor to understanding the esotericism of Charles Williams, but I hope that my analysis will also prove valuable for researchers interested in Waite, who, despite his centrality in the modern occult network, has had very little attention paid him in the thirty years since Gilbert's important biography.

To establish Williams as an actor in the occult network we must do the same for his texts. Another central tenet of ANT that informs my current project is the assumption that nonhuman actors also contribute to networks of the social—receiving, modifying and mediating actions just as humans do, though in a manner unique to their particular category (animal, vegetable, mineral, text, yo-yo, etc.).[69] ANT has most often explored this concept in connection to the relations between humans and technology, but the text is another nonhuman actor that must be taken into consideration—one that is perhaps easier to conceptualize as actor than a houseplant or a chihuahua—given the clear potential for impact, influence and mediation. Thus, in addition to the human actors that performed an array

---

69. For Latour on the need to widen our perspective of the actors that contribute to the creation, function and identification of the social to include "other types of material like documents, writings, charts, files, paper clips, maps, organizational devices, in brief intellectual technologies," see *Reassembling the Social*, 74–78. Cf. Michael, *Actor-Network Theory*, 5; Jackson, "Toward an Analytical and Methodological Understanding," 30; Rita Felski, *The Limits of Critique* (Chicago: The University of Chicago Press, 2015), 163–64.

of associations and relations, the modern occult network was continuously actuated by the liturgies of ritual, the secret knowledge documents of orders like the Golden Dawn, particular symbols and images, widely published knowledge texts such as Waite's histories, and, perhaps most influentially in the wider view, by the poetic or fictional texts produced by occultists such as Dion Fortune, Blackwood, Yeats and Williams. For ANT sociologists like Latour, such nonhuman actors lose their social significance when the traces of their influence have disappeared. Speaking specifically of technology, however, Latour hopes that "when objects have receded into the background for good, it is always possible—but more difficult—to bring them back to light by using archives, documents, memoirs, museum collections, etc., to artificially produce, through historians' accounts, the state of crisis in which machines, devices, and implements were born."[70] This social archaeology has enormous ramifications for the study of literature. Like all text, Williams's fiction is itself an archive within an archive—each novel a nodal point through which strains of modern esoteric belief can be rediscovered and rehabilitated.

This textual archaeology can be pursued from a number of disciplinary perspectives, but some of the sharpest digging tools, particularly for evaluation of fiction, are provided by literary criticism. This is true for all texts, of whatever genre or media, but, as I will discuss further in Chapter Three, the relationship between fiction and esoteric theory and practice has generated a unique form of narrative that is at the same time veridically intentioned and notably fantastic. Motivated by a desire to maintain a shroud of secrecy even in the public forum of published fiction and poetry, authors incorporating ritual, secret knowledge and abstruse symbol into narrative have tended to utilize the abstraction of less realistically-inclined narrative modes. Moreover, inspired by the inherently creative and adaptive nature of esoteric knowledge, authors of occult fiction have continued to pursue syncretism and innovation, very often finding

---

70. Latour, *Reassembling the Social*, 81.

themselves working with the tropes and narrative modes of "popular" cultural forms where such occult literary invention has already occurred, such as fantasy, the gothic and science fiction, resulting in an array of integrated cultural actors which Christopher Partridge has termed "occulture."[71] Beneath these layers of innovation and abstraction, authors from best-selling nineteenth-century novelist Edward Bulwer-Lytton to contemporary magician/scribe Alan Moore have used fiction to explore experiences or share information not publically discussed elsewhere.[72] In some such cases, literary criticism of occult fiction can provide us with the clearest possible window into particular currents or individuals about which little else is known.[73]

After establishing Williams's historical relationship to other modern occult figures and concepts, therefore, this book turns to literary criticism to analyze his engagement with esoteric knowledge through the refracted context of his novels, bringing the occultist dimensions of his work "back to light" by treating his novels as nodes in the modern occult network.[74] Themes, settings, and characters informed by occult theory and symbolism—particularly modern interpretations of kabbalah, alchemy, and magic—are identified and interpreted in light of the historical context in which Williams

---

71. Christopher H. Partridge, *The Re-Enchantment of the West: Alternative Spiritualities, Sacralization, Popular Culture, and Occulture* (London: T & T Clark International, 2004), esp. I:4–6, 69, 85. On the creative narrativity of occult knowledge see Kilcher, "7 Epistemological Theses," 147, and further discussion in Chapter Three, p. xxx.

72. Moore's *Promethea* series, for example, is itself a work that assumes a radical consanguinity of narrative and reality, relying on a Hermetic metaphysical framework in doing so. See Wouter J. Hanegraaff, "Alan Moore's *Promethea*: Countercultural Gnosis and the End of the World," *Gnosis: Journal of Gnostic Studies* 1 (2016): 234–58.

73. See, e.g., Mark Morrisson's attempt to grasp how theories formed in physics and chemistry affected modern alchemical concepts (and vice versa) via the fiction of occultists from Bulwer-Lytton to Charles Williams (*Modern Alchemy*, 22–28, 31–32), and Susan Johnston Graf's investigation of Algernon Blackwood's Golden Dawn affiliation via his fiction (*Talking to the Gods: Occultism in the Work of W.B. Yeats, Arthur Machen, Algernon Blackwood, and Dion Fortune* (New York: State University of New York Press, 2015), 81).

74. On the potential offered to literary criticism by ANT's emphasis on texts, among other objects, as social actors, see Felski, *The Limits of Critique*, 162–66.

encountered them, thus reestablishing what Umberto Eco terms the "referential power" of signifiers that are easily misunderstood because the forum of interpretation is too far removed from their historical context.[75] It is not only the novels themselves that require the "bringing back to light" Latour describes, but also the various esoteric signifiers found throughout his fiction. The bulk of these symbols, allusions and references to occult practice are related to magical, kabbalistic and alchemical phenomena, much of it encountered in the F.R.C. I will thus focus my interpretation of occult elements of Williams's fiction in the context of these four esoteric traditions.

A central assumption that this book relies upon (and hopes to substantiate) is that certain works of fiction rely for their narrative construction on a dual relationship between experience and expression. From this viewpoint, though it is possible to read Charles Williams's novels as stand-alone objects, they can be more comprehensively interpreted by analyzing the experiential dimensions that emerge from biographical data; conversely, these same experiential dimensions (and their corresponding belief structures) can be better understood when viewed through the prism of the novels, which are, in part, narratives that strive to authenticate and explore these experiences. There is clear danger of authorial fallacy in such a methodology; it must be pursued with caution, rooting interpretation within biographical dimensions that can be, or are already, well established, while remaining aware of the ultimate impossibility of extracting meaning that is either true to authorial intent or separable from the subjective functions of reader interpretation, including my own. However, I proceed in spite of this danger of fallacy for three reasons. First, while I agree with Latour that it is impossible for a text to communicate meaning commensurably from author to recipient,[76] this difficulty should not be allowed to prorogue the possibility of

---

75. Umberto Eco, *The Limits of Interpretation* (Bloomington; Indianapolis: Indiana University Press, 1990), 5.
76. Bruno Latour, *An Inquiry into Modes of Existence: An Anthropology of the Moderns*, trans. Catherine Porter (Cambridge, MA: Harvard University Press, 2013), 247.

clarifying an author's assumptions, beliefs, intentions and priorities through analysis of putatively fictional writings. Second, Williams's tendency to, like other occultists, explore certain aspects of esoteric knowledge and experience only in fiction leaves us with no better approach to understanding his engagement with occultism and his place in its intellectual and social networks. Third, the likelihood of revealing crucial aspects of biography and personal philosophy via criticism of the products of authorship are perhaps more enhanced in Williams's case than in that of most any other writer of fiction. T.S. Eliot certainly saw his friend's work in this light, writing shortly after Williams's death, "I can think of no writer who was more wholly the same man in his life and in his writings."[77] As Bosky observes, the level of hyperreality in Williams's fiction is unique: "Only Williams… provides such conviction and demands such belief, while still insisting upon plot-devices which—apparently—even he regarded as dramatically incredible."[78] If anyone committed an authorial fallacy, says Sørina Higgins, "it was Williams himself," so acute was the degree of closeness he drew between life and fiction.[79] There is an inextricable relationship between Williams's personal belief structure and his work, a bond so transparent that we can see beyond the boundaries of the novels—guided by their dim glow—into the shadows that have obscured the question of his interest in occultism.

This analysis of occult elements of Williams's life and fiction thus aims to bring the venerable traditions of literary and theological study of his work together with relatively new historical approaches to esotericism, expanding the network of Williams scholarship in the process. I begin in Chapter One by highlighting pertinent elements

---

77. T.S. Eliot, preface to *All Hallows' Eve*, by Charles Williams (New York: Noonday, 1948), xi.

78. Bernadette Bosky, "Charles Williams: Occult Fantasies/Occult Fact," in *Modes of the Fantastic: Selected Essays from the Twelfth International Conference on the Fantastic in the Arts*, ed. Robert A. Latham and Robert A. Collins (London: Greenwood, 1995), 178. Cf. Cavaliero, *Poet of Theology*, ix.

79. Sørina Higgins, "The Matter of Logres: Arthuriana and the Inklings," in *The Inklings and King Arthur: J.R.R. Tolkien, Charles Williams, C.S. Lewis and Owen Barfield on the Matter of Britain*, ed. Sørina Higgins (Berkeley, CA: Apocryphile, 2017), 52.

of biography for both Williams and Waite, followed by a comparison of the central tenets of their philosophies and an illustration of the manner in which both men integrated Christian and occult elements into their belief systems—Williams relatively unproblematically, Waite with a greater degree of complex identity politics. In Chapter Two I reconstruct Williams's initiatory trajectory in the F.R.C. from the rituals and records of his attendance in the order's meeting minutes. I then assess the question of the F.R.C.'s occult lineage by comparing its structure and ritual language to that of the Golden Dawn, which, I argue, is in many ways a genetic precursor of Waite's order. Chapter Three analyzes the relationship between Williams's F.R.C. experiences and the construction of his fiction, developing a theory of interchange between narrative and the lived fantasy of esoteric practice. After reviewing the central themes and content of the novels, I illustrate the interconnections between artistic process and personal experience in Williams's work by evaluating several passages that indicate a direct interplay between the novels and the F.R.C. ritual environment.

The next four chapters analyze Williams's relationship to occultism in the context of three esoteric traditions essential to both the author and most modern occult systems. Chapter Four places Williams's obscure fictional renderings of kabbalistic symbolism in the context of Waite's modern adaptations of imagery derived from the Jewish mystical tradition, particularly occultist interpretations of the "middle pillar" of the Tree of Life; connections between this symbolism and the tarot; and Shekinah, a feminine aspect of God immanent in the world, who Williams frequently encountered in the F.R.C. as a "Guide of Paths" to mystical attainment. Chapters Five and Six evaluate the one area of Williams's occult engagement that has received significant research attention in the past—his interest in magic. Chapter Five discusses Williams's development of a concept of magic as a "high-priestess" tradition of ancient wisdom pertaining to the successful achievement of mystical attainment—a central goal of modern magic. I then evaluate this "higher magic" in the context of the ritual engagement with language, movement and image in the

INTRODUCTION: THROUGH THE PORTAL

F.R.C., revealing a number of phenomenological similarities to the practices of other modern occult orders, which tended to share the F.R.C.'s goal of elevating consciousness through techniques such as visualization and meditation. Chapter Six interprets the magical elements of Williams's theory of coinherence, as well as his use of ritual magic to elevate his libido for poetic and mystical purposes, in the context of fictional portrayals of these practices. Building from this analysis, I identify a consistent magical ethic based on a dichotomy between selfish and selfless intention—a contrast resonant with the approach to magic taken by many other occultists—and situate Williams's attraction to magic in the context of "reanimation"—a psychologically motivated turn to magic in order to experience a more enchanted view of the world and the place of the self in human society. Chapter Seven examines the importance of alchemical philosophy and symbolism to Williams's system and occult experiences. In particular, I focus on the relevance of modern spiritual alchemy to the transmutations of body, psyche and spirit presented in the novels. In all four chapters, Williams's engagement with these esoteric traditions is explored through literary analysis of his seven novels of fantastic fiction, in dialogue with the wider historical context to which these works allude.

This book does not, regrettably, have the scope to focus on the impact of earlier developments in the esoteric traditions that interested Williams. The influence of these movements is strong, particularly that of Renaissance and early modern permutations of kabbalah, alchemy, and magic. However, the author's modern esoteric influences have received far less attention and recognition—no work currently exists which has taken advantage of the radically expanded view of modern occultism offered by recent research such as that of Wouter J. Hanegraaff, Alex Owen, Marco Pasi, Egil Asprem, Henrik Bogdan, and Olav Hammer. This book also does not attempt to add to the already significant amount of biographical data available, which was much enhanced by Lindop's biography, a thorough, well-researched account of Williams's life which exhaustively explores the complex strands of the author's personal and intellectual involvements, including his occult activities. One exception to this caveat is in-depth research into Williams's experiences in the F.R.C., an area that has not been as thoroughly explored and which is vital for understanding the extent of his esoteric activities. While I will touch briefly on the fascinating realms of word and myth presented in his volumes of poetry, close analysis of his verse is also outside the purview of this volume.[80] Finally, a word on research motivation: this book focuses exclusively on relations between Williams and occultism, but I have as little wish to categorize him primarily as an occultist as I do to see him branded as solely Christian. It is my continuing aim in this exploration of his occult life and fiction to maintain the state of critical flexibility for which Williams himself advocated: Upset with the critic S.L. Bethell's overtly Christian interpretation of Shakespeare, Williams moaned dramatically, "Let us—O let us leave that great ambiguous figure, his own ambiguity!...We ought to remain content with 'half-knowledge'; the 'irritable reaching' after identity of doctrine is as dangerous on one side as on the other."[81]

I conclude this exploration of Williams's occult life and fiction by evaluating its reflections in the attraction to occultism displayed by one of his characters—Roger Ingram of *Shadows of Ecstasy*. Roger chooses, despite the disapproval of most of his friends and family, to follow Nigel Considine, perhaps the most consummate occultist of Williams's magician characters. As several critics have noted, Considine represents both critical and approbatory stances toward modern occult practice.[82] The process of writing and editing between 1925 and 1932 may have been, among other things, a part of Williams's explo-

---

80. For sustained analysis of Williams's poetry, some of it touching on esoteric elements, see Roma A. King, *The Pattern in the Web: The Mythical Poetry of Charles Williams* (Kent, OH: Kent State University Press, 1990).
81. Charles Williams, "*Time and Tide* Review of *Shakespeare and the Popular Dramatic Tradition*, by S.L. Bethell, 1944," in *The Image of the City*, ed. Anne Ridler (Berkeley: Apocryphile, 2007), 39.
82. McLaren, "A Problem of Morality," 121–24; Grevel Lindop, *Charles Williams: The Third Inkling* (Oxford: Oxford University Press, 2015), 111; Ashenden, *Charles Williams*, 98.

ration of his own place in the modern occult network. The novel is thus helpful in addressing a number of important questions: What attracted Williams to esoteric concepts and imagery? Which ideas was he prepared to accept? Which must be rejected? How did concepts like spiritual alchemy, magic and the achievement of mystical experience through ritual fit with his Christian faith? A connection between Roger and his creator can only be suggestive, but the novel is certainly, like all of Williams's fiction, a vehicle for negotiating and translating occult ideas and experiences. By interpreting the novels with historical awareness of these experiences and their wider context in esoteric epistemology and modern occult practice, we can uncover processes of interior and exterior exploration that still reverberate between the lines of his fiction.

CHAPTER 1
LIFE AND TIMES
CHRISTIAN OCCULTISM IN MODERN ENGLAND

Superficially, there was nothing especially distinguished about Charles Walter Stansby Williams. He spoke with a lower middle class London accent, and appeared at first sight, as T.S. Eliot noted, as a "plain, spectacled man of rather frail physique."[1] There was nothing to mark him out as one who walked, by the end of his life, among the literary elite of modern England, or one that appeared to followers and admirers as a spiritual guru; a holy exemplar. Yet, said Eliot, once he made himself known—particularly once he began to speak—people were beguiled by "his liveliness, his intelligence and his amiability." If they were really alert they might even notice "a kind of extra perceptiveness…a spiritual sense."[2] C.S. Lewis told a friend that Williams was "ugly as a chimpanzee" but so radiant that "as soon as he begins talking he is transfigured and looks like an angel. He sweeps some people quite off their feet and has many disciples. Women find him so attractive that if he were a bad man he

---
1. T.S. Eliot, "The Significance of Charles Williams," *Listener*, 19 December 1946, 894. Cf. Carpenter, *The Inklings*, 73; Lindop, *Charles Williams*, vii.
2. Eliot, "The Significance of Charles Williams," 894.

could do what he liked either as a Don Juan or a charlatan."[3] This charisma seems to have emerged from a fascination with "what he had to say and how he said it"[4]—the result of what one of his followers called "extraordinary intellectual and spiritual powers"[5]— but also from an intangible mystique that Williams wrapped round both his exterior persona and his perception of the world—an overarching mythos accumulated from Arthurian legend, biblical imagery and occult symbolism into which those that interacted with him were pulled as major and minor characters. "I had a dark suspicion," said Phyllis Jones, a long time lover, "That he was not born of ordinary parents but that Merlin or some other magician brought him."[6] Such reactions to Williams are indicative of an insistent hagiography that rose among his friends and followers and coloured the early decades of Williams study.[7] Fortunately, recent decades have seen more careful biographical approaches, particularly by Grevel Lindop, that have shed light on the life of a passionate writer, a devoted but distracted husband, an active socialite and workaholic, and above all a man of paradoxical act, belief and intention: Charles Williams loved many women but seems only to have consummated this love with one; he adored the concept of royalty but held left-wing

---

3. C.S. Lewis to Arthur Greeves, quoted in Carpenter, *The Inklings*, 101. Cf. Cavaliero, *Poet of Theology*, 3–4.
4. M. Joyce Taylor, "Charles Williams," unpublished recollections, 1983, CWSA II.A.1.
5. Alice Mary Hadfield, *An Introduction to Charles Williams* (London: Robert Hale, 1959), 16.
6. Phyllis Jones to Charles Williams, Bodleian MS Res. c. 320, mixed undated II, c. 1929-30m f.47a, quoted in Lindop, *Charles Williams*, 129. Jones is writing in the 1920s, imagining herself talking to her future grandchildren about Williams.
7. Alice Mary Hadfield's two biographies, *An Introduction to Charles Williams* (1959) and *Charles Williams: An Exploration of his Life and Work* (1983), though indispensable to our knowledge of Williams's life, are particularly problematic in this area as she seems to have felt a responsibility to Williams to keep particular aspects of his life secret. See Lindop, *Charles Williams*, 136. Cf. Reilly, *Romantic Religion*, 148–49. As Lindop observes, "The reverential tone of much that was written about Williams after his death has obscured interesting sides of him" ("Charles Williams and His Contemporaries," 15). Lindop's biography goes a long way toward addressing this deficiency. For other helpful biographies see David Llewellyn Dodds, *Charles Williams* (Woodbridge, Suffolk: Boydell, 1991), 316–29; Cavaliero, *Poet of Theology*, 1–8.

politics dear enough that he half hoped the Russian Revolution would succeed;[8] he espoused saintliness but practiced a secretive sadomasochism with young female devotees for most of his adult life. His life and work is typified by a strange tension between contradiction and harmonious synthesis, and therein is its continuing source of magic.

Williams lived and breathed the productive freneticism of London until the last few years of his life, when he was relocated to Oxford to escape the bombings of WWII. Born in Holloway on 20 September 1886, his family relocated to Islington in 1889.[9] After spending his teen years to the north of the metropolis in St Albans, Williams would return to spend most of his life living in Hampstead, studying in Bloomsbury, and working in Holborn and Tooting. The moves from place to place in childhood were precipitated by poverty. His father, a clerk, lost his job due to blindness and opened an art supply store in St Albans with the help of a relative; the store never fared well and Charles's career prospects suffered as a result. Pure ability, however, won out. With the help of scholarships he attended St Albans Grammar School from 1899 to 1901 and then began commuting daily to a pre-degree program at University College London in January 1902. His UCL scholarship would have carried over to fund a full BA, but Williams was forced to withdraw after only a year because the family could no longer afford the additional costs. Here fate would have cut the career of an influential literary figure off at the stem, but better fortune was in store. Fred Page, a friend Charles met at his first job at the Methodist Book Room in Holborn, found him a job at the London offices of the Oxford University Press (OUP) in the "Paper, Printing, and Proof-Reading Department," where he began work on 9 June 1908 and never left.[10]

Even in childhood, Williams lived an inward-focused existence; myth and fantasy dotted the pages of books and also sprang forth

---

8. Lindop, *Charles Williams*, 67.
9. On the following details from Williams's childhood see ibid, 6–28; Carpenter, *The Inklings*, 76–77; Hadfield, *Introduction to Charles Williams*, 12–29.
10. *Introduction to Charles Williams*, 35.

into life. At five, a bout of measles left him extremely near-sighted but his condition was undiagnosed and he did not wear glasses as a child.[11] This or another childhood illness may have caused a lifelong nervous tremor that kept him from physical activity—he showed little interest in sport and was not fit to fight in WWI.[12] Thus, though he would always emphasize the value of physical sensation, the full gamut of this avenue of experience was unavailable to him from a young age, a deprivation that no doubt contributed to his love of reading and learning. His father's influence likely deepened his habit of imagination—Richard Walter "Stansby" Williams had an enquiring mind and a large, diverse collection of books.[13] He published a significant number of his own short fiction pieces and approached his son's education with an emphasis on avoiding dogma —teaching young Charles to pursue a multivalent perspective that sought legitimacy in a variety of angles taken to every issue.[14] The young Charles was thus provided with both a model of the intellectual spirit and a constant spring from which it could be fed.

The literariness and inward, mythopoeic focus of the young Williams would manifest early in a lived approach to fantasy. In adolescence he and a boyhood friend, George Robinson, invented a mythical East European kingdom called "Silvania" and frequently crossed its imaginal borders until well into their late teens, along with Charles's sister Edith. Lindop relates one Silvanian experience that indicates an early interest in ritual, a taste which would later manifest in his enthusiastic participation in the rites of the F.R.C.: In Silvania the boys founded the "Order of the Golden Cross" and went through an initiatory "Ceremony of Installation of Knight Imperial of the Golden Cross."[15] Williams brought this same love of story and

---

11. Lindop, *Charles Williams*, 5–6.
12. Ibid, 47. Charles's sister Edith theorized that his nervous tremor was caused by psychological difficulties—which often led to outbursts—experienced in his teens as a result of the family's financial difficulties and resulting marital stress (Edith M. Williams, "Memories of Early Days at Home," CWSA IV.B/5,4a).
13. Edith M. Williams, "Memories of Early Days at Home," CWSA IV.B/5,5–5a.
14. Carpenter, *The Inklings*, 77.
15. Lindop, *Charles Williams*, 15; Carpenter, *The Inklings*, 77. This experience indicates

ritual to his participation each Sunday in Anglican services. This boyhood enjoyment led to his confirmation in 1901 and a lifelong passion for sacred rites—Christian or otherwise.

Myth and ritual continued to define his life as he reached adulthood. In 1917 he married Florence Conway after nine years dating, but was rarely happy in married life. The birth of a son, Michael, in 1922, only seems to have contributed to a sense of feeling overwhelmed by the rigours of material life, demands increasingly at odds with his poetic soul.[16] Perhaps to overcome this dissatisfaction, Charles involved himself in many extramarital affairs. These were never actually consummated so far as we know, but they did involve physical relations of a different sort and consumed much of his time and energy in letter writing and romantic excursions. Much of this time was spent with Phyllis Jones, the second love of his life. The two met in 1926 when Phyllis joined London's OUP branch, and quickly fell in love. As he had done with his wife, Williams romanticized Phyllis, this time as three different women—"Celia," the poetic ideal of Phyllis, literally "the manifestation of divine glory in female human form";[17] "Phillida," her earthly counterpart, and "Circassia," the aspect of Phyllis that engaged with Williams in strange, mildly sadomasochistic rituals that he seems to have begun in his relationship with Phyllis, but which he would continue long after,[18] apparently motivated by a combination of simple lust and a complex practice of artistic and magical sublimation, intended to transmute the forces of eros into artistic energy.[19] In an unknown number of

---

an early knowledge of Freemasonry and/or Rosicrucianism. Williams's source for this knowledge is unknown.

16. Lindop, *Charles Williams*, 85–88.
17. Ibid, 139.
18. See ibid, 140. Lindop covers Williams's relationship with Phyllis Jones (Mcdougall) in detail, based on a collection of letters held in a restricted archive at the Bodleian Library in Oxford. See 123–31; 135–48; 157–60; 172–80; 181–83; 204–6; 221–23; 246–50. Ashenden publishes a number of excerpts from letters lent to him by Jones and analyzes Williams's relationship with Celia in light of his Romantic Theology (*Charles Williams*, 189–231).
19. See Lindop, *Charles Williams*, 340. This concept is discussed in greater detail in Chapter Six.

relationships with young admirers, he established himself as schoolmaster and his partners as pupil—setting out essays on subjects that suited the moment and person in question and threatening punishment if they were not completed satisfactorily. Sometimes these punishments were actually carried out—Phyllis received smacks on the hand or commands to bend over a desk or chair for a light, firm hit to a more erogenous zone. Phyllis, like most of the others, played along enthusiastically, even when, at its heights, these relationships went from master and pupil to master and slave.[20] "I am sadistic towards you," he admitted to Phyllis. He excused this as a sort of benign mastery for the purposes of instruction,[21] but the reality of his proclivities seems closer to the "constantly present" sadism identified by Humphrey Carpenter than Hadfield's hagiographic claim that Williams "had a quality that enabled him to walk in this fire and not be consumed."[22] Hadfield's statement has some merit, as Williams was more than capable of sustaining deep, meaningful relationships without any erotic element at all, while other romantic relationships seem not to have involved any sadomasochism.[23] Even in those that did, his actions were certainly condemnatory by today's standards, but more difficult to situate ethically in his own time: he always seems to have operated with some understanding of a need for consent, and his partners maintained positive views of his impact on their lives, with the notable exception of Lois Lang-Sims, whom he met in his Oxford days.[24]

We cannot know for sure that Phyllis was the first woman whom Williams persuaded to join him in such rituals, but it is noteworthy that the first documented occurrences of this ritualistic behaviour happened just after Williams ceased his involvement in the ritualistic

---

20. Ibid, 139–40.
21. Charles Williams to Phyllis Jones, 29 October 1930, quoted in Hadfield, *Charles Williams: An Exploration*, 104–5.
22. Carpenter, *The Inklings*, 84; Hadfield, *Charles Williams: An Exploration*, 90.
23. See Lindop, *Charles Williams*, 197, 230–32.
24. Ibid, 340. The relationship between Lang-Sims and Williams is discussed in Chapter Six.

activities of the Fellowship of the Rosy Cross. Remarkably, Williams seems to have kept his involvement with Waite's order a much better secret than his romantic flings, though it was only after his death that the sadomasochistic flavour of some of these relationships was revealed. Hadfield, a friend, coworker and devoted follower from their meeting in 1933 to Williams's death in 1945, knew so little about his involvement that she confused the F.R.C. with the Hermetic Order of the Golden Dawn, assuming Williams and W.B. Yeats, a member of another branch of the Golden Dawn, to be partners in ritual.[25] His wife knew nothing of the order, wanted to know nothing, and was able to state definitively, despite this level of awareness, that it had not affected her husband in any way.[26] As will become clear in the course of this book, however, Williams's ten years in the F.R.C. had an enormous influence on his thought, enriched the diverse symbolic toolbox from which he constructed his fiction and poetry, and satisfied, for a time, his yearning for experience via ritual.

Away from the secretive corners of his private life, Williams slowly acquired professional success through hard work, prolific publication, and a network of friends and contacts that helped publish and promote his work. One of the most impactful of these friendships was formed in 1934 when influential literary patron, Lady Ottoline Morrell, introduced him to T.S. Eliot. As Lindop points out, both men were committed to a "Christian mysticism enriched by a knowledge of other mysticisms," so it is no surprise that they saw value in each other's work.[27] Eliot seems to have felt particular affinity with Williams's interest in the Matter of Britain, telling Charles shortly after their meeting that he had never met someone interested in the Arthurian legends "in quite the same way as

---

25. Hadfield, *Charles Williams: An Exploration*, 29. Cf. Carpenter, *The Inklings*, 98.
26. Lindop, *Charles Williams*, 78.
27. "Charles Williams and His Contemporaries," 10. On Eliot's exploration of various mystical movements, including occultism, Bergsonian philosophy, and a Christian mysticism motivated by the work of Evelyn Underhill, see Donald J. Childs, *T.S. Eliot: Mystic, Son and Lover* (London: Athlone Press, 1997), 1–52.

myself"[28]—high praise from a man who produced one of the most seminal twentieth-century contributions to Arthurian mysticism with "The Waste Land."[29] Their decade-long friendship would result in Eliot publishing Williams's last two novels, commissioning him to write a history of witchcraft, and promoting his work following his friend's death.

Another friendship begun shortly thereafter was to prove even more impactful for Williams's legacy. In March of 1936 he received a letter from Clive Staples Lewis, who had just read *The Place of the Lion* and wrote to Williams to declare it "one of the major literary events of my life," comparable to his discoveries of George MacDonald, G.K. Chesterton and William Morris.[30] Lewis invited Williams to come up to Oxford to meet with the Inklings, a group of writers and intellectuals who had formed in Oxford in 1933 with Lewis at its fulcrum.[31] For the remainder of his life, Williams revelled creatively and socially in his interaction with this group, a forum in which he met a number of influential writers, including J.R.R. Tolkien. Lewis and Tolkien helped Williams refine his late poetry and his last novel, *All Hallows Eve*,[32] and he influenced their work in turn, particularly their fantastic fiction. Lewis told him that the last chapter of *That Hideous Strength* (1945) was based on Williams's concept of coinherence—a belief that the bodies, minds and souls of each human being inhere in each other by virtue of the indwelling spirit of the divine. Williams was actually less than enthusiastic about this, as he worried in a private letter that the world would attribute his ideas to Lewis.[33] He had the same worry about Lewis's *A Preface to Paradise Lost* (1942), an analysis of Milton's epic that Williams felt was motivated by his own lectures on the topic, given at Oxford after Lewis and Tolkien

---

28. T.S. Eliot to Charles Williams, 7 October 1934, Bodleian Ms. Res. c.137, f.2.
29. On the Arthurian mysticism of both Eliot and Williams see Moorman, *Arthurian Triptych*. On Williams alone see Dodds, *Charles Williams*.
30. C.S. Lewis to Charles Williams, 11 March 1936, Bodleian Ms. Res. c.137, f. 2.
31. For a brief history of the Inklings see Carpenter, *The Inklings*, 67.
32. Lindop, *Charles Williams*, 395.
33. Ibid, 278.

conspired to get him a lectureship in 1940.³⁴ Interestingly, Lewis seems to have experienced a similar worry in reverse. In a letter of 1938, he mock-jealously condemned Williams for "getting steadily better" since their meeting two years earlier, and predicted, perhaps somewhat patronizingly, that Williams would come to eclipse him: "I begin to suspect that we are living in the 'age of Williams' and our friendship with you will be our only passport to fame. I've a good mind to punch your head when we next meet."³⁵ Nothing of the sort came to pass—it was, ironically, Williams's association with the Inklings that would ensure the continued currency of his work.

Williams also had a part to play in the writing of what is arguably the Anglo-American world's most famous work of fantastic fiction—Tolkien's *The Lord of the Rings*, written between 1937 and 1949. Williams sat on many occasions with Lewis and others, listening as Tolkien read from his work-in-progress. Shortly before his death, Williams was the first person to read *The Fellowship of the Ring* and *The Two Towers* in continuous typescript, after which the two authors discussed the manuscript at length.³⁶ As a number of critics have suggested, it is likely not coincidence that the magical objects of several Williams novels seem to directly presage the ring that must be borne by Bilbo and Frodo Baggins in Tolkien's epic.³⁷ Just as Frodo must cast the ring desired by the sorcerous demi-god Sauron into Mount Doom, so must Williams's heroes return the occult powers of the graal of *War in Heaven*, the stone of *Many Dimensions*, and the tarot trumps of *The Greater Trumps* to the supernatural realm from whence they came. Williams's influence on Tolkien was likely less pronounced than the impression made on Lewis. Though the two men were good friends during Williams's lifetime, Tolkien recalled misgivings about his character and found some of his work "distaste-

---

34. Ibid, 314.
35. C.S. Lewis to Charles Williams, 7 June 1938, Bodleian Ms. Res. c.137, f. 2.
36. Lindop, *Charles Williams*, 410. Cf. Duriez and Porter, *The Inklings Handbook*, 6.
37. See, e.g., Caleb Crain, "What We're Reading: Charles Williams," *New Yorker*, 13 March 2013, http://www.newyorker.com/books/page-turner/what-were-reading-charles-williams.

ful."[38] Lewis, on the other hand, was, in Tolkien's words, "bowled over."[39] He thought Williams a great thinker of his day, and a man of whom it was not absurd to say, "He will in the end stand as the great English poet of this age."[40]

Lewis's slightly overwrought prediction reflects the fact that though Williams is recognized more for his novels today, it was as a poet that he centrally defined himself. He published seven volumes of verse, to varying degrees of acclaim. Two late publications, *Taliessen Through Logres* (1938) and *The Region of the Summer Stars* (1944) are often considered to represent the culmination of his evolution towards a unique poetic voice. These poems—interwoven, like the novels, with layers of esoteric symbolism—form Williams's Arthurian cycle, on which he worked for decades. He began research around 1911, consulting works like Jesse Weston's *From Ritual to Romance* (1920), which proposed the Holy Grail as a universal, pre-Christian symbol, James Frazer's *The Golden Bough* (1890), and Waite's *Hidden Church of the Holy Graal* (1909), but had difficulty actually doing much writing of the poems until the 1930s, when he published several early instalments in *Heroes and Kings* (1930/31).[41]

Williams was as varied in his publications as he was prolific—perhaps as a result of too easily accepting commissions. He was always in need of funds and recognition and could scarce afford to turn down projects as diverse as biographies of James I (1931) and Elizabeth I (1936); plays written for local dioceses such as *Thomas Cranmer of Canterbury* (1936) and *Judgement at Chelmsford* (1939); more than one hundred articles and reviews published with weekly magazine *Time and Tide*;[42] and commissions for theological texts such as

---

38. Carpenter, *The Inklings*, 121.
39. Ibid.
40. C.S. Lewis, "Charles Walter Stansby Williams (1886–1945): An Obituary," *Oxford Magazine* 63 (24 March 1945). Cf. Curtis, "Charles Williams," 139.
41. Lindop, *Charles Williams*, 42–44; David Llewellyn Dodds, "Continuity and Change in the Development of Charles Williams's Poetic Style," in *The Rhetoric of Vision: Essays on Charles Williams*, ed. Charles A. Huttar and Peter J. Schakel (Lewisburg, VA: Bucknell University Press, 1996), 194.
42. Lindop, *Charles Williams*, 130, 284.

The Descent of the Dove (1939), a short history of Christianity sprinkled with elements of Williams's heterodox theology, and *He Came Down from Heaven* (1938), a series of essays that apply a mix of literary criticism and theology to the Bible and, again, expound on some of Williams's own unique concepts. In 1941, in response to a commission from Eliot in his editorial position at Faber and Faber, Williams published *Witchcraft*, a history of magic that, unfortunately, ends with the Salem trials of 1692, thus denying us a straight-forward impression of his thoughts on modern occult theory and practice. He also produced a number of works of literary criticism. His lack of formal education caused him to read widely and autodidactically, resulting in a unique understanding of the nature of poetry and how to read it.[43] He brought this original poetics, honed, Lindop argues, by decades of teaching at the Evening Institute in Tooting and the City Literary institute in Holborn,[44] to a number of critical works, including *The Figure of Beatrice* (1943), a study of Dante's *Divine Comedy* (1320) that intermixes criticism with religious expression, interpreting Dante's idealization of Beatrice in light of Williams's own theology of romantic love. *The Figure of Beatrice* thus reflects a philosophy of mystical eros already developed in *Outlines of Romantic Theology*, written in the early 1920s but rejected by OUP after its reader, Bishop Strong of Oxford, rejected it as too unorthodox.[45]

"BUT ABOUT THIS REALITY OF YOURS..."

Whether he was writing theology or poetry, history or fiction, a full-length work or a review for *Time and Tide*, Williams could not help but infuse his work with elements of his heterodox philosophy. A quick elucidation of three central concepts is necessary before proceeding much further: the "way of affirmation," "Romantic Theology," and "coinherence." All three of these principles are based on a

---

43. "Charles Williams and His Contemporaries," 4–5.
44. See Lindop, *Charles Williams*, 130, 286.
45. Carpenter, *The Inklings*, 104. *Outlines* was not published until 1990.

wholesale rejection of materialist ontologies. Williams insisted on the reality of a spiritual realm, but, as in most esoteric systems, not one isolated in transcendence. For him the spiritual intricately connected to, and upheld, the visible phenomena of the material world, reflecting the Hermetic belief in an integrated cosmos in which the natural and supernal worlds reflect and enrich each other. This maxim, sometimes known as the doctrine of correspondences, proposes that the physical world, or microcosm, temporally reflects the eternal stasis of the macrocosm, variously conceived as a world of ideas or forms in the Platonic sense, as a realm of (usually ineffable) divinity, or as an unseen world populated with various spirits, elementals, demons and intelligences.[46] Williams describes the doctrine of correspondences as both a perennial wisdom universal to all creation and human experience, and as a specific historical tradition handed down from Near-Eastern antiquity: "It is a very ancient idea; it was held before Christianity and has been held during Christianity; it was common to Christians, Jews, and Mohammedans."[47] He interpreted the doctrine of correspondences both as "the idea that man is a small replica of the universe," and as an "imagination of relation in the universe."[48] In the first interpretation man is the microcosm, in the second all of nature plays this role; both conceptions are common in the history of esoteric thought. In the latter concept, the worlds above and below are perceived to be linked through acausal relationships of sympathy and/or similarity. This perception of inextricable unity between microcosm and macrocosm creates relationships between apparently dissimilar phenomena based on a logic of analogy or similitude, violating the laws of physics

---

46. Antoine Faivre lists the concept of correspondences as one of four definitive identifiers of esoteric thought (Faivre, *Access to Western Esotericism*, 10–15). Cf. B. J. Gibbons, *Spirituality and the Occult: From the Renaissance to the Modern Age* (London: Routledge, 2001), 6–7.

47. Williams, "Index of the Body," 82. On Williams's understanding of correspondences and the doctrine's importance to his belief system, see Ashenden, *Charles Williams*, 131–39, 166–69; R.A. King, "Occult as Rhetoric", 167; Reilly, *Romantic Religion*, 153–56; McLaren, "A Problem of Morality," 111.

48. Williams, "Index of the Body," 82, 83.

as understood since Descartes.⁴⁹ This infinity of possible relationships had important artistic implications for Williams, as it assumed what Michel Foucault calls a "homosemanticism,"⁵⁰ a semiotic state in which any signifier could relate productively to any other, enabling a Romantic imaginative and esoteric innovator like Williams to produce multivalent symbolic and interpretative possibilities in his poetry and prose. The doctrine of correspondences was also important to Williams's magical practices, as I will discuss further in Chapter Six, but its most significant ramification was, for him, the incarnation of Christ. As a living manifestation of God in nature, Christ modelled the interdependence of the human and the divine: "As above, so below," wrote Williams, "As in him, so in us."⁵¹ The intricate divine/human entanglement established by the incarnation had repercussions for man as microcosm in Williams's system, as he followed in a long line of esoteric and mystical thinkers who sought the means of human movement between micro- and macrocosm—mystical ascension from material to divine realms via the link between human mind and divine mind, human soul and divine soul, a journey made by a number of characters in his novels, including the Archdeacon Julian Davenant of *War in Heaven*, who moves through the "narrow channel" between the worlds when he ascends to "undreamed perfection" in the denouement.⁵²

One of Williams's most repeated maxims reflects the importance of cosmic correspondence to his thinking: "This also is Thou; Neither is this Thou."⁵³ Phenomena are one with the divine—a relation of

---

49. For a survey of the history of correspondent cosmologies from Plotinus to Emanuel Swedenborg to modern occultism, see Hanegraaff, *A Guide for the Perplexed*, 129–34.
50. Michel Foucault, *The Order of Things* (London: Routledge, 2002), 54.
51. Charles Williams, *The Figure of Beatrice: A Study in Dante* (New York: Noonday Press, 1961), 10. Cf. Urang, *Shadows of Heaven*, 58.
52. Charles Williams, *War in Heaven* (Grand Rapids, MI: William B. Eerdmans, 1980), 254.
53. See, e.g., *War in Heaven*, 137; *Descent of the Dove*, 7. Cf. Cavaliero, "Introduction," 8. The maxim likely recalls the Advaita Vedanta declaration of cosmic unity: "tat tvam asi" (that art thou) and its opposite "atat tvam asi" (thou art not that), but Williams himself was unsure of its provenance. He "once supposed it to come from Augustine" but had been "informed by experts that it was not so," and was "otherwise ignorant of

matter to spirit which led Williams to refer often to God as "the Unity"[54]—so they are "Thou," but they can never actually be the distant ineffable divine and are divided from it by original sin and primordial brokenness, so they are also not Thou. Williams thus asserted that all material life and experience is a reflection of the divine and emerges from it, leading him to a conclusion far from consistent with orthodox Christianity—that evil, despair and sin were as much of God as any other phenomena. Julian Davenant comforts himself with this thought as he goes voluntarily to try and save a friend and the Holy Grail from the clutches of an evil coterie of black magicians. He feels an "overwhelming desolation," but realizes that "'This also is Thou,' for desolation as well as abundance was but a means of knowing That which was All."[55] The Archdeacon reflects Williams's unequivocal adherence to the monism suggested by the doctrine of correspondences, an insistence on holism that required the rejection, wherever possible, of dichotomy. Enthusiastic about the potential for astrological symbolism to "direct attention to principles at work both in the spatial heavens and in the structure of man's body," Williams argued that such connections completely elide the spatial with the spiritual: "'As above, so below' ran the old maxim, but even that dichotomy is doubtful."[56]

This unitive cosmology informs a key tenet of Williams's philosophy and lifestyle—the "way of affirmation," a path for the mystic life that skews toward the Romantic embrace of physical experience,

---

its source" (*Descent of the Dove*, 7). Certainly the Advaita Vedanta motto was known to Western mystics: Williams would have encountered at least the second half of the slogan, "Thou art That," in the course of the last ritual he ever performed with the F.R.C. See "The Ceremony of Consecration on the Threshold of Sacred Mystery for the Watchers of the Holy House," (Amsterdam: Bibliotheca Philosophica Hermetica, A.E. Waite Collection, 1926), 7.

54. As seen frequently, for example, in *Many Dimensions*. See, e.g., 63, 192, 198. Cf. McLaren, "A Problem of Morality," 8, 111. Williams would also be referring to the trinitarian unity of God when using this term, as well as the kabbalistic ideal of the male and female aspects of the divine as united in their higher aspects, while divided in their lower.

55. *War in Heaven*, 240. Cf. 180–81.

56. Williams, "Index of the Body," 83.

material phenomena and semiotics. He was disgusted with what he referred to as a vestigial Manicheaism still embedded in Christian theology, "the vague suggestion that the body has somehow fallen further than the soul," and therefore that the natural, physical world should be rejected in favour of a focus on the spiritual.[57] Williams described this "Way of Rejection," or "the Negative Way,"[58] as an attempt to "eject all things until there was nothing anywhere but He."[59] In contrast to this asceticism he emphasized—and lived—the way of affirmation, following a path to the divine illuminated by the symbols and experiences of the phenomenal world.[60] The way of rejection retained value for him as an ethic of "definition, discipline, and refusal,"[61] but affirmation held a stronger grip, as indicated by the power he found in word and symbol, his adoration of the female body, and his love of ritual. Artistically, affirmation could be the ultimate criterion for the value of a work. In a letter to a friend he praised George Bernard Shaw as a dramatist, religious teacher and prose writer, but branded him as "manichaean" because "he doesn't really *like* life...his figures are Whistlerian: they have no significant detail."[62] For Williams, those who avoided such dualisms "might apprehend most easily the divine imagery of matter,"[63] discovering the divine through the signposts of the natural world and the myths and rituals that arise from them.

Even more vital to the way of affirmation was eros.[64] In Williams's system, the correspondence between divine and human meant that

---

57. *Descent of the Dove*, 57. Cf. *Outlines of Romantic Theology*, 9; Ashenden, *Charles Williams*, 65; Ridler, "Introduction to *The Image of the City*," xxxviii.
58. Williams, *Figure of Beatrice*, 9. *Descent of the Dove*, 58.
59. Williams, *Descent of the Dove*, 58.
60. On the ways of affirmation and negation see Williams, *Figure of Beatrice*, 9; "Way of Affirmation," 154. Cf. C.S. Lewis, "Williams and the Arthuriad," in Charles Williams and C. S. Lewis, *Arthurian Torso, Containing the Posthumous Fragment of the Figure of Arthur* (Oxford: Oxford University Press, 1948); Ashenden, *Charles Williams*, 56–62; Ridler, "Introduction to *the Image of the City*," xxxix–xl.
61. Williams, *Descent of the Dove*, 58.
62. Charles Williams to Thelma Mills, 1931, Bodleian MS Eng. Lett. 136.
63. Williams, *Descent of the Dove*, 58.
64. On the connection between the two, see *Figure of Beatrice*, 15–16.

all human experience could lead the soul in the direction of God, including, as with the Archdeacon, desolation. No aspects of experience were more valuable for this purpose than love and sexual desire —the manifestation of divine love in physical form. This is the basis of Williams's "Romantic Theology," a "science of God" with echoes,[65] as Stephen Medcalf observes, in Plato's concept of perceiving "the beautiful itself" through a lover.[66] Romantic Theology dictates that love, like ritual, can actually generate a feeling of unity with the divine if properly directed, by virtue of a parallel between the experience of human desire and a longing for union with God. The experience of falling in love produces "a new state of consciousness" which transmutes the body and mind of the lover, so that "his soul itself will enter upon a new state, becoming conscious of [the] grace of God."[67] Romantic love is thus a mystic practice centred squarely on the affirmation rather than the rejection of the images of the world[68]—one reaches for the body (nature), mind or soul of God by "affirming" or embracing the body, mind or soul of one's beloved. As Robert Reilly notes, the heading of "romantic experience" enabled the coming together of a diverse range of values, concepts and practices drawn from Williams's wide set of reading and influences. "Like Coleridge he was forever aiming at synthesis."[69] Of Williams's unique philosophical concepts, Romantic Theology displays perhaps the greatest degree of programmatic syncretism and its accompanying bricolage; elements of (affirmative) Christian mysticism, Dantean metaphysics, the ethos of the Romantics, kabbalah and alchemy are evident in its construction.[70]

---

65. *Outlines of Romantic Theology*, 7.
66. Stephen Medcalf, "The Athanasian Principle in Williams's Use of Images," in *The Rhetoric of Vision: Essays on Charles Williams*, ed. Charles A. Huttar and Peter J. Schakel (Lewisburg: Bucknell University Press, 1996), 27–28. The relevant passages noted by Medcalf are *Symposium*, 201D–212C and *Phaedrus*, 244A–257A.
67. Williams, *Outlines of Romantic Theology*, 15–16. Cf. *He Came Down from Heaven* (Grand Rapids, MI: William B. Eerdmans, 1984), 83–113.
68. Carpenter, *The Inklings*, 104.
69. Reilly, *Romantic Religion*, 10.
70. For more on Romantic Theology see Williams, *Outlines of Romantic Theology*; *He*

Correspondence between above and below also underpins "coinherence,"[71] a third pillar of Williams's unique philosophy. He took this patristic term, used to describe the indwelling of each member of the Christian trinity in each other, and extended it to the furthest cosmic extent of divine/human relations in order to establish what Barbara Newman calls a "reciprocity of being" with each other person on the planet.[72] He believed that this existential unity made possible the practice of "substitution," in which one person aware of their coinherence with another could offer healing or support via their correspondent connection.[73] Any form of pain, suffering and hardship could be transferred, effecting healing in the suffering party while only temporarily hurting the healer. This "substituted love" could take place across time and space,[74] and did not necessarily require the participation of the beneficiary. Towards the end of his life, as is abundantly reflected in his last two novels, Williams began to interpret all of his previously developed ideas through a coinherent filter. Where his artistic, theological and interpretive work had thus far been oriented around a quest for mystic oneness with the divine self within, by the mid-1930s he had begun to emphasize union on a more interpersonal level. A poem delivered during a toast at an annual dinner at the City Literary Institute in March of 1939 reflects the magnitude of this shift. Speaking to an audience who would likely not have understood the patristic term let alone his unique translation of it, Williams dropped "coinherence" into short text, reflecting the degree to which the concept was on his mind.[75]

Came Down, 88–110; "Sensuality and Substance," in *The Image of the City and Other Essays*, ed. Anne Ridler, 68–75 (Berkeley: Apocryphile, 2007). Cf. Mary M. Shideler, *Theology of Romantic Love: Study in the Writings of Charles Williams* (Grand Rapids, MI: Eerdmans, 1966); Ashenden, *Charles Williams*, ix, 6, 63–65; Lindop, *Charles Williams*, 110–11.

71. On coinherence see Williams, *Descent of the Dove*, 234–46. Cf. Newman, "Companions of the Co-Inherence," 6–13; Wendling, "'Flesh Knows What Spirit Knows'," 7.
72. Newman, "Companions of the Co-Inherence," 6.
73. See Williams, *He Came Down*, 114–33. Cf. Lindop, *Charles Williams*, 92, 156, 282.
74. Williams, *He Came Down*, 130.
75. "During the First Introduction," poem written for the annual dinner of the City Literary Institute, held at St. Ermin's hotel on 25 March 1939, CWSA.

Indeed, within a month he had drafted a promulgation for a secret society of his own, the "Order of the Co-Inherence," which his followers came to call the "Companions of the Co-Inherence," or "the Household."[76] Membership was mostly made up of close friends and followers. Williams intended to invite Eliot to join, and Lewis is known to have used substitution to relieve his wife's pain as she was dying of cancer,[77] but there is no evidence that either ever joined the order. The founding of the order was likely motivated in part by Williams's F.R.C. background, though there were some notable differences: The Companions was a much more loosely organized group—they had no constitution and were committed to meet only four times a year. In place of a structure and belief system rooted in hundreds of years of masonic and Rosicrucian tradition, the single axis of the Companions was the prophet of coinherence himself. Williams had made himself the master of a secret society, one that Lindop believes to have survived for roughly fifty years after his death.[78] The order's promulgation dictated that its function be *per necessitatem*, Christian," and Williams considered submitting it for "episcopal consideration," indicating that he saw the order as an extension of his Anglican belief and practice.[79] Episcopal approval, however, would have been unlikely. Like the unorthodox belief system out of which coinherence was founded, Williams's order was probably networked too closely to occultist precursors, including the F.R.C. Members of the group were dedicated to secrecy; there seems to have been a sort of initiation

---

76. See Hadfield, *Charles Williams: An Exploration*, 158–61; Lindop, *Charles Williams*, 290–93.
77. On Eliot see Lindop, "Charles Williams and His Contemporaries," 12, on Lewis see Nevill Coghill, "The Approach to English," in *Light on C.S. Lewis*, ed. Jocelyn Gibbs (London: Geoffrey Bles, 1965), 63.
78. Grevel Lindop, "Charles Williams: Magician, Inkling" (lecture, Treadwell's Books, London, UK, 10 November 2015). Lindop was still aware of people practicing substitution as of 2015.
79. Draft of "the Promulgation" for "The Order of the Coinherence," with cover letter, April 1939, Bodleian Ms. Res. c. 137, f. 1. Cf. Lindop, *Charles Williams*, 291; Hadfield, *Charles Williams: An Exploration*, 174.

ritual in some cases;[80] and the elements of ritual and magical practice in the act of substitution seem as connected to Williams's personal occult knowledge and experience as they were to his Christian faith. Because of its acausal, trans-temporal function, the practice of substitution is, as several critics have argued, inherently magical in both its praxis and its theoretical underpinnings.[81]

THE "DEAD MASTER"

One week after the official Allied victory in Europe in 1945, Charles Williams died unexpectedly of complications following surgery to repair adhesions in his intestines.[82] His legacy has never reached the heights that Lewis playfully suggested, but a significant group of friends and acquaintances laboured to achieve lasting recognition for him following his death. His friend Gerard Hopkins, nephew of Gerard Manley Hopkins, wrote in a 1945 obituary in the *Bookseller* that a "circle of devotion" had arisen around Williams by the time of his death.[83] In addition to Eliot and the Inklings, this circle of writers, friends and disciples included Dorothy L. Sayers, who spoke of Williams as the "Dead Master," a "source from which others received the waters of truth."[84] W.H. Auden appears to have met Williams only twice, but described these meetings as among his "most unforgettable and precious experiences."[85] He appears to have deeply understood Charles's lived blend of art, myth and philosophy: "You're the only one since Dante who has found out how to make poetry of theology and history," he told Williams.[86] Novelist Mary Butts, once a

---

80. As indicated in a letter to Alice Mary Hadfield, 10 May 1940. See Lindop, *Charles Williams*, 327.
81. See, e.g., Newman, "Companions of the Co-Inherence," 20; Gauntlett, "Charles Williams, Love & Shekinah," 24.
82. Lindop, *Charles Williams*, 9, 420.
83. Curtis, "Charles Williams," 143.
84. Dorothy L. Sayers, introduction to *James I*, by Charles Williams (London, Arthur Barker, 1951), ix, quoted in Curtis, "Charles Williams," 143.
85. Quoted in Reilly, *Romantic Religion*, 149. Cf. Lindop, *Charles Williams*, 275–76.
86. W.H. Auden to Charles Williams, 11 January 1945, Bodleian Ms. Res. c.137, f.2.

student of Aleister Crowley and one of the co-authors of his influential *Magick: Liber ABA* (1912–13), seems to have seen Williams as a spiritual leader favourable to the more Christian belief system she developed later in life. Describing him as "by far the best witness—to the heart of the matter," Butts told Williams that she intended to write the first comprehensive critical study of his work, though this was never published.[87] Kingsley Amis and Phillip Larkin were both struck by Williams during their time as his students at Oxford—while Larkin did not "give a fart for his poetry," he did admire his fiction.[88] Also while in Oxford, Williams developed a relationship with playwright Christopher Fry. Robert Gittings has shown that *Witchcraft* had a significant influence on the development of the characters and themes of Fry's *The Lady's Not for Burning* (1948), with particular sections of dialogue drawn almost verbatim from Williams's text.[89] Canadian folk rocker Bruce Cockburn never met Williams, but he cites his influence, particularly *The Place of the Lion*, as a central source of inspiration for his album *Dancing in the Dragon's Jaws*.[90] M. John Harrison, a leading modern day fantasy and SF author, was also struck by *The Place of the Lion*, listing it as one of his top ten books.[91] We do not know if Williams ever met Dennis Wheatley, a fellow novelist of occult fantasy and horror, but Williams's novels may have had an effect on the younger writer: Wheatley's tales of black magic follow Williams's script of introducing a supernatural array of forces into the world until the forces of good ultimately

---

87. Mary Butts to Charles Williams, January 1935, in *The Journals of Mary Butts*, ed. Natalie Blondel (New Haven, CT: Yale University Press, 2002), 442. Cf. Lindop, *Charles Williams*, 266–68. On Butts, her relationship with Crowley and her occult fiction, see Amy Clukey, "Enchanting Modernism: Mary Butts, Decadence, and the Ethics of Occultism," *Modern Fiction Studies* 60, no. 1 (Spring 2014).
88. Lindop, *Charles Williams*, 364.
89. Robert Gittings, "The Smell of Sulphur: 'The Lady's Not for Burning' Now," *Encounter* (Jan 1978): 75–78. Accessed CWSA I.A.v.3/c.
90. Curtis, "Charles Williams," 162.
91. M. John Harrison, "M. John Harrison's Top Ten Books," *The Guardian*, 28 October 2002. "Once you've read Williams," says Harrison, "You won't need to read CS Lewis, which is a relief."

triumph, often by divine intervention.[92] His first novel appeared in 1933, at the tail end of a period in which Williams saturated the occult fiction market with five novels in three years.

In short, Williams is culturally important not just in his own right, but because of the influence he had on others. These connections, particularly with Eliot and the Inklings, have ensured that he is still read today.[93] However, because these figures were not themselves involved with the modern occult network, analysis resultant from their interest in him, particularly the large body of research oriented around the Inklings as a sort of hub of Romantic Christianity, has hindered rather than helped our understanding of Williams's links to esoteric figures, groups and concepts. There is no question, however, that occult practice and symbolism were vital to the lived fantasy that enriched both his work and the day-to-day banality of his life. In addition to his involvement with the F.R.C., he "knew a great deal" about magic and witchcraft,[94] felt that the astrological zodiac had "great significance" for understanding the correspondent unity of the universe,[95] and displayed clear knowledge of the "Banishing Ritual of the Pentagram," a popular occult protection device.[96] He owned at least two tarot decks, and seems to have been fascinated enough by their symbolism to use it as the basis for the entire thematic structure of *The Greater Trumps*. He frequently turned to kabbalah as a symbolic hermeneutic with which to transcribe and explore his ideas and experiences.[97] Thus, though far too many Williams scholars have claimed that he only "dabbled" in the occult,[98] he was a student in a number of esoteric schools—a pupil at once playful and serious, as an artist must be.

---

92. See Keith Neilson, "Dennis Wheatley," in *Supernatural Fiction Writers*, ed. E.F. Bleiler (New York: Charles Scribner's Sons, 1985), 624–25.
93. Winship, "Novels of Charles Williams," 285.
94. Hadfield, *Introduction to Charles Williams*, 116.
95. Williams, "Index of the Body," 83.
96. Lindop, *Charles Williams*, 335–36.
97. See, for example, a letter (reproduced in ibid, 335) wherein Williams programmatically arranges a lover's mythical names according to the schema of the Tree of Life.
98. Winship, "Novels of Charles Williams," 114.

Those around him sensed Williams's esoteric mindset. Though his friend Alice Mary Hadfield was unsure of the extent of his occult activities, she sensed that he possessed "hidden knowledge" and "lived and expressed a 'mystery.'"[99] Eliot placed him on the edge of the supernatural: "At ease in human society, I am sure that he would have remained equally composed if a ghost, an angel or an evil spirit had entered the room."[100] When he first took up with the Inklings, Williams met Owen Barfield, an influential follower of Rudolf Steiner's esoteric school of Anthroposophy, founded as a breakaway, more Christian arm of the Theosophical Society in 1912. Barfield's identification with Williams was unequivocal: "I have just been talking to someone who told me I was an Anthroposophist," Williams reported after the meeting.[101] At some point during his time in Oxford he came home to his lodgings to find a group of friends and acquaintances experimenting with an Ouija board. Most of the group had approached the encounter reluctantly and had not produced much in the way of results—that is until Williams arrived. "'Charles came in the middle and joined in,' one participant recalled, "And the thing just went mad!...The thing went absolutely batty!...Just shot around the board like *that!*'"[102] This wartime anecdote must be taken with many grains of salt but at the very least it illustrates the perception others had of Williams as a man in touch with mysterious forces.

Divination by Ouija board aside, it is clear that Williams was socially, practically and intellectually connected to the modern occult network. Trying to identify particular nodal influences and connections in this network is a complex, not altogether achievable process. He was an autodidact—encouraged to read widely by his father and

---

99. Hadfield, *Introduction to Charles Williams*, 11.
100. Eliot, "The Significance of Charles Williams," 894.
101. Lindop, *Charles Williams*, 308. Hadfield reports that Steiner's followers also found Anthroposophical elements in Williams's poetry (Hadfield, *Introduction to Charles Williams*, 80). Barfield was also a member of the Inklings, but Williams's relationship with him was limited.
102. Lindop, *Charles Williams*, 303.

freed from any canonical constrictions which a graduate education might have placed on him, he appears to have absorbed poetry, fiction, history and philosophy from all corners of the known intellectual and creative worlds. Robert Reilly concludes from Williams's frequent literary allusions that his reading seems to have included "all the important critical and creative literature from the time of the English romantics" and much other material besides, particularly mystical texts from figures such as Pseudo-Dionysius, St John of the Cross, and the contemporary works of Evelyn Underhill, who Williams knew personally.[103] At least two major influences anticipated Williams's fusion of esoteric knowledge with symbolic poetic expression: William Blake, who Williams read "in his entirety,"[104] and W.B. Yeats. Williams sensed a kinship between his own thought and the vast esoteric system that emerges from Yeats's cosmic history, *A Vision* (1925), which the long-time Golden Dawn adept claimed to have written primarily at the behest of several cosmic entities via the mediumship of his wife.[105] Sometime in the early 1920s, Williams read Walter Scott's *Hermetica* (1924) in the course of editing it for the OUP.[106] This four-volume work included translations of the *Corpus Hermeticum* and the *Asclepius*, both texts which heavily informed Renaissance Hermeticism and, in turn, significantly influenced modern occult thought. A number of early modern sources also informed his esoteric perspective: He expressed admiration for Hermetic thinkers like Pico and Agrippa and, more than any other figure in this period, found consanguinity in the magical and alchem-

---

103. Reilly, *Romantic Religion*, 9. Williams was less impressed with Underhill's thoughts on mysticism than he was with the large amount of "authentic sayings" she included in *Mysticism: A Study in the Nature and Development of Man's Spiritual Consciousness* (1911). Williams also appears to have read *Practical Mysticism* (1915) and *The Essentials of Mysticism* (1920), both of which, he says, are a valuable "psychological examination of the [mystic] Way" (Charles Williams, "Introduction," in *The Letters of Evelyn Underhill* ed. Charles Williams (London: Longmans, 1943), 17, 32.
104. Duriez and Porter, *The Inklings Handbook*, 84.
105. Charles Williams, "Blake and Wordsworth," in *The Image of the City*, ed. Anne Ridler (Berkeley, CA: Apocryphile, 2007), 59; Lindop, *Charles Williams*, 280; Hadfield, *Charles Williams: An Exploration*, 31.
106. Lindop, *Charles Williams*, 95.

ical writings of fellow Englishman Thomas Vaughan, inspired by his view of the incarnation of Christ as the key to the mystery of the correspondent union of spirit and matter.[107] Among the many works of esoteric scholarship produced by influential figures in the modern occult network, Williams read Westcott's *Numbers: Their Occult Power and Mystic Virtues* (1890), as well as his translation of sections of a sixteenth-century German translation of the Hebrew *Sepher Yetzirah* (*Book of Formation*), a late antique text influential in the medieval development of kabbalah.[108] He also read at least two works by G.R.S. Mead, founder of the Quest Society (a gathering of occult researchers of a more critical, historical bent), *Quests Old and New* (1913) and *Fragments of a Faith Forgotten* (1900), a survey of antique Gnosticism.[109]

These textual sources, no doubt joined by many others that have gone untraced, significantly influenced the development of Williams's esotericism, but he primarily encountered occult knowledge through two specific social circles, absorbing much through conversation and personal experience. The first of these circles was a bi-weekly meeting which Williams attended regularly from 1919 to 1939 at the vicarage of the Reverend Arthur Hugh Evelyn Lee,[110] an Anglican curate and long-time member of two branches of the Golden Dawn—Waite's Independent and Rectified Rite of the R.R. et A.C. and, following Waite's disbanding of this order in 1914, the Stella Matutina, a separate branch of the Golden Dawn that more clearly emphasized practical magic. Another I.R.R. and Stella Matutina member also attended these meetings—Daniel Howard Sinclair Nicholson. As Lindop suggests, through Nicholson and Lee, Williams may have had access to some of the occult knowledge received

---

107. Charles Williams, *Witchcraft* (Wellingborough: Aquarian Press, 1980), 223–24, 229–31. Cf. Ashenden, *Charles Williams*, 118–30. For Vaughan on the incarnation see, e.g., "Anima Magica Abscondita: Or a Discourse of the Universal Spirit of Nature," in *The Works of Thomas Vaughan: Eugenius Philalethes*, ed. Arthur Edward Waite (London: Theosophical Publishing House, 1919), 93.
108. Lindop, *Charles Williams*, 95. Westcott titled his translation *Sepher Yetzirah: The Book of Formation and the Thirty Two Paths of Wisdom* (1893).
109. Ibid, 95–96.
110. See ibid, 63–66, 96.

through involvement with these alternate Golden Dawn offshoots, though the two occultists would have had to break their order vows to give him specific knowledge of the rituals they had encountered.[111]

ARTHUR EDWARD WAITE

Williams met Lee and Nicholson in the course of editing their collection of English mystical verse, which featured poetry from a number of figures associated with modern occultism, including Crowley, Underhill, Yeats, Machen, and Machen's close friend A.E. Waite, who was to prove an even more influential source for the esoteric Christianity of Charles Williams than the two Stella Matutina adepts. Waite and Williams met on 4 September 1916, after Williams read Waite's thesis on Arthurian mysticism, *The Hidden Church of the Holy Graal*, and felt moved to send him his recently published first volume of poetry, *The Silver Stair* (1912).[112] Sensing a kindred spirit, Waite invited him to his home, a visit which was repeated at least once before Waite invited Williams to join the new secret society he had founded in 1915, the Fellowship of the Rosy Cross.

Like Williams, Waite made his way onto the intellectual stage of modern England in spite of a mediocre education and obstructive social and financial circumstances.[113] Born in Brooklyn on 2 October 1857, Waite immigrated to England after the death at sea of his father, a ship's captain, a year later. He was able to attend school for even less time than Williams; partly because of financial circumstances, he dropped out around age fifteen to intern as a clerk.[114] He then tried to make it as a writer of poetry and short fiction, mostly fairy tales.

---

111. Ibid, 65, 96, 331. For more on Williams's relationship with Lee and Nicholson, see Ridler, "Introduction to *the Image of the City*," xxvi.
112. For details of Waite and Williams's relationship, including meeting, see Gilbert, *A.E. Waite*, 148–49; Lindop, *Charles Williams*, 56; Gauntlett, "Charles Williams, Love & Shekinah," 9–10; Ashenden, *Charles Williams*, 5; Willard, "Acts of the Companions," 270.
113. See Arthur Edward Waite, *Shadows of Life and Thought* (London: Selwyn & Blount, 1938), 14–18.
114. Ibid, 46. Cf. Gilbert, "The Masonic Career of Arthur Edward Waite," 2.

Though he was successful in publishing in a number of minor periodicals between 1876 and 1886,[115] he was not able to make ends meet and ultimately found a more profitable writing life in scholarly approaches to mystical and esoteric materials.[116] He wrote dozens of books and hundreds of articles on a variety of topics, including Christian mysticism, alchemy, ritual magic, Freemasonry, the tarot, kabbalah, Martinism, Arthurian mysticism, and Rosicrucianism. He also translated or edited collections of work by many figures important to the history of Western esotericism, including the German alchemist and medical innovator Paracelsus, Thomas Vaughan, and Éliphas Lévi. He was also heavily involved with two periodicals dedicated to occult scholarship—his own *The Unknown World*, which produced 11 issues after he founded it in 1894, and the well-read *Occult Review*, to which he frequently contributed in addition to working as editor of the "Periodical Literature" feature from 1911–1931.[117] The tarot deck that he designed along with Pamela Colman Smith is still in use today as a tool for divination and meditation.[118]

Although many of Waite's books saw little of the light of day—particularly his poetry and fiction—others were relatively successful, particularly in the esoteric community. Some are still used as resources for academic research,[119] though Waite's work is often historically and philologically suspect, perhaps weakened by his lack of education. More problematically, his primary motivation was always to promote his mystical philosophy, as openly stated in the

---

115. Gilbert, "The Masonic Career of Arthur Edward Waite," 3n7.
116. Detailed accounts of Waite's publishing history can be found throughout Gilbert, *A.E. Waite*. Cf. R.A. Gilbert, *A.E. Waite: A Bibliography* (Wellingborough, Northamptonshire: Aquarian Press, 1983).
117. *A.E. Waite*, 91, 101.
118. On Waite's collaboration with Smith to produce the influential "Rider-Waite" tarot deck, see ibid, 138.
119. See, e.g., Henrik Bogdan, "Freemasonry and Western Esotericism," in *Handbook of Freemasonry*, ed. Henrik Bogdan and Jan A.M. Snoek (Leiden: Brill, 2014), 297–98; Betty Jo Teeter Dobbs, *The Foundations of Newton's Alchemy: Or, 'the Hunting of the Greene Lyon'* (Cambridge: Cambridge University Press, 1975), 10; Philip Beitchman, *Alchemy of the Word: Cabala of the Renaissance* (Albany: State University of New York Press, 1998), numerous citations.

introductions of many of his books.[120] This last quality makes his work less useful to scholars today, but it probably contributed to its impact in the modern occult world. Aleister Crowley, the most well-known magician of Waite's day, showed little public respect for his fellow occultist but admitted privately in a letter that he would not have been as easily able to access occult knowledge without Waite's textual contribution: "Waite certainly did start a revival of interest in Alchemy, Magic, Mysticism, and all the rest."[121] Hanegraaff argues that Waite has had more impact than any other in the English-speaking world in promoting the very concept of a specific esoteric current in Western culture,[122] noting that, due to the lack of any higher level academic work, Waite was the "virtually unavoidable authority" for anyone looking for a historical framework for the various esoteric traditions until the late twentieth century.[123] Gilbert view of Waite's impact on the academic study of esotericism is less guarded: "His idiosyncrasies and carelessness over minor details do not weaken the foundations he laid; his work was sound enough for it to carry the superstructure of modern scholarship when it begins to build, as it must, upon his researches."[124] This prediction of a coming increase in scholarship of esoteric currents, made in 1987, has come true. Waite, however, has received little credit for building the foundations of the discipline, and even less research dedicated to his life and work.

In addition to his historical and philological interest in esoteric subjects, Waite involved himself heavily in various groups founded in the midst of the occult revival. After the death of his sister, Frederica, in 1874, Waite moved away from the Roman Catholic faith in which he had been brought up by his mother, though he mirrored

---

120. See Principe, "Historiography of Alchemy," 395, for an especially harsh critique of Waite's translations of alchemical texts.
121. Aleister Crowley to Louis Wilkinson, 7 April 1945, quoted in Gilbert, *A.E. Waite*, 11.
122. Hanegraaff, *Esotericism and the Academy*, 248. Cf. 249–52. Joscelyn Godwin expresses a similar opinion (*The Theosophical Enlightenment* (Albany, NY: State University of New York Press, 1994), 346).
123. Hanegraaff, *Esotericism and the Academy*, 249.
124. Gilbert, *A.E. Waite*, 161.

Williams's continuing passion for ritual.[125] He was also like Williams in that he never tired of searching for religious knowledge and experience in the myths and symbols of Western civilization. He turned to Spiritualism following his sister's death, sinking himself into Spiritualist literature from 1878 and then beginning to attend seances in 1885 in an effort to contact her in the spirit realm. He does not seem to have been successful, but he continued to validate Spiritualist phenomena at the time of the writing of his autobiography, *Shadows of Life and Thought*, in 1938.[126]

From this late perspective, Waite recalled himself becoming more immersed in the esoteric via the allure of fiction. He read the occult novels of Edward Bulwer-Lytton: *Zanoni* (1842), *A Strange Story* (1862), and *The Haunted and the Haunters* (1859). George MacDonald's *Phantastes* (1858) was "an epoch at this stage" because it illustrated the immanent God in nature.[127] Around the same time he read Blavatsky's *Isis Unveiled* (1877), which presented a complex, entangled universalist system that was, like Waite's own search for spiritual meaning, partly motivated by the reading of fiction.[128] Waite disliked its anti-Christian bias, but even in 1938, after decades spent positioning himself in opposition to groups like the Theosophical Society, he had to admit that Blavatsky's work was "helpful as an *omnium gatherum* [we might say "catch-all"] of esoteric claims and pretences, a miscellany of magic and its connections."[129] This was an older more cynical Waite—as a young man in the 1880s he was impressed enough to involve himself with Blavatsky's Theosophical Society, first established in New York in 1875. He began attending the London

---

125. Gilbert, "The Masonic Career of Arthur Edward Waite," 11.
126. Waite, *Shadows*, 62, 87. Cf. *Studies in Mysticism and Certain Aspects of the Secret Tradition* (London: Hodder and Stoughton, 1906), 134; Gilbert, *A.E. Waite*, 48–53.
127. Waite, *Shadows*, 66–67. On immanence in *Phantastes* see Aren Roukema, "The Shadow of Anodos: Alchemical Symbolism in Phantastes," *North Wind: A Journal for George MacDonald Studies* 31 (2012): 49–50.
128. See Ingvild Sælid Gilhus and Lisbeth Mikhaelsson, "Theosophy and Popular Fiction," in *Handbook of the Theosophical Current*, ed. Olav Hammer and Mikael Rothstein (Leiden: Brill, 2013), 454, 456–67.
129. Waite, *Shadows*, 67–68.

Lodge in 1884, at the residence of A.P. Sinnett, another leading Theosophist and author of the influential *Occult World* (1884). Waite met Blavatsky and seems to have been impressed despite his lack of belief in her mediumship, but it was with Sinnett, who frequently encouraged Waite's publishing career, that he formed a real bond.[130]

Isis Unveiled also brought Éliphas Lévi to Waite's attention. He thus acknowledged a "general debt" to Blavatsky's work, as he would spend much of the next two decades translating the French occultist's work and popularizing it in England.[131] Lévi became a sort of prophet or spiritual father to Anglo-American occultists in the *fin de siècle* and beyond, a source, as Gilbert observes, of doctrine that could be hardened to ideology: "Ideas that were born of Lévi's imagination became enshrined as occult dogmas."[132] Lèvi's concepts were not simply conjured from the thin air of the imaginal, but his adaptations of older esoteric knowledge forms were certainly seminal and epochal. These included the concept of an all-pervading medium called the "Astral Light" that could be controlled by the trained will of the magician—an extrapolation of mesmerist and contemporary physical theories regarding a universal fluid believed to permeate all matter—and a parallel between the kabbalistic symbolism of the ten sephiroth and the greater trumps of the tarot. Both are core occultist concepts to this day.[133] Waite's translation and promotion of Lévi's work thus contributed to positioning him as a key actor in the modern occult network.[134]

From early on Waite displayed a fascination with secret societies

---

130. Ibid, 86–89; Gilbert, *A.E. Waite*, 77–78.
131. For Waite on his interest in Lévi see Waite, *Shadows*, 67–68, 92–98. Cf. Gilbert, *A.E. Waite*, 76, 88.
132. *A.E. Waite*, 89.
133. See Gilbert, *A.E. Waite*, 89. On Lévi's Astral Light see Julian Strube, "The 'Baphomet' of Eliphas Lévi: Its Meaning and Historical Context," *Correspondences* 4 (2016): 64–69; Egil Asprem, "Pondering Imponderables: Occultism in the Mirror of Late Classical Physics," *Aries* 11, no. 2 (2011): 142.
134. Waite was not impressed, however, with the English disciples of Lévi. He continued, with many reservations, to admire the French occultist to the end of his life, but he felt that his English occult followers "should be commemorated in a new Dunciad" (*Shadows*, 99).

—in 1888 and 1891 he tried to form groups around a "new religion...at once scientific and aspirational, positive and mystical,"[135] but both endeavours failed. He would not lose the desire to form and lead his own order, but for the next two decades he was happy to actively involve himself in the secret societies of others, most of them related to Freemasonry. He became the ninety-ninth member of the Hermetic Order of the Golden Dawn in January 1891 and had ascended through the grades to the initiatory level of "Philosophus" by 1892, but left for several years after this point because he was troubled by an undisclosed legal matter affecting some of the leading members. He remained abreast of the order's affairs, however, and re-entered in 1896; by 1899 he had made the decision to pass into the Golden Dawn's second, inner order, the Rosae Rubae et Aurae Crucis (R.R. et A.C.), which required magical training and initiation via the Golden Dawn's two part "Adeptus Minor" ritual, still one of the most impactful occultist rituals and one that, as we will see in Chapter Two, Waite clearly admired.[136]

As the nineteenth century bustled energetically into the twentieth, however, Waite was losing patience with some of his fellow occultists and abandoning his connections with the central figures with whom he had helped build an influential subculture. He later claimed disgust for Westcott and Mathers, the prime movers of the Golden Dawn, loathing their "buskined struttings and their abysmal ignorance of the suppositious arcana which they claimed to guard."[137] The Golden Dawn reproduced by mitosis in the middle of the first decade of the new century, producing three new orders from

---

135. Waite, "A New Light of Mysticism," *Light* 8, no. 402 (15 September 1888): 462. Cf. Gilbert, *A.E. Waite*, 93–94.
136. For the history of Waite's involvement in the Golden Dawn, see Waite, *Shadows*, 121–33; Gilbert, *A.E. Waite*, 109–26; *A.E. Waite: A Bibliography*, 11.
137. Waite, *Shadows*, 99. Cf. 221. As Gilbert explains, Waite's later polemics likely do not represent his attitude in the *fin de siècle*. Mathers was ostracized in occult society in general as of 1900 because of a split in the Golden Dawn, while Waite was likely still angry at Westcott in 1938 because he had been a part of preventing Waite's election to Celebrant in the Societas Rosicruciana in Anglia (S.R.I.A) in 1908 (Gilbert, *A.E. Waite*, 130).

the dying body of its parent. Waite played the executioner role in this death, taking control of the order's Isis Urania temple in London in 1903, at the head of a splinter group known as the Independent and Rectified Rite of the Rosae Rubeae et Aurae Crucis (I.R.R.), which he would lead until 1914.[138] At this point he finally founded an order all his own. The Fellowship of the Rosy Cross launched in 1915; for Waite, it was the apex of his involvement with secret societies.

Waite involved himself with countless other esoteric groups as well. In 1901 he sought Freemasonic initiation and by 1902 had reached the degree of Master Mason, at which time he was free to seek participation in at least ten distinct "Higher" rites and degrees, motivated, Gilbert argues, by a desire to gather material for the eventual founding of his own order.[139] He travelled as far as Scotland and Switzerland to take part in rituals that particularly fascinated him, always in a search of "a deeper insight into the meaning and symbolism of Ritual."[140] From 1908 he was vice-president of Mead's Quest Society,[141] a role he also performed for the short-lived Alchemical Society, founded in London in 1912.[142] His membership in these latter two groups was public rather than secret, thus further increasing his reputation and influence in modern esoteric circles. Waite was aware that all this represented an unusual degree of occult social engagement: in 1903, after joining the Sphere group led by actress Florence Farr—a sub-circle of the Golden Dawn—he wrote in his diary, "I look shortly to be the most initiated man in Europe."[143]

Waite thus engaged personally, at times intimately, with many leading occult figures; Sinnett, Blavatsky, Westcott, Mathers, Mead and Farr represent only a shortlist. He made contact outside his own social and initiatory circles as well. He had a long and productive

---

138. See Waite, *Shadows*, 228.
139. Waite, *Shadows*, 161; Gilbert, *A.E. Waite*, 128. Cf. 124–32; "The Masonic Career of Arthur Edward Waite," esp. 13.
140. Waite, *Shadows*, 161; Gilbert, *A.E. Waite*, 129–30.
141. See Gilbert, *A.E. Waite*, 103, 110–12; Owen, *Place of Enchantment*, 49.
142. Morrisson, *Modern Alchemy*, 33.
143. Gilbert, *A.E. Waite*, 117.

meeting with Rudolf Steiner during the Anthroposophist's 1912 visit to London,[144] and corresponded with French Martinist Dr. Gerard Encausse, better known as Papus, who seems to have encouraged Waite to found a non-masonic English branch of Papus's "Order of St. Martin."[145] Perhaps it was the latent author in him that helped form strong bonds of friendship with Arthur Machen, who briefly joined him in the Golden Dawn. Waite supported Machen after his wife's death in 1902; Machen reciprocated by acting the wingman during Waite's short affair with his sister-in-law, resulting in the two coming together to publish *The House of the Hidden Light* (1904), an obscure text of mystical eroticism edited from letters exchanged between them.[146] One of the relationships that most affected Waite's reputation however, was far from friendly. He probably met Aleister Crowley at some point, most likely during the latter's short-lived involvement with the Golden Dawn,[147] but the two men do not seem to have interacted much. Nevertheless, Crowley took time to publicly flagellate Waite's personality and philosophy in his periodical, *The Equinox*, and novel, *Moonchild* (1923), in which Waite appears thinly disguised as the inept and unnecessarily verbose magician Edwin Arthwait, a "stupid pedant...in the fetters of his own egoism [who] pronounced himself father and grandfather of all spiritual science, in language that would have seemed stilted and archaic to Henry James."[148] Waite must have been aware of these attacks, but never responded directly—though Crowley, a one-time protégée of Mathers, was very likely a secondary target in Waite's dismissal of the

---

144. Ibid, 127.
145. Gilbert, "The Masonic Career of Arthur Edward Waite," 11; *A.E. Waite*, 121.
146. See Gilbert, *A.E. Waite*, 60–75.
147. On Crowley's initiatory activity in the Golden Dawn, see Ellic Howe, *The Magicians of the Golden Dawn: A Documentary History of a Magical Order, 1887–1923* (Wellingborough: Aquarian, 1985), 192–94.
148. Aleister Crowley, *Moonchild* (London: Sphere, 1972), 147. Cf. 148–53, 161–65, 169–71, 187–89; R.A. Gilbert, "The One Thought That Was Not Untrue," in *Aleister Crowley and Western Esotericism*, ed. Henrik Bogdan and Martin Starr (Oxford: Oxford University Press, 2012).

Golden Dawn founder as a "mentor stultorum" (teacher of fools).[149] Unfortunately, Crowley's polemical attacks on Waite appear to have been influential. The magician's vituperations were followed up by similar, though less vitriolic rejections from a later generation of occultists, including Ithell Colquhoun and Israel Regardie.[150] Such attacks might seem to reinforce Waite's perception of himself as separate from the occultist stream, but the time taken by such central occult actors to denigrate his ideas and person suggests that he was a major player in the social and intellectual development of modern Anglo-American esotericism, a man against whom new players on the occult scene could seek to dialectically position themselves. By joining the F.R.C., Williams placed himself under the intellectual and spiritual tutelage of one of the most prominent and experienced occultists in modern Britain.

OCCULT IMAGINATION AND THE SECRET TRADITION

It is no surprise that Williams discovered a striking consanguinity with Waite upon reading *The Hidden Church of the Holy Graal*; he shared many values and elements of belief with his F.R.C. "Imperator." As with Williams, the doctrine of correspondences was central to Waite's mystical and esoteric belief system, "the one Catholic and Hermetic axiom for a root principle of philosophy...the universal sacramental doctrine."[151] The metaphysics that underpinned Waite's central priority of mystic reunion with the divine were based on this

---

149. Arthur Edward Waite, *The Book of Ceremonial Magic* (Forgotten Books, 2010), 2, http://www.forgottenbooks.org/info/9781605065762.
150. Ithell Colquhoun, *Sword of Wisdom: Macgregor Mathers and the Golden Dawn*, 1st. American ed. (New York: Putnam, 1975), 231–33; Regardie, *Complete Golden Dawn*, 1:19. Regardie had a more balanced view of Waite: he cited him on tarot knowledge and admired some of the rituals of the F.R.C, but ultimately denigrated his writing style and Christian occult perspective. See, e.g., ibid, 7:62.
151. Arthur Edward Waite, *The Secret Tradition in Alchemy: Its Development and Records* (London: Kegan Paul, Trench, Trubner, 1926), 267. Cf. *The Secret Doctrine in Israel: A Study of the Zohar and Its Connections* (1913, repr. New York: Occult Research Press, n.d), 58; *The Holy Kabbalah* (London: Williams and Norgate, 1929), 224.

doctrine, as were the more practical elements needed to achieve this goal—ritual elevation of consciousness via symbol- and image-based visualization techniques. Waite also shared—and likely influenced—Williams's affirmative way. His turn toward affirmative mysticism was likely promulgated partly by the neo-Romantic sentiments of modern occultism in general, but he also found inspiration in the thought of Louis Claude de Saint-Martin, a French mystic and Freemason. Saint-Martin, says Waite, who started reading the Frenchman along with Lévi in his teens, defied the historical trend of asceticism among mystics by keeping "his finger always on the pulse of the world."[152] Waite mirrored Williams in affirming some role for negative self-renunciation in mystical attainment. However, "the price of the new birth is not the wanton torture of our nature proposed by unbridled asceticism." For Waite, as for Williams, the complete renunciation of self and world was an "error of enthusiasm."[153]

This affirmation of human experience in the natural world led Waite in the same direction as Williams—toward Romantic love. As discussed further in Chapters Two and Four, Waite saw the sexual and emotional love between man and woman as correspondent to a mystical desire that draws divided aspects of self and soul together, and also reflective of love exchanged between masculine and feminine aspects of the divine itself, as expressed in kabbalah. Here as well, however, affirmation faded into negation at the highest level of attainment, as the state of love encountered by the mystic was no longer one of human emotion or desire, but a state in which love eradicates distinctions between self and others and "conforms the whole man with its object."[154]

Crucially, however, much engagement with the phenomenal awaited the adept before this mystical state could occur, and here

---

152. Arthur Edward Waite, *The Life of Louis Claude De Saint-Martin, the Unknown Philosopher, and the Substance of His Transcendental Doctrine* (London: Philip Wellby, 1901), 52.
153. Ibid, 252.
154. Arthur Edward Waite, *The Way of Divine Union* (London: William Rider and Son, 1915), 310.

Waite joined Williams in embracing the faculty of imagination. Williams valued the sense of imagination he found in English Romanticism, where it was emphasized, in the words of Coleridge, as "a synthetic and magical power" that could achieve the "balance or reconciliation of opposite or discordant qualities," thus, for both Romantic and mystic, allowing the grasp of all things in their correspondent unity: "Imagination," said Coleridge, is "the soul that is everywhere, and in each; and forms all into one graceful and intelligent whole."[155] Williams took up a similar idea in his commentary on Wordsworth's *Prelude*. For the "true Romantic," said Williams, quoting from the concluding stanzas of the poem, imagination is "but another name for absolute power/ And clearest insight, amplitude of mind, and Reason in its most exalted mood."[156] Though he may have encountered these concepts through the Romantics, Williams's emphasis on the power of imagination has esoteric ramifications, as early modern Hermetic views of the imagination provided much of the inspiration for German and English Romanticism. Building on ideas found in texts dating back at least as far as the late antique *Corpus Hermeticum,* Giordano Bruno conceived the imagination as the principal tool of magical and mystical processes because of its ability to transcend the divide between material and spiritual. Paracelsus proposed a similar link between soul and matter, while Jacob Boehme envisioned the universe as the product of the imagination of God—all three radical concepts significantly influenced the macrocosmic reach of the Romantic imagination.[157] The boundaries between esotericism and Romanticism are thus frequently blurry, as each has informed the other since the first eighteenth-century stirrings of the latter movement.[158]

---

155. *Biographia Literaria*, 14.
156. Williams, "Blake and Wordsworth," 60 (from *The Prelude*, 14.192).
157. Antoine Faivre, *Theosophy, Imagination, Tradition: Studies in Western Esotericism* (Albany, NY: State University of New York Press, 2000), 101, 106. For an example of the preeminent role of imagination in the *Corpus Hermeticum* see "A Discourse of Hermes to Tat, His Son: that God is Invisible and Entirely Visible," in Brian P. Copenhaver, *Hermetica* (Cambridge: Cambridge University Press, 1992), 18.
158. On the many intersections between esotericism and Romanticism, see Wouter J.

It is no surprise, then, that imagination was vital to the esoteric and Romantic Waitean system that Williams encountered in the F.R.C., where the path to mystical experience was paved with imaginal engagement with material sensations and semiotics. The value of symbol and experience was based on what Waite called a "philosophical pantheism" which, true to his esoteric, correspondent epistemology, "identifies the universe with God."[159] "Ideas in the absolute order are conceived only by representation, which is the mode of symbols and sacraments," said Waite, expressing a value for ritual, image and sacrament which he attributed to his childhood experiences in the Catholic Church.[160] A wide variety of signifiers were essential to providing mystical access to a metaphysical space behind the sign; through the reflection of divinity in the objects and symbols of the material world, the adept "forges the strong chains of union binding all worlds together."[161] As Antony Borrow argues, Williams's way of affirmation implicitly embraces symbolism in the same way, to the degree that even dark images, or experiences as evil as death, madness, sorrow and loss, show an aspect of God and direct humans toward him.[162] "All images are, in their degree, to be carried on," said Williams, "Mind is never to put off matter; all experience is to be gathered in."[163]

For both men, however, material semiotics were,

Hanegraaff, "Romanticism and the Esoteric Connection," in *Gnosis and Hermeticism from Antiquity to Modern Times*, ed. Roelof Van den Broek and Wouter J. Hanegraaff (New York: State University of New York Press, 1998); *New Age Religion and Western Culture*, 415–21; Gibbons, *Spirituality and the Occult*, 2, 17–18, 98.

159. Waite, *Shadows*, 259. In present day terminology, Waite's system is best described as "panentheistic," a term which describes the material world as permeated with spirit, but not itself divine.

160. Waite, *Studies in Mysticism*, 248. Cf. *Shadows*, 22: "The beginning of a life at the Altar was laid thus early. No one can speak for another; but in my case at least, certain spiritual seeds were sown thereby."

161. Waite, *Studies in Mysticism*, 48–49.

162. Antony Borrow, "The Affirmation of Images," *Nine* 3 (1952), 327, 329, quoted in Reilly, *Romantic Religion*, 158.

163. Williams, *Descent of the Dove*, 60.

in Waite's words, "always, and of necessity, insufficient" in and of themselves.[164] The adept "must pass beyond the signs, to reach a threshold of experience within...where signs no longer lead and Sacraments have served their purpose."[165] In short, the mystic journey reaches a point of imagelessness that is fundamentally individual and internal, a state that can be neither encountered nor explained through word and symbol, a state that is "pure intelligence in deep contemplation."[166] Such descriptions of an ontologically ineffable layer of reality, the experience of which is imageless and indescribable, are consistent with the majority of mystical and occult worldviews in the period and for millennia before.[167] The view of image, word and symbol as nevertheless vital to the mystic journey is also common; as David Katz notes, there are libraries full of texts designed to help others achieve "putatively ineffable experiences" which "in some oblique sense at least, describe mystical experiences after they have transpired."[168] Katz observes that the perception of boundaries of the "sayable" in mystical traditions has resulted in an amazing diversity of imaginative forms intended to convey the meaning and content that have structured experiences otherwise deemed ineffable.[169] Within the context of Western culture specifically, however, affirmative imagination has been specifically connected to esoteric practice. Egil Asprem has shown that the imaginal theory and practice of the esoteric traditions has important roots in medieval Christian thought, particularly popular contemplative

---

164. Waite, *Studies in Mysticism*, 248.
165. Waite, *Shadows*, 277.
166. Ibid, 238; *Divine Union*, 234.
167. William James famously described the attribution of ineffability to religious experience as one of two *sine qua non* primary characteristics of mysticism (the second quality is the noetic, intuitive nature of mystical knowledge claims). See William James, *The Varieties of Religious Experience: A Study in Human Nature* (London: Longmans, Green, 1902), 380. Cf. Joshua Gunn, "An Occult Poetics, or, the Secret Rhetoric of Religion," *Rhetoric Society Quarterly* 34, no. 2 (2004): 32.
168. Steven T. Katz, ed., *Mysticism and Language* (Oxford: Oxford University Press, 1992), v.
169. "Mystical Speech and Mystical Meaning," in *Mysticism and Language*, ed. Steven T. Katz (Oxford: Oxford University Press, 1992), 32–33.

practices and the concept of imagination as a faculty that enables negotiation between human and divine mind, as put forward by the Scholastics, themselves working from Aristotle and the neo-Platonists, usually through Arab philosophers like Avicenna and Averroes.[170] Still, Asprem maintains the overall structure of a distinction put forward by Antoine Faivre, between the Christian *via negativa* and an esoteric approach to imagination more representative of Williams's way of affirmation. This valuation for a path of active imagination preceding the ultimate negativity of attainment is seen in occultism, where "both magically and theosophically oriented practices emphasize development of imagery as the path of practice, while holding up some ineffable experience of transcendent insight as the ultimate goal."[171]

Indeed, this tension between symbol and ineffability sits at the heart of esoteric theory and practice. It stems, at least in part, from the neo-Platonic concept of the "One"—the divine source from which all existence continuously emanates—as cosmically ubiquitous but also concurrently absolutely unknowable and indescribable. Symbol came to be seen, particularly in the context of the Renaissance revival of the gnostic, Hermetic, and kabbalistic traditions that expanded on this conception,[172] as the primary vehicle with which to imagine or express the nature of the One, who, as Umberto Eco describes, "is not only unknowable and obscure but...being independent of any deter-

---

170. Egil Asprem, "Esotericism and the Scholastic Imagination: The Origins of Esoteric Practice in Christian Kataphatic Spirituality," *Correspondences* 4 (2016): 6–19.
171. Ibid, 11. Cf. Faivre, *Access to Western Esotericism*, 12; T.M. Luhrmann, *Persuasions of the Witch's Craft: Ritual Magic and Witchcraft in Present-Day England* (London: Picador, 1989), 202–07.
172. On neo-Platonism, Renaissance Hermeticism, kabbalah, gnosticism and the development of a particular approach to symbol that has significantly influenced the development of modern hermeneutics and strategies of expression, see Eco, *The Limits of Interpretation*, 18–20. The reader should be aware that the term "gnosticism" describes a tradition with the same amount of historical flux and differentiation as "esotericism," a term with which it is often conflated (See Hanegraaff, "Forbidden Knowledge," 234). To get a sense of the history of gnosticism and the diversity of movements and concepts gathered under the term, see Michael Allen Williams, *Rethinking "Gnosticism": An Argument for Dismantling a Dubious Category* (Princeton: Princeton University Press, 1996).

mination, can contain all of them and is consequently the place of all contradictions."[173] This combination of transcendence and "emanational continuity"[174]—being all and not being at all—produced the tension between valuation and rejection of symbolism seen in the way of affirmation. In the holistic monism espoused by Waite, Williams and most other esoteric thinkers, the images and symbols created or encountered by the imagination are tripartite: they are divine in themselves as a result of emanation from the One, yet radically dissimilar from its unknowable transcendent nature, while remaining correspondently reflective of it and also of each other. Because of this neo-Platonic tripartite function, the esoteric traditions have tended to view symbols as the most effective means of communicating, however imperfectly, the experience of direct mystical knowledge of the divine and its inextricable oneness with all other forms of existence.[175] Esoteric knowledge has, in this sense, remained attractive to symbolists and surrealists as much as occultists because of its performative power. It helps the individual to think, perceive, and imagine acausally and intuitively—gnostically. Writing to Phyllis Jones, Williams spoke of mystical attainment in a way that reflects this esoteric affirmation of symbol: the "re-union of man and God" he said, is a work "which is pursued everywhere and at all times, from which nothing is alien and to which all things are directed."[176] Given this all-encompassing inclusion of all signs and all experience as a part of the mystic quest—expressed, it must be noted, in 1929, just as Williams was entering his most prolific period of fiction writing—the bardic fluidity of image, symbol and ritual language found in his novels seems aimed at an identical goal.

As Williams rose to the highest levels of F.R.C. initiation, his role changed from esoteric student to teacher. He was now expected to communicate the path to attainment learned in the order through

---

173. Eco, *The Limits of Interpretation*, 18.
174. Ibid.
175. Ibid.
176. Charles Williams to Phyllis Jones, January 1929, Bodleian MS REs. c. 320/I, letter 34, quoted in Lindop, *Charles Williams*, 153.

the same semiotic set in which he had encountered it.[177] Waite called this body of symbolism the "Secret Tradition."[178] The Secret Tradition is both the invaluable knowledge gained from mystic union with the divine,[179] and, concurrently, the path laid out by those few who have returned from their transcendent experiences.[180] It is "the history of the human soul, its origin, its transmigrations, and its destiny."[181] There are only a chosen few initiates, who Waite calls "the Holy Assembly,"[182] able to identify the esoteric substrate of the Secret Tradition beneath exoteric forms of doctrine. These initiates might come from any cultural, temporal or doctrinal background, but the perennial tradition of knowledge that they are able to access and communicate is universal, though it will be expressed by members of the Holy Assembly in historically specific terms. Waite specifically identified the Secret Tradition with esoteric knowledge, based on the fact of its hiddenness: "The true student of Theosophia in its widest meaning believes in the existence of a knowledge—which in effect is occult science—handed down from remote ages."[183] Like many esoteric thinkers, Waite thus saw the Secret Tradition as a body of secret knowledge passed down from ancient Greece and the Near

---

177. This shift is explained in detail in Chapter Three.
178. References to the Secret Tradition can be found throughout Waite's work, beginning in *The Doctrine and Literature of the Kabalah* (London: The Theosophical Publishing Society, 1902). Cf. Gilbert, "The Masonic Career of Arthur Edward Waite," 16–17; A.E. Waite, 97; Hanegraaff, *Esotericism and the Academy*, 248.
179. Waite's concept of union with the divine owes much to the Christian mystical tradition, particularly Meister Eckhart (1260–1329), often credited with introducing to Christian circles the idea that the divine lives within the self and can be discovered there. See Dan Cohn-Sherbok and Lavinia Cohn-Sherbok, *Jewish and Christian Mysticism: An Introduction* (New York: Continuum, 1994), 111–12. A full contextualization of Waite's mystical philosophy within the history of Christian mysticism is still to be written. Waite himself wrote frequently on the subject, however, particularly in *The Way of Divine Union* and *Studies in Mysticism*.
180. For the essence of Waite's beliefs on the praxis of achieving mystic union see *Shadows*, 235–45; Gilbert, *A.E. Waite*, 163.
181. Waite, *Studies in Mysticism*, 254.
182. Waite, *Shadows*, 170–71.
183. Waite, *Holy Kabbalah*, 10. This is a rare usage of the phrase "occult science" for Waite in this period (1929). We should assume that he intends the term to mean "hidden knowledge" rather than modern occult science.

East, and thus historically derived and subject to minor culturally specific permutations.[184] However, he also emphasized the Secret Tradition's "eternal pre-existence."[185] In this view it existed "before the world was with God" and is a form of knowledge universally accessible through individual gnosis.[186]

Similar concepts of an "ancient wisdom narrative" are found in virtually every esoteric belief system since the Renaissance, where it formed, as Hanegraaff illustrates, "the conceptual foundation of the initial 'referential corpus' of Western esotericism."[187] Modern occultism followed exuberantly in this lineage. Most, if not all, of Waite's occultist peers would have held similar beliefs, but, given his youthful enthusiasm for the French occultist's writings, Waite may have been initially influenced by Lévi's identification of a "pure religion" behind all other religions, its roots in kabbalah but more easily found in Catholicism since the time of Christ, though Catholics themselves rarely find it.[188] This religion, said Lévi, "exists and it has always existed in humanity; but it had to be concealed by the sages, because the vulgar have been incapable of comprehending it. It is the tradition of all the great sanctuaries of antiquity, it is the philosophy of nature, it is God living in humanity and in the world."[189] Such concepts are at the core of the programmatic syncretism of modern occult projects, which, like the Secret Tradition, sought to ahistorically assemble knowledge from a variety of esoteric traditions for the purpose of revealing a hidden, perennial truth beneath them. Hane-

---

184. See *Doctrine and Literature of the Kabalah*, 10–12. *Holy Kabbalah*, 15, 25; *Secret Doctrine in Israel*, 16; *The Secret Tradition in Freemasonry* (London: Rebman, 1911), 1:ix.

185. Waite, *Holy Kabbalah*, 16. Cf. ibid. 15, 574; *Doctrine and Literature of the Kabalah*, 10–12, 123, 127, 490; *Secret Doctrine in Israel*, 19; *The Secret Tradition in Freemasonry* (London: Rebman, 1911), 2:379.

186. *Secret Doctrine in Israel*, 19; *Holy Kabbalah*, 15.

187. Hanegraaff, *Esotericism and the Academy*, 73. Cf. 5–76. Hanegraaff borrows the term "referential corpus" from Faivre (*Access to Western Esotericism*, 6).

188. "The Beginnings of Occultist Kabbalah: Adolphe Franck and Eliphas Lévi," in *Kabbalah and Modernity: Interpretations, Transformations, Adaptations*, ed. Marco Pasi, Kocku von Stuckrad and Boaz Huss (Leiden: Brill, 2010), 24–26, 119–20. Cf. Strube, "'Baphomet' of Eliphas Lévi," 44–47.

189. "'Baphomet' of Eliphas Lévi," 47 (translation Strube's).

graaff observes this consanguinity between Waite's Secret Tradition and similar occult theses and goes one step further, arguing that in addition to having much more in common with occultists such as Lévi than it may appear at first sight, Waite actually contributed significantly to the growth of the very idea of a secret esoteric tradition underlying Western culture.[190] Waite's gathering of a bricolage of symbol to represent and communicate the claims of the Secret Tradition is also typical of the affirmation of symbolism and imaginal interaction consistent with esoteric mystical practice. Thus, the Christian theology of Waite and Williams must be fitted with the cosmotheistic valuation of material phenomena that contributes to the heterodox universalism of Romantic Theology and the Secret Tradition.

CONSTRUCTING A CORDON SANITAIRE
PART I: OCCULTISM VS. MYSTICISM

For Williams, a man who embraced multivalence and resisted dualism, this heterodoxy doesn't seem to have produced as much tension as it did for Waite. Despite his panentheistic cosmology, his significant involvement with modern esoteric groups and individuals, and the major role he played in perpetuating the occult revival, for most of his life Waite denied any connection to occultism, dichotomously presenting himself as a mystic instead. This problematic and very blurry distinction has persisted largely unquestioned in contemporary scholarship and has almost completely infused the field of Williams studies, where it is usually deployed to distance Williams from occultism as well. Scholars of Waite's life and work owe R.A. Gilbert a great debt, as his 1987 biography is clear, concise, and faithfully represents its subject in almost every regard. However, Gilbert too faithfully follows Waite's construction of a distinct dichotomy between occultism and magic on the one hand and his own Christian

---

190. Hanegraaff, *Esotericism and the Academy*, 248–52.

mystical philosophy and practice on the other;[191] the result has been a distortion of Waite's place in the modern occult network.

Waite stated in his biography that he began turning "far from things occult" as early as 1890, when he was "moving ever further from the false dreams of occult philosophy and practice."[192] However, these recollections represent a highly problematic simplification of his relationship with modern occult ideas and society. It is certainly true that he frequently criticized occultists and distinguished his own concepts and practices from theirs, first as a "true student of occultism,"[193] and later as a mystic with no connection to the "Pandora's box of modern occult speculations.[194] His critique of occultism revolved around two central problems with modern applications of esoteric knowledge. First, he felt that occultists wilfully ignored the historical context of the traditions they mined for symbolism. Waite attacked groups such as the Theosophical Society for their "lush growth of weedy wonder and concern over things occult," pursued along "putative paths of power and distracted paths of research," rather than in a proper historical vein.[195] His other central contention was that occultism was dangerous because of its connection (almost synonymous in Waite's mind) with practical magic. He followed the centuries old Christian accusation that magical power was evil because it was a desire after personal power—the Secret Tradition but "misdirected terribly by perverted will."[196] He concluded that such material desires faced occultists with the danger of never turning toward the only responsible goal of esoteric theory and practice—mystical attainment. "Phenomenal occultism and all its arts," he said in 1913, "Indifferently connect with the tradition of the

---

191. See, e.g., Gilbert, *A.E. Waite*, 12–13. Cf. *A.E. Waite: A Bibliography*, 11.
192. Waite, *Shadows*, 127, 146.
193. Waite, *Doctrine and Literature of the Kabalah*, 11.
194. Waite, *Divine Union*, 26.
195. Waite, *Shadows*, 145; *Divine Union*, 26. Cf. *Secret Tradition in Alchemy*, 46.
196. Waite, *Shadows*, 185. Cf. *The Book of Ceremonial Magic*, 336.

mystics: they are the path of illusion by which the psychic nature of man enters that other path which goes down into the abyss."[197]

Waite's actual attitude toward occultism, however, is much more complex than this statement allows. As Ronald Decker and Michael Dummett note in their study of Waite's tarot, he worked hard to create the image of himself as a "fastidious scholar repelled by the grandiose and irrational pretensions of occultism," but this picture was an illusion performed by a man "as committed to occultism as any of those whom he so scornfully rebuked."[198] Each of Waite's criticisms of modern occultists contains elements of hypocrisy. His attack on the ahistorical "weedy wonder" of occultists is not without basis, and he certainly did possess a wider scope of historical knowledge than most of his peers. We have seen, however, that his Secret Tradition was assembled with the same taste for bricolage as other occult systems, and, as we will see in the case of the rituals of the F.R.C. in the next chapter, with the same degree of disembedding from their original historical context.

Waite's attempt to draw a stark dichotomy between "phenomenal" occultism and his own mysticism is similarly problematic. Such a distinction is based on a common association between occultism as concerned with practical magic and mysticism as focused on the acquisition of enlightenment and/or ancient, usually secret or experiential, knowledge. However, as Robert Galbreath observes, most practicing occultists would not accept a separation of theoretical knowledge from personal participation and development of the self.[199] On the surface of things Waite sets himself apart from this group as he very much encourages such a separation, but the closer look at his actual philosophy and practice taken in this book shows that he merged speculative esoteric knowledge with practical, ritual activities intended to transmute the self and elevate consciousness in

---

197. Waite, *The Book of Ceremonial Magic*, 2. Cf. *Studies in Mysticism*, 244–45.
198. Ronald Decker and Michael Dummett, *A History of the Occult Tarot, 1870–1970* (London: Duckworth, 2002), 136.
199. Galbreath, "Explaining Modern Occultism," 17–18. Cf. Hanegraaff, *New Age Religion and Western Culture*, 422.

precisely the manner that Galbreath describes. Though Waite's ultimate goal was "to lose the symbols in their meanings,"[200] his imaginal and ritualistic practices indicate that he certainly continued to value (and exploit) the image-laden systems of the esoteric traditions in much the same way as his modern occult contemporaries, at the same time as he looked to Christian mysticism. Other perspectives on Waite's system that have received much less attention than Gilbert's view, particularly in the field of Williams studies, would agree. Alison Butler maintains Waite's distinction between magic and mysticism, but argues that he "embraced the mystical and religious aspects" of occultism, while Antoine Faivre, who has been enormously influential in establishing the contemporary academic study of esotericism, felt that Waite's thought was "resolutely in the line of the occultist movement of his period."[201] At times such views of Waite rely on accentuating the far more inclusive language of his earlier publications (when he had not yet begun to distance himself from occultism), but at all times in his life we find a disconnect between Waite's stated opposition to occultism and his actual practice.[202]

Waite's binary opposition between occultism and his own mystical philosophy supports Gerd Baumann's theory that between every such opposition, constructed for the purposes of defining the self in relation to a projected "other," there is a liminal space in which

---

200. Arthur Edward Waite, "The Pontifical Ceremony of Admission to the Grade of Adeptus Minor, 5=6," (Amsterdam: Bibliotheca Philosophica Hermetica, A.E. Waite Collection, 1916), 49.
201. Alison Butler, "Arthur Edward Waite," in *The Occult World*, ed. Christopher Partridge (Abingdon, Oxon: Routledge, 2015), 283; Faivre, *Access to Western Esotericism*, 82.
202. Waite was less strictly opposed to practical occultism when writing anonymously. He wrote several texts on the tarot under the pseudonym "Grand Orient," instructing those naturally suited to "the priesthood of practical magic" in the ways of tarot divination (*A Manual of Cartomancy*, 4th ed. (London: William Rider and Son, 1909), 2). As Grand Orient, Waite was separated from the anti-occult brand of his scholarly and mystical public persona, thus freeing him to express a valuation of occultism that more accurately represented the stance he lived outside of the polemics in his books. See, e.g., the preface to the 1909 printing of *Manual of Cartomancy*: "the byways of practical occultism are not without their importance" (v).

a ternary principle will inevitably be found.²⁰³ Baumann offers Edward Said's famous concept of Orientalism as an example of one of three types of identity construction in which such a third principle will be operative. Baumann recalls that Said's presentation of the construction of Western identity as rational and progressive, as opposed to non-Western others as superstitious and backwards, includes a component in which Westerners treasure this non-Western other for the spontaneity and richness which they perceive their own culture to have lost, and seek to incorporate these elements back into Western culture in order to regenerate it.²⁰⁴ Waite is an individual example of such "reverse mirror-imaging."²⁰⁵ He constructed his identity as a mystic by rejecting occultism as mysticism's phenomenal other, concerned only with the insignificant intrigues of practical magic and the development of personal power, all the while freely incorporating those aspects of occult thought and practice that he continued to value into his belief system. Latour notes that such processes are essential to the formation of new groups or networks in society. In Latour's ANT terms, Waite's binary represents an attempt to "trace or retrace the boundary of a group" by declaring other groupings within that group "as being empty, archaic, dangerous, obsolete, and so on." Other modern esoteric thinkers are thus designated as an occult "anti-group" to the circle of texts, esoteric phenomena and individuals that Waite was drawing around him.²⁰⁶ It is no coincidence that Waite began to intensify his polemics against "occultism" at exactly the time that he was establishing the I.R.R. as "a mystical instead of an occult construction" of the Golden Dawn.²⁰⁷ When such new social groups are carved out of existing

---

203. Gerd Baumann, "Grammars of Identity/Alterity: A Structural Approach," in *Grammars of Identity/Alterity: A Structural Approach*, ed. Gerd Baumann and Andre Gingrich (New York: Berghahn Books, 2006), 33–36.
204. Ibid, 20–21.
205. Ibid, 20.
206. Latour, *Reassembling the Social*, 32.
207. Waite, *Shadows*, 228. Cf. Howe, *The Magicians of the Golden Dawn*, 254–56. Waite's development of the I.R.R. from the Golden Dawn's point of fracture is discussed in more detail in Chapter Two.

groups, Latour notes, "their spokesperson looks rather frantically for ways to *de-fine* them. Their boundaries are marked, delineated, and rendered fixed and durable."[208]

This construction of identity through artificial duality has been a common story in the history of Western esotericism. On a grand scale, the boundaries and characteristics of individual or group belief systems are often delineated by the various polemical discourses used to group particular phenomena into the "wastebasket" of esoteric culture: Asprem describes this process as a "proliferation of disjunctions," wherein beliefs and practices that appear phenomenologically similar are drawn into binary relationships similar to Waite's vocal rejection of occultism.[209] Many modern occultists dislocated Christian and Enlightenment rationalist polemics in order to set themselves off from these more normative networks, but Waite was not the only one to reverse this disjunction and speak dismissively about occultism from the standpoint of an occultist. Mead eschewed "esotericism" and "occultism" as "corrupting rather than helpful" in his founding of the Quest Society,"[210] despite the society's clear mandate to research the forms of knowledge often included under the headings of both terms. At the same time as Waite and Mead began to designate an occult anti-group, two leading Italian esotericists, Julius Evola and Mario Manlio Rossi, published harsh critiques of the central schools and figures of the occultist network in which they operated.[211] These discursive actions were possible, as Alex Owen has shown, because of the fluidity of the terms in question: "In practice...the different strands of occultism and mysticism were so

---

208. Latour, *Reassembling the Social*, 33.
209. See Asprem, "Esotericism and the Scholastic Imagination," 30. Asprem builds on the discourse analysis of Kocku von Stuckrad in *The Scientification of Religion: An Historical Study of Discursive Change, 1800–2000* (Berlin: Walter de Gruyter, 2014), 25–55.
210. G.R.S. Mead, "'The Quest'—Old and New: Retrospect and Prospect," *Quest* 17, no. 3 (April 1926): 297.
211. Roberto Bacci, "Transmutation and Homogenization of Consciousness in Italian Esotericism During the Fascist Period: Mario Manlio Rossi's *Spaccio Dei Maghi* and Julius Evola's *Maschera E Volto Dello Spiritualismo Contemporaneo*," *Correspondences* 2, no. 2 (2014): 195.

closely interwoven that even those who were familiar with the finer points of esotericism used the terms interchangeably...It was generally understood by serious adherents and popularizers alike...that 'mysticism' was simply another way of saying 'occultism.'"[212] The fluidity of these terms does not mean that particular viewpoints predicated on them could necessarily be reconciled,[213] but certainly all parties were free to use them in whatever manner suited their (often polemical) processes of identity formation.

An intriguing passage in *Studies in Mysticism* (1906) suggests that Waite was quite aware of the discursive power of transforming referents and contrasting them against each other. Waite argues that there are certain terms between which an opposition becomes constructed over time, "although it is not justified by their primary significance." He gives the example of the "very clear differentiation" which has come to exist between "occult" and "mystic," and admits that "fundamentally speaking, the two words are identical." Despite their original similarity of meaning in earlier times, Waite states that we have come to understand the occultist as the disciple of one or all of "the secret sciences"—he gives the examples of alchemy, astrology, divination, and magic—while the mystic "has no concern as such with [their] study."[214] Given this clear awareness of the constructedness of binary uses of these terms, Waite's dichotomy between the occultist other and his own mysticism should be seen as a boundary quite purposefully carved across an otherwise diverse esoteric spectrum in which the distinction between the two was actually much more complex. At the time he discussed these discursive aspects, Waite regarded the two terms as largely analogical, but in later years he put up a high boundary fence between them, strung with the sharp barbwire of polemic. Meanwhile, his actual position continued to occupy Baumann's liminal ternary space, as he never stopped interacting

---

212. Owen, *Place of Enchantment*, 21–22. Cf. 47.
213. Ibid, 47–48.
214. Waite, *Studies in Mysticism*, 5–6.

with the esoteric traditions in a manner that reflected much of the zeitgeist, function, and ethic of modern occultism.

This reevaluation has been necessary because Waite's artificial dichotomy between occultism and mysticism, often connected to a similar distinction between magic and mysticism, has been projected onto Williams.[215] However, if we cannot separate Waite himself from occultism by virtue of his artificial binary, a connection to Williams is doubly uncertain. There is, moreover, little evidence of similar discursive actions on Williams's part. The closest he comes to such a differentiation is a statement in "The Index of the Body," an essay on the doctrine of correspondences: "The word 'occult' has come into general use, and is convenient, if no moral sense is given it simply as itself. It deals with hidden things, and their investigation. But in this case we are concerned not so much with the pretended operations of those occult schools as with a certain imagination of relation in the universe, and that only to pass beyond it."[216] Williams's statement is more reflective than Waite's rhetoric of the complex structure of rejection and approbation with which both men approached occultism. Like Waite, Williams seems aware of the discursive fluidity of the term "occult"; unlike his F.R.C. Imperator, he is happy to continue using the term, with an ambiguous caution as to its "moral sense." For him the term is a productive referent for the study of "hidden things" to which much of occult, Theosophical, modern alchemical and Spiritualistic research was dedicated.[217] Dichotomous thinking similar to Waite's appears more clearly in the dismissive reference to "occult schools," contrasted with imaginal access to the macrocosmic via the symbols of the microcosmic, reinforced by the insistence that one must "pass beyond" this interaction with the

---

215. See, e.g., Scott McLaren, "Hermeticism and the Metaphysics of Goodness in the Novels of Charles Williams," *Mythlore*, no. 3–4 (2006): 3; King, *The Pattern in the Web*, 165; Ashenden, *Charles Williams*, 52, 55.
216. Williams, "Index of the Body," 83.
217. See Richard Noakes, "The 'World of the Infinitely Little': Connecting Physical and Psychical Realities Circa 1900," *Studies in History and Philosophy of Science Part A* 39, no. 3 (2008): 324.

divine semiosis present in language, image and nature. As with Waite, however, the phenomenal remains essential to all but the final step on the mystic ladder. Williams continues on to discuss the doctrine of correspondences in relation to the zodiac, distinguishing a higher astrology of the divine body from a lower "debased astrology" of prophecy.[218] Williams cautions that this latter form is to be avoided, but notes that the images of the zodiac also offer "a kind of macrocosmic-microcosmic union of a more serious and more profitable kind." This is the movement, via meditation upon the principles represented by astrological symbolism, from the "spatial" to the "spiritual" heavens.[219] Fixed upon correspondent monism, Williams engaged with a wide repository of symbolism—esoteric and otherwise—in order to achieve, through ritual and visualization, the elevation of consciousness that would provide inner transmutation and access to higher planes of existence—a goal and the means to that goal which lay at the heart of modern occult practice. It is this gaze through the spatial to the spiritual that led Eliot to call him "a catholic student of the occult."[220]

OCCULTISM VS. CHRISTIANITY

Waite's influence has also been used to reinforce the cordon sanitaire assumption that Williams, as a Christian, could not possibly have involved himself with occultism with any degree of seriousness. Despite Waite's belief that the Secret Tradition could be found beneath any form of religious doctrine, most Williams scholars have insisted on seeing him as exclusively Christian. This projection allows the assertion that the esoteric traditions Williams discovered in Waite's writings and in the F.R.C. had "already been Christian-

---

218. Williams, "Index of the Body," 83.
219. Ibid.
220. T.S. Eliot, "Dante's Beatrice: Knower, Known and Knowing," *The Times Literary Supplement*, 24 July 1943, 358.

ized."[221] This interpretation can be traced back to Gilbert's biography, where he argues, despite Waite's claim to have lost his faith in Catholicism at an early age, that "he not only maintained his church attendance but became a strident apologist for the Faith."[222] Gilbert presents Waite's belief system as a Christian translation of various esoteric currents, grounding his argument on the fact that Waite drew extensively from Christian imagery and tradition in designing the rituals and theology of the F.R.C.[223] However, the F.R.C. also relied heavily on other traditions, particularly alchemy, kabbalah and Rosicrucianism, and though Christian mystical interpretation of these traditions was important to Waite, he was also insistent that they be seen in their authentic historical sense, not merely in their "Christianized" versions.[224] Ultimately, Christianity joined all other traditions as a sphere of dogma and symbol that could guide the initiate toward attainment, but, as Imperator Waite assured neophytes of the F.R.C., could not in itself provide access to "that infinite realm which lies behind the woven circle of official religion."[225]

---

221. McLaren, "Hermeticism and the Metaphysics of Goodness," 3; Ashenden, *Charles Williams*, 1, 71, 120.
222. Gilbert, *A.E. Waite*, 23. In an article published twenty-five years after his 1987 biography, Gilbert adjusts his position on Waite's relationship to Catholicism: "[Waite] could eschew Catholic dogma while retaining its ritual, its atmosphere, and his own interpretation of the doctrines of the mystics of the Church." Gilbert presents a much more accurate picture in this later research, aligning Waite less with the church and more with "a stable community of fellow believers who engaged in the "practical mysticism" of his Rosicrucian Order" (Gilbert, "The One Thought That Was Not Untrue," 251). Unfortunately, Gilbert's earlier presentation has played a much more defining role in Williams studies.
223. Gilbert, *A.E. Waite*, 142, 146.
224. Waite, *Doctrine and Literature of the Kabalah*, 121.
225. Arthur Edward Waite, "The Ceremony of Reception into the Grade of Neophyte, 0=0," (Amsterdam: Bibliotheca Philosophica Hermetica, A.E. Waite Collection, 1916), 45. This universalism is also emphasized in the ritual for the Zelator grade: "The path of your symbolic progress in this Grade has brought you from the Court of the Temple into the Holy Place. Beyond it is a Holy of Holies, and yet beyond is another Mystery of Religion, leading by successive stages to a central place of experience, unto which all faiths testify, which all set forth in types" ("The Ceremony of Advancement in the Grade of Zelator, 1=10," Amsterdam: Bibliotheca Philosophica Hermetica, A.E. Waite Collection, 1916), 27).

Waite *did* frequently express Secret Tradition concepts in Christian terms, but this was a question of cultural background rather than doctrinal superiority. Mystical experience, he explained, is provoked by "some particular circle of faith...intellectually this fact rooted each mystic in that faith which was his originally."[226] Mystical experience was thus "catholic to all ages," all places, and all traditions, the "universal religion."[227]

Williams was more visibly and specifically Christian than Waite. As an "unswerving son" of the Church of England,[228] he wrote plays for local dioceses, published theological works, attended services throughout his life and at one point even penned the liturgy for a service at Saint Paul's, London, at the request of the Bishop of Chichester.[229] However, he would not have been interested in the exclusivity assumed by the cordon sanitaire. He would likely have looked quizzically upon Hadfield's statement that he was "the great protagonist of Christianity as alone among religious revelations exposing and defining the glory of mortal flesh," particularly since, as we have seen, he disdained Christianity's dualistic aversion to physicality.[230] Anglicanism was an ideal forum for Williams, as Hadfield herself observes,[231] because of its flexibility—the Church of England has had its orthodoxies and its orthodox, but ultimately it provided Williams enough theological space to develop his own unique blend of Christian, mystical, and occult observance. Indeed, for some this space appeared so wide as to extend as low as hell itself. Literary critic Theodore Maynard decided that Williams was a Satanist after

---

226. Waite, *Divine Union*, 321.
227. Ibid, 319; Waite, *Holy Kabbalah*, 132. Cf. "Thomas Vaughan and His *Lumen De Lumine*," in *The Hermetic Papers of A.E. Waite: The Unknown Writings of a Modern Mystic*, ed. R.A. Gilbert (Wellingborough, Northamptonshire: Aquarian Press, 1987), 90.
228. Hadfield, *Introduction to Charles Williams*, 131.
229. A manuscript of this liturgy is in the Bodleian, Ms. Res. c. 137, f. 3, in a collection donated by Anne Ridler, who attached a note to the document indicating that she did not think the service ever took place.
230. Hadfield, *Introduction to Charles Williams*, 85. For similar views, see Reilly, *Romantic Religion*, 177; Shideler, *Theology of Romantic Love*, 1.
231. See Hadfield, *Introduction to Charles Williams*, 131, 170.

reading his *Poems of Conformity* (1917),[232] while Lewis reports that one of the Inklings, Charles L. Wrenn, "*almost* seriously expressed a strong wish to burn Williams, or at least maintained that conversation with Williams enabled him to understand how inquisitors had felt it right to burn people." Lewis and Tolkien agreed with Wrenn that Williams was "eminently combustible."[233]

These associations with heresy are outlying responses to Williams's unusual set of interests and philosophies, the latter made rather tongue in cheek, and the former eventually retracted (see note). However, they indicate his interest in religious thought that was far from conventionally—or specifically—Christian. He was not afraid to invoke the universalizing tendencies of mysticism and the ancient wisdom tradition when he saw them as improvements to Christian doctrine. A note found in Williams's as-yet-unpublished "Commonplace Book," a collection of materials for a long-planned cycle of Arthurian poetry that finally manifested in *Taliessen Through Logres* and *The Region of the Summer Stars*, indicates that he shared at least a degree of Waite's conception of Christ as cosmic and universal.[234] Notes analyzing the deities of pre-Christian cultures—Odin, Astarte, Mithras, Quetzalcoatl—as particular forms of the universal truth offered by Christianity, show his broad search for symbols that could express the nature of the divine. His reading of Prescott's *History of the Conquest of Mexico* (1853) led him to wonder if the Mayan deity Quetzalcoatl was not in fact another physical manifestation of the same divine urge that led to the incarnation of Christ: "Would the

---

232. Maynard wrote a scathing review of the collection, though later retracted his accusation of Satanism after meeting the poet, saying that Williams had "established for himself a philosophical point of contact between Paganism and the Christian Faith." Quoted in Kerryl Lynne Henderson, "'It Is Love That I Am Seeking': Charles Williams and the Silver Stair," in *Charles Williams: A Celebration*, edited by Briane Horne, 131–52 (Leominster, Herefordshire: Fowler Wright, 1995). Cf. Lindop, *Charles Williams*, 73–75.

233. Walter Hooper, ed. *The Collected Letters of C.S. Lewis, Volume II* (New York: Harper Collins, 2004), 283. Cf. Curtis, "Charles Williams," 145.

234. I am grateful to David L. Dodds and to the Charles Williams estate for providing me with access to this unpublished manuscript. Pagination follows the typed manuscript as reproduced by Dodds, here p. 104–6.

traditions about him make him contemporaneous with Christ—and if so, would they be another result of the 'assumption of the manhood (the world, mankind, matter,) into God' in the Incarnation?"[235] This thinking is rooted in theological debates that had been ongoing in more liberal Christian circles since the nineteenth century, in which the historical Jesus was radically expanded into a "Cosmic Christ" that could be found in all geographies, temporalities and cultures, a universalizing tendency that appealed to modern esoteric figures like Theosophist Alice A. Bailey, who developed a Christology which incorporated the Christian messiah as "an inclusivist, perennialist, and pan-religionist figure."[236]

Those involved in such speculations often continued, as Williams did, to identify as Christians, despite establishing significant intellectual distance between themselves and the mainstream. In a 1939 letter to his wife, Williams indicates that he was aware that his metaphysics cast a net far wider than the Sea of Galilee. He had been asked to attend a conference on the subject of how to present the Christian faith in contemporary society, but doubted whether he was the man for the job: "Am I a Christian? I don't know, but I know what Christianity possibly may be."[237] This response indicates Williams's sometimes ambivalent posture towards codified religion. He was not without his criticism of the Church, particularly its denigration of eros. He may have been speaking as much about himself as of D.H. Lawrence when, in the same year, he admired the accentuation of sex and the body put forward by this "convinced and rhetorical heretic." "The Church," he argued, "Owes more to heretics than she is ever

---

235. Commonplace Book, 106.
236. Sean O'Callaghan, "The Theosophical Christology of Alice Bailey," in *Handbook of the Theosophical Current*, ed. Olav Hammer and Mikael Rothstein (Leiden: Brill, 2013), 101. Cf. 106–9. Waite also preached the doctrine of the Cosmic Christ. See *Divine Union*, 182.
237. Charles Williams to Florence Williams, 27 November 1939, in Roma A. King, ed. *To Michal from Serge: Letters from Charles Williams to His Wife, Florence, 1939–1945* (Kent and London: Kent State University Press, 2002), 34.

likely (on this earth) to admit."[238] Thus, even at a time when his writings display a more dominant influence from Christianity than in previous publications, he was willing to embrace the value of intellectual and philosophical challenge, preferring fluidity and multivalence over a reification of idea. "A great curiosity ought to exist concerning divine things," he wrote in 1938, "Man was intended to argue with God."[239] This approach to religion—perhaps best described as a heterodox Christianity that opened out onto universalism—is illustrated by Romantic theology, wherein "Romantic lovers in any part or in any age of the world have achieved their proper end under whatever creed they professed. The present business is merely the formulation of Christian theology; not a denial or correction of others."[240]

A similar universalism is visible in Williams's treatment of esoteric ideas and symbolism. He was aware of the incompatibility which others assumed between Christian knowledge and the esoteric claims and practices of magic, kabbalah and Rosicrucianism. He told his friends very little about his involvement with the F.R.C.,[241] partly because vows of secrecy prevented him, but perhaps also because, as his good friend John Pellow theorized, "He probably—and rightly—had an inkling that I would take the Occult very seriously."[242] Though, as we will see, knowledge and experience of esoteric concepts informed his theories of coinherence and Romantic Theology, when writing about them in works he perceived as theological, he largely explored them in an isolated Christian context; he felt, for example, that the Zohar of kabbalah was "extraordinarily valuable" to Romantic Theology, but did not include it in his book on the subject because it was "not part of historic Christian thought."[243] Yet,

---

238. Williams, "Sensuality and Substance," 69 (originally published in *Theology*, May 1939).
239. Williams, *He Came Down*, 33.
240. *Outlines of Romantic Theology*, 8.
241. See Hadfield, *Introduction to Charles Williams*, 80.
242. John Pellow to Alice Mary Hadfield, 30 July 1976, CWSA IV.D.i/a.
243. Williams, *Outlines of Romantic Theology*, 55n.

he does not seem to have experienced this feeling of incompatibility in the construction of his personal belief system. As will become clear in the following analysis of Williams's esoteric life and fiction, his fluid, syncretistic intellectual approach resulted in an incorporation of Christian theology with occult experience, theory and practice that shows little concern for the dichotomous thinking typified by the cordon sanitaire.

CHRISTIAN OCCULTISM

The assumption that Waite and Williams could not have strayed from Christian orthodoxy, viewed as a reified tradition in necessary opposition to a similarly inflexible category of occultism, has obscured the possibility that Williams's thought could be concurrently Christian and esoteric, which was, as Thomas Willard concludes, exactly the blended system that Waite offered to Williams via his books and the ritual experience of the F.R.C.[244] Indeed much contemporary criticism of esoteric and occult currents continues to be affected by the assumption of a polar binary between Christianity and the occult. Of course, this dichotomy has not simply apparated out of thin air—it reflects cultural discourses such as those that have resulted from the variety of Christian and Enlightenment rationalist critiques that have helped form our conception of esoteric knowledge over the centuries. The contrast thus created was perpetuated by the nineteenth-century reversal I have already discussed, in which a number of occultists embraced Christian polemics against esoteric knowledge as a crucial strategic element in defining their own identity through alterity. Aleister Crowley is the most famous example. After a childhood spent in a strict Plymouth Brethren community, he set himself up in polar opposition to Christianity and its traditional values, embracing

---

244. Willard, "Acts of the Companions," 278. Both Grevel Lindop and Gareth Knight propose the same unproblematic conflation. See Lindop, *Charles Williams*, 3; Knight, *Magical World of Charles Williams*, 11. Knight, a former member of Dion Fortune's Society of Inner Light, has himself synthesized occult and Christian worldviews (King, *Ritual Magic in England*, 158).

practical magic, experimenting with a wide range of sexual acts, and identifying himself as the great Beast of Revelation.[245] Such opposition to Christianity has been defined by scholars such as Marco Pasi and Leon Surette as one of the defining characteristics of modern occultism.[246]

The virulent anti-Christian stance taken by some occultists is an important feature of the movement and certainly should not be ignored, but ultimately Crowley's approach to Christianity was a minority position. Most occultists occupied Baumann's ternary—the liminal space that will inevitably be found between binary opposites.[247] Anna Kingsford, an influential member, for a while, of the Theosophical Society, and founder of the Hermetic Society (a precursor to the Golden Dawn), developed an esoteric Christianity similar to that of Waite, though more radical. Her heterodox theology denied a historical basis for Christianity, did not elevate it above other religions and did not see Jesus as the sole route to salvation—but she adhered to a Christian identity nonetheless.[248] Éliphas Lévi is also an important example. He valued magic and kabbalah as part of the ancient wisdom that originated with Zoroaster, but he also asserted that Christianity became the true guardian of these traditions at the time of the birth of Jesus, after which esoteric knowledge pursued outside the Roman Catholic church—itself unable to see the

---

245. See Henrik Bogdan and Martin Starr, eds, *Aleister Crowley and Western Esotericism* (Oxford: Oxford University Press, 2012), 3–5. For a reliable, succinct biographical introduction to Crowley, see Marco Pasi, *Aleister Crowley and the Temptation of Politics* (Durham: Acumen, 2014), 10–21.

246. Pasi, "Occultism," 1366; Surette, *Birth of Modernism*, 94.

247. For more inclusive approaches to the relationship between modern esotericism and Christianity, see Owen, *Place of Enchantment*, 21; James Machin, "Towards a Golden Dawn: Esoteric Christianity and the Development of Nineteenth-Century British Occultism," *The Victorian* 1, no. 1 (2013); Liz Greene, *Magi and Maggidim: The Kabbalah in British Occultism, 1860–1940* (Sophia Centre Press, 2012), 125.

248. Joscelyn Godwin shows that Kingsford was a very important influence on other occultists who merged Christianity with esoteric thought, including Annie Besant, a leader of the Theosophical Society, and her friend and fellow explorer of esoteric knowledge, the Rev. C.W. Leadbeater (*The Theosophical Enlightenment*, 346) Cf. Janet Oppenheim, *The Other World: Spiritualism and Psychical Research in England, 1850–1914* (Cambridge: Cambridge University Press, 1985), 189.

truth hidden beneath its dogmas—lost all legitimacy.[249] Annie Besant applied the "occult understanding of Christian teachings" revealed in her *Esoteric Christianity* (1901) to the Theosophical Society when she took over its leadership in 1907, mingling previously anathema Christian elements with the usual blend of Eastern spirituality and Western esotericism.[250] These are only a few examples of the complex interrelations between modern esoteric movements and Christianity. This tangled web indicates the need to avoid the binaries constructed by occultists like Waite and Crowley as they sought to clarify the boundaries of their esoteric philosophies.

Charles Williams occupied a similar position in the liminal space between the artificial binaries of orthodox Christianity and occult thought. Like Waite he rejected particular elements of occult practice, but in the main he saw his life, work and theology enriched by synthesis with esoteric currents. Both Waite and Williams were enthusiastic members of a significant group of Christian esotericists that, as Jocelyn Godwin describes, faced "the blustering of the theologians" and preferred mysticism over the external workings of the Church, rejected associations between the Church and political powers, prioritized Jesus over the petulant Yahweh of the Old Testament, read the scriptures symbolically rather than literally, and emphasized tolerance and universalism but never quite abandoned the idea of Christian superiority over other religions.[251] Add to this Williams's involvement with Waite's masonic Rosicrucian society, his interest in astrology, the tarot, alchemy and kabbalah, and his private experimentation with magical ritual for the purposes of mystical and

---

249. Hanegraaff, *Esotericism and the Academy*, 245–47. Strube, "'Baphomet' of Eliphas Lévi," 46–47; Gilbert, *A.E. Waite*, 88.

250. Owen, *Place of Enchantment*, 48. Cf. George D. Chryssides, "The New Age," in *The Cambridge Companion to New Religious Movements*, ed. Olav Hammer and Mikael Rothstein (Cambridge: Cambridge University Press, 2012), 249; Oppenheim, *The Other World*, 190–93.

251. Godwin, *The Theosophical Enlightenment*, 227. Cf. Susan Greenwood, "Gender and Power in Magical Practices," in *Beyond New Age: Exploring Alternative Spirituality*, ed. Steven Sutcliffe and Marion Bowman (Edinburgh: Edinburgh University Press, 2000), 140.

artistic excitation, and it is hard to see how we can any longer identify him as anything but both a devout Christian and an enthusiastic occultist.

CHAPTER 2

THE FELLOWSHIP OF THE ROSY CROSS
A MODERN OCCULT EXPERIENCE

There is no better example of Williams's interaction with modern occult theory and practice than the blend of Rosicrucianism, Freemasonry, kabbalah, alchemy, and magic that he encountered in his ten year involvement with the F.R.C. Prior to the release of Gilbert's Waite biography, Williams was widely believed to have been a Golden Dawn initiate,[1] based on reports from friends who stated that he confided to them that he was a member.[2] Despite this association with the Golden Dawn, however, early scholars tended to ignore its ramifications, despite puzzlement regarding the occult materials in his novels and poetry.[3] One reason for this was a feeling that there was not enough information: Anne Ridler acknowledged that the Golden Dawn materials seemed to have had "considerable" influence on Williams,[4] but complained that

---

1. See, e.g., Hadfield, *Charles Williams: An Exploration*, 29–31; Cavaliero, *Poet of Theology*, 4–5; Reilly, *Romantic Religion*, 162.
2. Ridler, "Introduction to *the Image of the City*," xxiii.
3. Two exceptions are Bosky, "Even an Adept"; Chad Walsh, "Charles Williams' Novels and the Contemporary Mutation of Consciousness," in *Myth, Allegory and Gospel*, ed. John Marwick Montgomery (Minneapolis, MN: Bethany Fellowship, 1974).
4. Ridler, introduction to *The Image of the City*, xxiv.

it was "extremely difficult to get at the truth" of the nature of his involvement.[5] Yet, even if the extent of his personal engagement remained mysterious, the rituals of the Golden Dawn had been publicly available for analysis since before the time of Williams's death;[6] opportunity was available to contextualize at least some occultist aspects of his work. Given the cordon sanitaire approaches that have been applied to his involvement with the F.R.C., it is far more likely that infamy, rather than obscurity, lay behind the lack of research interest in the Golden Dawn.[7] Simple obscurity is not much of an explanation; the F.R.C. remains more mysterious today than the Golden Dawn ever was, with very little scholarship devoted to the order itself, aside from Williams's participation. To a degree this reflects a difference in notoriety. The Golden Dawn had star power: Yeats, Crowley, Farr, Blackwood, Machen. The F.R.C. had Charles Williams.

Gilbert's revelation that Williams was involved in the F.R.C. rather than the Golden Dawn thus cast the author's occult activities in a more, not less obscure context. Where at least a murky idea of the Golden Dawn's ritual environment could have been derived from its rituals and knowledge lectures, F.R.C. materials were almost impossible to come by. Despite this difficulty, scholars began to pay attention to Williams's Rosicrucian activities—probably at least in part because Gilbert's portrayal of the F.R.C. as "wholly mystical" and "wholly Christian" eased the perceived irreconcilable tension

---

5. Ibid, xxiii. Cf. xxiv–xxvi.
6. Abbreviated forms of the rituals were published as early as 1909–10 by Aleister Crowley in *The Equinox* I, nos. 2 and 3. The rituals of the Stella Matutina, the version of the Golden Dawn Williams would have to have been a part of due to his age (he was 17 when the original Golden Dawn dissolved), were published in Israel Regardie, *The Golden Dawn*, 4 vols. (Chicago: Aries Press, 1939). Cf. Bogdan, *Western Esotericism*, 127–28.
7. Research on the Golden Dawn is much more widely available than for the F.R.C. For original rituals and knowledge lectures see Francis King, ed. *Astral Projection, Ritual Magic and Alchemy: Golden Dawn Material by S.L. Macgregor Mathers and Others* (Rochester, VT: Destiny, 1987); Regardie, *Complete Golden Dawn*. For the history of the order see Howe, *The Magicians of the Golden Dawn*; Gilbert, *The Golden Dawn*.

between Williams's Christian and occult interests.[8] Subsequent analysis has tended to follow a dichotomous view of the F.R.C. as mystical and Christian and the Golden Dawn as magical and occult.[9] Ashenden, for example, cautions that it is essential to distinguish between the F.R.C. and the Golden Dawn because the latter group pursued goetic magic, "that is rather more 'black' than 'white,'" and was involved in "serious public scandal,"[10] while the F.R.C. offered Williams an orthodox Christian experience: "Those who misunderstand or know next to nothing about the nature of Waite's Rosicrucianism fear that Williams spoke from a position outside the boundaries of Christian orthodoxy. That was not the case. In fact his use of that tradition enabled him, after developing his own distinctive mythical framework and mythically charged language, to speak remedially from within Christian culture."[11]

Like most simplistic binaries, this dichotomy has some accuracy. Waite certainly hoped to distance his order from "lesser circles of initiation" like his old order,[12] a distinction expressly based on the Golden Dawn's interest in more practical forms of ritual magic. However, as other Williams critics have noted—some with disdain,[13] others more intrigued[14]—the F.R.C. has much more of the occult about it than has generally been acknowledged, and certainly displays many of the trappings of its parent order. Though Alison Butler, also following in Gilbert's line, assures us that the F.R.C. is a "new creature and not a further evolution of the Golden Dawn magical system,"[15] a more complex genealogical picture emerges

---

8. Gilbert, *A.E. Waite*, 142.
9. For Gilbert's account of Williams's F.R.C. involvement, see *A.E. Waite*, 149. Accounts that rely on Gilbert include Willard, "Acts of the Companions," 269, 272–73; Newman, "Companions of the Co-Inherence," 3–4; Mordecai, "Charles Williams and the Occult," 266–67; King, "The Occult as Rhetoric," 165–66; King, *The Pattern in the Web*, 11–12.
10. Ashenden, *Charles Williams*, 3.
11. Ashenden, *Charles Williams*, viii.
12. Waite, "Neophyte," 41.
13. Mordecai, "Charles Williams and the Occult," 267–68.
14. Bosky, "Even an Adept," 34.
15. Butler, "Arthur Edward Waite," 285.

once the rituals, professions, and constitution of the order are held up for examination. In the following analysis of Charles Williams's initiatory experiences, I will deconstruct the distinction between the F.R.C. and occult groups like the Golden Dawn to show that while Waite's order was certainly Christian and mystical it also drew important methods and concepts from its parent order, and shared the central modern occult aim of spiritual attainment.

MASONIC ROSICRUCIANISM

Placing the F.R.C. in its modern occult context through comparisons with the Golden Dawn is both natural and productive, as the latter society was very much a parent to its rebellious stepchild. Both orders were influenced by a number of previous Rosicrucian groups. The first and arguably most influential of these orders never actually existed. This was the original "Fraternity of the Rosy Cross,"[16] the purported authors of two manifestoes mysteriously released in early seventeenth-century Germany: the *Fama Fraternitatis* (1614) and the *Confessio Fraternitatis* (1615). This secret brotherhood claimed that the body of their founder, Christian Rosenkreutz, had recently been discovered in a hidden tomb, his body unmarked by time though it was 120 years after his death. As I will discuss further on, this legend played an important role in the rituals and symbolism of both the Golden Dawn and the F.R.C., but other Rosicrucian orders would also play a role. Though the brotherhood announced in the *Fama* was almost certainly fictional, the manifestoes kindled real interest in the concept of a Rosicrucian secret society in the seventeenth century.[17] The English Hermeticist Robert Fludd immediately came to the

---

16. *Confessio Fraternitatis*, printed in Francis Yates, *The Rosicrucian Enlightenment* (London: Routledge, 2002), 251–60.
17. On the history of Rosicrucianism see Christopher McIntosh, *The Rose Cross and the Age of Reason: Eighteenth-Century Rosicrucianism in Central Europe and Its Relationship to the Enlightenment* (Leiden: Brill, 1992); *The Rosy Cross Unveiled: The History, Mythology and Rituals of an Occult Order* (Wellingborough: Aquarian Press, 1980); Bogdan, *Western Esotericism*, 63–66.

defense of the mysterious order against charges of heresy in *Apologia Compendiara Fraternitatem de Rosea Cruce* (1616) and Francis Bacon referred to the Rosicrucians in *New Atlantis* (1627) as one of the sources of inspiration for his utopian "order of priest-scientists."[18]

The Rosicrucian myth also provided exciting narrative materials for a group of secret societies that *did* exist: the Freemasons. Casual associations were made by masons in the seventeenth century, and by the 1720s some rites were claiming roots in Rosicrucianism.[19] By mid-century, the first Freemasonic group to definitively establish itself in a Rosicrucian mode emerged—the Gold- und Rosenkreuzer, founded ca. 1763 in Sulzbach.[20] This order established the grade structure that would influence a later fringe Freemasonic group with Rosicrucian connections: the Societas Rosicruciania in Anglia (S.R.I.A.—founded 1865–66), which in turn provided the grades for the Golden Dawn's Westcott, Woodman, and Mathers, all members of the S.R.I.A. before they founded their new occult order in 1888.[21]

The F.R.C. shared these roots in masonic Rosicrucianism. Waite was also involved with the S.R.I.A.,[22] in addition to participation in a variety of other rites and degrees. His research led him to conclude that the existence of the brotherhood of the manifestoes was unlike-

---

18. Bogdan, "Freemasonry and Western Esotericism," 287; *Western Esotericism*, 71–72.
19. Bogdan, "Freemasonry and Western Esotericism," 287.
20. Roland Edighoffer, "Rosicrucianism II: 18th Century," in *Dictionary of Gnosis and Western Esotericism*, ed. Wouter J. Hanegraaff (Leiden: Brill, 2006), 1015; Bogdan, "Freemasonry and Western Esotericism," 291.
21. On the Gold- und Rosenkreuzer, see McIntosh, *The Rosy Cross Unveiled*, 82–94. For its grade structure, see 89; for its links to the S.R.I.A. see 109. Cf. Bogdan, *Western Esotericism*, 128; "Freemasonry and Western Esotericism," 291–92; Gilbert, "The Masonic Career of Arthur Edward Waite," 6. Another fictional Rosicrucian group lay behind the Golden Dawn as well, as Westcott claimed to have received authorization for the founding of the order from a high-ranking adept named Anna Sprengel, a supposed member of a pre-existing German branch of the Golden Dawn. Most scholars agree, however, that Westcott likely created both Sprengel and the German Golden Dawn to legitimize the founding of his own order. See Bogdan, *Rituals of Initiation*, 125; Asprem, *Arguing with Angels*, 47; Gilbert, *A.E. Waite*, 105–7; Howe, *The Magicians of the Golden Dawn*, 25; Christopher McIntosh, "'Fraulein Sprengel' and the Origins of the Golden Dawn: A Surprising Discovery," *Aries* 11, no. 2 (2011).
22. See Gilbert, *A.E. Waite*, 130–31.

ly,[23] but like the founders of the Golden Dawn he saw no harm in using the myth as a symbolic vehicle for the transformative journey of the adepts in his order. He portrayed the Fellowship as "the guardian of a path of symbolism communicated in Ritual after the manner of the chief Instituted Mysteries, past and present." The F.R.C. was therefore the heir of past secret societies, including previous Rosicrucian groups based in the "Speculative Art" of Freemasonry.[24] In the twenty-first article of the "Constitution and Laws of the Fellowship," Waite specifically connected the F.R.C. to the rise of masonic Rosicrucian groups like the Gold- und Rosenkreuzer, saying that the history of the Fellowship, "in one of its forms…is referable to the third quarter of the 18th century."[25] In one of the order's higher rituals, he pronounced the F.R.C. to be the "final evolution" of the "early history of the Rosy Cross."[26]

This latter statement seems to draw a genealogy that originates in the *Fama Fraternitatis* and runs through the Gold- und Rosenkreuzer, the S.R.I.A. and the Golden Dawn before culminating in the F.R.C. Waite's twelve year on-again-off-again membership in the Golden Dawn was his most impactful encounter with masonic Rosicrucianism. This membership ended with the Golden Dawn itself, as Waite joined with Reverend W.A. Ayton and Marcus Worsley Blackden to lead a minority of the R.R. et A.C. in schism, resulting in the eventual breakup of the order. Waite and his fellow revolutionaries took control of the Golden Dawn's Isis Urania temple in London on their way to founding the I.R.R., after releasing a manifesto which declared themselves interested in a "mystical" approach that they felt had typified the order in its early years, before "the ascendancy of a single chief" (Mathers) had directed things toward a "lower occultism."[27] This declaration seemed to bewilder other members of the order,

---

23. Waite, *Doctrine and Literature of the Kabalah*, 365.
24. See the constitution of the F.R.C, printed in Gilbert, *A.E. Waite*, 183–85.
25. Ibid, 184.
26. Waite, "Adeptus Minor," 38.
27. "The Manifesto of 24 July 1903," in Gilbert, *A.E. Waite*, 177–78. Cf. Waite, *Shadows*, 228; Howe, *The Magicians of the Golden Dawn*, 254–56.

many of whom joined together to form the Stella Matutina. The manifesto exploited a semantic ambiguity very much in the vein of the artificial dichotomy between mysticism and occultism that Waite would begin to perpetuate from this point forward. J.W. Brodie-Innes, who would become one of the leaders of the Stella Matutina, reflected this discursive confusion: "What is meant by a 'mystical trend' and by the 'lower occultism' is obscure,"[28] he told Waite in a letter, and indeed, as is usual with such dichotomies, the realities on the ground were muddled. It is clear that Waite saw the I.R.R. as a direct descendant of the Golden Dawn, in which "the Rite went on, as if no revolutions had occurred."[29] Examinations of magical ability that had been a required part of initiation into the R.R. et A.C. were eschewed, as were practices focused on the development of magical potentialities within the self and the invocation of angelic and demonic principles, but the Golden Dawn's rituals, structures, and primary aims of adeptship maintained a strong presence. Moreover, though the I.R.R. has been portrayed as "in direct opposition" with the "magical agenda" of the Stella Matutina because of its "Christian mystical emphasis,"[30] the remaining similarities in the ritual activities of the two orders and the continued cooperation between them tells another story. Once he had consolidated control of the Isis Urania Temple, Waite seemed quite willing to work with the Stella Matutina as another valid branch of the Golden Dawn. The two orders signed a concordat in 1907 that established official lines of communication, and on at least one occasion Waite stood in as "Adeptus Exemptus" in the Stella Matutina temple in London.[31]

In 1914 Waite closed the Isis-Urania Temple for good, partly because of infighting over the authenticity of the cipher documents whose "discovery" by William Westcott had provided the materials

---

28. Quoted in Howe, *The Magicians of the Golden Dawn*, 253.
29. Waite, *Shadows*, 228.
30. Butler, "Arthur Edward Waite," 284.
31. Waite, *Shadows*, 221–25.

for the founding of the Golden Dawn.[32] In 1915 he launched the F.R.C., taking nineteen members of the I.R.R. with him, their intention, Waite declared in the order's constitution, to create an initiatory society "concerned only with the quest and attainment of the human soul on its return to the Divine Centre."[33] This language would also seem to further a divide between a "mystical" F.R.C. and the practical concerns of occultism, yet the ultimate aim of Golden Dawn adepts was also mystical; namely, the elevation of the self toward union with a higher, or divine self, a goal accomplished through concepts and symbolic systems discovered in Rosicrucianism, astrology, kabbalah, the tarot, alchemy, Freemasonry, and ritual magic among a variety of other esoteric traditions.[34] Moreover, the more mystical focus of the I.R.R. and F.R.C. did not sever the umbilical cord along which occult symbol, ritual, philosophy and practice flowed from their mother order.

As in the Golden Dawn, F.R.C. initiates interacted with materials from the symbolic systems of the Secret Tradition through active imaginative and meditative ritual practices, seeking the elevation of consciousness that would allow themselves to become aware of the divine within—"a revelation of Eternal Mind unto the mind of man."[35] Waite found much of the symbolic content he required in the masonic Rosicrucian heritage he had discovered in the Golden Dawn, much of it extracted directly from its rituals. Though he distanced himself and his order from the Golden Dawn in later years, in fact the first seven rituals of the F.R.C. still bear evident similarities to those of its genealogical ancestor, a result of years of reworking them for the I.R.R. and then incorporating much of what remained into the F.R.C.[36] In concluding this chapter I will compare the

---

32. Gilbert, *A.E. Waite*, 122–23. For the complicated history of the cipher documents see Howe, *Magicians of the Golden Dawn*, 1–25; Asprem, *Arguing with Angels*, 49.
33. Gilbert, *A.E. Waite*, 182.
34. See Owen, *Place of Enchantment*, 73, 76. Cf. Howe, *Magicians of the Golden Dawn*, xi–xiii.
35. Waite, "Neophyte," 10. I expand on this imaginative activity in Chapter Five.
36. See Gilbert, *A.E. Waite*, 137.

"Adeptus Minor" rituals of the two orders in order to illustrate this Golden Dawn lineage.

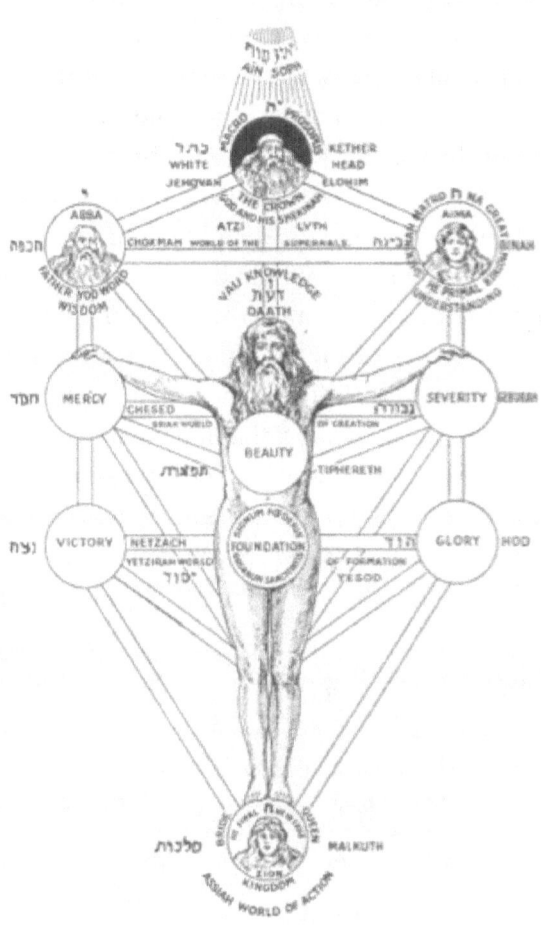

Figure 1: Diagram of the Tree of Life; frontispiece from The Secret Doctrine in Israel *(1913).*

Waite also followed Mathers and Westcott in adopting the grade structure established by the Gold- und Rosenkreuzer and tying this hierarchy to that of the kabbalistic Tree of Life, deploying the complex imagery of the ten *sephiroth* of kabbalah in order to programmatically syncretize an intricate symbolic network.[37] The Tree of Life schematic had been in development from the medieval period, used by Jewish kabbalists to pictorially organize the hierarchical arrangement of the ten sephiroth—macrocosmic aspects or principles that continuously emanate out from *Ain Soph*,[38] the ultimate divine principle that is, like the neo-Platonic One, both all things in their summation and an ineffable principle of nothingness.[39] Just as in the Golden Dawn, F.R.C. initiates visualized themselves rising through the order's grades by symbolically ascending along the paths of the Tree of Life, stepping from *sephira* to sephira.[40]

Each initiatory ritual involved the imaginative opening of at least one path between the sephiroth so that the adept could proceed further up the tree toward mystic union. For example, the path of *Resh* was opened for a Frater Theoreticus seeking to advance to the grade of Practicus, thus allowing the adept to envision themselves advancing from *Yesod* to *Hod*, the sephira equivalent to the Practicus grade.[41] Each path and each sephira, the adept was told, were equivalent to different "modes and aspects of consciousness."[42]

---

37. On the Golden Dawn's use of the ten sephiroth to organize its diverse network of symbolism, see Asprem, "Kabbalah Recreata," 146–47; Bogdan, *Western Esotericism*, 121. For its grade structure see Howe, *The Magicians of the Golden Dawn*, 15–16; Bogdan, *Western Esotericism*, 122.
38. These terms are more commonly transliterated as *sefirot* and *Ein Sof*, but these spellings were common among English speakers in Williams's time, including Waite, from whom he derived many of his kabbalistic ideas and images. For the purposes of continuity, I will employ Waite's spellings of these and other terms rendered from Hebrew throughout.
39. For a brief but informative summary of the complex concept of the sephiroth, see Joseph Dan, *Kabbalah: A Very Short Introduction* (Oxford: Oxford University Press, 2006), 41–45. On Ain Soph see 39–41. These concepts are discussed in greater detail in Chapter Four. For Waite's depiction of the chain of being emanating from Ain Soph, see Figure 1.
40. On the possibilities for mystical attainment offered by contemplation of the sephiroth see Waite, *Doctrine and Literature of the Kabalah*, 376; *Secret Doctrine in Israel*, 106; *Holy Kabbalah*, 290, 474; *Shadows*, 230.
41. "The Ceremony of Advancement in the Grade of Practicus, 3=8," (Amsterdam: Bibliotheca Philosophica Hermetica, A.E. Waite Collection, 1916), 12. See Figure 1.
42. "The Ceremony of Reception in the Portal of the Fourth Order," (Amsterdam: Bibliotheca Philosophica Hermetica, A.E. Waite Collection, 1916), 20.

THE FELLOWSHIP OF THE ROSY CROSS

Liz Greene argues that the Tree of Life was valuable to Waite as an imaginative aid but not in terms of a rational system.[43] However, the F.R.C.'s grade structure and its use of the sephirotic tree to organize symbolism from a number of diverse traditions indicate that he, like the founders of the Golden Dawn, was motivated by both the opportunity for logical taxonomy and the elevation of mystical imagination. Characteristic of programmatic syncretism, Waite followed the Golden Dawn in disembedding particular aspects of sephirotic symbolism from their kabbalistic context and reapplying them in order to structure the order's rituals, provide symbolic fodder for the imagination, and express the perennial knowledge of the Secret Tradition. Significant differences remained between the two orders. As we will see in Chapter Five, the F.R.C. did not step away from magical practices entirely, but its praxis was certainly more abstract, focused on less phenomenal goals, and performed outside a consciously acknowledged theurgical tradition. Waite also eschewed the Egyptian symbolism that was popular in the Golden Dawn,[44] and adjusted the grade structure so that it more faithfully reproduced the sephirotic symbolism of kabbalah, adding a fourth order to the three of the Golden Dawn in order to better correspond to the four hierarchical worlds occupied by the sephiroth.[45] Despite these differences in structure and practice, Waite's development of the F.R.C. initiatory system remained heavily influenced by his time in the Golden Dawn and, to a lesser extent, the S.R.I.A. and other masonic orders. The ritual and symbolic environment in which Williams flourished was born out of the heritage of masonic Rosicrucianism, adapted to the needs and priorities of modern occult practice.

---

43. Greene, *Magi and Maggidim*, 324.
44. See Gilbert, *A.E. Waite*, 123.
45. See Figure 1. On the concept of the four worlds see Gershom Scholem, *Kabbalah* (New York: Meridian, 1990), 119–20. For an explanation of this concept within an F.R.C. ritual see Arthur Edward Waite, "The Ceremony of Reception in the Portal of the Third Order, Being the Second Portal Grade," (Amsterdam: Bibliotheca Philosophica Hermetica, A.E. Waite Collection, 1916), 20–21.

THE PATHS OF THE TREE OF LIFE

Charles Williams was initiated into the entry grade of Neophyte on 21 September 1917, joining the Salvator Mundi Temple of the F.R.C., assembled at the Imperial Hotel on London's Russell Square.[46] From the ritual text, we can assume that he entered the temple, its lights extinguished to simulate divine darkness, from the west side of the room, a "hoodwink" over his eyes and a coarse black garment draped about his body. Passing through a doorway into the room, he was perceived to be passing through a portal into the sacred space of the temple.[47] He was not permitted to make any movement of his own, but was led by two officers: a "Guide of Paths" to instruct his movement, and a "Lucifer" (light bringer) to light his way in the dark.[48] He was led to the middle of the temple where stood a black altar, its colour symbolic of the fallen state of humanity and the alchemical state of putrefaction.[49] On the west side of the room two other officers waited to cleanse the initiate—an "Aquarius" with water, and a "Thurificans" with fire. Williams would not at first have been able to see them, but from his place facing east at the altar, he faced the "three celebrants" of the ritual, each, like the other officers, draped in different coloured robes, and decorated with various insignias relevant to their role and level of initiation.

The "Master of the Temple," who led the ritual, sat enthroned on the southeast side of the room, the "Warden of the Temple" on the north side of the east wall, and between them the "Guide of Paths."[50]

---

46. The following account of Williams's F.R.C. involvement is constructed from the minutes and rituals of the F.R.C. accessed in the Waite Collection at the Bibliotheca Philosophic Hermetica. The minutes are contained in the *Records of the Sacred Temple* (2 volumes) for the F.R.C, and *Records of the Holy House* (2 volumes) for the Ordo Sanctissimus Rosae et Aureae Crucis, a separate inner society which encompassed the society's Third and Fourth Orders.

47. For an imaginative reconstruction of Williams's first ritual experience as he passed through the Neophyte grade, see Lindop, *Charles Williams*, 60–63.

48. Waite, "Neophyte," 21–24, 36.

49. Ibid, 37. The alchemical aspects of F.R.C. symbolism are discussed in Chapter Seven.

50. Ibid, 37–38.

These figures were arrayed according to the symbolism of the Tree of Life, which is commonly attributed with three pillars—a masculine pillar symbolic of light and mercy on the right, formed from the sephiroth of *Chokmah*, *Chesed* and *Netzach*; a feminine pillar of darkness and judgment on the left, made up of *Binah*, *Geburah* and *Hod*, and a middle pillar that began in *Malkuth* and ascended the Tree of Life to the highest manifestation of the divine in *Kether*.[51] This middle pillar found balance between the right and left and played a vital symbolic role in the F.R.C. by displaying the path of mystical ascent. The Master of the Temple represented the masculine pillar of light, the Warden the feminine pillar of darkness, and the Guide of Paths the middle pillar.[52] To emphasize the pillar symbolism, the Guide of Paths also sat between a black pillar and a white—symbolism extracted from the Freemasonic tradition by both the Golden Dawn and the F.R.C. and matched to the Tree of Life. The middle pillar represents a marriage of male and female principles, but the Guide of Paths also took a symbolically feminine role—that of Shekinah, the feminine aspect of divinity in kabbalah—as he or she guided initiates up the middle pillar toward the zenith of mystical experience.

Williams was officially given his chosen secret order name of "Qui Sitit, Veniat" (He who is thirsty, come), derived from Revelation 22:17. He then made a vow to follow the laws of the order and never to share its "Rites, Proceedings or its Knowledge,"[53] a promise he seems not to have broken. The Lucifer then gave him the secret step, sign, grip and words allocated to the Neophyte grade.[54] These elements

---

51. See Figure 1. See Chapter Four for a more in-depth discussion of sephirotic symbolism in the F.R.C.
52. Waite, "Neophyte," 38–39. Cf. "The Ceremony of Advancement in the Grade of Practicus, 3=8" (Amsterdam: Bibliotheca Philosophica Hermetica, A.E. Waite Collection, 1916), 34. The Neophyte ritual also emphasizes the relation between these three figures and the three "supernal" sephiroth—Chokmah at the head of the male pillar, Binah at the head of the female, and Kether, the highest stage of the Tree of Life, at the head of the middle pillar ("Neophyte," 15–16).
53. Ibid, 26.
54. See ibid, 34.

could be used by the adept in further repetitions of the ritual, or, in the case of the step and grip, at the next level of initiation. Waite, influenced by Freemasonry and reflecting the programmatic syncretism of occultism, allocated these items, as well as a mystical number,[55] a planetary body, a mystical title, an angel, and often an alchemical element, to each grade. From Zelator to Philosophus, the lower four grades, each initiatory level also corresponded to one of the four beasts of Ezekiel,[56] as well as a set of "Divine and Angelical Names" that were referable to a particular "quarter of the heavens" and one of the four Aristotelian elements assumed by alchemists to make up the building blocks of matter: fire, water, earth, and air, understood in the F.R.C. as the "Four Sacramental Elements" that make up the earthly personality of humankind.[57] The step, given only in the Neophyte ritual, was indicated by a series of foot movements. In the case of the Neophyte ritual, the sign was formed by a particular hand gesture which was linked to the number 10—sacred both to the Neophyte grade and, because it indicated the sephiroth in their completeness, to the order as a whole. The grip—a particular ritual handshake also of masonic origin—represented the number 10 as well.[58] Once the transmission of this ritual knowledge was complete, the Lucifer removed the coarse black robe—representative of "the unpurified life of earth"—from Williams's body and clothed him in the ritual garb of the Neophyte: a black robe with a collar of white silk, wrapped about the waist with a cord of brown and red, symbolizing the various alchemical stages of the candidate's purifica-

---

55. The mystical number was formulated by adding together the number of numbers represented by each sephiroth. Thus, the mystical number for the Zelator grade, equivalent to Malkuth, the tenth sefira, was 55—formed by adding the first ten digits of the numerical system together. Crowley explains this process in *Liber LVIII*, or "An Essay Upon Number." See "The Temple of Solomon the King," *The Equinox* 1, no. 5 (March 1911): 106.
56. Waite, "Portal of the Third Order," 29–30.
57. Ibid, 30. For the specific applications of the elements see "Practicus," 35; "The Ceremony of Advancement in the Grade of Philosophus, 4=7," (Amsterdam: Bibliotheca Philosophica Hermetica, A.E. Waite Collection, 1917), 33; "Zelator," 31.
58. "Neophyte," 34.

tion.[59] Around his neck was placed the "Mystical Badge of the Fellowship in the World of Action"—a red calvary cross.

On this particular occasion the Neophyte ceremony was followed by the "Festival of the Equinox," a ritual always held to celebrate both the autumnal and vernal equinoxes, occasions at which the F.R.C. usually appointed members to positions of leadership. On 19 April 1918 Williams achieved passage into the Zelator grade, considered equivalent to the element of earth and the sephira of Malkuth, the closest realm of divinity to the material world. As in much of the kabbalistic tradition, Malkuth was related to Shekinah, the "abiding and indwelling presence" of God immanent in the world;[60] thus, the secret words ("Adonai Malkah") and mystical number (55) of Zelator also connected to Shekinah.[61] On this occasion, as in most of the other rituals, the temple was decorated with banners on the east side, each one inscribed with the Hebrew letters pertaining to the paths along the Tree of Life which the initiate would need to follow to achieve the next mode of consciousness or level of initiation in their mystical/initiatory ascent—the grade of Theoreticus.[62]

Having advanced to the initiatory point of Yesod, Williams had now moved from the "fourth mystical world" of *Assiah*,[63] the kabbalistic "World of Action, which is that of manifested things," to the world of "Formation" or *Yetzirah*,[64] equivalent to the F.R.C.'s Second Order. His experience in the rituals of the next three grades—Theoreticus, Practicus, and Philosophus—followed a consistent masonic pattern in which the secret words, grips, steps and signs of the previous grade would need to be given by the postulant in order to ascend to the next grade, though the postulant could be "prompted if

---

59. Ibid, 35.
60. "Zelator," 40.
61. "The Ceremony of Admission to the Grade of Adeptus Exemptus, 7=4," (Amsterdam: Bibliotheca Philosophica Hermetica, A.E. Waite Collection, 1916), 30.
62. Ibid, 31.
63. "Neophyte," 16.
64. "The Ceremony of Advancement in the Grade of Theoreticus, 2=9," (Amsterdam: Bibliotheca Philosophica Hermetica, A.E. Waite Collection, 1916), 12.

need should be."[65] Each ritual continued to encourage meditation on the symbolic principles exemplified by the planets, sephiroth, and "macrocosmic elements"[66]—the moon, Yesod and air for the Theoreticus; Mercury, Hod and water for the Practicus; and Venus, Netzach and fire at the grade of Philosophus.[67] The second order grades also took more time to perform a function that had also been important in the lower grades of the Golden Dawn: education. In the F.R.C. this occult instruction was almost solely focused on kabbalah, particularly the symbolism of the Tree of Life and Shekinah, whose mystically erotic quest for union with her divine masculine spouse offered a model for the adept, as they visualized themselves achieving their own marriage with a divine aspect within.[68]

Williams achieved these grades within the course of a year, rarely missing a meeting. After his advancement to Philosophus, he was given the role of "Aquarius"—a minor ceremonial office carried out in the Neophyte and Zelator rituals—for a six-month period. On 7 July 1919, Williams was inducted into the Third Order—equivalent to the kabbalistic world of *Briah* (Creation). This time induction into the next grade, Adeptus Minor, required him to pass through two rituals. On 7 July, he and four others were postulants in "The Ceremony of Reception in the Portal of the Third Order," and on 26 August he was "raised on the cross of Tiphereth" in a ritual that involved,[69] as it did in the Golden Dawn, being literally bound to a cross in symbolic emulation of Christ's death. This crucifixion was part of a well-crafted narrative of life, death and resurrection that united the three Third Order grades.[70] Before his mock crucifixion, Williams entered and exited a sanctuary designed after the tomb of Christian

---

65. Ibid, 15.
66. Ibid, 7.
67. Ibid, 31; "Practicus," 34-35; "Philosophus," 32-33.
68. "Theoreticus," 29-30; "Practicus," 31-32; "Philosophus," 22, 30-32. See Chapter Four, p. xxx.
69. *Records of the Holy House*, 20.
70. See Arthur Edward Waite, "The Ceremony of Admission to the Grade of Adeptus Major, 6=5," (Amsterdam: Bibliotheca Philosophica Hermetica, A.E. Waite Collection, 1916), 34, for a summary of this ritual structure.

Rosenkreutz;[71] both experiences represented the mystical death presaging rebirth. Following his crucifixion he was given his own "Wand of Office" and the black robes he had worn in the lower order were replaced with new, white garments, representing the completion of his initiatory journey of self-purification.[72]

Williams seems to have enjoyed these initial Third Order rituals; in the course of the next two years he participated in the Portal ritual on five occasions, and in the Adeptus Minor ritual on nine. He was also very active in the lower two orders during this period, acting in several official capacities: Thurificans for six months, and Lucifer for nearly a year. He held the more significant Warden of the Temple office for six months, and on 26 September 1921 he was invested as Master of the Temple, which, Imperator Waite would have told him in the installation ritual, is "the highest office which I can bestow on you in this temple."[73] Williams's involvement in the F.R.C. reached a peak as Master of the Temple. His duties included leading rituals, appointing junior officers, and keeping minutes of each meeting. He was appointed Master of the Temple twice more, in 1923 and 1924. Each appointment represented a period of intense involvement, after which he would appear at meetings more sporadically until he took on another leadership role. In addition to increasing both his profile in the order and his level of ritual engagement, the Master of the Temple role likely resulted in an almost rote understanding of Waite's esoteric concepts—particularly in the area of kabbalah. Williams would have been required to recite long passages—he told Ridler that he memorized them for greater ritual effect[74]—in which he instructed various postulants on the spiritual and initiatory signifi-

---

71. "Adeptus Minor," 15.
72. Ibid, 34–35. See Chapter Seven for an illustration of the alchemical implications of these garments.
73. "The Installation of a Master of the Temple in the Worlds of Formation and Action," (Amsterdam: Bibliotheca Philosophica Hermetica, A.E. Waite Collection, n.d), 4.
74. Ridler, "Introduction to *The Image of the City*," xxiv–xxv.

cance of esoteric concepts such as the paths and sephiroth of the Tree of Life.

F.R.C. Grade	Corresponding Sephira
First Order	**Assiah—World of Action**
Neophyte (0=0)	
Zelator (1-10)	Malkuth
Second Order	**Yetzirah—World of Formation**
Theoreticus (2=9)	Yesod
Practicus (3=8)	Hod
Philosophus (4=7)	Netzach
Third Order	**Briah—World of Creation**
Adeptus Minor (5=6)	Tiphereth
Adeptus Major (6=5)	Geburah
Adeptus Exemptus (7=4)	Chesed
Fourth Order	**Atziluth—World of Emanation**
Adeptus Exaltatus (0=0 in Supernis)	Daath

Figure 2: The grade system of the F.R.C.

Williams was elevated to "Adeptus Major" on 5 June 1923, surrounded by other adepts of Waite's new inner order, the Ordo Sanctissimus Rosae et Aureae Crucis (O.S.R. & A.C.), which was formed from the Third and Fourth orders in 1922.[75] The Adeptus Major ritual repeated the Adeptus Minor pattern of death and rebirth, though this time the symbolic power of Shekinah once again took prominence. The Adeptus Major was considered to have passed along the sephirotic path of *Kaph* to the sephira of Geburah, a feminine, left pillar aspect of God that was symbolic of judgment and severity, though this was, at least in the kabbalistic symbolism prioritized by Waite, a severity of love.[76] The principles of judgment and severity aligned with the mystical death the adept had to undergo before experiencing mystic oneness; in this grade, intoned the

---

75. Gilbert, *A.E. Waite*, 143. The acronym follows Waite's usage.
76. Waite, "Adeptus Major," 56.

presiding Celebrant in Chief, "You are taught how to die" (30). This "Divine Darkness," however, to which the adept was led along "one of the Paths of Shekinah" (29), was ultimately the precursor to a "Bridal Night" (43). Following this mystical death, the initiate was conceived to have encountered a mystical "marriage" (43) between the self of the lower soul, represented by Shekinah, and the higher self of the soul's lover, "Christ mystical" (41).

The grade of "Adeptus Exemptus" finished off the Third Order triad of life, death and resurrection by focusing on the nature and duties of the resurrected, purified adept that, ideally, had been created by the successful union of the material and divine aspects of the self.[77] However, complete attainment had not quite been reached at this stage of Williams's journey along the sephirotic paths, which had now reached the masculine sephira of *Chesed*, or mercy. The "union of subject and object has already begun," the Adeptus Exemptus ritual declared, but it was not until the Fourth Order that the mystic union of the divided parts of the self would be complete.[78] Williams's initiation into the Adeptus Exemptus grade on 10 July 1924 was a strange one, as another adept seems to have performed the ritual in the role of postulant while Williams and a third aspirant looked on.[79] After achieving the grade of Adeptus Exemptus, Williams attended an O.S.R. & A.C. ritual only once in the next year, as he had been appointed to his third term as Master of the Salvator Mundi Temple (on 30 September 1924) and was busy attending lower order rituals. This does not reflect a lack of interest in goings-on in the upper temple. Williams was expected to accede to a leadership stage in the lower orders now that he had graduated to Adeptus Exemptus: "He who attains the Grade of Exempt Adept is an ordained priest and teacher, who comes down into the lower Sephiroth of the Third Order for the celebration of the Mysteries therein, and is also reflected into the Second and First Orders, where he is

---

77. "Adeptus Exemptus," 23.
78. Ibid.
79. This may have happened in the other grades as well, but it is only in this case that the meeting minutes clearly indicate this likelihood.

represented by the Master of the Temple."[80] Thus, though Williams had already worked as Master of the Temple twice before, the Adeptus Exemptus ritual confirmed his knowledge and leadership development through the process of initiation, officially ordaining him as a master fit for the spiritual and psychological development of lower order initiates.

On 1 July 1925, however, the O.S.R. & A.C. suddenly regained prominence in his occult life, as the first rituals of the Fourth Order were performed, taking Williams, along with the other leading adepts of the F.R.C., into the ultimate stage of the order's ritual progression. Throughout July 1925, the O.S.R. & A.C. held multiple performances of "The Ceremony of Reception in the Portal of the Fourth Order" and its partner ritual "The Ceremony of Contemplation on the Further Side of the Portal." Williams went through the portal on 22 July and then through the further side of the portal on 29 July. This portal symbolized the ascent of the adept up the Tree of Life to the sephiroth known as the "supernals"—Binah, Chokmah and Kether. Waite considered these sephiroth to be out of range of the living, however, and instead envisioned the initiate's final goal on the Tree of Life to be the hidden sephira of *Daath*, or Knowledge. "Daath," the presiding Celebrant in Chief instructed gathered adepts in the Adeptus Exemptus ritual, "is the Mediator between the upper and lower Sephiroth. It conciliates on the right and the left. It is the equilibrium in the height, and a place of ineffable union where God is known of the heart."[81] In other words, Daath represented a place of absolute mystical experience, the eradication of the divide between subject and object, lower and higher selves, man and God. The mystical ascension to Daath did not, however, mean the initiation into another grade, as there were no further grades above Adeptus Exemptus. At one point a ritual does refer to entrance in the Fourth Order as attainment of "that Grade which may be called Adeptus

---

80. Waite, "Adeptus Exemptus," 5.
81. Ibid, 45.

Exaltatus,"[82] but this is the closest Waite ever comes to identifying a grade structure equivalent to the higher reaches of the Tree of Life, as there was no rank or hierarchy in the Fourth Order. Instead, all initiates were "joined or integrated in the Holy Assembly."[83] Waite seems to have felt that the social hierarchies of human sodalities had no place among the Holy Assembly of initiates who had achieved mystic union with the supernatural divine.

With his successful passage into the Fourth Order, Williams's active involvement with Rosicrucian occultism (that we know of) was coming to a close.[84] After participating three times in the Adeptus Minor ritual in August and September of that year, on 16 September he took part for the only time in the rarely performed "The Ritual of Return in Light on the Threshold of the Holy Supernals," which did not perform an initiatory function, but served to educate Fourth Order adepts about the nature of the path of return from mystic union, as well as its incumbent responsibilities. For the next two years he continued to attend both Salvator Mundi and O.S.R. & A.C. meetings sporadically, but his interest seems to have been waning. He did not attend any of the lower temple's equinox or solstice celebrations during this time, though it was generally expected that

---

82. Waite, "Portal of the Fourth Order," 19.
83. Ibid, 7–8.
84. Two scholars have recently proposed that Williams was a member of both the F.R.C. and a later branch of the Golden Dawn. Edward Gauntlett proposes that Williams's involvement with the Golden Dawn is substantiated by his use of the name "Golden Dawn" when referring to his initiatory activity, his documented personal acquaintance with Yeats, and his possession of a sword that he is known to have kept in a cupboard in his office (Hadfield, *Explorations*, 106). Gauntlett observes, supported by Gilbert, that the F.R.C. did not use swords in their rituals, while Golden Dawn members were required to obtain one. See Gauntlett, "Charles Williams, Love & Shekinah," 22. Grevel Lindop also feels it quite likely that Williams was an initiate of either the Stella Matutina or Waite's I.R.R. (*Charles Williams*, 66). The latter option is not possible, however, as Waite disbanded the order in 1914 and we know that he and Williams did not meet until 1916. Williams's membership in the Stella Matutina remains an intriguing possibility, but there is no evidence to confirm it. Williams could have met Yeats through any number of literary connections or in his work with the O.U.P. His ownership of a sword is certainly a worthy piece of evidence to support Guantlett's position, but if possession of a sword were direct proof of Stella Matutina involvement, historical membership in the order would be very high indeed.

members attend these rites.[85] On 29 June 1927, Williams played the role of "Second Spokesman" in a new Fourth Order ritual written by Waite in 1926, "The Ceremony of Consecration on the Threshold of Sacred Mystery," created, according to Gilbert, as a bridging ritual between the Third and Fourth Orders.[86] This was to be his last known involvement with the F.R.C. The minutes record that he sent his regrets for absence from the celebration of the next autumnal equinox, but following this Frater Qui Sitit, Veniat disappears from the records.

It is unclear why Williams left the F.R.C., but the simple application of Occam's razor may be called for on this question. It is probably not a coincidence that he performed the only ritual he had yet to experience in his last known involvement with the order. Having experienced all the rites, a certain curiosity would have been satisfied and, like a reader reaching the end of a good page-turner, Williams may simply have chosen to close the book on the F.R.C. His involvement in Waite's order thus displays his character as poet, artist, and dramatist. As long as he was involved in the ceremonial, as long as new stories and new symbols waited to be revealed, the F.R.C. held his interest. Though Williams was heavily involved in the communal aspects of the order for a number of years, and was thus willing to frequently repeat his participation in many of its rituals for the sake of other members seeking to ascend to higher grades, we have seen that the intensity of this attachment seems to have faded in later years. With his commitment to the other members waning, and having experienced all there was to experience, Williams seems to have naturally drifted away. He certainly continued to value both his relationship with Waite (the two stayed in limited contact until at least 1931)[87] and his time in the order, as indicated by instructions given to a friend to bury his F.R.C. regalia after his death[88]—a gesture

---

85. Waite, "Portal of the Fourth Order," 145.
86. R.A. Gilbert, personal correspondence, 30 August 2013. See Lindop, *Charles Williams*, 144, for a brief description of the ritual.
87. Ashenden, *Charles Williams*, 6.
88. Lindop, *Charles Williams*, 423.

that seems to indicate both his attachment to the F.R.C. and a commitment to his vow of secrecy. This vow is also a potential answer to the question of why Williams claimed to be in the Golden Dawn rather than the F.R.C.: He may simply have seen this small lie as a convenient way to conceal the actual nature of his involvement. This solution is purely conjectural, but the advantages of such a strategy are clear. This method would have allowed Williams to let his friends and family know that he was attending the meetings of a secret Rosicrucian society—even walk through the doors in broad daylight—but still keep them almost entirely in the dark.

Williams's dedication to secrecy is another indication that it is problematic to brand his F.R.C. experiences as "wholly Christian." The vow of the F.R.C. initiate has much more in common with esoteric traditions like Freemasonry and Rosicrucianism, and, in Williams's modern occult context, orders like the Golden Dawn, than with mainstream Christian denominations, which tend to make their doctrines available to as many prospective converts as possible. Though Christian imagery, mythology and theology have remained central in masonry and Rosicrucianism, the secret rituals of orders like the F.R.C. present a stark contrast to such a proselytizing ethic. In addition to the fact that they were not available to non-initiates, the rituals of the F.R.C. contain passages of untranslated Latin, as well as symbolism that is incomprehensible without familiarity with particular forms of esoteric knowledge, particularly alchemy and kabbalah. This secrecy is perpetuated by an instinct completely opposite to that of Christianity: the "counsel enjoined upon" the adepts of the Holy Assembly was, said another Waitean adept, to "'cast not thy pearls before swine.'"[89] Like most occult groups, the F.R.C. considered the majority of the human race morally, spiritually and intellectually unfit for the ancient wisdom of esotericism.[90]

---

89. Philip S. Wellby, "Arthur Edward Waite, October 2nd, 1858–May 19th, 1942: A Personal Tribute," *Occult Review* 69, no. 3 (July 1942): 103.
90. Dion Fortune's view of esoteric knowledge is indicative of the occultist mainstream: "The knowledge guarded by the secret fraternities is too potent to be given out indiscriminately, and is guarded, not as a sordid trade secret, but...for the safety of the

Waite remained active with the F.R.C. until his death. As would be expected, he also kept his vows of secrecy, referring only vaguely to his prize order. As of 1987, Gilbert was able to report that a small group identifying as the F.R.C. was still in existence, "albeit in a somewhat reduced and altered form."[91] Though I do not have a source that is willing to go on the record, I can verify Gilbert's report to some degree, as I have been told in personal conversation with an active British Freemason that the F.R.C. operated until at least the mid-1980s in London, and that it still exists today, though largely inactive, in New Zealand. Also of interest, though contradictory to this testimony, is the presence, at least online, of a group claiming to have revived Waite's order with temples in the United Kingdom, Brazil, France, Italy, the United States and Australia, in addition to New Zealand.[92]

THE F.R.C. AND THE GOLDEN DAWN: THE ADEPTUS MINOR RITUALS

Before shifting my focus from Williams's life to his fiction, I would like to illustrate the extent to which Waite's order was connected to the modern occult network by looking more closely at similarities between the Adeptus Minor rituals of the Golden Dawn and the F.R.C. Williams went through "The Pontifical Ceremony of Admission to the Grade of Adeptus Minor" on thirteen recorded occasions —twelve as observer or celebrant and one as an initiate—so it is likely, particularly because of his preference for reciting ritual text from memory, that its powerful imagery was still well in mind as he wrote his novels, particularly those he developed in the recent after-

---

public." Human nature must be regenerated, in Fortune's view, before it will be ready for the ancient wisdom that the occult schools have guarded for millennia (Dion Fortune, *Sane Occultism* (London: Aquarian, 1987), 112–13). Cf. Luhrmann, *Persuasions of the Witch's Craft*, 274.
91. Gilbert, *A.E. Waite*, 197.
92. See "Frater Deo in Vita Aeterna, "The Fellowship of the Rosy Cross: Its Founder and Its History," website of the Fraternitas Rosae Crucis, http://fellowship.rosy-cross.org/history.

math of his F.R.C. involvement.[93] The Golden Dawn's "Ceremony of the Grade of Adeptus Minor" is one of the most well-practiced and frequently adapted rituals in occult history. This ritual was written by Mathers in 1892 as part of the founding of the R.R. et A.C., along with its partner, the "Ritual of the Portal of the Vault of the Adepti,"[94] though he claimed to have received the rituals from unidentified secret chiefs in Germany.[95] Waite highly valued the Adeptus Minor ritual, so much so that he believed it to be above Mathers's talents. "There is nothing to suggest," Waite stated suspiciously, "That it ever came out of the same mint as the Rituals of the Golden Dawn."[96] Waite did not propose an alternative theory of authorship; he may simply have wished to cast doubt on the connection between a ritual he treasured and Mathers, to whom he and the other founders of the I.R.R. attributed responsibility for the Golden Dawn's turn from mysticism to "the lower occultism" of practical magic.[97] In fact, there are many factors that support Mathers's authorship, including the clear similarity of style and purpose to the Ritual of the Portal and the ritual's snug fit with the rest of the Golden Dawn system. Few scholars apart from Waite would question Mathers's authorship.[98]

---

93. His experiences seem to have had a long-lasting impact. Lindop convincingly theorizes that the Adeptus Minor ritual was the impetus for a scene in *Judgement in Chelmsford*, in which the climax features a young woman being bound to a cross. This play was written in 1939, fourteen years after Williams is last known to have partaken in the Adeptus Minor ritual (Lindop, *Charles Williams*, 294).

94. The full text of these rituals is available in Regardie, *Complete Golden Dawn*, 7:2-61. Regardie also made the rituals available in his 1939 compendium of Golden Dawn materials, but later discovered that these were Stella Matutina versions which had undergone significant revision. His 1984 volume reproduces rituals given to F. Leigh Gardner between 1894 and 1896, now held in the Yorke Collection at the Warburg, University of London. See Bogdan, *Western Esotericism*, 127–28 for this publication history. Waite's Adeptus Minor ritual is also available in Regardie's *Complete Golden Dawn* (7:92–126). For a summary of the Golden Dawn's Adeptus Minor ritual see Howe, *The Magicians of the Golden Dawn*, 85–88.

95. Howe, *Magicians of the Golden Dawn*, xvii. Cf. Bogdan, *Western Esotericism*, 125–26.

96. Waite, *Shadows*, 226. "The Golden Dawn" here refers to the first, outer order of the society.

97. "Manifesto of 24 July 1903"

98. See Howe, *Magicians of the Golden Dawn*, xvii; Bogdan, *Western Esotericism*, 125; Gilbert, *The Golden Dawn*, 35.

Waite denigrated the Golden Dawn's rituals as part of his general attempt to delineate a separate mystical network for himself and the F.R.C. He described them as "a mass of confused Symbolism," and could admit them only one point of importance: "The notion of a Candidate ascending the Tree of Life."[99] Golden Dawn scholars, particularly those with connections to the order, have been just as anxious to disassociate the F.R.C. and its ritual materials from its parent order. Israel Regardie, an influential Stella Matutina initiate, shows some admiration for the F.R.C. scripts and advises adepts that Waite's Adeptus Major ritual could prove attractive, particularly to those looking to move up the initiatory ladder past the Adeptus Minor level where the original Golden Dawn rituals left off.[100] Ultimately though, he concludes that "there is almost no relationship between the teachings originally laid down [in the Golden Dawn] and the later biblical emphasis introduced by Waite," a distinction echoed by Francis King, a member of another group with historical ties to the Golden Dawn—Dion Fortune's Society of the Inner Light.[101] Gilbert agrees, acknowledging that the F.R.C.'s structure remained congruous to the Golden Dawn, but suggesting that Waite's removal of Egyptian and pagan references made the symbolism "wholly Rosicrucian and Christian."[102] These distinctions seem to channel a binary expressed by occultist Gerald Yorke, and used by Christopher McIntosh to differentiate the F.R.C. from the Golden Dawn. Yorke divides Hermetic orders, which "include some Christianity and don't stress it," from Rosicrucian orders, which "are primarily Christian but draw on other pre-Christian sources." McIntosh relies on this dichotomy to distinguish Waite's "Rosicrucianized" order from its "Hermetic" precursor.[103] This distinction aims to describe an actual difference in occult method and intention between the two orders, but it commits the same crime of simplification as

---

99. Waite, *Shadows*, 230. Cf. 125, 218–19.
100. Regardie, *Complete Golden Dawn*, 7:62.
101. Ibid, 1:18–19; King, *Ritual Magic in England*, 112.
102. Gilbert, *A.E. Waite*, 123.
103. McIntosh, *The Rosy Cross Unveiled*, 117. Cf. 113–15.

Waite's dichotomy between mysticism and occultism. Yorke's binary is the reverse of the cordon sanitaire that has been used to distance an orthodox Christian Charles Williams from occultism—it reifies non-existent categorical polarities in order to distance itself from a tradition (Christianity) to which it remains connected through myriad historical and cultural threads. In doing so, it blurs our perception of the significant cultural and intellectual space that is shared by Rosicrucian, Hermetic, mystical and occult currents.

In order to better comprehend historical, philosophical and social relationships between the various groups and figures that have moved in and out of these esoteric currents, we must avoid the generalizations of discursive polarity and seek the greatest practical degree of specificity. While acknowledging difference between groups like the Golden Dawn and the F.R.C., we can still very productively look past artificial binaries constructed by actors like Waite, Regardie and Yorke to see many important points of agreement and shared heritage. This consanguinity is perhaps most clearly indicated by a comparison of the two Adeptus Minor rituals. It is historically no surprise that this should be so, as Waite had been adapting and rewriting Mathers's rituals for use in the I.R.R. since 1905.[104] Both rituals are crucial to the overall plot structure of their orders—namely the journey of the adept, through transmutation of the self, to mystical union with a higher (often divine) self. This journey is represented through three primary symbolic systems: the story of Christ, the myth of Christian Rosenkreutz, and, as in all the rituals of both orders, the sephirotic symbolism of kabbalah. In both societies, the Adeptus Minor grade's link to Tiphereth is symbolically representative of the point in the initiatic journey where adepts prepared themselves, through a process of personal transmutation, for spiritual attainment.[105]

This process of transformation is extensively represented in both rituals by the life, death, and rebirth of Jesus Christ. A number of

---

104. Gilbert, *A.E. Waite*, 137.
105. See Owen, *Place of Enchantment*, 77.

ritualistic acts are performed to symbolize the spiritual transmutation achieved by Christ in these three stages. As in the F.R.C., Golden Dawn initiates were bound to a cross. The postulant, "a member of the Body of Christ," was seen to "spiritually bind" themselves to the "Cross of Suffering," thus accepting hardship for the self as a process of death and rebirth.[106] Both rituals also feature the postulant being marked on the forehead, feet, palms, and breast by a dagger dipped in wine.[107] The script uttered during this part of the ritual, which guides the adept through the transformation represented by the Christ journey in order to achieve the mystical elevation of consciousness, is unchanged in Waite's rewrite.

Christ symbolism is pervasive in the Third Order F.R.C. rituals, particularly in the Adeptus Minor ritual. Waite frequently relies on two aspects of the image of Christ, both of them specifically related to the esoteric milieu. The first is Christ as "the Great Exemplar of initiation" who expressed the mystic path not just in word and symbol, but also in the manner of his own life—a biographical encounter that can be reenacted in every soul.[108] This importance of the literary/historical model of the Christ-life to the mystic journey is the leading focus of both Adeptus Minor rituals, where, the F.R.C. initiate was told, "all its symbols and ceremonies, with all its epochs, are depicted as a figurative Mystery of the Christ-Life enacted in your own life and your proper personality."[109] Christ, Waite said in *The Way of Divine Union*, "Goes before us eternally, rising from grade to grade in our consciousness."[110] This exemplar role is perhaps the strongest Christian element of the F.R.C., but it does not distinguish the order from occultism. In addition to the many other symbolic patterns functioning alongside Christ imagery in Waite's order, a number of leading figures in the modern occult revival saw the Christ-life as a vital emblem of the mystic journey. Rudolf Steiner taught that

---

106. Regardie, *Complete Golden Dawn*, 7:41.
107. Waite, "Adeptus Minor," 28–29; Regardie, *Complete Golden Dawn*, 7:43.
108. Waite, "Adeptus Minor," 37. Cf. Waite, *Divine Union*, 185, 320.
109. Waite, "Adeptus Major," 33.
110. Waite, *Divine Union*, 182.

Christ's initiatory process of death and rebirth made public the esoteric secrets previously accessible only to initiates in Egyptian and Greek mystery cults.[111] Blavatsky rejected conventional Christianity, particularly the "disagreeable, racist god of the Hebrew scriptures," but valued "the true Christianity of Jesus—the great Socialist and Adept, the divine man who was changed into an anthropomorphic God."[112] The Golden Dawn, meanwhile, based its entire Adeptus Minor ritual on the concept of Jesus as exemplar, relying far more than the F.R.C. on language drawn directly from New Testament passages pertaining to the biblical significance of the Christ-life. "It is written," R.R. et A.C. postulants were told, "If ye be crucified with Christ, ye shall also reign with Him."[113]

This loosely translated passage from 2 Timothy 2:12 also speaks to a second, related understanding of the relationship between the life of Christ and that of the adept. This is the discovery of "Christ-mystical,"[114] who is equivalent to the aspect of the divine self that, via the cosmic unity inherent in Waite's immanent cosmology, resides within each human self. The aspect of the divine encountered in this way is not the historical Jesus, but the "cosmic Christ" that Jesus also discovered in himself, becoming the exemplar of mystical attainment in the process.[115] The realization of the cosmic Christ is a coming to awareness of the God "immanent in the universe,"[116] who is "known only by incarnation in each of us," an "indwelling...in consciousness."[117] McIntosh proposes that the F.R.C. differed markedly from the Golden Dawn in this sense, along the lines of his Rosicrucian/Hermetic distinction: "In Waite's order...everything is done by the participants in a spirit of reverence towards the Godhead rather than

---

111. See Cees Leijenhorst, "Steiner, Rudolf," in *Dictionary of Gnosis and Western Esotericism*, ed. Wouter J. Hanegraaff (Leiden: Brill, 2006), 1088.
112. H.P. Blavatsky, *Collected Writings, Volume VIII, 1887* (Wheaton, IL: The Theosophical Publishing House, 1966), 77. Cf. Godwin, *Theosophical Enlightenment*, 292.
113. Regardie, *Complete Golden Dawn*, 7:43; repeated 49.
114. Waite, "Adeptus Minor," 11.
115. Waite, *Divine Union*, 182.
116. Ibid, 321.
117. Ibid, 206, 34. Cf. 240, 321.

identity with it."[118] The adepts of the F.R.C., however, were not simply kneeling in pews in adoration, though certainly this remained a priority for Christian adepts like Williams. In Waite's conception of mystic union the adept was seen to achieve a "Christ-state" within,[119] equivalent to union with a higher, divine self. In *The Way of Divine Union*, written as he was completing the rituals for the F.R.C., Waite specifically frames this Christ-state as a repetition of the achievement of Jesus of Nazareth: a "deification"[120] through discovery of the cosmic Christ within: "When we awaken to consciousness therein, each can say unto each: I am the Resurrection and the Life."[121] These exact words were the first intoned by Golden Dawn initiates as they ritually rose from the dead in their own Adeptus Minor ritual;[122] in copying this famous declaration of divinity by Jesus (see John 11:25), adepts in both orders marked the achievement of their own "Christ-state."

This concept of spiritual attainment as union with the cosmic Christ has roots in earlier Christian mystical tradtions, but can also be productively situated with concepts expressed by other modern esoteric thinkers. Anna Kingsford and Edward Maitland, for example, used terminology similar to Waite's in their valuation of the figure of Christ: "Man, ascending by evolution from the material and lowermost stratum of existence, finds his highest development in Christ."[123] As Joscelyn Godwin observes, in this conception Christ is not a historical figure but "the state of the regenerated man, in whom

---

118. McIntosh, *The Rosy Cross Unveiled*, 117.
119. Waite, "Philosophus," 31; "Adeptus Major," 35.
120. Waite, *Divine Union*, 313.
121. Ibid, 187. Waite did not see this "virtual becoming into God" as in any way heretical, but as a proper interpretation of the history of Christian mystical thought. See, e.g., ibid, 39n4, 195, 313.
122. Regardie, *Complete Golden Dawn*, 7:50.
123. Anna Kingsford and Edward Maitland, *The Perfect Way: Or, the Finding of Christ* (London: J.M. Watkins, 1909), 154. Kingsford and Maitland were also like Waite (and Williams) in their emphasis on the symbol of Christ as a combination of divinity and humanity—the point where "the two streams, the ascending and the descending, meet; and the man knows and understands God."

the soul has become united with the Divine Spirit."[124] Waite himself was unsure about the "historicity of Christ," but concluded that the question was irrelevant to the "Great Quest" for union with the cosmic Christ, which is "catholic to all ages."[125] Neither of these Christologies—the cosmic Christ or Christ exemplar—were unique to modern occultism, but it is clear that they were attractive to many of the esoteric thinkers working in this setting. Perpetuated by groups such as the Theosophical Society and the occultist network underpinned by the Golden Dawn, they have continued to be central concepts in twentieth and twenty-first century alternative religious systems, particularly the New Age movement.[126]

In addition to the Christ story, both Adeptus Minor rituals review the legend of Christian Rosenkreutz, reenacting his entombment and the discovery of his undecayed body after 120 years. In both rituals the discovery of the tomb is equivalent to the rediscovery of the secret narrative of ancient wisdom held to have "existed from time immemorial."[127] The tomb also has a variety of other important symbolic connections. Along with Christ's resurrection from a different sepulchre, the discovery of Rosenkreutz's tomb represents the final stage of mystical rebirth.[128] The tomb is also seen as a microcosmic representation of the universe, entered by the adept "as a door that is entered at birth."[129] Conversely, it is also instrumental, as a repository of correspondent symbolism, in the adept's transcendence of the material universe—"a temple opening from earthly into spiritual life."[130] Given the symbolic importance of the tomb, both orders focused on its aesthetic arrangement. Waite seems to have highly valued the R.R. et A.C.'s design of the tomb, as he incorporated the same construction, with some minor changes, into the F.R.C.'s

---

124. Godwin, *Theosophical Enlightenment*, 337–38.
125. Waite, *Divine Union*, 320–21. Cf. 319, 322.
126. See Hanegraaff, *New Age Religion and Western Culture*, 189–90. Hanegraaff notes that "it is remarkable how often New Age authors talk about Christ."
127. Regardie, *Complete Golden Dawn*, 7:43; Waite, "Adeptus Minor," 37.
128. Regardie, *Complete Golden Dawn*, 7:50.
129. Waite, "Adeptus Minor," 13.
130. Ibid, 14.

temple. Part of this similarity is due to the fact that both orders followed the description of the tomb given in the *Fama Fraternitatis*,[131] and thereby incorporated the tomb's heptagonal structure, placed a brass altar in its centre inscribed with various mottoes, and painted triangles on the ceiling and floor. However, Mathers also made a number of additions, all indicative of the modern occult taste for bricolage. For example, the four Hebrew letters of the kabbalistic divine name, the Tetragrammaton—*Yod, He, Vau,* and *He*—were inscribed on the altar, but with a further innovation that reflects the importance of Christological symbolism to the ritual: Mathers followed the Christian kabbalistic synthesis of Johann Reuchlin (1455-1522), a German Hebraist who added the letter *Shin* in the middle of the Tetragrammaton to form *Yeheshuah*, the Hebrew name of Jesus, which is the "key word" of both Adeptus Minor rituals.[132] Though Waite rejected Christian kabbalah on a scholarly level, he seems to have valued Reuchlin's formulation in this case, as he included it in the F.R.C.'s recreation of the tomb.[133]

Waite also included other adaptations he discovered in the Golden Dawn. A rose with twenty-two petals was set into the triangle on the ceiling, and said to be in symbolic correspondence with the twenty-two paths of the Tree of Life, while the triangle itself was said to represent the three supernal sephiroth and made correspondent to the light side of the Tree of Life.[134] The black triangle on the floor represented the "Averse and Evil" sephiroth of the *Qlippoth*—the dark side of the Tree. Around the triangle was written, "He Descended into Hell."[135] The triangles on the ceiling and floor thus represented the adept's Christ-life traversal of both the dark and light "phases of

---

131. See Yates, *The Rosicrucian Enlightenment*, 246–47, for the original *Fama Fraternitatis* account. For the Golden Dawn tomb description see Regardie, *Complete Golden Dawn*, 7:48. For the F.R.C.'s description see Waite, "Adeptus Minor," 44.
132. See Scholem, *Kabbalah*, 198; Bogdan, "Freemasonry and Western Esotericism," 298–99.
133. Waite also expresses support for the Yeheshuah formulation in Waite, *Life of Louis Claude De Saint-Martin*, 241.
134. Regardie, *Complete Golden Dawn*, 7:55; Waite, "Adeptus Minor," 59.
135. Waite, "Adeptus Minor," 57; Regardie, *Complete Golden Dawn*, 7:55.

our being."[136] Between this spectrum of dark and light there is all conceivable colour, and thus the seven walls of both tombs were decorated with the seven colours of the rainbow. All colours can be found in the three supernals, but each of these colours was related to one of the lower seven sephiroth. The adept who made the symbolic journey along the paths of the Tree of Life, including the synthesis of all colours, which is "blackness and bordereth on the Qlippoth," gained the right to be known by "the Mystic Title of Hodos Chameleonis, the Path of the Chameleon, the Path of Mixed Colors."[137] The reconstruction of Christian Rosenkreutz's tomb is thus an excellent example of the programmatic syncretism common to both the Golden Dawn and the F.R.C.; this aspect of the Adeptus Minor rituals incorporates symbolism from a variety of traditions in order to better systematize the original Rosicrucian narrative of death and regeneration and expand its perennial scope.

Waite did not incorporate imagery into his rituals as indiscriminately as occult groups like the Golden Dawn, but he still drew from whatever symbolic set suited his Secret Tradition purposes.[138] The F.R.C.'s constitution declared an attachment to a "Christian mode" of interpretation of esoteric symbolism,[139] but it should be clear by this point that this Christian mode was heterodox in the manner of the esoteric Christianity of figures like Kingsford, Besant, and Lévi. Moreover, though the F.R.C. deployed a more clearly Christian hermeneutic than the Golden Dawn, this difference between the two orders cannot be used to substantiate an artificial Christian/occult

---

136. Waite, "Adeptus Minor," 57.
137. Regardie, *Complete Golden Dawn*, 7:54. The Hodos Chamelionis concept adapted pre-existing kabbalistic applications of colour symbolism to the sephiroth. See Sanford L. Drob, *Kabbalistic Metaphors: Jewish Mystical Themes in Ancient and Modern Thought* (Northvale, NJ: J. Aronson, 2000), 50.
138. An indicative example that goes beyond Waite's favoured traditions of alchemy and kabbalah is found in the Zelator ritual, where the astrological symbol of "the Sacred Swastika" is described as "a great astronomical symbol which speaks to those who can interpret concerning the Divine in the universe." The meaning of the symbol is then deconstructed using occult numerology. See Waite, "Zelator," 18.
139. "Constitution & Laws of the Fellowship," printed in Gilbert, *A.E. Waite*, 184.

dichotomy. The Golden Dawn's Adeptus Minor ritual relies more on direct biblical quotation than the F.R.C. version does,[140] while Waite's rituals rely more centrally on sephirotic symbolism. Finally, any attempt to brand the F.R.C. as "wholly Christian" must come face to face with Waite's universalism. We have seen that the preference for a Christian mode of interpretation does not extend past the level of doctrine and is therefore no longer of consequence at the imageless stage of the mystic journey. As Imperator Waite told assembled F.R.C. initiates attending workings of the Neophyte ritual: "We are dealing, my Brethren...not alone with the question of religion but with its heart and centre, behind all the external differences of systems and churches and sects."[141]

Having made my case for the occult entanglements of Waite's order, however, I want to emphasize that becoming aware of similarity does not require us to ignore difference. Significant distinctions remain, in particular those that arose from Waite's dichotomous rejection of the practical concerns of occultism. Though the two Adeptus Minor rituals have much in common, the Golden Dawn's version was intended to accompany a period of intense study into various methods of practical magic, such as divination, scrying, and astral travel.[142] R.R. et A.C. postulants would also spend time crafting magical implements such as wands and daggers, practicing Enochian magic for purposes as diverse as invoking angels and playing four person "Rosicrucian chess," and developing their powers of clairvoyance.[143] Moreover, while the ultimate achievement of initiation was understood in terms of spiritual enlightenment in both orders, many Golden Dawn adepts also understood mystical attainment as a source of power with which to achieve these magical goals.

However, though Waite rejected such earthly concerns as having nothing to do with the mystic path, the difference between his

---

140. See, in particular, Regardie, *Complete Golden Dawn*, 7:39-40.
141. Waite, "Neophyte," 45.
142. Regardie, *Complete Golden Dawn*, 7:42.
143. Howe, *Magicians of the Golden Dawn*, 288–89; Regardie, *Complete Golden Dawn*, 43; Gilbert, *The Golden Dawn*, 67; Owen, *Place of Enchantment*, 74–75.

approach and such magical praxis can easily be overstated. As Alex Owen has shown, the Golden Dawn's exploration of magical techniques "was seen as part of the process of attaining the great gift of occult wisdom, which presages the kind of enlightenment for which the true Adept strives."[144] The adepts of the F.R.C. certainly worked within a different value system when it came to practical occultism, but they too sought the esoteric wisdom of the Secret Tradition; moreover, their quest for attainment was achieved through imaginative, meditative and ritualistic practices that, as I will illustrate further in Chapter Five, had some kinship with the Golden Dawn's explicitly magical approach. Moreover, most of the R.R. et A.C. training in practical magic was intended for personal use, rather than deployment in a ritual setting, thus dramatically reducing the magicity of the Golden Dawn ritual experience itself. It is also likely that only a few order members applied their magical knowledge to their personal lives once they had passed the magical knowledge examinations required for full R.R. et A.C. membership. As Ellic Howe notes, there are only a few records of R.R. et A.C. trained magicians performing magical operations.[145] Thus, the actual ritual setting of the two orders was much more similar than usually portrayed. Rather than a far-flung Christian and/or Rosicrucian satellite of the modern Hermetic world, the F.R.C. was an asteroid moving in close orbit with its parent planet, the Golden Dawn. The symbolic and narrative congruities between the Adeptus Minor rituals are indicative of the degree to which Charles Williams's ritual experiences in the F.R.C. were firmly situated in the modern occult network. Without understanding the F.R.C. as an actor within this network, we cannot begin to properly comprehend the rich initiatory experience that he discovered there. With this awareness, both readers and critics will be able to gain better access to the complex tapestry of esoteric images and practices that Williams sowed through his novels.

---

144. Owen, *Place of Enchantment*, 76.
145. Howe, *Magicians of the Golden Dawn*, 104.

Figure 3: The High Priestess. Pamela Colman Smith and Arthur Edward Waite, printed in The Pictorial Key to the Tarot: Being Fragments of a Secret Tradition under the Veil of Divination *(London: William Rider & Son, 1911), 77.*

CHAPTER 3

FICTION AND EXPERIENCE

Once through the portal of the Fourth Order of the F.R.C., Williams became a member of the Holy Assembly, considered to have successfully attained knowledge of the divine self within. True to Waite's conviction of the imagelessness of mystical experience, this initiation into the Fourth Order was considered an ascension beyond the assorted symbols of the Secret Tradition; as the adept rose, so he sank into ineffability. "Beyond this world," Williams heard as he passed through the portal, "No signs are given—no names or passwords spoken. This is therefore the great rite of the dissolution of symbols."[1] However, this dissolution was not permanent. Mystical experience was perceived as a momentary flash of gnostic insight, after which the mystic returned to an ordinary mode of sensory and semiotic experience, though now equipped with full awareness of the knowledge of the Secret Tradition.[2] In this enhanced state, the initiate became a master. Though the search for mystic union could be, as Waite admitted, "perhaps undeniably self-

---

1. Waite, "Portal of the Fourth Order," 8–9. Cf. "Adeptus Major," 34–35.
2. Waite, "Portal of the Fourth Order," 42.

ish,"[3] the Fourth Order "Adeptus Exaltatus" was asked to turn outward and accept a new task: to give back to the narratives and traditions that had contributed to their successful moment of attainment.

This shift was expressed in the symbolism of Daath, the hidden eleventh sephira, which Waite used to represent direct knowledge of the divine self within. In this sense, Daath performed two important symbolic functions for F.R.C. adepts. In its first, upward looking role it played "Mediator" between the aspects of divine consciousness represented by the higher, supernal sephiroth and those accessible through the lower seven stages modelled by the Tree of Life.[4] Its second, downward function was less focused on the attainment and transmutation of the self, and more centred on the spiritual well-being of the community. Here, Daath symbolized the role of the Holy Assembly adept as educator and communicator: "From the Word in Daath flow down those symbols which are thought and speech at the highest."[5] As Adeptus Exaltatus Williams thus became, like Daath, the "fontal source whence all the signs proceed."[6] His education in this reverse projection of the mystic way had begun already as an Adeptus Exemptus, where he was given a "solemn discharge or permit, whereby we are sent to preach the gospel of mystical life unto every prepared creature." The term "prepared creature" is significant, as it maintains the esoteric emphasis on secrecy and obscurity in

---

3. Arthur Edward Waite, *A Book of Mystery and Vision* (London: Philip Wellby, 1902), xii–xiii.
4. "Adeptus Exemptus," 45.
5. Ibid, 46. Waite's association of Daath with a final site of divine gnosis is relatively unique to his system. Occultists have usually envisioned rising beyond Daath, while the F.R.C. rituals also make no connection to another common association in modern magic, in which Daath appears as a "false sephira," a site of mystical abyss that must be passed through to proceed above or, as for the magician Kenneth Grant, a portal through which the adept could reach the back side of the Tree of Life—equivalent to the kabbalistic *qlippoth* (see *Cults of the Shadow* (London: Frederick Muller, 1975), 169–70.
6. "The Ceremony of Contemplation on the Further Side of the Portal, which Is 0=0 in Supernis," (Amsterdam: Bibliotheca Philosophica Hermetica, A.E. Waite Collection, 1922), 35.

order to ensure that the powerful knowledge of the esoteric traditions is not unveiled to ears that are not ready to hear. Thus, insists the ritual, this gospel must be "uttered in symbols only and clouded in forms of speech."[7] Prior to his initiation into the Fourth Order, Williams had absorbed the occulted symbolism of the Secret Tradition and directed it toward the achievement of individual mystical attainment. Now, as a member of the Holy Assembly, he was expected to generate it.

And generate he did. Williams's novels, like his poetry, are a bricolage of symbolism, jammed with biblical and literary allusions, references to Arthurian legend, and a significant number of characters and events compiled from his own life. Even more dominant however, at least in the first five novels, are elements of occult symbolism that Williams would have discovered in the F.R.C. Kabbalah and alchemy feature prominently, along with the trumps of the tarot, a variety of magical symbols and practices, and, perhaps most of all, narrative representations of mystical experience. Even the Fourth Order command to return from the state of illumination and express the way to its source can be found in the novels: The occultist Nigel Considine of *Shadows of Ecstasy* mirrors the language of the F.R.C. rituals when he states his view of the ultimate purpose of adeptship: "The true adepts care for nothing but to discover the secrets, and to enter into communion with ecstasy; and if they shall govern the world, as they shall, they will do it to make known to all men the things they themselves know."[8] Responding to a letter in which Williams outlined early ideas for *All Hallows' Eve*, T.S. Eliot told his friend that his current concept was missing this very proselytic aspect. "One of your most important functions in life," he told Williams, "Is to instill sound doctrine into people (tinged sometimes with heresy, of course, but the *very best* heresy) without their knowing it...This is not a matter of Gilding the Pill, but of introducing the maximum amount of Physic into the treacle: so don't forget to capture

---

7. "Adeptus Exemptus," 43. Cf. 5.
8. Charles Williams, *Shadows of Ecstasy* (Grand Rapids, MI: Eerdmans, 1978), 153.

the attention of the most inattentive."[9] Eliot missed the mix of playful generic thrill and intently serious theosophy that had typified Williams's earlier fiction, his knack for enfolding the "Physic" of the metaphysical in an attractive narrative shell.

THE UNBEARABLE LIGHTNESS OF FICTION

Williams began to write *Shadows of Ecstasy* a year after he received his first instruction to share Secret Tradition knowledge through symbolism in the course of the Adeptus Exemptus ritual. Initially called *The Black Bastard*, then *Adepts of Africa*, the novel was written in the summer of 1925, but only published, after significant revision, in 1933. Williams began the novel on 8 July 1925,[10] seven days after the O.S.R. & A.C.'s first performance of the portal ritual of the Fourth Order. On 22 and 29 July, Williams himself participated in the two rituals that inducted him into the Fourth Order, receiving the Adeptus Exaltatus command to share his mystic knowledge. Thus, while one influential critic has claimed that Williams wrote his novels only for the money,[11] I wish to suggest another likely motivation, one more attuned to the author's metaphysical and aesthetic priorities: The narrative flexibility of fiction allowed Williams to satisfy his Fourth Order responsibilities as a mystic leader and teacher without eliding the esoteric requirement to communicate Secret Tradition knowledge through veils of symbolism. He clearly sought profit from his novels, but, as I will show time and again in this book, there is a significant relationship between his F.R.C. experiences and the content and purpose of his fiction.

Though Williams felt his "real work" to be first poetry then literary criticism,[12] fiction offered him a cultural forum that could not be found in either of these modes, one which combined the ludic

---
9. T.S. Eliot to Charles Williams, 14 December 1940, Bodleian Ms. Res. c.137, f.2.
10. Dodds, *Charles Williams*, 319.
11. Carpenter, *The Inklings*, 95.
12. Charles Wiliams to Florence Conway, 15 September 1944, in *To Michal from Serge*, 223.

play of the fantastic with opportunities to express the cosmic concepts he was tasked to communicate. Few aspects of his fiction are left untouched by this shared priority: themes, symbols, settings and characters are spun on the wheel of his creative imagination and it is frequently the Adeptus Exaltatus that molds the clay. Many, including Williams himself, have doubted that he approached his fiction with the serious intent I am attributing to his Fourth Order adeptship. The claim that he wrote the novels simply to pad his often empty pocketbook is certainly not without merit—he himself related this motivation to his friends. Joan Harris, his secretary at Oxford Publishing House, recalled him saying that while poetry remained his first love, the "novels would be bread + butter."[13] In a 1925 letter to another friend, Williams described *Adepts of Africa* as a "wonderful" book, but appears to have been insecure about his move into fiction. "It is the joke of my life," he said, though he added, "And I love it as such."[14]

We should not attach too much importance to such denials of serious attachment. Glen Cavaliero has shown that he took this approach to most, if not all, of his work, arguing that Williams's claim that a true author should be able to go on churning out pages while riding the London Underground indicates "that he never took his writing too solemnly."[15] This combination of the playful and the serious extends to the novels, where we are certainly not expected to read meaning into each piece of action and characterization. Crucially, however, this superficial gloss must be balanced by evidence that Williams saw his novels as serious expressions of his coinherent mysticism. When Mary Butts first contacted Williams after reading three of his novels—"but chiefly *The Place of the Lion*"— with "the utmost delight," she asked about a rumour she had heard that he had repudiated his novels, having written them as a hoax,

---

13. Handwritten draft of reminiscences of Charles Williams by Joan Harris, undated, uncatalogued, CWSA.
14. Charles Williams to Olive Willis, 23 Dec 1925, quoted in Lindop, *Charles Williams*, 117.
15. Cavaliero, *Poet of Theology*, 4.

"with [his] tongue in [his] cheek."[16] Williams appears to have been somewhat incensed by this rumour—he did not allow his reply to be delayed by the post but sent an immediate telegram: "Repudiation all nonsense. Charles Williams."[17] He then followed up with a letter several days later: "I have never repudiated, never could and never should dream of repudiating (by God's mercy) anything real in the novels." He admitted to making jokes of them here and there, and to writing them partly for profit, but did not see why this should mitigate their metaphysical significance: "There is a temporal occasion for everything... But why the temporal occasion should be supposed to negative all spiritual existence I cannot see."[18] Williams's motivations for writing fiction cannot, therefore, be explained away by the profit motive. His letter to Butts suggests that alongside more frivolous and mundane purposes he enthusiastically affirmed fiction as a looking glass through which readers might step into the realm of "spiritual existence." Further belying the profit motive theory is the fact that the novels did not actually gain him much in the way of income, and provided his publishers with even less.[19] His predilection for occult motifs has even less of the sniff of capital about it; as early as 1930, Gollancz had warned him against topics like black magic and the Holy Grail, worried that they "would 'put off' many readers."[20] Despite the lack of success that greeted his fiction, Williams continued to produce it for the rest of his life, though his pace of publication slowed dramatically after the early thirties. There are any number of potential explanations for this slowdown: Gollancz would no longer accept his fiction,[21] he had a plethora of

---

16. Mary Butts to Charles Williams, 6 January 1934, quoted in Lindop, *Charles Williams*, 267.
17. Quoted in Lindop, *Charles Williams*, 268.
18. Charles Williams to Mary Butts, 10 Jan 1934, quoted in Lindop, *Charles Williams*, 268.
19. "I hate your losing money when I've made it through you," Williams told Victor Gollancz, after the latter had published his first four novels (Charles Williams to Victor Gollancz, 28 July 1932, CWSA I.F.xiii/c).
20. Victor Gollancz to Charles Williams, 19 March 1930, Bodleian Ms. Res. c.137, f.2.
21. Lindop, *Charles Williams*, 234. Gollancz rejected *Descent Into Hell* in January 1934.

commissions for other projects, and the novels clearly were not doing enough to "pay my child's school fees."[22] Despite these obstacles, he persevered. Even after the publication of *All Hallows' Eve* in the last year of his life, we know from his letters that another novel was in progress, the drafts of which have never been found.[23] Both pleasure and conviction drove him on: Writing fiction, he told Gollancz, offered "excitement and fun."[24] If we combine this claim with Williams's response to Butts, it's clear that in fiction he found a playful forum in which he could express Secret Tradition knowledge and other congruent theological concepts with the utmost seriousness.

In addition to providing an outlet through which to carry out the communicative task of the Adeptus Exaltatatus, fiction allowed Williams to explore mystical, magical and poetic aspects of his ritual experiences, encountered both in and outside of the F.R.C. Eliot spoke of Williams's constant presence in both "the material and spiritual world at once," and seemed to ascribe his fiction with the power to best share experiences that stem from the coming together of those two worlds in Williams's correspondent perception: "There are pages in his novels which describe, with extraordinary precision, the kind of unexplainable experience which many of us have had, once or twice in our lives, and been unable to put into words."[25] Two years later, in his introduction to a reprint of *All Hallows' Eve*, Eliot connected this type of experience to Williams's occult activities. Though he cautioned that not all that Williams had "borrowed from the literature of the occult" should be given complete credence,[26] he insisted that in drawing from the supernatural and the paranormal in his fiction, "Williams is telling us about a world of experience known

---

22. Charles Williams to Mary Butts, 10 Jan 1934.
23. Lindop, *Charles Williams*, 414.
24. Charles Williams to Victor Gollancz, 13 July 1932, CWSA I.F.xiii/d.
25. Eliot, "The Significance of Charles Williams," 895.
26. Eliot, preface to *All Hallows' Eve*, xv.

to him: he does not merely persuade us to believe in something, he communicates this experience that he has had."[27]

Eliot felt, however, that there was a limit to Williams's ability to communicate his metaphysical concepts and experiential knowledge. He observed that to an extent his friend's message "was beyond his resources, and probably beyond the resources of language...What it is, essentially, that he had to say, comes near to defying definition. It was not simply a philosophy, a theology, or a set of ideas: it was primarily something imaginative."[28] Eliot seems to have sensed the ineffable root of Williams's Adeptus Exaltatus message; the internal, non-narrative nature of his encounters with the supernatural. Eliot finds himself also unable to use language to describe the extent of Williams's vision, settling for the rather vague "something imaginative" as a bit of a placeholder. The term does, however, capture the fantastic, mythopoeic aspect of Williams's attempt to explore and express his mystical and, later, coinherent experiences through fiction. Of necessity, these encounters were channeled through symbol, metaphor, and allusion; Williams's perception and interpretation of his experiences were fundamentally narrative and creative.

Since Williams's time, there has been a significant increase in appreciation for the role of narrative in defining human experience. Paul Ricoeur sees narrative, understood as a temporal, plot-based mode of understanding, as an essential feature of human existence that makes time relevant to human comprehension.[29] Ricoeur characterizes human experience as having a "pre-narrative quality" in which there is no aspect of experience that cannot be spoken of as "incipient story," an action or desire straining toward expression.[30] Other narratologists have gone even further, denying the existence of

---

27. Ibid, xvi.
28. Ibid, xiii. Cf. Cavaliero, *Poet of Theology*, 161; Moorman, *Arthurian Triptych*, 89.
29. Paul Ricoeur, "The Human Experience of Time and Narrative," in *Reflection and Imagination: A Ricoeur Reader*, ed. Mario J. Valdes (Toronto: Harvester Wheatsheaf, 1991), 99.
30. Paul Ricoeur, "Life: A Story in Search of a Narrator," in *Reflection and Imagination: A Ricoeur Reader*, ed. Mario J. Valdes (Toronto: Harvester Wheatsheaf, 1991), 432.

a pre-narrative form of experience such as the "ineffable experience" from which the soul returned as Adeptus Exaltatus in the Fellowship of the Rosy Cross.[31] David Carr, for example, approves of Ricoeur's link between life and narrative but criticizes the view of narrative as "a cultural, literary artifact at odds with the real," which he finds in the work of Louis Mink, Hayden White, Roland Barthes, and, to a less radical extent, Ricoeur.[32] Extending Ricoeur's observations on the close relationship between time and narrative, Carr asserts that narrative is far from just a manner of describing an event. Rather, its structure is inherent in events themselves: "Far from being a formal distortion of the events it relates, a narrative account is an extension of one of their primary features."[33] Carr's argument works against the perception of narrative accounts of experiences as simple representations of events that have taken place in the past, as he persuasively asserts that experiences do not take place in a present that is demarcated from the past and future; rather, "The present is precisely a point of view or vantage point which opens onto or gives access to future and past."[34] Experiences encountered in the "present" derive their sense and meaning from experiences in the past, and from hopes or assumptions regarding the ramifications of the experience for the future. Other narratologists, including psychologist David Yamane, continue to insist on the existence of "core experiences" that are not accessible to scholars, thus upholding the category of ineffability. Narrative remains just as bound to experience for Yamane, however. Event accounts are "the primary way people concretize, make sense of, and convey their experiences," for Yamane, and are thus crucial to those attempting to understand them—including the

---

31. Waite, "Adeptus Exemptus," 21.
32. David Carr, "Narrative and the Real World: An Argument for Continuity," *History and Theory* 25, no. 2 (May 1986): 120.
33. Ibid, 117.
34. Ibid, 125.

experiencers themselves—since we cannot approach the actual ineffability of the moment.[35]

Whether you side with Carr's view or prefer to maintain an emphasis on "pre-narrative" experience, Yamane's point indicates that religious experiences, even specifically ineffable encounters such as those sought in the F.R.C., can *only* be accessed through the narratives of those activities. Human experience cannot be separated from narrative, just as a human life cannot be separated from its narrative distinctions, explanations, and extrapolations. An analysis of religious experience that does not "differentiate a core from its interpretations"[36] results in research that can establish a more complete picture of what the subject has encountered and continues to encounter. Crucially, narratological approaches to events described as religious or spiritual, such as mystical attainment or conversation with a supernatural being, have also suggested that previous narratives of experience like those found in myth or in holy texts are instrumental in formulating later experiences. The account of an experience is thus directly linked to the narrative process that constructed it, and neither can be separated from the other. A narrative of religious experience can thus help to understand the nature, purpose and psychological context of the experience itself, by highlighting processes of interpretation, concretization, and meaning making.[37] To put it more simply and more radically, by analyzing the

---

35. David Yamane, "Narrative and Religious Experience," *Sociology of Religion* 61, no. 2 (2000): 175–76.
36. Wayne Proudfoot, *Religious Experience* (Berkeley: University of California Press, 1985), 123.
37. For an example of application of narrative analysis to religious experience, see C.J. Bender, "Touching the Transcendent: Rethinking Religious Experience in the Sociological Study of Religion," in *Everyday Religion: Observing Modern Religious Lives*, ed. N.T. Ammermann (Oxford: Oxford University Press, 2007), 214. Bender's article analyses the way in which previous experience and socially derived religious assumptions help construct the experience—and a narrative of that experience—of a women who envisions Christ acting as her Reiki guide to an encounter with an ineffable divine figure. Cf. Ulrike Popp-Baier, "Religious Experiences as Narrative: Reflections on the Advantages of a Narrative Approach," in *Religious Experience & Tradition*, ed. A. Budriunaite (Kaunas: Vytautas Magnus University).

narrative of an experience, we analyze the experience itself. Williams did not intend his novels to function as straight-forward accounts of experiences encountered in the F.R.C., in his ritualistic activities with young women, in prayer and meditation, or in poetic ecstasy, but his Adeptus Exaltatus priorities, combined with his natural tendency toward metaphysical speculation and theologizing, led him to incorporate all these into the action, characterization, theme and symbol of his novels.

FANTASTIC NARRATOLOGY: THE LIMINALITY OF ESOTERIC KNOWLEDGE

Williams's decision to take time away from criticism and poetry to write fiction was thus motivated, at least in part, by his Adeptus Exaltatus commitment to teach while he entertained and, in the course of communicating his correspondent worldview and the value of mystical attainment, to explore the ecstatic experiences engendered by magico-mystical interaction with the symbols and practices of the esoteric traditions. Another important question remains, however: why rely on generic forms such as fantasy, the gothic, horror, detective mystery and science fiction? A simple initial explanation is that he quite enjoyed genre fiction. He told a friend that he decided to write the "thriller" that became *Shadows of Ecstasy* after reading one of Sax Rohmer's *Fu Manchu* novels,[38] and, as we will see, his fiction is also clearly informed by a number of other authors of the fantastic popular in the period. As I have shown, however, Williams did not take up fiction purely for its entertainment value. Thus, though his novels have elements of realism and drawing room banter that might be found in less fantastic works of the Victorian and modern period, they are centrally characterized by supernatural horror and divine sublimity, designed with the sole purpose of shocking the reader from a materialist or naturalist perspective. Williams follows the

---

38. Charles Williams to Olive Willis, 23 Dec 1925, quoted in Lindop, *Charles Williams*, 116.

general pattern of most fantastic modes of the period—the gothic, weird fiction, horror and even some science fiction (née scientific romance) all tended to feature the arrival of a supernatural presence, element, or object which must be dealt with by the characters in some manner and returned to the supernatural, or controlled and made an acceptable part of the natural world, a narrative pattern which Farah Mendlesohn calls "intrusive fantasy."[39]

There are significant differences between the structures and purposes of the seven novels, but at all points there is an assumed permeability, a wide, two-way bridge with nary a troll or tollgate, between the natural and the supernatural. For Franco-Bulgarian structuralist Tzvetan Todorov, this permeability gives rise to the very "sense of the fantastic" that drives the reader experience of the nineteenth and early twentieth century generic modes that Williams productively mixed together. Todorov defines the sense of the fantastic as "that hesitation experienced by a person who knows only the laws of nature, confronting an apparently supernatural event."[40] By "laws of nature" Todorov refers to the perspective of realism, and his definition of the fantastic encapsulates the experience of either character or reader as they encounter events that shatter this perspective. Both are caught in a liminal state in which they must choose whether what they are faced with is real—and therefore operating by previously unknown natural laws—or imaginary.

Each of Williams's seven novels attempt to create this liminal state of wonderment and doubt by shattering the reader's perception of barriers between natural and supernatural. Like contemporaries Arthur Machen, Algernon Blackwood and Evelyn Underhill, Williams's fiction seeks the violent monistic overthrow of both reductionist naturalism and the dualisms of theism and doctrinal Christianity. A letter to a friend indicates the centrality of this emphasis on correspondent unity to the novels: asked whether he could define

---

39. Farah Mendlesohn, *Rhetorics of Fantasy* (Middletown, CT: Wesleyan University Press, 2008), xxii, 114–15.
40. Tzvetan Todorov, *The Fantastic: A Structural Approach to a Literary Genre* (Ithaca: Cornell University Press, 1980), 25.

what, exactly, his books were about, Williams was unequivocal: "I always know—it's about the Holy Grail or the Stone of Suleiman or attacks by negroes. 'Back to Matter'! is my cry."[41] Williams thus chose to write in the fantastic mode precisely to perpetuate Todorov's hesitation, crying for his reader to question whether the perceived imaginary of the supernatural might not actually contain a divine real. Fantastic fiction offered him a unique opportunity to suggest permeability between the material world and the spiritual realm he saw infusing it. He sought to place the reader in a liminal state of hesitation between the two, a hesitation that had, for Williams, both a narrative function and an authentic, experiential dimension. In attempting to draw the reader to this state of hesitation, Williams shared a state of being in which he appears to have been frequently suspended. As Eliot mused, the supernatural "is just as natural to the author as our everyday world. And he makes our everyday world very much more exciting, because of the supernatural which he finds always active in it."[42] Fiction thus enabled a congruency between the state of mind of the reader and the encounter with the supernatural Williams experienced in the course of transforming psyche and consciousness in ritual settings such as the F.R.C.

Williams seems to have found occult phenomena especially useful for formulating this hesitation. In his case much of this attraction can be traced to his personal involvement with occult Rosicrucianism, but the very nature of esoteric knowledge itself is at play here as well, as it functions as a form of narrative that exists, almost by definition, in the state of liminality which the fantastic attempts to secure for its reader. As we have seen, Andreas Kilcher identifies esotericism as an epistemological phenomenon, one existing in an ongoing dialogical relationship to normative epistemological currents. As a result of this relationship, its traditions are subject to temporal historical and cultural interpretations, and are therefore the ongoing, shifting result of "ever new discursive negotiations and

---

41. Quoted in Hadfield, *Charles Williams: An Exploration*, 97.
42. Eliot, "The Significance of Charles Williams," 894.

displacements." Kilcher argues that esotericism is therefore a primarily "narrative, imaginal, aesthetic construction," with a tendency to adapt and reformulate myth and story that displays literary characteristics: "The epistemology of esotericism invents narratives of history, the cosmos, divinity, humanity, etc. It is built upon the *narrativity*, even the inventability (*inventio*) of knowledge."[43] Esotericism thus engages more openly and more freely with literary methods of knowing and expression than do most religious narrative traditions, adding layers of meaning and signification to similes, parables, metaphors, and images.[44] It proves useful to creators of literature precisely because of these concomitant functions. Not just Williams, but virtually every writer of fantastic fiction has found rhetorical power in the symbols, myths and allusions of the esoteric traditions.

For Joshua Gunn, this quality of inventio is what distinguishes occult discourse from more conventional religious attempts to explain the nature of the divine and religious experience. Where traditional religious narrative avoids neologism, relying on the tested (and often sacred) logos of sacred texts, Gunn argues that occult discourse probes the utmost extent of creativity.[45] It would be dangerous to pursue this simplification too far—some religions—Judaism (particularly kabbalah) and Hinduism come immediately to mind—have displayed astonishing degrees of semiotic reinvention and adaptation, while even traditions that discourage narrative reinvention still tend to experience radical innovation in certain circles, as seen in the examples of esoteric Christian syncretism discussed in Chapter One. Yet, approached with caution Gunn's observation is quite helpful for understanding the manner in which occult discourse has differentiated itself from more dominant Western religious currents. Even more pertinent to my current project is Gunn's identification of a "dynamic generative paradox" that rises from the

---

43. Kilcher, "7 Epistemological Theses," 147.
44. Ibid.
45. Gunn, "An Occult Poetics," 43.

tension between ineffable experience and the limitations of human semiotics to express it. In this conception, esoteric innovation leaps from the frustration of trying to narratively reproduce facts and encounters believed to be beyond narrative.[46] Again, we must avoid oversimplification: not all occultists were (or are) interested in mystical experience and some that were did not see it as necessarily ineffable, but in the case of Charles Williams, Gunn's observation points to a likely motivation for his decision to unleash esoteric knowledge upon a largely uncomprehending readership. The frustration of communicating linguistically inaccessible experiences and ontological dimensions may have prompted his frequent turn to arcane esoteric concepts, themselves often the product of attempts by others to express the inexpressible. In keeping with the quality of inventio, Williams continued to adapt and reinterpret the images and symbols he borrowed from the esoteric traditions.

Much of this adaptation came in the form of syncretism, as Williams freely associated a variety of symbols and images in order to satisfy his quasi-surrealist taste for multivalence. If a word or symbol in his fiction seems to stand in simple and stolid relation to a single referent, it is likely not because the author intended it so. His monistic worldview caused him to layer each character, each setting, each symbol in his work with as many points of signification as possible.[47] Boyhood friend George Robinson reported that even as a youth attending a local theological debating group in St Albans, Charles "had a knack sometimes of changing his position halfway through a debate in order to see what could be said for the other side—greatly to the bewilderment of the more [illegible] pudding brained

---

46. Ibid, 31. Cf. 32, 34–36, 41.
47. A number of critics have discussed Williams's taste for multivalence, particularly in Charles A. Huttar and Peter J. Schakel's excellent collection, *A Rhetoric of Vision: Essays on Charles Williams* (Lewisburg: Bucknell University Press, 1996). From this volume see Bosky, "The Inner Lives of Characters and Readers: Affective Stylistics in Charles Williams's Fiction"; Charles A. Huttar, "Introduction to *the Rhetoric of Vision: Essays on Charles Williams*," 23; Alice E. Davidson, "Language and Meaning in the Novels of Charles Williams," 50; Stephen Medcalf, "The Athanasian Principle in Williams's Use of Images," 32. Cf. Lindop, *Charles Williams*, 23.

brethren."[48] Williams seems to have maintained this fondness for paradox throughout his life. In his 1942 theological publication, *The Forgiveness of Sins*, he expresses frustration with the tendency of the language of theologians to slide "back into a one-sided use of that language. Their terms ought to be ambiguous; they ought to carry meanings at once in time and outside time."[49] Multivalence, then, remained the only semiotic approach to the ineffable, though even by this route Williams doubted the possibility of a divine vocabulary.[50] I could not agree more with Bernadette Bosky's argument that one of Williams's goals in writing novels was to achieve this semantic multiplicity, bypassing the limitations of non-fictional theological writing.[51] Bosky identifies three particular techniques that Williams employs to communicate his monistic vision: 1) phrases or sentences that create a paradoxical confluence of opposites, such as "Filial Godhead"[52] and "terribly good,"[53] and thus cause the reader to modify their outlook as a result of being emotionally struck by the collision of these opposites, ideally reaching an understanding that transcends their apparent conflict; 2) polysemy in single words or concepts; 3) use of pronouns or other references to subjects that enables a multivalence of character. Here, a single character's actions can be seen as both parochial and plot-inscribed *and* archetypal and metaphysically significant.[54] Bosky argues persuasively that in each of these three cases, Williams's ultimate goal

---

48. George Robinson to Alice Mary Hadfield, CWSA II.A.4, 8. Lois Lang-Sims reached a similar opinion about Williams after meeting him in 1943. See Charles Williams and Lois Lang-Sims, *Letters to Lalage: The Letters of Charles Williams to Lois Lang-Sims* (Kent, OH: Kent State University Press, 1989), 79.
49. Charles Williams, *The Forgiveness of Sins* (London: Geoffrey Bles, 1942), 17.
50. Ibid.
51. Bosky, "Affective Stylistics in Charles Williams's Fiction," 66.
52. Williams, *Shadows of Ecstasy*, 79. This term is actually Milton's (*Paradise Lost*, 6.722), but Williams's attraction to it is clear as it plays a significant role in Roger Ingram's exploration of mystical experience in the novel.
53. *Descent into Hell* (Grand Rapids, MI: William B. Eerdmans, 1979), 16.
54. Bosky, "Affective Stylistics in Charles Williams's Fiction," 61–67.

is to communicate otherwise indescribable experiences and, ideally, "do so in a language that will allow us to recreate the experience as we read."[55]

For Bosky, the particular experience that Williams is trying to share is his mystical awareness of the cosmic unity of man, nature and divinity. Indeed, Williams himself linked multivalence to mystical attainment in an essay on Yeats, another visionary writer whose symbolic method merged with his extensive experience with occult knowledge and practice in the Golden Dawn and Stella Matutina. The poetry of Yeats, who himself described a symbol as something that "entangles, in complex colours and forms, a part of the Divine Essence,"[56] was for Williams the exemplar of the semiotic pathway to attainment laid out by esoteric and fantastic imagery. The highest value of Yeats's references to magic, faery and alchemy, "is perhaps the continual suggestion of other possibilities than the normal mind is conscious of."[57] In this sense it is not so much the practical application of such occult concepts that matters, but their effect in achieving "the vision of a final attainment more perfect than faerie."[58] Williams followed Yeats and a host of other literary figures from Blake to Machen who gathered together the symbols of the Western spiritual traditions to guide readers toward transcendence. As an Adeptus Exaltatus writing fiction, he disseminated esoteric symbolism in much the same way that he had often encountered it as a Neophyte, Zelator or Adeptus Major—undiluted, unexplained and uninterpreted—simply presented in word or visual form in order to summon an inexpressible truth to the mind. In doing so, he created new esoteric products from out of his occult experiences, textual actors that took up a modest, but still active role in the modern occult network. The esoteric knowledge mediated in these texts is informed by Williams's unique philosophy and synthesized with images and

---

55. Ibid, 60–61.
56. W. B. Yeats, "The Symbolism of Painting," in *Essays and Introductions* (New York: Macmillan, 1961), 148.
57. Charles Williams, *Poetry at Present* (Oxford: Clarendon Press, 1930), 63.
58. Ibid.

concepts from other traditions, but this process of negotiation and adaptation is exactly that which drives the dialogical formation of esoteric knowledge.

THE NOVELS—INTRUSIONS OF THE SUPERNATURAL

Images, symbols and practices derived from modern occultism are a feature of all seven of Williams's novels, but they are most prevalent in the first four. In *Shadows of Ecstasy*, the fifth novel published but the first written, the sense of supernatural intrusion is not so palpable as in his later novels. Yet, modern English materialist sensibility is shattered by the invasion of the Allied Supremacies of Africa—a force both military and magical, composed largely of African troops but led by Nigel Considine, a figure of white colonial power. Considine and his forces have repossessed the entire African continent from the European powers and now threaten to reverse the pattern of colonialism altogether, invading Europe itself. The army that has landed on Britain's beaches is amorphous and surreal—only one African character features in the action, and the power of the invaders is not justified by a quantification of military might. The African troops are not material realities but unreal, anti-rational spectres. Their military strategy is symbolic martyrdom rather than systematic takeover. They use no planes, no bombs, only terror and a frenzied suicidal dance intended to dominate the British populace with "the fear of their own passions"[59]—their own capacity for inchoate madness. Thus, though they are technically of earthly origin, the Allied Supremacies perform the narrative function of the supernatural intrusion of the fantastic. The African forces, however, are a fringe concern in a novel centred entirely on their leader, the occultist Nigel Considine. Considine presents both reader and characters with a variety of occult phenomena that shatter the boundaries of the natural. He offers a number of convincing proofs to support his claim that he has developed a technique of sublimating human

---

59. Williams, *Shadows of Ecstasy*, 152.

passions, particularly desire, in order to grant himself magical power and an extended lifespan that stands at two hundred years. He possesses the ability to control both his followers and his foes with a method of magical hypnosis rooted in occult interpretations of nineteenth-century mesmerism, and seems close to achieving the goal sought by alchemists for centuries—the indefinite prolongation of the life of the physical body.

These claims combine with the amorphous presence of the African forces to engender Todorov's hesitation, creating and maintaining a sense of the fantastic. The reader is, potentially, left in a perpetual state of hesitation as to the reality of magical phenomena in the novel—they are empirically unjustifiable, yet the novel insists on their possibility. This sense is magnified, as in any fantastic narrative, by character response. Considine's quest to overcome death is analyzed through the eyes of a small group of Londoners, each representative of a particular socio-cultural demographic: Sir Bernard Travers, a medical doctor, represents rational skepticism; Ian Caithness, a vicar, represents institutional, dogmatic Christianity, sometimes impressively, but more often with clear failings. Inkamasi, a Zulu king held hostage by Considine, represents both a type of archetypal royalty and the perspective of the African other. Philip, Bernard's son, represents the Romantic theological viewpoint, his fiancèe Rosamond both the human object of his mystical desire and its selfish, superficial opposite. Romantic Theology's positive female viewpoint is represented by Isabel, Rosamond's sister, the wife of Roger Ingram, a poet and literary critic and, beside Considine, the novel's central actor. Williams places each of these archetypal characters in the position where they must choose a direction in which to move from their hesitation and reject or accept Considine's earth-shattering claims.[60] Each character voices the likely response of their socio-cultural demographic to modern occultism, likely embodying

---

60. Williams was fond of this mechanism; all of the novels feature diverse character responses to supernatural intrusion, particularly the first five. See Dodds, *Charles Williams*, 325; Urang, *Shadows of Heaven*, 71.

aspects of Williams's own multivalent perspective. A wide gamut of responses results, from the disinterest of the rational materialist Bernard to the open hostility of the Christian Ian Caithness. It is the sincere interest of Roger Ingram, however, which carries the plot. Roger elects to become Considine's disciple after the occultist shows him the mystical passion that underlies poetry, in a manner no one has been able to communicate to him before.[61] Roger is also fascinated by Considine's eternity project. When his master is shot dead by another disciple with the assistance of Caithness, Roger deliberates to the last about the possibility of a Christ-like resurrection to follow this Judas-like betrayal. Roger's thoughts on this in the last line of the novel perpetuate the hesitation of the fantastic beyond the novel's scope: "If—ah beyond, beyond belief! but if he returned..."[62] As Richard McLaughlin concludes in his 1950 review of the novel, we are left "a little uncertain of Williams's conclusions."[63] The author himself was enthusiastic about the hesitation between supernatural improbability and realistic expectation that was maintained with his ending: "The last pages make me all quivery in case he *should* come back," he told his publisher, Victor Gollancz, as he submitted yet another revised version of the novel.[64] Apparently Gollancz agreed, as *Shadows of Ecstasy* was finally published.

The next four novels continue to maintain the sense of the fantastic by bringing supernatural forces into the sitting rooms of mid-war Britain. In *War in Heaven, Many Dimensions* and *The Greater Trumps,* the divine ruptures into physicality—or, in Williams's correspondent terms, the physicality of the divine is revealed—in the Holy Graal,[65] a magical stone said to have been in the possession of Solomon, and the original deck of the tarot.[66] Again, plot, theme and

---

61. See Williams, *Shadows of Ecstasy*, 86–87, 133.
62. Ibid, 224.
63. McLaughlin, "Drama of Belief and Unbelief," 18.
64. Charles Williams to Victor Gollancz, 28 July 1932, CWSA I.F.xiii/e.
65. Williams follows the spelling he encountered in Waite's *The Hidden Church of the Holy Graal.*
66. On the role of mediatory objects in the first five novels, see McLaren, "A Problem of

character development are driven by a diversity of responses to these intrusions—some seek to possess these objects, others to return them to their supernatural origins. Some run from these manifestations of divinity, others pursue them. Most of the shape and gloss of these mediatory objects is drawn from the esoteric traditions, as are many of the techniques used by characters to respond to the invasion of the supernatural promulgated by these magical intruders.

Williams wrote *War in Heaven*, originally titled *The Corpse*, in 1926, but it too was rejected for publication until Joan Harris rescued it in 1930, just as Williams was about to throw it out. She sent it to Victor Gollancz, who published this and four subsequent novels.[67] Beneath a largely superfluous detective-thriller structure, in which a corpse is discovered in a publishing house and an inspector put on the case, *War in Heaven* orbits around the sudden discovery of the Graal in the cupboard of a small parish church by the Archdeacon Julian Davenant. The Graal provides a medium with which to bridge the gap between matter and spirit—to reveal the monistic physics of the incarnation—by virtue of the power it absorbed in "the high intensity of the moment when it was used."[68] The novel's central characters are arrayed in competing triads, some seeking to possess the Graal, others to protect it. Together with the Duke of the North Ridings and Kenneth Mornington, a publishing assistant, the Archdeacon forms a small band of modern day Arthurian knights questing for the Graal. Their goal, however, is not to possess the Graal but to secure it from three dark magicians—Dimitri, who wants to destroy the Graal, Manasseh, who wants to destroy *with* it, and the Satanist Gregory Persimmons, who seeks it both to enhance his magical power and to achieve mystic union with the dark principle he worships. These three are abetted by archeologist Sir Giles Tumulty, an erstwhile antagonist who achieves true villainy in an encore role in *Many

---

Morality," 109, 24. McLaren—erroneously in my opinion—includes *Shadows of Ecstasy* and *The Place of the Lion* in this category.
67. Reminiscences of Charles Williams by Joan Harris. Cf. Lindop, *Charles Williams*, 66, 123.
68. Williams, *War in Heaven*, 37.

Dimensions, but for now is more interested in empirical knowledge of the Graal's history and qualities. In the climactic scenes, the sorcerous triumvirate manage to possess the Graal and temporarily subdue the Archdeacon's group, killing Mornington with black magic. Ultimately, however, they are unable to defeat the Archdeacon because of his sedate connectedness to the power that is in the holy cup. In the midst of a dark ritual designed to use the Graal to marry the Archdeacon's soul to a thrall enslaved by Persimmons, the three sorcerers are summarily defeated by a manifestation of divinity that emerges from the Graal—Prester John, a mythical priest-king of the East. The denouement sees the Archdeacon mystically ascend into transcendence with the magical assistance of the holy cup, which quickly follows him to union with the supernatural principle that it represents.

A similar resolution occurs in *Many Dimensions*, published six months later in January 1931.[69] Chloe Burnett and her boss Lord Arglay, the Chief Justice of England, seek to restore a curious object called the "stone of Suleiman" to its rightful place "in the Transcendence."[70] The stone has been stolen from its Sufi guardians and is causing havoc in inter-war England because of its many abilities. It offers many of the powers dreamed of by modern occultists, including astral travel, telepathy, healing, and clairvoyance. It even enables time travel.[71] In addition to this range of powers, the original stone, a primordial unity of matter and spirit, can be multiplied into infinite copies with similar abilities, though this multiplication is understood in the novel as division because it represents the disintegration of the stone's correspondent unity. A host of political, corporate and scientific powers led by Giles Tumulty seek to divide the stone in order to achieve a wide spectrum of material goals—instantaneous transport and infinite wealth are just the beginning of the technological, economic and political possibilities it offers—but

---

69. Lindop, *Charles Williams*, 177.
70. Charles Williams, *Many Dimensions* (Grand Rapids, MI: William B. Eerdmans, 1979), 59. Suleiman is an English transliteration of the Turkish name for Solomon.
71. Williams, *Many Dimensions*, 20, 24, 101, 192, 198.

Chloe and Arglay take a course similar to the Archdeacon, intuitively aware that to abuse the stone's power for material purposes is a violation of its intertwined spiritual essence.[72] Chloe, in particular, swiftly becomes aware of the stone's higher nature and is disgusted by the greed of the other characters. She begins to respond to the stone's desire for reintegration with the divinity from which it has been separated, and eventually, with Arglay's assistance, returns it to its supernatural source, her spirit following as the Archdeacon's follows the Graal. This return of the supernatural intrusion to its source is typical of the point of climax in the narrative arc Mendlesohn identifies in the intrusive mode most common to fantasy in the period.[73]

The Greater Trumps sees a similar return, though this time the characters remain attached to their material surroundings. A young magician, Henry Lee (named after A.H.E. Lee) discovers the original tarot deck of which all others are imitations, in the possession of his future father-in-law, the hapless realist Lothair Coningsby. Henry, as fantastical trope would have it, is a member of a gypsy family that has functioned for generations as the high priests of a Holy of Holies in which a number of solid gold figurines whirl in an endless dance, representing the cosmic dance of divine principles. The figures are connected both to these powers and to the trumps of the tarot through the intricate connections of magical sympathy described by the doctrine of correspondences. Henry and the current high priest, his grandfather Aaron, seek to possess Lothair's tarot, in the belief that combining the deck and the figures will give them greater divinatory and magical power, thus elevating them "among the dancers" themselves.[74] When Lothair refuses to give them the deck, they attempt to kill him by releasing the elemental powers of air and water

---

72. Ibid, 159, 256. As we have seen, in Williams's monistic Romantic system such a dualist rejection of the correspondent relationships between above and below is the source of deep ethical failure. See McLaren, "A Problem of Morality," 111; Glen Cavaliero, introduction to *Witchcraft*, by Charles Williams, (Wellingborough, Northamptonshire: Aquarian, 1980), 4.
73. Mendlesohn, *Rhetorics of Fantasy*, 115.
74. Charles Williams, *The Greater Trumps* (Grand Rapids, MI: William B. Eerdmans, 1978), 30.

connected to two of the suits of the tarot deck (sceptres and cups). The supernatural invades with fury—a murderous storm of snow and wind arises, empowered and accentuated by occult forces. Lothair is saved only by the intervention of his sister, Sybil, "a woman of great power" who is impervious to the riotous elements,[75] and his daughter Nancy, Henry's fiancée, who breaks Henry's control over the storm. Things get worse, however, when all four of the elemental powers—earth, air, water, fire—are released by another of the Lee family and Nancy triggers an "invasion of the Tarots" in an attempt to control them. All is returned to normal by Sybil, the first of Williams's adept characters to practice coinherence, as she deploys an innate magus-like power over the invading elements and principles, using the deck to return them to the supernatural.

In *The Place of the Lion* the emphasis shifts from magical objects. A medieval grimoire or spellbook is consulted by Berringer, the leader of a small occult group, but it is the spell he utters from that book that invokes the divine principles of the macrocosm to manifest in the material world. These forces—equivalent to the nine Pseudo-Dionysian angelic hierarchies—loosely represent ideals of strength, intellect, greed, beauty, and so forth, manifested as the animals to which they most closely correspond in the microcosm. Thus, for example, power manifests as a lion, material desire as a serpent, and beauty as a butterfly. As had by now become standard for Williams, the intrusion of these forces upsets a contemporary England deluded by materialist assumptions. The novel's two central characters—the romantically entangled Anthony Durrant and Damaris Tighe—both greet the initial arrival of these supernatural forces with understandable skepticism, but, as usually occurs in the intrusive fantasy described by Mendlesohn's generic taxonomy,[76] both progress over the course of the narrative from denial to acceptance, accepting the assault on their reductionism by the angelic forms so that they can act as necessary to return them to the supernatural. It is largely

---

75. Ibid, 106.
76. Mendlesohn, *Rhetorics of Fantasy*, 115.

Anthony who achieves this. He battles with two members of Berringer's secret society who seek power from the invading principles and thus come to embody them—one taking the amorphous shape of a lion, the other of a serpent. In the process of defending himself against these strange antagonists, Anthony himself begins to identify with an animalian principle, that of the Christ-spirit discovered within through mystic rebirth, which takes the form of an eagle. In the course of a mystical experience into which he is thrust by staring into the eyes of the comatose Berringer, Anthony ascends from a dark abyss by becoming aware of himself as the eagle. In his newly illuminated state, he attempts to save his friend Quentin—driven mad by fear of the terrifying supernatural—and joins Richardson, an ascetic of the negative way who plays foil to Anthony's active, affirmative mystic path as both fight to restore balance to the world. Anthony eventually transforms into a modern day Adam, gaining command over nature through language-based invocation and returning the angelical principles to their supernal home.[77] *The Place of the Lion* is the first of the novels to see a reduction in occult imagery, though "modern Gnosticism or what appear to be its equivalents" is still very much at work.[78] The angelical principles are released through magical invocation by a group that seems to represent a satire of occult society; Anthony's mystical attainment has connections to spiritual alchemy and to the discovery of the higher self within sought in the F.R.C.; and his restoration of the principles through angelic *revocation* is certainly a sort of redemptive magic.

---

77. See Williams, *Place of the Lion*, 202.
78. Ibid, 80. There may also be connections to late antique Gnosticism, which is directly referenced in a conversation between Anthony and Richardson (ibid), and may have served, via Mead's *Fragments of a Faith Forgotten*, as impetus for the novel's animal imagery. For example, though there are a variety of potential sources for this symbolism, and Williams was probably influenced by more than one of them, Mead's book may have influenced the manner in which the characters take on the animal aspects of the principles whose nature is most congruent to their desires. *Fragments* features an account of the Gnostic teacher Basilides (100–200 CE), who taught that when animal natures "appear round the soul, they cause the desires of the soul to become like to the special natures of these animals" (George Robert Stow Mead, *Fragments of a Faith Forgotten* (London: Theosophical Publishing Society, 1900), 276–77).

However, the tools used to reveal the supernatural are not as connected to the esoteric traditions as in the earlier novels. Though the strange menagerie of animal symbols that Williams uses instead is hardly easier to comprehend, the relative lack of occult imagery unfamiliar to most readers may help explain why many have found *The Place of the Lion* more easily accessible than other works.[79]

Williams wrote his next novel, *Descent into Hell*, in 1933, but Gollancz turned it down and it did not appear until 1937, when Faber and Faber published it at the behest of T.S. Eliot.[80] In the interim, Williams, possibly despairing of publishing this sixth novel, revived the character of Lord Arglay and projected him into a setting that is conceptually similar to *Descent into Hell*. The result was his only short story, "Et in Sempiternum Pereant."[81] Walking in the countryside along a road that, like eternity, seems to curve forever ahead until it meets up back behind him, Lord Arglay feels that he has stepped out of both time and space. He comes upon a path that leads off from this infinite revolution and takes it to a small dark cottage, inside which he discovers a tear in the fabric of the natural, a billowing mass of smoke and flame that connects to the abyss. The sense of chaos produced by the greater trumps and angelical principles is gone, replaced by the cold grip of the weird. Where the novels provide scientific, theological or mythical subtext for their supernatural intrusions, here neither the mysterious flame nor the presence of the cottage itself are explained, resulting in the creeping tingle of the uncanny that hovers throughout. Williams seems to have two aims in "Et in Sempiternum Pereant," both evolved from *Descent into Hell*: a depiction of the underworld, as much psychological as actual, and a presentation of coinherent substitution, which was now gathering importance in his life and beginning to suffuse his metaphysics. As Arglay stands in the cottage, resisting the psycho-spiritual pull of

---

79. See, e.g., Sørina Higgins, "1931: 'The Place of the Lion' Summary," 14 January 2015, https://theoddestinkling.wordpress.com/2015/01/14/the-place-of-the-lion/
80. Lindop, *Charles Williams*, 273.
81. Charles Williams, "Et in Sempiternum Pereant," *London Mercury* 33, no. 194 (Dec 1935).

hatred, an emotion he has always struggled with, another figure staggers in, consumed completely by the hellish forces swirling around them. Arglay attempts to "offer himself to it, to make a ladder of himself" for the figure to ascend rather than descend the ladder of Jacob offered by the smoke billowing up and down in the cottage.[82] He is unsuccessful, but his sacrifice does allow him to escape back onto the ever-curving road, symbolic of existential materiality.

Williams did not adjust this narrative thread when it eventually appeared in *Descent into Hell*. Now the world of the dead is seeping into the living lands of Battle Hill, a post-WWI purpose-built community north of London. Pauline Anstruther must deploy the methods of coinherent substitution to rescue an ancestor who has been trapped in the spirit realm. Before she can do so, Pauline must first deal with another supernatural manifestation—a threatening doppelgänger that manifests as a result of her fear of its coming. She is assisted with both these challenges by Peter Stanhope, a playwright and coinherent adept who, like the Archdeacon, Isabel Ingram and Sybil Coningsby, is a character already fully developed in spiritual balance and self-empowerment at the opening of the novel. Meanwhile, portals to other supernatural realms have been opened in Battle Hill. Lily Sammile, an allusion to Lilith and Samael, demonic figures said in kabbalistic texts to have had sexual relations with Adam and Eve,[83] opens a gateway to hell in a shed near the cemetery. Meanwhile, Lawrence Wentworth, a local historian, is having dreams in which he slides down a rope into a hell of his own creation, a hell inflamed by his lust for actress Adela Hunt, the star of a play that Stanhope has written and is directing for performance locally. Adela is more interested in a younger man; the rejected Wentworth spends his unrequited energies on the creation of a succubus with which he satisfies his passions. At the novel's conclusion, the historian reaches the end of the rope, a psychological descent into "the blankness of a

---

82. Ibid, 157.
83. Williams likely learned of these figures from Waite's *Secret Doctrine in Israel* (101–04). The novel directly references Lilith (*Descent into Hell*, 204)

living oblivion, tormented by oblivion" (221), an abyssal nothingness described, as in "Et in Sempiternum Pereant," in terms of an infinite, self-perpetuated geometry: "the bottomless circles of the void."[84]

The boundary between the natural world and the supernatural spirit realms is just as permeable, if not more so, in *All Hallows' Eve*, published in early 1945 but written in 1944, developed from a play that Williams began writing in 1941, alternately titled *Frontiers of Hell, How the Devil, The Lady and the Witch* and *The Devil and the Lady*. In it a lady and her black magician lover plot to sacrifice their daughter in a satanic ritual, with the goal of enabling the lady's protege to bear the Devil's child so that Satan can become incarnate on Earth.[85] The novel moves away from this plot somewhat, but vestiges remain: Satan may not be born on earth, but a black magician, Simon Leclerc, takes a leading role. Simon's abilities trigger the hesitation of the fantastic: he possesses magical power enacted through the reversal of the divine names of kabbalah, a technique learned among French occultists in the nineteenth century; he has, like Considine, extended his lifespan to at least two centuries; and he magically created two copies of himself who are off in Russia and China attracting large followings via displays of power and a superficially salvific message of love, even as their original does the same in England after having already attracted an "enormous following" in America.[86] The "Lady" of this sorcerer Antichrist is no longer a co-conspirator; Lady Wallingford has been demoted to virtual thralldom, but she still supports LeClerc's use of their daughter Betty in a series of ambitious magical experiments designed for one purpose—exploration of the realm of the dead and dominion over it. As in *Descent into Hell*, this supernatural world overlaps, surrounds and infuses the space of the material world. Through LeClerc's magical experiments, Williams reverses the direction of intrusion from his earlier novels. Instead of supernatural forces breaking into the

---

84. *Descent into Hell*, 222.
85. Lindop, *Charles Williams*, 348–49.
86. Charles Williams, *All Hallows' Eve* (New York: Noonday, 1948), 30.

natural world, Leclerc sends Betty into the otherworld. On one such journey she meets two denizens of the dead lands, the central protagonist Lester Furnival and her self-absorbed friend Evelyn. Both have lingering claims to the world of the living; Lester, in particular, seeks reconciliation with her emotionally estranged husband Richard. Eventually, concern for Betty's wellbeing and love for Richard draw her into the material world, leading to a sequence of events in which Leclerc, the prophet of a perverse Romantic Theology, is overcome by Lester's selfless acts of coinherent substitution. Coinherence is subtly present in the self-sacrificial actions of characters like Sybil Coningsby, but these last two novels stress the concept much more, with less focus on the mystical realization of the unity of God, human, and world which dominates the earlier fiction.[87] This transition suggests that the Fourth Order priorities of the F.R.C. may have begun to fade for Williams by the mid-1930s, or that, while he may still have seen himself as a mystic teacher, his vision was shifting from Waite's Secret Tradition to the theories that would shortly lead to his formation of the Companions of the Co-inherence.

THE GOTHIC OCCULT

Descent into Hell and *All Hallows' Eve* also double down on ghoulish tropes that Williams employed in *War in Heaven*, and to a lesser degree in *Shadows of Ecstasy*,[88] but seems to have moved away from in the middle three novels: depictions of black magic, sorcerers, succubi and similar phenomena, which are rooted in the urge to terror and abjection seen in gothic and horror literature, as well as longstanding polemical discourses against esoteric traditions like magic and witchcraft. Indeed, these two cultural currents have often intersected and

---

87. As noted by Ashenden, *Charles Williams*, 114.
88. Williams's planned alterations for the novel suggest that it was written in a more grotesque vein before its revisions in the early thirties. "I suspect some of this will be 'unpleasant,'" he told Gollancz, referring to an unknown scene, "So I will cut out some of it. Especially the baby" (Charles Williams to Victor Gollancz, 18 June 1930, "Shadow of Ecstasy: Alterations," CWSA I.F.xiii/a).

informed each other. Gothic literature has mythologized the esoteric since its mid-eighteenth century origins in Horace Walpole's *The Castle of Otranto, A Gothic Story* (1764). Just as the esoteric traditions appealed to primordial ancient wisdom, the gothic, at least in its early period, looked backwards, reinventing a decaying, sensuous Europe to replace the rigid, classical model envisioned by the Enlightenment.[89] Esotericism and the gothic have most productively mixed in the rejected terrain created by discourses arrayed polemically against esoteric knowledge. Gothic fiction has explored esoteric phenomena in a relatively positive light at times—the Rosicrucian adepts of Bulwer-Lytton's *Zanoni* for example—but far more often traditions such as magic and alchemy are exploited for the cultural associations created by rationalist and/or Christian polemics. Thus, even Bulwer-Lytton, though authentically engaged with a wide variety of esoteric concepts, gave us the depraved sorcerer Margrave in *A Strange Story*, a figure with a gothic heritage going back at least as far as the dark magus Vathek and his witch mother Carathis in William Beckford's *Vathek* (1786).

Such characters and the demonic rites they pursue were attractive to gothicists seeking to invoke sensual passions in their readers, particularly fear and terror.[90] This sensuality was pursued for a number of reasons, including the Romantic counter to Enlightenment rationalist and industrialist currents which, in a more nuanced modern form, centrally informed most aspects of Williams's fiction. Two other common motivations for the emotive invocation of the gothic seem to apply to Williams as well. First, gothic terror has sometimes been perceived to draw audiences closer to either the psychological or supernatural unknown, often conceived as an encounter with the sublime, following Edmund Burke's 1757 concept

---

89. David Stevens, *The Gothic Tradition* (Cambridge: Cambridge University Press, 2000), 9–10; Glen Cavaliero, *The Supernatural and English Fiction* (Oxford: Oxford University Press, 1995), 23; Glennis Byron and Dale Townshend, eds, *The Gothic World* (London: Routledge, 2014), xxxvi.

90. See Stevens, *Gothic Tradition*, 46, on this and other central characteristics of the gothic.

of an experience of astonishment, most easily provoked by fear, in which "the mind is so entirely filled with its object, that it cannot entertain any other, nor by consequence reason on that object which employs it."[91] Second, the monstrous figures that provoke these scenes—such as LeClerc and the sorcerers of *War in Heaven*—can be seen as manifestations of the buried fears of the unconscious—both of the individual mind of the author and of the collective cultural mind, as described by Julia Kristeva's psychoanalytic concept of abjection.[92] Kristeva proposes that we abject, or throw off, the ambiguous, contradictory aspects of our being that keep us from feeling like harmonized selves. We abject these aspects into uncanny forms, and though we do this out of an unconscious instinct for psychological self-preservation, we immediately fear the manifestations that we have created.[93] Esoteric phenomena are particularly useful in producing this abjected other—the magus and the witch, the kabbalist and the alchemist—constructed others of Western monotheism—*already existed* in an abjected state by the eighteenth century arrival of a specifically identifiable gothic mode.[94] It is no surprise then that the gothic would turn to such figures in order to reflect the repressed contradictions of the self and its wider communities.

Williams did not himself participate in these processes of abjection—his experience with occultism and embrace of esoteric

---

91. Edmund Burke, *A Philosophical Enquiry into the Origin of Our Ideas of the Sublime and the Beautiful* (London: Dodsley, 1764), 53–54. A number of critics have commented on the connections between the gothic and the production of Burke's sublime. See, e.g., Vijay Mishra, *The Gothic Sublime* (Albany: State University of New York Press, 1994), 17, 23, 25; Clive Bloom, "Introduction: Death's Own Backyard," in *Gothic Horror: A Reader's Guide from Poe to King and Beyond*, ed. Clive Bloom (London: Macmillan, 1998), 11; Stevens, *Gothic Tradition*, 46, 50–51.
92. See Jerrold E. Hogle, "Introduction: The Gothic in Western Culture," in *The Cambridge Companion to Gothic Fiction*, ed. Jerrold E. Hogle (Cambridge: Cambridge University Press, 2002), 3–4.
93. As described by Hogle ("The Gothic in Western Culture," 7). Cf. Julia Kristeva, *Powers of Horror: An Essay on Abjection*, trans. Leon S. Roudiez (New York: Columbia University Press, 1982), 4–6, 10.
94. On the abjection of religion see Kristeva, *Powers of Horror*, 17–18.

concepts removed him from such polemical perspectives. He did, however, take advantage of the gothic's long-standing reliance on abjected esoteric knowledge to paint images like the infinite hell of Lily Sammile's infernal shed or the dark rituals that assault Mornington and the Archdeacon, with the purpose of arousing the sublime through terror of the abjected (let us just call it abject terror). To an extent, as we will see in Chapter Six, such depictions represent a critique of self-absorbed magical perspectives in modern occultism, but characters like LeClerc, Dmitri and Sammile are rooted much less in personal experience than in this shared gothic/esoteric lineage of abjection. In his Commonplace Book Williams seems to refer to the process of achieving sublimity through abject terror as an encounter with the "grotesque," one of three ways "in which all things can be seen." Along with "vision"—which already possessed mystical dimensions for the author—the grotesque joins "lust" as a mode of perception that acts not just in a degraded fashion but "in, so to speak, a transcendent way."[95] This brief note is not expanded upon in his published writings but its ramifications echo through the pages of the last two novels and *War in Heaven*. Even *The Place of the Lion* carves from the macabre, particularly a scene in which a huge, paranormal snake oozes from the decaying body of the occultist who has identified with its supernal identity.[96] Such passages have the potential to create the "breathless and unexplainable dread of outer, unknown forces" of H.P. Lovecraft's "weird tale,"[97] a form closely entwined with the gothic mode.[98] Williams's Christian occult supernatural was unknown and dreadful, but it was also ultimately good. In the terms he placed in the mouth of Peter Stanhope, the divine was a "dreadful goodness" and nature is "'full of terror'"[99]—full, in

---

95. Commonplace Book, 110.
96. Williams, *Place of the Lion*, 116.
97. Burke, *The Sublime and the Beautiful*, 65–67.
98. On overlapping distinctions between gothic, horror and weird fiction, see Alex Murray, "'This Light Was Pale and Ghostly': Stewart Home, Horror and the Gothic Destruction of 'London,'" in *London Gothic: Place, Space and the Gothic Imagination*, ed. Lawrence Phillips and Anne Witchard (London: Continuum, 2010), 70–71.
99. Williams, *Descent into Hell*, 16–17.

Williams's immanent perspective, of the sublime presence of God. Though it resists associations with what is conventionally understood as religion, the gothic has, like the occult, joined other post-Enlightenment cultural modes in contributing to what Christopher Partridge calls a "significant sacralizing effect" in Western culture—a reinvigorated spirituality that skirts secularist and rationalist rejection of the sacred and supernatural by guising itself in imaginative and fantastic forms.[100] Williams aimed to effect precisely this invigoration when deploying gothicized images of dark sorcerers and the yawing maw of hell—"grotesque" images that could guide the reader to a vision of the divine through terror, because "This also is Thou."

IN THE NETWORK OF OCCULT FICTION

The gothicized esoteric deployed in Williams's fiction does not reflect his modern occult experiences, but it is indicative of a number of intertextual relationships visible in his work, many of which mediate occultist fictional influences. The gothic tradition was far from Williams's only source of narrative influence. His love of fiction began in childhood, with, among others, Jules Verne, Charles Dickens, Thomas Macaulay, Alexandre Dumas, Anthony Hope's *Prisoner of Zenda* (1894—the source of Williams's mythical kingdom of Silvania), Nathaniel Hawthorne, and the adventure stories of Max Pemberton.[101] He described the novels of May Sinclair as having "a quite unusual attraction" for him as a young man.[102] More specifically, his novels show signs of mediating the influence of earlier texts with esoteric elements: Glen Cavaliero suggests that Joris-Karl Huysman's classic Satanist fiction, *La-Bas* (*Down There*, 1891) may have informed

---

100. Partridge, *Re-Enchantment of the West*, 1:5. Cf. 1:4, 40, 69, 85. For a discussion of this sacralizing effect in relation to the ability of gothic terror to provide a "flawed vehicle to the transcendent," see Victoria Nelson, *Gothika* (London: Harvard University Press, 2012), 16.
101. George Robinson to Alice Mary Hadfield, CWSA II.A.4, p. 1; Lindop, *Charles Williams*, II, 14–15.
102. Williams, "Introduction," 8.

ESOTERICISM & NARRATIVE

Williams's meticulous descriptions of a black mass and other goetic rites in *War in Heaven*.[103] H. Rider Haggard is another potential influence, particularly on *Shadows of Ecstasy*, where Roger affects to quote from Haggard when greeting Inkamasi, the Zulu King. Haggard's Ayesha—a virtually immortal European exerting absolute power over a group of warlike Africans via magical power (*She*, 1886-87)—seems a likely prototype for Considine. Another likely literary source for Williams's portrayal of occultists is *Zanoni*, which, like Waite (and most other occultists) he quite admired.[104] Some of his known reading in adulthood seems to be mediated in similar fashion. We have seen that *Fu Manchu* was part of the motivation for writing *Shadows of Ecstasy*. Indeed, it is possible to see how Considine and his African army could have evolved from the ethereally powerful Manchu and his "yellow peril" over the course of eight years rewriting. Williams read Arthur Machen's *The Great God Pan* (1894), which has proved very popular in occult and neo-pagan circles, as part of the research for his Arthurian poetry epic. The discovery of the Holy Grail in a small Welsh village in Machen's "The Great Return" (1915) may have motivated *War in Heaven*'s similar device,[105] and more generally Williams may been influenced by Machen's conflation of a gothic mode with occult themes, also extracted from personal experience with masonic Rosicrucian ritual materials (in the I.R.R.). Some of the chilling gothic vastness of the last two novels—the feeling of a supernatural presence in the armchair facing—may have derived from Machen.

R.H. Benson's *The Necromancers* is another potential source for

---

103. Cavaliero, *The Supernatural and English Fiction*, 108.
104. *Poet of Theology*, 56. Williams refers to Bulwer-Lytton's concept of "the Guardian of the Threshold" as something heard "in old tales of magic" in *Descent into Hell* (70). It is uncertain whether he purposefully continues Bulwer-Lytton's mythologization of the concept, or had forgotten its actual origin, or if it had become so ubiquitous in occult circles that Williams truly thought it to be a more venerable part of the magical tradition.
105. As observed by Martin Moynihan in "Charles Williams and the Occult," paper presented to the Oxford C.S. Lewis Society, Oxford, 3 June 1986: transcript in CWSA II.B.199, 3.

some of the more ghoulish presentations of occultism.[106] Laurence Wentworth's obsession with a succubus form of Adela Hunt has something of significance in common with Benson's Laurie Baxter. Baxter is also tempted toward damnation by an evil spirit in the form of his beloved, in this case the illusory reflection of his dead fiancée; like Wentworth, it is Baxter himself who summons this demon (with the help of others present at a Spiritualist séance). Both Wentworth and Baxter are presented as harsh critiques of the act of projecting love and desire past living subjects in order to satisfy a selfish craving for what has been lost. Benson derides Baxter's spiritualist experiments with the pejorative "necromancy," a polemic Williams seems to emulate in his portrayal of Leclerc's necromantic attempts to infiltrate the supernatural. Where Benson is unabashedly critical, however, Williams occupies a much wider value range, balancing criticism with enthusiasm.[107]

Several critics have pointed out that Evelyn Underhill's *Column of Dust* seems to be a model for much of Williams's fiction;[108] indeed, Underhill's novel has many of the same preoccupations with the supernatural. Like Williams's characters, in the course of summoning a spirit or elemental into the material world, Underhill's heroine, Constance Tyrrel, "had found a little hole in the wall of appearance; and, peeping through, had caught a glimpse of that seething pot of spiritual forces whence, now and then, a bubble rises to the surface of things."[109] There are more specific commonalities as well: as in Machen's "The Great Return," the Holy Grail is discovered in a small country chapel,[110] and a model of relationship similar to Romantic Theology appears at several points, also specifically connected to

---

106. See Dodds, *Charles Williams*, 319.
107. Williams referenced Benson's novel as a source on necromancy in his Commonplace Book, 23.
108. Reilly, *Romantic Religion*, 9; Dodds, *Charles Williams*, 319; Heath-Stubbs, *Charles Williams*, 13; Cavaliero, *The Supernatural and English Fiction*, 108. Williams also read Underhill's *Mysticism* (1911) in preparation for his Arthurian cycle (Lindop, *Charles Williams*, 44).
109. Evelyn Underhill, *The Column of Dust* (London: Methuen, 1909), 32.
110. Ibid, 139.

Dante's Beatrician vision.[111] Underhill also shares Williams's tendency to stretch symbol and allegory to the point of didacticism, extolling various mystical virtues and concepts at the expense of narrative quality. Williams seems to have sensed this, as he criticized the novel for its failure to live up to its "possibilities of wit, terror, and sublimity. The wit is there," he drowsed critically, "But hardly the terror or sublimity."[112]

THE NOVELS OF AN ADEPTUS EXALTATUS

Whether Underhill accomplished the feat or not, Williams certainly seems to have taken the same narrative task on himself, though his talents tended more to sublimity than wit. The novels do frequently attempt the latter, particularly via literary puns and allusions, but it is an encounter with the chill and wonder of the supernatural that Williams seems to have been more anxious to offer his readers. In addition to the grotesque of gothic terror, he deployed the other two ways "in which all things can be seen": "Lust," as the initial stage of Romantic Theological attainment, is an important ingredient, though the novels do not spend much time on romance. More pressing is the "vision" of the transcendent—the means of accessing the fleeting moment of mystic oneness that was the aim of F.R.C. initiation. It is toward this goal that Williams directed most of the modern occult theory, symbolism and practice referenced in the novels. He enfolded the esoteric knowledge of the Secret Tradition—particularly that derived from kabbalah, alchemy and ritual magic—into his fiction for the same reason that Waite included it in the ritual elements of his Rosicrucian order: as a ladder up which the mystic could clamber to attainment, taxonomically structured with the symbolism of the ten sephiroth. Much of this esoteric imagery reflects the historically specific adaptations of the modern occult milieu, and a good portion of this shows signs of being directly derived from the F.R.C. Problem-

---

111. Ibid, 158, 302.
112. Williams, "Introduction," 10.

atically, some of this material is deployed in a manner that all but another F.R.C. adept would have had difficulty contextualizing. To some degree this was the point—as we have seen, such obscure imagery lent to a quasi-surrealist symbolic method that Williams hoped would offer a glimpse of the ineffable, reflective of the paradoxical expression of the inexpressible which Gunn sees as the driver behind occult innovation. Williams was thus a real-life manifestation of Glyndon, the aspiring adept of *Zanoni*, also written by a Rosicrucian (allegedly) author exploring esoteric concepts via the narrative and philosophical flexibility of the fantastic. Glyndon refracts the spiritual fascinations of his creator—and anticipates those of Williams—when he appears in the novel's preface as an aged Rosicrucian sage who has written *Zanoni* as a true account of higher Rosicrucian knowledge, shrouded by a veil of fiction: "a truth for those who can comprehend it, and an extravagance for those who cannot."[113]

However productive such obscurity might have seemed for authors like Williams and Bulwer-Lytton though, in the former's case it has likely been a major factor in his novels' lack of broad appeal. Francis King could not state the case better when he describes Waite's "heterodox version" of the Golden Dawn system as "the key without which the deepest and inmost meaningfulness of Williams can never be unlocked."[114] As Thomas Willard notes, this is a key that has eluded even the most attentive readers.[115] Williams's audience cannot possibly expect to glimpse his meaning from hermeneutical horizons that do not include F.R.C. experience, or, usually, even basic knowledge of esoteric thought systems. Several critics have noted

---

113. Edward Bulwer-Lytton. *Zanoni: A Rosicrucian Tale* (1842; repr., Blauvelt, NY: Rudolf Steiner, 1971), 14. The evidence for Bulwer-Lytton's Rosicrucian involvement is scant, but he claimed to be an initiate of an unknown "Rosicrucian Brotherhood." See Edward Bulwer-Lytton to Hargrave Jennings, 2 July 1870, in Victor Bulwer-Lytton, *The Life of Edward Bulwer, First Lord Lytton*, 2 vols. (London: Macmillan, 1913), 2:41–42. Regardless of the extent of his Rosicrucianism, he certainly shared Williams's serious interest in the esoteric traditions.
114. King, *Ritual Magic in England*, 112.
115. Willard, "Acts of the Companions," 278.

important relationships between the rituals of the F.R.C. and particular symbols, themes and plots in his work,[116] but much more needs to be done. The rest of this book analyzes occult elements of Williams's fiction in depth; in many cases we will see that the F.R.C. acted as a central mediator for his discovery and interpretation of esoteric knowledge. At this point, however, I would like to examine several aspects of his fiction which are directly related to the specific ritual experiences Williams encountered on his journey to the state of Adeptus Exaltatus.

At several points Williams uses his fiction to comment on the very nature of ritual experience itself. At certain junctures he treats ritual experience with appreciation for its hieratic potential, but there are also corresponding critiques of occult societies. *The Place of the Lion* offers a satirical portrayal of occultists not ready to confront the supernatural immensity of the powers they invoke. Berringer, the occultist who draws the angelical principles into rural England, is the leader of a small occult study group that conducts mysterious meetings on a monthly basis. The extent of the group's activities is never made clear, but their main focus is on Berringer's theory of "thought-forms"—images of divine principles that can be "moulded" through meditation.[117] The novel's tone is not critical of these experiments in and of themselves, but the majority of Berringer's followers are presented, in Damaris's terms, as "absurd creatures" practicing a "fantastic religion."[118] Though they have worked to "shape" the divine thought-forms—to invoke them, in other words, for the purposes of personal magical power—when the "ideas, energies, realities, whatever you like to call them" actually do break into the world, the

---

116. Lindop has shown how *The Masque and the Manuscript*, a 1926 play written for performance at Oxford Publishing House, is linked to the ritual death of the F.R.C. initiate in Waite's Adeptus Major ritual (*Charles Williams*, 134–35). Gavin Ashenden has made some interesting connections between "The Ceremony of Consecration on the Threshold of Sacred Mystery," a rarely performed ritual which Williams only experienced once, and symbolism used in *Shadows of Ecstasy* and *Many Dimensions* (Ashenden, *Charles Williams*, 34–39).
117. See Williams, *Place of the Lion*, 23, 29.
118. Ibid, 20.

occultists are powerless to control them.[119] Gathered to hear a lecture from Damaris, they run from the room when they hear the ghostly hiss of an actual divine principle manifesting in the room as a great serpent.[120] This suggestion that many occultists lack the personal strength to deal with the cosmic energies they seek to control is found again in *Shadows of Ecstasy*. Mottreux, the Judas of Considine's disciples, cannot control his lust for some jewels in Considine's care and kills him as a result. After their leader's death, the rest of the group is torn apart, motivated by the material distractions of greed, fear and revenge. Roger quickly rejects the idea of continuing association with them, though he acknowledges that he would gladly continue to pursue the mysteries if Considine were to return.[121]

Their disciples are failures, but the characterization of Berringer and Considine is more ambiguous. They represent a more approving stance toward esoteric groups, specifically an approbation of the power of the hierophant to connect the worlds of spirit and matter through the magic of ritual. Both men take the role Williams would have observed in Waite as Imperator of the F.R.C., or taken himself during his three stints as Master of the Temple. Berringer has named his house *The Joinings*, clearly indicating his intent "to try and see the world of principles from which this world comes,"[122] a goal that fits with Williams's own occult intentions. Foster, one of Berringer's followers, describes him in terms of a Holy Assembly adept—as a Guide of Paths able to direct others to mystical awareness of the otherworld: "I know that this man was able sometimes to see into that world, and contemplate the awful and terrible things within it, feeding his soul on such visions; and he could even help others towards seeing it, as he has done me on occasions."[123]

Considine takes on a hieratic role when Roger, Philip and Sir Bernard visit his home for dinner. After the meal, he conducts his

---

119. Ibid, 28.
120. Ibid, 33.
121. Williams, *Shadows of Ecstasy*, 216.
122. Williams, *Place of the Lion*, 53.
123. Ibid, 53–54.

guests into a long high room divided by a curtain of a deep, vivid sapphire-blue. Williams's description of the space summons to mind the image of a temple—a sacred space from any religion perhaps, but with a veil reminiscent of the Hebrew Holy of Holies. Behind the curtain of this inner sanctum there are musicians playing a haunting melody that triggers a mystical encounter in all but the rationalist Bernard—Roger's consciousness is altered via contemplation of Milton's poetry, Philip's through physical adoration of the lines and curves of Rosamond's body. When the music stops and the two men have returned from reverie, Roger envisions Considine as an idealized master of occult ritual. Though he wears an ordinary dinner jacket, the sapphire drapes behind transform him into

> a figure in hieratic dress, motionless, expectant, attentive, having power to give or to withhold...His hands were by his sides, his head was a little thrown back, his eyes were withdrawn as if he meditated, and behind him the vast azure hung as if it were a cloak some attendant had but that moment removed and still held spread out before he folded it.

For Roger, Considine's charismatic immensity has the power to transform perception: "Imagination made itself visible before him and overwhelmed him with its epiphany."[124] As discussed further in Chapter Five, this elevation of imagination, seen as a visionary power that could elevate consciousness via interaction with image and symbol, was a central goal of occult societies like the Golden Dawn and the F.R.C. The descriptions of Considine here and in the following scene, wherein his disciple Nielsen seeks his approval to commit suicide in an attempt to defeat death,[125] likely owe much to Williams's own hieratic experiences in the F.R.C.

Considine does not conduct Roger and Philip beyond the temple veil to encourage their mystical illuminations, but in *The Greater*

---

124. Williams, *Shadows of Ecstasy*, 81.
125. Ibid, 84–85.

Trumps the characters frequently pass through the curtains veiling the dancing figurines in their sacred chamber. Here we find some of the most vivid suggestions of the power of ritual to energize the imagination and sacralize the mundane. Nancy has entered the chamber before, but when she does so with Henry, holding the trumps of the tarot and walking with magical intent, she "felt the difference; what had on the previous night been a visit of curiosity, of interest, was now a more important thing. It was a deliberate repetition, an act of intention, however small; but it was also something more." Repetition and intention distinguish ritual from ordinary action; this, combined with her interaction with the symbols of the tarot, evokes an experience radically different from her previous entry into the temple of the figurines. This experience is Romantic Theological: "By her return, and her return with Henry, she was inviting a union between the mystery of her love and the mystery of the dance. As she stood, again gazing at it [the dance], she felt suddenly a premonition of that union, or of the heart of it."[126] As with Philip's experience in Considine's drawing room, the ritual environment and the symbols it contains help Nancy realize the connections between her love for Henry and the possibility of mystical attainment. Williams presents this as an act of inward discovery: "It must be in herself that the union must be, in a discovery of some new state...there was no other place nor other means, whatever outward change took place. All that she did could but more deeply reveal her to herself."[127]

Here Williams displays an understanding of mystical attainment common in modern occultism—the reunion of a lower self bound to materiality with a higher form within, sometimes of divine nature. The idea of the division of the psyche or soul into a lower entity and a higher form that exists in constant unity with the divine was not new to modern occultism. It can be found in Christian mysticism at least as far back as Meister Eckhart,[128] with roots in Christian concepts of

---

126. Williams, *Greater Trumps*, 93.
127. Ibid.
128. Like Williams (and Waite) Eckhart posited that God and the soul are always already one, and the divine aspect of the soul simply awaits discovery within. His

theōsis (divinitization/deification) based on Pauline theology, and in kabbalah beginning with its Jewish origins in twelfth-century Iberia.[129] These concepts can be compared to the older Hindu notion of the *atman*, the universal self held to be in eternal correspondence with the divine *Brahman*.[130] These various strands, particularly the Christian and kabbalistic heritages, are visible in the Golden Dawn and the F.R.C., in both of which union with the higher self was the highest aim. Moina Mathers, wife of Samuel MacGregor and also a leader in the Golden Dawn, described the higher self as equivalent to "the Christ that *can* be within,"[131] presaging a prayer of adepts in the F.R.C.'s Adeptus Minor ritual: "Through all the grades of the Christ-hood, give unto us the realisation of the union, that we may attain that self which is in Thee."[132] Given the importance of union with the higher self in the Golden Dawn, it is no surprise to find similar language in the R.R. et A.C.'s Adeptus Minor ritual: "In Thee I am

---

Christian mysticism was much less affirmative, however, as for Eckhart, like the majority of Christian mystics dating back to the patristic period, the task of the mystic was to empty oneself of material distractions through perfect self-annihilation in order to be able to understand this oneness. See Cohn-Sherbok and Cohn-Sherbok, *Jewish and Christian Mysticism*, 111–12; Robert K.C. Forman, *The Innate Capacity: Mysticism, Psychology and Philosophy* (New York: Oxford University Press, 1998), 9.

129. On theōsis, see Stephen Finlay and Vladimir Kharlamov, "Introduction," in *Theosis: Deification in Christian Theology*, ed. Stephen Finlan and Vladimir Kharlamov (Cambridge: James Clarke, 2006), 1–8. Kabbalah divided the soul into several parts, including an earthly soul or self and a higher *neschamah* or, in the later philosophy of Isaac Luria, *jechidah*. See Scholem, *Kabbalah*, 157.

130. As with most forms of esoteric knowledge, modern occultism saw a variety of adaptations of the higher self concept. The term "higher self" seems to have gained popularity as a result of its use by Madame Blavatsky. See, e.g., *Studies in Occultism* (London: Sphere, 1974), 12. Cf. Marco Pasi, "The Varieties of Magical Experience: Aleister Crowley's Views on Occult Practice," *Magic, Ritual, and Witchcraft* 6, no. 2 (Winter 2011): 152. The experience was alternately known as union with or awareness of the "Divine Genius," "Higher Genius," or "the Holy Guardian Angel." See Pasi, "Varieties of Magical Experience," 52, 147; Bogdan, *Western Esotericism*, 143–44. For a general summary of the concept of the higher self in the esoteric traditions, see Hammer, *Claiming Knowledge*, 55.

131. Moina Mathers (as Vestigia Nulla Retrorsum), "Know Thyself," in *Astral Projection, Ritual Magic, and Alchemy: Golden Dawn Material by S.L. Macgregor Mathers and Others*, ed. Francis King (Rochester, VT: Destiny, 1987), 152.

132. Waite, "Adeptus Minor," 27.

Self," says the postulant in prayerful pose, "And exist in Thy Selfhood from Nothing. Live Thou in me, and bring me unto that Self which is in Thee. Amen."[133]

"THE END OF DESIRE"—
THE DISCOVERY OF THE HIGHER SELF

The F.R.C. rituals connect the discovery of "the higher self which is in Thee" to a concept called "the end of desire."[134] "Behold," says the initiate at the conclusion of the Adeptus Minor ceremony, "I am that which I sought, and the end of my desire is with me."[135] This characterization of attainment as the end of desire represents the belief that desire will be unnecessary once the initiate realizes that all longed-for objects have been a part of the self all along. Specifically, the ultimate target of desire, the divine mind, has been in the human mind; divine awareness in human consciousness.[136] It is this end that Chloe achieves when she experiences unity with the stone of Suleiman. Williams refers to "the end of desire" in several novels, but never so clearly as in *Many Dimensions*, where he frequently uses the phrase to allude to mystic union.[137] "The End of Desire," says the Hajji, the Sufi

---

133. Regardie, *Complete Golden Dawn*, 7:40.
134. Waite, "Portal of the Fourth Order," 15.
135. Waite, "Adeptus Major," 60. Cf. Waite, "Portal of the Fourth Order," 31–32.
136. Waite often described the union of higher and lower selves as a coming together of mind or consciousness: "The Mind of God is our own Mind in the God-state...There is no other source of knowledge" (Waite, *Shadows*, 239). See *Shadows*, 237 for a more detailed discussion of the concept.
137. Williams, *Many Dimensions*, 42–45, 95, 102, 115, 129, 262. Williams enjoyed applying the same type of multivalence he gave to symbols to words and phrases. Here, the term "end of desire" clearly connects to the F.R.C. rituals, but was likely derived from other literary and philosophical sources as well. Oneness with God and nature was frequently understood as the consummation of erotic desire by the Romantics. Williams would certainly have encountered, for example, Blake's "The Question Answer'd": "What is it men in women do require?/ The lineaments of Gratified Desire." (See Irving Singer, *Courtly and Romantic*, vol. 2, *The Nature of Love* (Cambridge, MA: MIT Press, 2009), 283–95, for a full elaboration of Romantic eros and mystic fulfilment). Williams may also have been familiar, as Waite certainly was, with Louis Claude de Saint-Martin's concept of *l'homme de désir* ("man of desire" or "man of aspiration"). The man of desire is he who is so possessed of a soul that aspires for God that he

guardian of the stone, is both what the stone offers to those who seek it, and what it is in itself (43). In his typical illusive fashion, Williams is no clearer than this in the novel about the meaning of the phrase, but here the word "end" signifies both the goal of desire and the cessation or fulfilment of it. The former meaning has important ramifications for Romantic Theology: Chloe and Arglay, like many male/female duos in Williams's novels, guide each other toward a realization of the unity of all things in God (represented by the stone of Suleiman) and the potential for the self to realize this unity as well. In this sense, the end, or purpose, of desire—often physical—is mystic union.[138] Chloe's desire for the divine principle within the stone effects the second meaning of the phrase—the cessation of desire—achieved in the mystic state of awareness of the primordial oneness of self, nature and divine. Having aligned her will to the divine will of the stone, its divided types flow back to the archetypal original that Chloe holds in her hands (260). In her desire to understand and serve the stone, Chloe has become identical to it. Thus, when the stone has achieved union with itself, she too experiences attainment. With typical multivalence, Williams describes this as both union with the stone—representative of higher divine principles—and union within. Lord Arglay sees Chloe standing "her in herself"—a reference to the lower, material self discovering the higher self within. After she provides a path for the stone to return to its supernatural point of origin, the attained Chloe is described as "clothed in the beauty of the End of Desire" (262). Williams thus connects the F.R.C.'s occult formulation of the discovery of the higher self to the Platonic concept that lies at its root: the ability to contem-

---

is able to discover the spark of divinity that still remains within the self from its prelapsarian state of full unity with the divine. My thanks to Wouter Hanegraaff for pointing out this connection. For a brief summary of Saint-Martin's concept see Arthur McCalla, "Saint-Martin," in *Dictionary of Gnosis and Western Esotericism*, ed. Wouter J. Hanegraaff (Leiden: Brill, 2006), 1027.

138. The relationship between Chloe and Arglay is not primarily physical, though there are hints of sexual tension between the two characters (see, e.g. Williams, *Many Dimensions*, 250). For Chloe's recognition that the end of her desires lies beyond physicality see p. 51. Cf. Gauntlett, "Charles Williams, Love & Shekinah," 19.

plate "the divine beauty itself, in its unique form" through the desire aroused by "obvious beauties" such as those of the human body.[139]

The end of desire and the higher self come together again in *Shadows of Ecstasy*, where a series of existential discussions between Roger and Considine on poetry and magic culminate in an experience that makes further conversation unnecessary. Considine is in the midst of describing the history and praxis of his transmutation of body and consciousness when Roger suddenly cries out, "And the end...what is the end?"[140] Considine answers only by turning to his disciple and looking deep into his eyes. This hypnotic gaze thrusts Roger into reverie, a vision of drowning and then emerging exultant from a great sea. Before this alchemical baptism can occur, however, Roger must discover the divinity within himself. He hears again a line from Milton that had accompanied his mystical experience in Considine's drawing room: "And thus the Filial Godhead answering spake."[141] In this earlier event the line had echoed internally as Roger reflected on the meaning of a portion of the Godhead that is filial, or subordinate, to another higher aspect. In doing so, he realized *himself* as the filial Godhead—"it was he that answering spake" (79). Now, cast into reverie by Considine and recalling the line from Milton and the realization of his higher self that went with it, Roger is thrust into the sea, representative of complete knowledge of God and the unity of all things: "Could a man's body be always...infiltrated with this sea, he might always know!" Now it is the sea who utters Milton, and hearing it Roger becomes one with the water, "ocean calling to ocean," and rejoices in "an ecstasy that controlled itself in great tidal breaths."[142]

---

139. Plato, *Symposium*, 211c–11e. In the same way, Chloe "sees the beautiful through that which makes it visible" (ibid, 212a). Plato's concept also clearly underpins Romantic Theology, though any number of intermediary sources may stand between Williams and *The Symposium*.
140. Williams, *Shadows of Ecstasy*, 203.
141. Ibid, 203. Cf. *Paradise Lost*, 6.722.
142. Williams, *Shadows of Ecstasy*, 205. The sea has a great number of potential allusive points, but here too the F.R.C. context may be at work. After achieving the grade of Practicus, the initiate was instructed that in the "Secret Church in the heart" the light

Just as Williams learned in the F.R.C., however, Roger cannot immerse himself in the sea of mystical experience for long. Considine pulls him from his reverie: "It may be known and believed," he tells Roger, "It can't be lived thus. But it can be found and lived" (206). Williams would have have heard similar words in the course of the F.R.C.'s "Ritual of Return in Light," where he was told that the soul of the adept goes up through paths and sephiroth "even unto Daath" but "does not cross the threshold, save only in intimations of vision" and "comes back therefrom because of its mission to the world."[143] Considine thus plays the role of F.R.C. Imperator for Roger, first providing the appropriate ritual atmosphere and leadership in his drawing room, then casting him into further reverie with his hierophantic gaze, and finally showing him the path of return to a life that is mundane but enriched by attainment. In all three cases, Roger's achievement is expressed in the terms encountered by his creator's occult ritual experience in the F.R.C.

Williams expands on the end of desire and higher self concepts in two other novels, adding layers of meaning to their original occult context. The climactic scenes of *War in Heaven* add a third possible interpretation of the end of desire—an inverted understanding that associates mystical and magical activity with an utter nihilism in which desire—and therefore the very quest for mystic union with the divine centre itself—cannot exist. The Greek sorcerer Dmitri's motivation in trying to destroy the Graal is simply to hasten the conclusion of things to their end, at which point Gregory Persimmons and Manasseh, his partners in trying to obtain the Graal, will realize "what the end of desire and destruction is" (145). He invokes the term only to suggest that there is nothing beyond this end but the void; the end of desire is annihilation. For his partner Persimmons, however,

---

of the supernal sephiroth is "sphered in the Waters of Understanding, the Great Sea of Binah" (Waite, "Practicus," 39). Seen in this context, Roger's mystical experience is at its height when this supernal light is discovered within himself, in the complete intuitive understanding of God that is represented by Binah.

143. Arthur Edward Waite, "The Ritual of Return in Light" (Amsterdam: Bibliotheca Philosophica Hermetica, A.E. Waite Collection, 1924), 8.

the end is much like it was for the adepts of the F.R.C., though aimed at a different locus of divinity. He seeks "a rapture of iniquity"—union with a dark force suggestive of Satan (168). Though Gregory embraces Dmitri's magical power and knowledge, he senses that the Greek's abyssal translation of the "end of desire" is a perversion of his own. He feels himself hanging "above the everlasting void" as he watches Dmitri murder Kenneth Mornington with black magic, and recoils from it: "Was this the end of victory and lordship and the Sabbath, and this the consummation of the promises and of desire?" (217; we can read "consummation" and "end" as equivalent here). Gregory's doubt that this could be the end he seeks is exploited by the Archdeacon Davenant in the midst of the three magicians' attack on him and the Graal. Davenant senses Gregory's weakening resolve in the face of the void and responds by presenting himself to Persimmons's spirit as a source of salvation, again invoking the metaphysical satiation of the end of desire: "The Archdeacon presented himself to that spirit...as a means whereby the satisfaction of all desire might meet it."[144] The attack on the Archdeacon is a failure and serves only to summon Prester John, the power that guards the Graal. Prester John offers the same redemptive end to Gregory as the Archdeacon, announcing that if he can sacrifice himself as he has attempted to sacrifice others, "there shall be agreement with you also in the end, for you have sought me and no other."[145] Persimmons responds by giving himself up to the police for a recently committed murder, a first step toward the redirection of his desire and the achievement he has been seeking. Both Gregory's quest and Dmitri's anti-quest are significant reinterpretations of the F.R.C.'s understanding of the end of desire, but both illuminate its essential principles in a manner consistent with the calling of a Fourth Order adept. Dmitri's nihilism provides a foil to the affirmative mysticism of occult ritual, while

---

144. Williams, *War in Heaven*, 241.
145. Ibid, 246. For a lengthy discussion of the ambiguities of Gregory's character and his surprise redemption, see Ashenden, *Charles Williams*, 104–14.

Gregory's quest for an experience of dark rapture echoes that of the F.R.C. initiate, despite his illusion of seeking a different goal.

A similar expansion occurs in *Descent into Hell*, this time with the higher self. Williams plays with the concept in order to create an opposition between two ethereal forms of the self that appear to Pauline Anstruther—a shadowy doppelgänger produced by fear, and a supernal ideal that replaces the doppelgänger once she has moved past her fear with the help of Stanhope, sacrificing her own well-being to take on the fear of the spirit of her ancestor. The higher self that faces Pauline once this action is complete is identical to the girl's earthly appearance but it is an "immortality,"[146] a manifestation of her divine self. Here too, mystical ecstasy is the tie that brings together Pauline's "original" and its earth-bound "translation" (171). This ecstasy, however, is produced by a different process than in the earlier novels, where mystical experience is usually derived from ritual, poetry, or contemplation. Pauline's experience of her higher self recalls Prester John's instruction to Persimmons to seek self-sacrifice, as she attains union within herself via the substitution of herself for another. This reinterpretation of the higher self concept thus reflects Williams's shift in emphasis towards coinherence in his later years.

The examples of Chloe, Roger, Gregory and Pauline indicate that Williams did not rely only on image and symbol to communicate the nature of mystical experience. He has often been criticized for failing to create convincing personas. The accusation of an early biographer in the *Bookman*—"his characters are inverted robots, utterly thoughtful and entirely inhuman"—has been frequently repeated, particularly regarding his characterization of women.[147] Indeed, his

---

146. Williams, *Descent into Hell*, 171. For other interpretations of the nature of Pauline's supernal self, see Newman, "Companions of the Co-Inherence," 12; Medcalf, "Athanasian Principle," 39–40. These authors discuss the Platonic and Christian mystical influences on Williams's formation of Pauline's higher ideal, influences which also, as we have seen, informed the occultist conception of the higher self.

147. Eustace Portugal, "Charles Williams," *Bookman*, March 1932, 314. For later examples, see Rayner Heppenstall, "Books in General," *New Statesman and Nation*, 21 May

FICTION AND EXPERIENCE

characters are often formulaic and superficial, particularly those who are most ideal; Chloe Burnett, Sybil Coningsby, the Archdeacon and Peter Stanhope leave one longing for at least a minor vice that might add realism. But, as Gunnar Urang observes, Williams's characters are not primarily intended to be rounded representatives of real human personality[148]—they are ultimately constructed for the purposes of allegory, usually in order to present various viewpoints, as seen in the array of responses to the invasive supernatural. In the case of characters who experience the end of desire in the discovery of the higher self, Williams embeds his own F.R.C. experiences into the fabric of their development. In learning of themselves as the sea and the stone, Roger and Chloe represent Williams's own discovery of existential kinship with nature and the divine; Pauline's encounter with her "original" mirrors Williams's later connection between the discovery of the higher self and coinherent self-sacrifice. Even Gregory, though he journeys to the divine via paths of goetic magic, murder and cruelty, reflects the desire for union with which F.R.C. adepts were expected to approach their own experiences. These characters thus serve a dual function: they allowed Williams to explore his own occult experiences through the production of fiction and, more importantly for his Adeptus Exaltatus role, they act, like the F.R.C.'s Guide of Paths, as narrative role models for readers seeking their own mystical attainment.

OCCULT FICTION, OCCULT LIFE

These examples of occult mystical concepts that made their way, with varying degrees of translation, from the F.R.C. into the novels, support the likelihood that Williams's Adeptus Exaltatus responsibilities were part of his motivation for writing fiction. We cannot be sure what degree of mystical attainment he actually achieved, though T.S.

1949, 532; Hadfield, *Introduction to Charles Williams*, 82; Cavaliero, *Poet of Theology*, 161–62.
148. Urang, *Shadows of Heaven*, 71. Cf. Dodds, *Charles Williams*, 320.

Eliot spoke of "states of consciousness of a mystical kind" that Williams "knew, and could put into words."[149] His novels indicate that he at least possessed a heritage of image, symbol and experience from which he could imagine the process of illumination, and the frequency of his depiction of mystical attainment reinforces the likelihood that he had at least some personal experiences in which he felt himself to have achieved elevated states of consciousness that brought him closer to awareness of the aspect of the divine within. His deployment of the higher self and end of desire concepts shows that he felt it important, in his Adeptus Exaltatus role, to semiotically express the way to such experience in the generative, paradoxical encounter of ineffability and description. Understanding the Fourth Order priorities that Williams likely had on his mind during the writing of his fantastic fiction allows a more comprehensive view of the motivation behind the themes, symbols and characterization in his work. The reader is able to access the significance of Chloe's mystic quest, or sense the subversive metaphysical twist behind the redemption of Gregory Persimmons, without being previously aware of concepts such as the end of desire, let alone its F.R.C. context. However, the examples above indicate that knowledge of the occult ritual experiences that Williams encountered in the F.R.C. can add rich layers of interpretation to our analysis of his work, especially if this context is understood in relation to the F.R.C.'s Golden Dawn heritage and, partly by extension, its connection to the wider modern occult milieu.

As a fiction writer, Williams was, as one reviewer noted, "on a plane all his own,"[150] but this reciprocal marriage of life and fantasy was not unique to him. It can be found in a number of other fantasy authors of the day, many of them also involved with occultism. Indeed, modern esoteric activity was itself so layered with elements drawn from the fantastic or in dialogue with its modes, tropes, and

---

149. Eliot, preface to *All Hallows' Eve*, xvii.
150. Richard McLaughlin, "Chasing the Grail in England," review of *War in Heaven*, by Charles Williams, *Saturday Review*, 1 October 1949, 16.

images, that SF/fantasy writer Brian Stableford has called the zeitgeist of figures like Blavatsky and Crowley "lifestyle fantasy."[151] This term captures the occultist urge to enchant the mundane by adding layers of myth and flair to daily life—the late Victorian and Edwardian version of twenty-first century cosplay. Samuel Mathers adopted the Highland name MacGregor and often used the aristocratic title of "Comte de Glenstrae," claiming an ancestral link to Ian MacGregor of Glenstrae—a Jacobite aristocrat—that likely had little genealogical substance.[152] We could simply dismiss such actions as forms of nomenclatural class struggle, but they are more than simply "tartan-hued pretensions."[153] Mathers's attempt to claim Scottish aristocracy emerged from his fascination with Celtic myth, as well as his tendency to infuse fantastic elements of pomp and hierarchy, including those discovered in his masonic and occult activities, into the course of everyday life. W.B. Yeats, who got to know Mathers during the course of a decade together in the Golden Dawn, felt that his enormous capacity for imagination made him a living exhibition of the Romantic movement, a "necessary extravagance" to whose incredible claims people reacted not with incredulity but knowing acceptance. Mathers was a character in a living mythology, a "figure in a play of our composition."[154] Yeats himself is well known for developing multiple personas based on his concept of the "mask," a purposefully developed alternate personality that he believed could help him become closer to his higher self, which he saw as something antithetical to the personality of the lower self. To overcome this binary, Yeats constructed mask identities in opposition to each other, hoping to overcome the divide between lower and higher selves through dialectical antinomy. Lifestyle fantasy characters like "Michael Robartes," an occult scholar and dreamer, and the Irish

---

151. Brian M. Stableford, *Historical Dictionary of Fantasy Literature* (Lanham, MD: Scarecrow Press, 2005), xxiv.
152. Howe, *The Magicians of the Golden Dawn*, 38–39. Aleister Crowley followed Mathers in adopting pseudo-aristocratic titles and assuming Scottish aristocratic heritage.
153. Ibid, 39.
154. W.B. Yeats, *Autobiographies* (London: Bracken, 1995), 187.

Nationalist "Owen Aherne," a man of action, served this antinomial purpose, as well as providing an antidote for the passivity he felt was encouraged by the modernist doctrine of "sincerity and self-realisation."[155]

Williams took a less purposeful but similar approach to lifestyle fantasy. His immersion in Silvania extended into adulthood, especially within the context of the Arthurian legends. In one of his last master-servant relationships with young women, for example, he took on the persona of Taliesin, the Arthurian bard, while Lois Lang-Sims alternated between roles of princess, schoolgirl and, most of all, the slave girl "Lalage." We have seen that Phyllis Jones received similar mythical treatment. She was "Celia," "Phillida," and "Circassia," while he played the role of her master Urban, "Ambassador to the Imperial and Urbane Government,"[156] apparently exacting small physical punishments when Jones did not satisfy the requirements of her "August Lord."[157] This love for lived fantasy extended well beyond his private romantic relationships. The masonic Rosicrucian temple of the F.R.C. offered a lived experience of fantastical enchantment: In addition to engagement with a plethora of images and symbols derived from bygone eras and exotic cultures, adepts had opportunity to act out an antique ritual posture while enacting roles such as Master of the Temple—positions which also granted a sense of hierarchical presence not available in ordinary life. A further incidence of lifestyle fantasy is also a clear indication of the close relationship between Williams's life and fiction. Writing a pageant for the Diocese of Chelmsford in 1939, he insisted on doing so as Peter Stanhope. He lived the life of *Descent into Hell*'s playwright hero throughout the writing and enactment of *Judgement at Chelmsford*,

---

155. *Per Amica Silentia Lunae* (London: MacMillan, 1918), 34–35. For more of Yeats on the mask concept see ibid, 34; *Autobiographies*, 469. Cf. Ellmann, *Yeats*, 75–77; Ronsley, *Yeats's Autobiography*, 78–82.
156. Phyllis Jones to Charles Williams, 10 January 1927, quoted in Lindop, *Charles Williams*, 138.
157. Phyllis Jones to Charles Williams, 1927, quoted in Lindop, *Charles Williams*, 139. Cf. 138–40.

even insisting that any correspondence be sent to Peter Stanhope care of Charles Williams at Oxford Publishing House.[158]

Williams thus reflected an occultist tendency for lifestyle fantasy, a fictionalization of the "real" often carried out, as in the case of Yeats, with the intention of accessing a higher real. In Williams's case this current flowed both ways—as his life was lived in fiction, so his fiction emerged from his life, often with very little to mitigate its transposition. This too was common among modern occultists, many of whom turned to fiction to share their alternative spiritualities. Dion Fortune wrote her own philosophy of therapeutic occult psychology into four occult novels, also infusing her passion for pagan concepts such as the Great Goddess.[159] A collection of occult detective fiction, *The Secrets of Doctor Taverner* (1926), is based on her psychological experiences under the mentorship of Dr. Theodore Moriarty,[160] who seems to be the basis for Taverner—skilled esoteric psycho-healer by day, powerful occult adept by night. The Taverner stories will seem quite unbelievable to most readers—at best they will encounter the hesitation of the fantastic. Fortune, however, claimed that they were not only written from experience, but also "toned down to make them fit for print."[161] Edward Bulwer-Lytton is an important precursor to occult fiction writers like Fortune and Williams. His interest in magic, Rosicrucianism, mesmerism, geomancy and astrology informed his authorship of novels like *Zanoni* and *A Strange Story* and went on to influence the belief systems of occultists from Blavatsky to Williams himself—an impact via fiction that leads Joscelyn Godwin to call him the most important figure of Victorian occultism.[162] Algernon Blackwood, a member of both the Golden Dawn and Waite's I.R.R., frequently explored occult

---

158. Ibid, 285–86.
159. Susan Johnston Graf, "The Occult Novels of Dion Fortune," *Journal of Gender Studies* 16, no. 1 (March 2007): 47–48.
160. See Butler, "Dion Fortune and the Society of the Inner Light," 316.
161. Dion Fortune, *The Secrets of Doctor Taverner* (Wellingborough, Northamptonshire: The Aquarian Press, 1989), 10.
162. Godwin, *Theosophical Enlightenment*, 128.

concepts in novels such as *The Human Chord* (1910), *The Promise of Air* (1918), and *The Bright Messenger* (1921). Blackwood was secretive about his involvement in numerous occult groups, which included the Theosophical Society, the Golden Dawn, and the Quest Society. As Susan Johnston Graf has observed, the only way to acquire some of the details of Blackwood's occult encounters—or understand the metaphysics that emerged from these experiences—is through his fiction, which, like that of Williams, frequently espouses or condemns concepts that closely coincide with the occult systems with which he was involved.[163] These are just a few examples from a long list of esoteric thinkers and practitioners who have mixed life and fiction to explore esoteric knowledge and experience. As they have done so, they have created new symbols, practices and archetypal characters that occultists or other followers of alternative spiritual traditions could use to construct their syncretic belief systems.

Even Waite, likely one of the primary intellectual influences for many of the occultist fiction writers above, attempted to share his belief system via narrative, releasing two collections of faerie stories: *Prince Starbeam* (1879) and *The Golden Stairs* (1893). As in so many other areas of Charles Williams's spiritual and mythopoeic life, therefore, Waite may also have influenced his initiate's turn to fiction as a vehicle for expressing the inexpressible. Waite was a passionate reader, collector and even erstwhile writer of penny dreadfuls—the often formulaic pulp novels that brought fiction to all levels of Victorian society.[164] He wrote two early volumes of criticism in which he studied and catalogued Victorian pulp stories, and thus represents an early, if not the earliest, example of a critic found insisting on the historical value of the penny dreadful in the study of literature and culture.[165] This critical interaction had important personal elements

---

163. Graf, *Talking to the Gods*, 81.
164. See Gilbert, *A.E. Waite*, 26–30.
165. As argued by Gilbert and, more substantially, by Christine Ferguson. See Gilbert, *A.E. Waite*, 28; Christine Ferguson, "Reading with the Occultists: Arthur Machen, A.E. Waite, and the Ecstasies of Popular Fiction," *Journal of Victorian Culture* (2016): 5–9.

as well. Waite notes in his autobiography that he may not ever have become interested in occultism had not popular fiction developed his taste for romantic enchantment in boyhood.[166] Both Gilbert and Christine Ferguson have shown that this movement from fiction into esoteric practice constituted a permanent entanglement of fantasy and spiritual quest—as Waite grew more advanced in his roles of occult mystic and esoteric scholar, he gained a greater and greater appreciation for the ability of fiction to instigate mystical experience.[167]

Given this appreciation, it is possible that Waite himself played a role in encouraging Williams to carry out his Fourth Order responsibilities through fiction. While there seem to have been a number of motivations behind Williams's 1925 decision to take up fiction, his induction into Waite's Holy Assembly likely played an important role. As a newly initiated Adeptus Exaltatus, he turned to the very esoteric symbolism which had provoked his ritual experiences in order to communicate them. As shown by his projection of F.R.C. concepts such as the end of desire and the higher self into his novels, there is meaningful, experiential purpose behind his deployment of occult symbolism and concepts. Esoteric images and ideas, many of them the specific product of modern occultism, do not merely decorate the walls of his fiction—they erect them. The remainder of this book will focus on Williams's fictional application of kabbalah, magic and alchemy, three rich, complex traditions that were central to his philosophy and the occult elements of his lifestyle fantasy. As with all the other literary, religious, and historical narratives that he employed in his novels, Williams did not intend all allusions to these esoteric traditions to complement his serious exploration of belief and experience. A magician might be a gothic anti-hero like LeClerc or a coinherent adept like Stanhope; the Philosophers' Stone functions as a playful reference in one moment, and a symbol of the

---

Waite's research on penny dreadfuls can be found in "By-Ways of Periodical Literature" (1887), and "Dealings in Bibliomania" (1904).
166. Waite, *Shadows*, 36.
167. Ferguson, "Reading with the Occultists," 7–8. Gilbert, *A.E. Waite*, 90.

cosmic unity of divine and nature in another. Differentiating between play and seriousness, accident and intention, can be difficult. Caution is required when drawing connections between Williams's life, fiction and proselytic attempts to communicate knowledge of coinherence and the mystic path. In many cases, however, the context of Williams's background and heterodox theology, combined with provably relevant occult concepts—especially those of A.E. Waite—provides enough of a guiding framework for productive analysis of the deployment of occult phenomena in his fiction. With the combined literary/historical method with which I have approached the shared phenomena of Williams's life and fiction, we can better understand the meaning and intent of his obscure esoteric references —alllusions and signifiers that seem independently mysterious but become clearer when viewed as part of a greater tradition.

CHAPTER 4

KABBALAH

CHARLES WILLIAMS
AND THE MIDDLE PILLAR

The mystic images of kabbalah were essential to Charles Williams's perception of the universe and his expression of its structure. Kabbalah informed his Romantic Theology, provided the symbolism that underpinned the programmatic array of the F.R.C.'s ritual environment, and aesthetically enriched the variegated landscape of his fiction and, as Roma A. King has shown in detail, his poetry.[1] The extent to which kabbalah informed his thought is indicated by his frequent reliance on its symbolism in his letters. The Tree of Life, in particular, provided a poetic geometry with which he frequently organized thoughts or facts. This might take the form of matching elements of a person's personality to various aspects of the sephiroth, as he did in a letter to Joan Wallis, with whom he carried on one of his longest sadomasochistic relationships. Williams matched the lower half of the sephirotic tree with five names he had given her, with her real name attributed to Malkuth,

---

1. *Pattern in the Web*, 15–16. King's analysis of the kabbalistic background of Williams's poetry is valuable, but kabbalah is treated as a monolithic tradition, rather than a historically variable current in which Williams was situated in a particular place and time, and subject to specific cultural influences.

the sephira considered most reflective of material existence.[2] In a letter to Anne Ridler he used a kabbalistic hermeneutic to assess the spiritual maturation of the Earl of Rochester (about whom he was writing a biography). He was a man, said Williams, reflecting the map of his own internal development in the F.R.C., who he doubted "had reached Tiphereth, or even Netzach—though perhaps he had dimly mounted to Yesod."[3] In another letter Williams told a friend that it had become clearer to him, following a performance of *Judgement at Chelmsford*, that "the whole thing represents the Sephirotic Tree."[4] In an unpublished summary of the play, Williams reveals this structure, with central characters made symbolically equivalent to the left and right pillars of the Tree, and "Chelmsford," the personification of the diocese of Chelmsford, ascending to "full perfection" via the middle way between the two pillars.[5] Such projections of sephirotic symbolism into mundanity indicate that kabbalah was not simply attractive to Williams as window dressing for his poetry and fiction, but was integrated into the very fabric of his perceptual and communicative self, an entwining that was the result not just of intellectual and aesthetic exposure to kabbalah, but many evenings spent imagining mystical ascension through the sephirotic limbs of the Tree of Life in the ritual setting of the F.R.C.

He acquired kabbalistic knowledge from Waite outside the F.R.C. as well. Ridler notes that though it was his reading of *The Hidden Church of the Holy Graal* that led Williams to make contact with Waite, it was *The Secret Doctrine in Israel* that interested him the most.[6] No doubt Williams would have been particularly attracted to Waite's somewhat anachronistic accentuation of kabbalah's focus on

---

2. Charles Williams to Joan Wallis, 4 October 1940, quoted in Lindop, *Charles Williams*, 335.
3. Charles Williams to Anne Bradby (Ridler), 9 November 1934, quoted in Lindop, *Charles Williams*, 243.
4. Charles Williams to Phyllis M. Potter, 8 August 1939, Bodleian, Ms Res. c.58/1, f.4.
5. Charles Williams, outline of *Judgement of Chelmsford*, Bodleian Ms. Res. c.58/2, f.1. Cf. Lindop, *Charles Williams*, 294. For an additional example, in which Williams matches two coworkers to the left and right pillars of the Tree, see ibid, 126.
6. Ridler, introduction to *Image of the City*, xxv.

the correspondence between divine and human male-female relationships—the philosophical *sine qua non* of Romantic Theology.[7] Waite was not the only source available, however. He seems to have consulted an entry on "Cabala" in the 1902 edition of *The Jewish Encyclopedia*,[8] and also read Westcott's translation of the late antique *Sepher Yetzirah*, which provided foundational concepts for the later development of kabbalah. He would likely also have extensively discussed the subject during his bi-weekly meetings with Lee and Nicholson, absorbing the distinctly modern adaptations of kabbalah to which they were exposed as members of the Stella Matutina. Another influence came much earlier on in life—in 1931 Williams told a professor at Duke University that he had been exposed to Jewish religious thought in his youth: "My father had a very strong feeling for the Jewish tradition—and to some extent he passed this on to me."[9]

The "Jewish tradition" as a whole is much more extensive than kabbalah itself. While kabbalists often claim that their tradition is at least as old as Moses, the first historically distinguishable kabbalists can be traced to twelfth century France and Spain, with important centres appearing first in Provence, then in Castile and Catalonia. The Zohar, by far the most important kabbalistic text, was either written or compiled in Gerona in the late thirteenth century, likely by a group of authors/compilers who pseudopigraphically presented the text as the written teachings of Simeon bar Yochai, a famous second-century rabbi.[10] There are important precedents to the influential

---

7. The connection between the two is evaluated by Gavin Ashenden. See *Charles Williams*, 40–55.
8. Williams notes that he consulted volume 3 of 12, where God is described as "the negation of all negation" (Commonplace Book, 170). This is consistent with the Encyclopedia's "Cabala" entry.
9. Charles Williams to Lewis Chase, 23 July 1931, quoted in Lindop, *Charles Williams*, 191.
10. See Ada Rapoport-Albert and Theodore Kwasman, "Late Aramaic: The Literary and Linguistic Context of the Zohar," *Aramaic Studies* 4, no. 1 (2006): 6–7, for a review of the history of the writing of the Zoharic literature, and Boaz Huss, "Translations of the Zohar: Historical Contexts and Ideological Frameworks," *Correspondences* 4 (2016): 81–128, for the fascinating history of its translation and adaptation in a number of different

Iberian kabbalah, such as the *Sefer Yetzirah*, which first introduced the concept of the sephiroth, but the Jewish scholars in Iberia and Provence significantly altered the ideas of this earlier text, expanding the ten aspects of God to a seemingly infinite variety of symbolic and metaphysical systems.[11]

At its core, kabbalah simply means "that which has been received." It denotes an esoteric body of wisdom said to have been given to Moses on Sinai and communicated since then through secret, oral channels and beneath the surface layers of the text of the Torah, intended by Moses to contain both an immediately apparent exterior meaning and an interior, esoteric meaning that must be deciphered by the kabbalist. "Kabbalah" thus refers more to a particular origin and form of knowledge transmission than a specific body of dogma.[12] The term has evolved, however, to indicate a particular spiritual tradition that is rooted in Jewish mysticism but has developed over time in a number of other cultural contexts, particularly in early modern Christian Europe and among Western alternative religious groups in the last century and a half. While many kabbalists claim an *a priori* basis for their tradition,[13] most historians emphasize that no such perennial current of kabbalah exists; rather, the tradition exhibits notable cultural and philosophical diversity.[14] There are, however, particular phenomena that tend to mark diverse strands of belief as "kabbalistic," including the concepts of Ain Soph, the ten

---

cultural and linguistic settings. Many sources are available on the history, beliefs and practices of kabbalah. Some of the most authoritative available in English are Scholem, *Kabbalah*; *Major Trends in Jewish Mysticism*, 3rd ed. (New York: Schocken, 1974); Dan, *Kabbalah*; Moshe Idel, *New Perspectives in Kabbalah* (London: Yale University Press, 1988).

11. Dan, *Kabbalah*, 16–17.

12. Ibid, 2.

13. Some kabbalists have claimed to access secret knowledge in an intuitive, visionary manner, direct from the divine source. Waite himself posits this as a possibility. For most kabbalistic thinkers, however, the chain of knowledge extending from Moses is a more vital source (Dan, *Kabbalah*, 3).

14. See, e.g., Dan, *Kabbalah*, ix–x; Scholem, *Kabbalah*, 87; Hava Tirosh-Samuelson, "Gender in Jewish Mysticism," in *Jewish Mysticism and Kabbalah: New Insights and Scholarship*, ed. Frederick E. Greenspahn (New York: New York University Press, 2011), 222.

sephiroth, and the Shekinah, the female aspect of God manifest in the material world. Even these concepts however, are not completely ubiquitous and have seen a variety of interpretations over the centuries.[15]

A.E. WAITE AND MODERN OCCULT KABBALAH

Waite's application of kabbalistic concepts was as unique as any other. He did not, of course, see his interpretation as subjectively defined or historically situated, though he did frequently portray kabbalah as historically and culturally diverse in his scholarly works. He believed, however, that most kabbalistic interpretations formed after the thirteenth-century Zoharic period were lesser, erroneous forms of the original, and that he alone among modern kabbalistic thinkers had been able to reappropriate these concepts for students of kabbalah in his own time. Even more significantly for understanding the kabbalah of Charles Williams, Waite believed that he, as a member of the Holy Assembly, had identified the key elements in Zoharic kabbalah that best reflected the perennial wisdom of the Secret Tradition. It was this set of symbols and concepts that Williams encountered in his F.R.C. ritual experience, and found so attractive in *The Secret Doctrine in Israel*. This was not, however, the purely Zoharic kabbalah that Waite claimed. His adapations had much in common with other modern occult developments, despite his protestations to the contrary—framed along the lines of his usual anti-occult polemics. As I will discuss in this chapter, much of the kabbalistic content of Williams's novels is predicated on—or at least congruent with—Waite's interpretations of concepts including the middle path on the sephirotic tree, the link established by occultists between sephirotic symbolism and the tarot, and a correspondence of divine and human eros, which Waite called the "mystery of sex." It is

---

15. See Dan, *Kabbalah*, 5–8, 41. Dan gives precedence to the sephiroth as the most specifically identifiable kabbalistic concept, though even this is not a completely reliable signifier.

important therefore, to take a moment to situate Waite's approach to kabbalah in its modern occult context, in order to get a sense for how Williams's kabbalah is connected—intellectually, experientially and intertextually—to the modern occult network.[16]

In his three books on kabbalah Waite scolded occultists,[17] particularly Lévi and Mathers, for relying on later translations of the Zoharic literature, such as the limited number of texts available in the *Kabbala Denudata* (1684) of Christian Knorr von Rosenroth,[18] rather than going back to the true source of the doctrine.[19] Those who relied on Mathers's influential *The Kabbalah Unveiled* (1887), a partial translation of Rosenroth's work into English, received an even harsher scolding.[20] The result, Waite believed, of occultist reliance on sources too far removed from the Zoharic font, was that they were "disposed to accept everything indiscriminately as part of the genuine tradition."[21] Waite's complaint was not without substance. Occultists in the period had little access to original sources and often had to rely on truncated translations like Mathers's as they interpreted various

---

16. In *Ritual Magic in England*, Francis King states that he completed a lengthy analysis of the influence of Williams's experience with the system of kabbalistic imagery developed in the Golden Dawn and passed through Waite (in what King feels to be a degenerated form) to the F.R.C. (King, *Ritual Magic in England*, 112). Such an analysis is sorely needed, but regrettably King either does not seem to have completed this research or was not able to find a suitable publisher, as no such publication seems to exist.
17. *The Doctrine and Literature of the Kabalah* (1902); *The Secret Doctrine in Israel* (1913); *The Holy Kabbalah* (1929). *Shadows of Life and Thought* (1938) also contains passages important for understanding Waite's view of kabbalah.
18. Some of these are from the Zoharic era, while some are later interpretations of disciples of Rabbi Isaac Luria of Safed (1534–72) (Allison P. Coudert, "Christian Kabbalah," in *Jewish Mysticism and Kabbalah: New Insights and Scholarship*, ed. Frederick E. Greenspahn (New York: New York University Press, 2011), 165).
19. E.g. Waite, *Holy Kabbalah*, 423; *Doctrine and Literature of the Kabalah*, xviii, 358; *Shadows*, 96–99. On the impact of the *Kabbala Denudata* in modern occultism see Asprem, "Kabbalah Recreata," 145.
20. Mathers's publication contained three books/units of the Zohar, translated into English through the Latin prism of von Rosenroth: "The Book of Concealed Mystery," "The Greater Holy Assembly," and "The Lesser Holy Assembly."
21. *Doctrine and Literature of the Kabalah*, xiv.

esoteric systems.[22] Moreover, their interpretive approach could be radically all encompassing. The modern approach to kabbalah was typified by programmatic syncretism: as Waite noted, occultists aligned kabbalah with the Chaldean Oracles, Zoroastrianism, the Druids, Norse myth, ancient Egypt, and even, as seen in the writings of Blavatsky and other Theosophists, with ancient wisdom produced in the Far East.[23] Occult kabbalah was thus, said an aggravated Waite, almost completely ahistorical. Worse, once plucked from its specific historical context, kabbalah was frequently elevated to the status of the universal source of all other religions.[24] Waite holds Lévi responsible for this "inauguration of a new epoch"[25] in which kabbalah is considered to be "a religion behind all religions," a master key without which other spiritual systems could not be intelligibly interpreted, particularly in the case of Christianity.[26] Unsurprisingly, Waite also criticized occultists for overemphasizing the importance of practical magic in Jewish mysticism, which he also felt to be the result of unfamiliarity with the actual Zohar. He stated that occultists were only interested in kabbalah for its finite value—for its observa-

---

22. Egil Asprem, "Contemporary Ritual Magic," in *The Occult World*, ed. Christopher H. Partridge (Abingdon: Routledge, 2014), 386.
23. *Doctrine and Literature of the Kabalah*, 125. On Blavatsky's orientalization of kabbalah see *Isis Unveiled*, vol. 2, 212–250, especially 215, 219, 236, 245. Cf. Marco Pasi, "Oriental Kabbalah and the Parting of East and West in the Early Theosophical Society," in *Kabbalah and Modernity: Interpretations, Transformations, Adaptations*, ed. Boaz Huss, Marco Pasi, and Kocku von Stuckrad (Leiden: Brill, 2010), 158.
24. Among a number of figures, Waite criticizes Blavatsky for this approach *(Doctrine and Literature of the Kabalah*, 434; *Holy Kabbalah*, 520), as well as Mathers *(Doctrine and Literature of the Kabalah*, 307, 358; *Holy Kabbalah*, 423; *Shadows*, 96–99), and Lévi *(Doctrine and Literature of the Kabalah*, 179, 398, 401; *Holy Kabbalah*, 488, 491).
25. *Holy Kabbalah* reads "the invention of a new and gratuitous phase" (493).
26. Waite, *Doctrine and Literature of the Kabalah*, 407. For Lévi on the universality of kabbalah see *The Book of Splendours* (Wellingborough, Northamptonshire: Aquarian Press, 1983), 29. The complexity of Waite's actual stance towards modern occult kabbalah is revealed via comparison of this passage, written no later than 1898, with a passage from *Studies in Mysticism*, published in 1906. Here Waite states that concepts were drawn into kabbalah "from various sources, and chiefly from Egypt and Assyria," contradicting his usual emphasis on the Hebrew provenance of kabbalah (Waite, *Studies in Mysticism*, 258).

tions on physiognomy, numerology, astrology and magic[27]—and thus produced a "debased Kabbalism" that was "not even a reflection" of the "authentic Tradition of Israel."[28]

Waite's adaptations of kabbalistic concepts certainly lacked the purposeful application to magical practice seen in the Golden Dawn, where the symbols of the Tree of Life were involved in methods to increase personal magical power, such as the Middle Pillar ritual discussed further below. However, the F.R.C.'s use of sephirotic symbolism for visualization and meditation had, as I will argue in Chapter Five, lingering elements of magical praxis. Moreover, his aspersions against the universalism and ahistorical syncretism of occultist kabbalah ring hollow when we consider that his Secret Tradition had similar epistemological foundations. At the same time that Waite scolded modern occultists for reinterpreting kabbalah to suit their own interests, he himself prioritized interpretations that best suited pre-existing Secret Tradition concepts and rejected everything else. Ironically, much of this differentiation from traditional Jewish kabbalah may have derived from the fact that Waite himself probably did not read any more of the Zohar than other occultists before 1906, after which time he read a French translation by Jean de Pauly that was quite unreliable because translated with a bias toward discovering Christian mystical concepts in the Zoharic texts.[29] Prior to this point, though he finished *The Doctrine and Literature of the Kabalah* in 1898 and published it in 1902, Waite could not have read the Zohar in the original, as he did not read Aramaic, which makes up the majority of its corpus, or Hebrew, also found in its pages.[30]

---

27. *Doctrine and Literature of the Kabalah*, 149–50.
28. *Holy Kabbalah*, 9; Waite, *Secret Tradition in Alchemy*, appendix II, "Kabalistic Alchemy."
29. As Waite himself admitted (*Holy Kabbalah*, 8n1).
30. Waite says in his autobiography that he learned Latin and Greek in his teens, but never mentions acquiring Aramaic and Hebrew (*Shadows*, 42). Despite the fact that Waite frequently cites the Zohar in his books, Gershom Scholem assumes that he was compelled to rely on de Pauly's translation "owing to his own ignorance of Hebrew and Aramaic" (Scholem, *Major Trends*, 208). As we have seen, however, Waite must have used other Latin, French or English sources as well.

Thus, though he managed to form a view of kabbalah through alternate sources that was good enough to be commended by Gershom Scholem,[31] a prestigious scholar of Jewish mysticism, Waite could be just as prone to misinterpretations and reformulations of the "original" kabbalah as any other occultist in the modern period; his approach mirrored the very ahistoricism and syncretism that he so often criticized.

The very concept of a Secret Tradition has much in common with the occult approach to kabbalah. We have seen that Waite's system followed the programmatic syncretism of most modern occult systems, anachronistically reapplying material from a variety of traditions in order to reveal a hidden, perennial truth behind them. An important part of Waite's construction (or, in his mind, discovery) of the elements of the Secret Tradition involved disembedding kabbalistic phenomena from various contexts and reinventing, reinterpreting and reapplying them according to the dictates of his personal mystical priorities. There are a number of key examples of this disembedding, particularly, as I will discuss shortly, in relation to the symbolism of Shekinah and the sephiroth. Most of these adaptations are the result of his growing conviction that the Zohar directly communicated knowledge intended for the achievement of mystical attainment. Scholars including Gershom Scholem and Joseph Dan have argued that a concept of mystic union similar to that found in Christian mysticism did not exist in Zoharic kabbalah. While such ideas can be found in the thought of Abraham Abulafia (1240–ca.1291) and in Hasidism, the concept has been rare in kabbalah until modern times.[32] Waite himself did not express support for a kabbalistic

---

31. Scholem, *Major Trends*, 208. Overall, Scholem's view of Waite was ambivalent. In *Major Trends* (1941) he complimented only *The Secret Doctrine in Israel*, judging the earlier *Doctrine and Literature of the Kabalah* as of "little value" (212n25). Earlier he had published a review critical of *The Holy Kabbalah* (*Orientalistische Literaturzeitung* 7 (1931): 633–38), while a note on scholarship in *Kabbalah* concluded that Waite's works were "essentially rather confused compilations made from secondhand sources" (Scholem, *Kabbalah*, 203).

32. Scholem, *Kabbalah*, 160; Dan, *Kabbalah*, 8. A significant number of other scholars take Waite's view, including Moshe Idel (*Enchanted Chains: Techniques and Rituals in*

concept of mystic union in *The Doctrine and Literature of the Kabalah*. He was much more enthusiastic about the idea, however, in *The Secret Doctrine in Israel*, which aims more at mystical exploration than scholarship,[33] and *The Holy Kabbalah*, which largely synthesizes the two previous books.[34] This change was likely affected, at least in part, from reading the Zohar through the Christian mystical lens of de Pauly's translation.[35]

This is, however, a relatively minor wavering of Waite's Zoharic compass in comparison to his wholehearted embrace of the Golden Dawn's revolutionary adaptations of sephirotic symbolism. We have seen that the F.R.C. followed its parent order in organizing its grade system around the Tree of Life, and used this structure to syncretize symbolism from a variety of different esoteric traditions, including alchemy and the tarot. Other associations that had already been made by early kabbalists were maintained—such as the alignment of numbers and Hebrew letters to particular sephiroth, in addition to other symbols and aspects of nature, including the planets, astrolog-

---

Jewish Mysticism (Los Angeles: Cherub Press, 2005), 3–4, 6–11, 19–26, 34–35, 64–69; *New Perspectives in Kabbalah*, 59–73) and Arthur Green, though even they admit, like Green, that to speak in terms of direct experience of God in the Zohar "was considered far beyond the bounds of propriety" (*Introduction to the Zohar: Pritzker Edition*, trans. Daniel C. Matt, vol. 1 (Stanford: Stanford University Press, 2004), lxvi).

33. See *Secret Doctrine in Israel*, vi–vii.

34. *Secret Doctrine in Israel*, 231; *Holy Kabbalah*, 375. Passages from Waite's 1902 publication are revised in *The Holy Kabbalah* to reflect Waite's later emphasis on the mystic potential offered by kabbalah. As with *The Doctrine and Literature of the Kabalah*, however, *The Holy Kabbalah* is presented as a "critical study of Jewish Kabbalah" (511), though Waite also states in his introductions that he is primarily concerned with drawing the spiritual elements of the Secret Tradition out of kabbalah, rather than focusing on exegesis or historical analysis, apparently without feeling these two research goals to be contradictory.

35. As argued by Scholem, *Major Trends*, 212. De Pauly's translation is unlikely to have been the only factor in this shift, however. Arthur Green argues the opposite, stating that Waite was actually motivated to publish *The Secret Doctrine in Israel* in order to "provide a counterweight" to de Pauly's Christianized translation (Arthur Green, "Shekhinah, the Virgin Mary, and the Song of Songs: Reflections on a Kabbalistic Symbol in Its Historical Context," *AJS Review* 26 (2002): 38n146). Most importantly, we have no way of knowing how much Waite's shift in emphasis is simply due to the fact that de Pauly's work provided him with an opportunity to read more of the Zohar, translation flaws or no.

ical signs, and the elements.[36] The antiquity of these ideas has led Liz Greene, one of the only scholars to analyse Waite's kabbalah in any detail, to conclude that he and other modern occultists largely recreated the essential doctrines of the Jewish schools.[37] The Golden Dawn, however, with Waite in its wake, followed Lévi in taking such associations to new heights, thus instigating what Bogdan calls a "new trend in Western esotericism," one that came to so thoroughly define modern occultism that present day practitioners are unaware that many elements of their kabbalistic practice would be unrecognizable to a kabbalist in Zohar-era thirteenth-century Spain.[38] Waite, like so many kabbalists before him, whether Jewish, Christian, occultist or a productive blend of these traditions, created his own unique form of kabbalah, one that had specifically modern esoteric characteristics, particularly in its application through ritual.

BECOMING SHEKINAH:
CHARLES WILLIAMS AND THE MIDDLE PILLAR

As noted already in my review of Williams's known F.R.C. experiences, the primary symbolic function of the sephiroth in Waite's order, as in the Golden Dawn before it, was to provide a visionary ladder on which initiates could imaginatively project themselves in the achievement of "successive states and stages of the soul which goes to God"[39]—the quest for a level of consciousness equivalent to a coming to awareness of the divine, higher self. A similar imaginative

---

36. See Dan, *Kabbalah*, 45, on the many symbolic associations applied to the sephiroth in early kabbalah.
37. See Greene, *Magi and Maggidim*, 308–22. Other analyses of Waite's kabbalah include Hanegraaff, *Esotericism and the Academy* (248–52) and J.H. Laenen, *Jewish Mysticism*, 266), both of whom conclude, in Laenen's words, that Waite based himself "rather uncritically" on modern occult sources such as Lévi. However, this conclusion goes too far the other way—while occult influences had an enormous impact on Waite, he rejected a number of popular occult concepts and embraced other kabbalistic notions, such as the Shekinah, in which other modern occultists showed little interest.
38. Bogdan, *Western Esotericism*, 122–23. Cf. Hanegraaff, "The Beginnings of Occultist Kabbalah," 108–09; Asprem, "Kabbalah Recreata," 133.
39. Waite, "Adeptus Major," 35.

engagement with the Tree of Life was seen in later Jewish mystical movements, including the important sixteenth-century school in Safed, the seventeenth-century messianism of Sabbatai Zevi, and Hasidism.[40] In the Zoharic literature to which Waite attributed the Secret Tradition legitimacy of kabbalah, however, the narrative of ascent is largely absent from the concern of the living mystic.[41] Waite's enthusiasm for the guidance offered by sephirotic geometry to those seeking mystical attainment was thus based not in the Zohar but in later kabbalistic interpretations, particularly those discovered in the Golden Dawn.

One such sephirotic symbol was the "middle pillar," a straight line seen to begin with Malkuth at the bottom of the Tree and ascend in progressive levels of consciousness and experience through Yesod, Tiphereth, Daath and Kether.[42] Initiates of both the Golden Dawn and F.R.C. visualized themselves ascending the Tree of Life in a zigzag pattern from sephira to sephira, in line with the pattern of initiation from grade to grade, but the middle pillar offered a straight path to attainment, particularly for the F.R.C. initiate.[43] The Golden Dawn differed from the F.R.C. in that it saw the middle pillar as a visualization tool that could be used to draw down power from its divine source in Ain Soph in order to effect a wide variety of magical purposes (particularly in later manifestations of the order such as the Stella Matutina).[44] However, the pillar was a two way street. It could also be used "as a map for man's return to his soul's source."[45] In the Golden Dawn's "Ritual for Spiritual Development," for example, the adept performed a ritual known as the middle pillar technique and

---

40. See Idel, *Enchanted Chains*, 47–51.
41. See ibid, 57.
42. See Figure 1.
43. See *Holy Kabbalah*, 201–02, for Waite's scholarship on the middle pillar.
44. For the Golden Dawn materials on the middle pillar see Regardie, *Golden Dawn*, 1:90, 179–82. Cf. Hanegraaff, "How Magic Survived," 369; *Guide for the Perplexed*, 110, 116.
45. Howe, *Magicians of the Golden Dawn*, xii. Waite also saw the middle pillar as multi-directional, describing it as the path on which "great influences come down" ("Neophyte," 39), but he disapproved of manipulating this divine power for the purposes of practical magic.

KABBALAH

then begged God to enable the archangel Metatron to bring "the 'Divine influx'" to the base of the pillar "to rend away the veils of darkness from my mortal vision" to enable "attainment to the eternal Glory."[46] The F.R.C.'s purpose was similar: for Waite, the middle pillar, which he also refers to as the "middle way," the "middle path," and the "*linea media*," represented a straight path to mystic union. As in the Golden Dawn the pillar is described as a path for the elevation of mind and consciousness: "The way of the soul's ascent...[is] one of ascent in mind...realisation of mind in God, consciousness in the supernal part of mind."[47] The discovery of the divine self within is thus an elevation of the human mind to a level at which it can attain direct gnosis via equivalency with the divine mind: "Mind explores itself and reaches thus a so-called Higher Mind."[48] There is a long-standing tradition in kabbalah of the ascent of the souls of the deceased via a cosmic pillar to paradise,[49] but as with other sephirotic formulations in the F.R.C. rituals, the portrayal of the middle pillar as a ladder for the living mystic is quite removed from Zoharic conceptions.[50] It is therefore yet another example of the tension between Waite's arch insistence on adhering only to Zoharic kabbalah and the actuality of his practice, which was typified by the modern occult tendency for symbolic disembedding and specifically influenced by the Golden Dawn's middle pillar concepts.

Both orders also dwelled on the importance of the middle pillar as a site of balance between the pillars of Mercy and Severity.[51] Moina Mathers applied this to the equilibrium that must be sought within the self, cautioning junior adepts that before making any big

---

46. Regardie, *Golden Dawn*, 3:248, 252, 259; Cf. Owen, *Place of Enchantment*, 77.
47. Waite, "Portal of the Fourth Order," 39.
48. Waite, *Shadows*, 238. Cf. Waite, "Portal of the Fourth Order," 39.
49. See Idel, *Ascensions*, 101–42.
50. See Idel, *Ascensions*, 57, 101, 120, on the post mortem nature of median pillar ascensions in Iberian Kabbalah.
51. As Mathers noted, the search for equilibrium is "a fundamental qabalistical idea" not limited to occultist kabbalah (*Kabbala Denudata: The Kabbalah Unveiled* (London: Kegan, 1926), 14). On the equilibrium between Mercy and Severity see Idel, *Enchanted Chains*, 50; Scholem, *Kabbalah*, 109; Greene, *Magi and Magiddim*, 63–65.

decisions or actions, let alone judging those of others, they should try to unite with the higher self, standing with their heads under the crown of Kether in the middle pillar, not leaning too far toward either Mercy or Severity lest they become unbalanced.[52] Union with the higher self also required finding equilibrium between opposing cosmic principles in the F.R.C.: "Between the Thrones of the East and the Altar are the two Pillars... They are symbols of Light and Darkness, Active and Passive, Mercy and Severity, Male and Female, the pairs of opposites in all things, ever seeking equilibrium, which is attained through union at the centre. Between them lies the Narrow Path of Ascent in the Spirit."[53] In a 1943 letter to Lois Lang-Sims, Williams includes a kabbalistic reference that indicates that concepts like the middle pillar were still central to his worldview sixteen years after leaving the F.R.C. He finishes the letter by wishing Lang-Sims the balance of the middle way: "In the Sephirotic tradition, the left side was Severity and the right was Mercy; together they were the Way of Benignity. So, be all things to you; so, all things in you."[54]

As in the Golden Dawn, two pillars visually flanked the middle way in the temples of the F.R.C. This symbolism indicates the orders' Freemasonic heritage, wherein similar pillars represented Boaz and Jachin, the pillars of Solomon's temple;[55] more importantly, however, they were syncretically linked to the left and right sides of the Tree of Life. In a number of rituals, an important figure could be found between the two pillars, known in the Neophyte and Zelator rituals as the "Guide of Paths" and in some of the higher rituals as the "Priestess of the Rite" or "High Priestess." This figure was considered the "Mediator and Reconciler" of the two opposing cosmic principles represented by the left and right pillars of Judgment/Severity and

---

52. Moina Mathers, "Know Thyself," 156–67. Cf. Bogdan, *Western Esotericism*, 143.
53. Waite, "Neophyte," 37. Waite draws on the Golden Dawn Neophyte ritual here. See Regardie, *Golden Dawn*, 6:19. Cf. Waite, "Portal to the Fourth Order," 43; "Neophyte," 16; *Secret Doctrine in Israel*, 35; *Holy Kabbalah*, 201.
54. Charles Williams to Lois Lang-Sims, 31 November 1943, in *Letters to Lalage*, 46.
55. Bogdan, *Western Esotericism*, 137.

Mercy.[56] Following the intellectual and philosophical urges prompted by a mixture of kabbalistic tradition,[57] occult convention and his own Secret Tradition priorities, Waite connected this physical manifestation of the middle pillar directly to another kabbalistic symbol that he highly valued—Shekinah.[58] As is usual with kabbalistic symbolism, the exact details of this myth vary, but the essential concept is that Shekinah once existed in a state of primordial union with the masculine aspect of God—often identified as Jehovah—but was cut off from him by a primordial catastrophe and thus exists, like man and nature, in a state of separation from the higher aspects of divinity. Shekinah is thus associated with Malkuth, the lowest of the ten sephiroth, though a higher feminine principle, connected to Binah, is said to remain in union with the masculine in the eternal realms represented by the supernal sephiroth. It is kabbalah that brought the understanding of Shekinah as female into Jewish tradition, but she predates twelfth-century Iberia, appearing in earlier texts as a principle of divinity immanent in the world.[59]

Shekinah is perhaps the most vital and frequently invoked symbol in the rituals of the F.R.C., particularly with reference to her quest for reunification with the masculine element of her divided self, a long-standing, cosmic drama that makes Odysseus's journey home to Penelope seem like a walk to the corner store. In this quest for unity, Shekinah served as a guide or model for the initiate. But she was not just a model for the mystic quest—because she was immanent in the material world she was also its *goal*. In this role, she

---

56. Waite, "Neophyte," 39. Cf. "Theoreticus," 12; "Neophyte," 22.

57. Waite was quite taken with the connection made between Shekinah and the middle pillar by kabbalists such as Joseph Gikatilla (1248–1305). See, e.g., *Gates of Light* (*Sha'are Orah*), trans. Avi Weinstein (London: Sage, 1994), 31–32, where Shekinah is discussed as a median of opposites of the left and right sides of the Tree of Life. Cf. Waite, "Zelator," 24; "Portal of the Fourth Order," 8; *Secret Doctrine in Israel*, 192, 196; *Holy Kabbalah*, 343.

58. For a brief review of the concept of Shekinah in kabbalah, see Dan, *Kabbalah*, 45–49. Scholem, *Major Trends*, 229–33; Green, "Shekinah"; Green, "Introduction," xlviii. For Waite on the subject, see *Secret Doctrine in Israel*, 190–234; *Holy Kabbalah*, 342, 351, 353.

59. Dan, *Kabbalah*, 46–47.

was the aspect of God to which adepts directed prayer and supplication.[60] Given that the F.R.C. was an initiatory society focused on ascending the sephiroth to mystical attainment, however, the "Guide of Paths" role was much the more important of these two. Said Waite: "The Divine Presence of Shekinah is still on this earth of ours, and the return journey by which all things are consummated in God is by and in union with her. She is the leader of the human race—or at least the elect therein—into the beatific state of *Atziluth*."[61] Already in the Neophyte ritual, the Guide of Paths is presented as one who can show the adept the "middle path [to] the return of the mind into union."[62] The Guide is clearly linked to the middle pillar in this ritual, but not to Shekinah, perhaps because Waite intended this symbolism to be revealed only to initiates in the rituals of higher grades, where the three are clearly linked.[63] Having achieved the grade of Philosophus, for example, the initiate learned that Shekinah's quest for reunion with the masculine presaged the symbolic mystical marriage that would take place in the Third Order. Anticipating the adept's ascension to the sephirotic level of Tiphereth at the Adeptus Minor grade, Williams as Master of the Temple would have described a similar trajectory for Shekinah. Assuming the sonorous tone of ritual, he would have framed the interior discovery of the higher self in terms of the grand unification of the divided God: "She has gone inward into the Christ-State, and the Beloved is hidden in the Lover."[64] Waite here followed a version of kabbalistic gender symbolism in which the reunion of the divided principles is symbolized by the marriage of Malkuth with Tiphereth.[65]

Williams would have informed the initiate that Shekinah would

---

60. Waite, "Adeptus Major," 10–11, 23.
61. *Secret Tradition in Alchemy*, 393. See Waite, "Philosophus," 30–32 for the F.R.C.'s clearest statement of its understanding of the symbolism of Shekinah and its importance to the mystic journey.
62. Waite, "Neophyte," 39. Cf. "Philosophus," 31; *Doctrine and Literature of the Kabalah*, 252; *Secret Doctrine in Israel*, 35, 255; *Holy Kabbalah*, 161–62, 394.
63. E.g. Waite, "Adeptus Exemptus," 8, 13, 27; "Portal of the Fourth Order," 8.
64. Waite, "Philosophus," 31.
65. See Tirosh-Samuelson, "Gender in Jewish Mysticism," 192.

no longer serve as Guide of Paths after the level of Tiphereth, given that both she and the adept who modelled her would have entered the wedded bliss of the Christ-state. This did not mean, however, that the adept actually lost Shekinah's guidance as they continued to ascend the Tree of Life. The symbolism of the mystic marriage would be repeated and emphasized in the Adeptus Major ritual: After the adept had experienced mystical death and symbolically risen from the tomb, a new manifestation of Shekinah also emerged from the tomb, now dubbed "Priestess of the Rite," and connected no longer to Malkuth but to Binah, the supernal feminine sephira that, together with the masculine Chokmah, usually represents permanent, unbroken divine unity in the kabbalistic tradition.[66] The Priestess reminded the adept that she had been his guide along the sephirotic pathways: "With you I have been in exile, O Brother, and with you I enter into liberation."[67] Shekinah continued her role as middle pillar guide in "The Ceremony of Reception in the Portal of the Fourth Order," this time as the High Priestess—a figure taken from the tarot who Waite also connects to Shekinah in the commentary to the Rider-Waite deck.[68] The stages of ascent up the middle pillar are visually displayed in the course of the ritual as the High Priestess walks in front of a procession with a banner marked with the sephirotic symbol of Daath, while lesser-ranked brethren walk behind with the banners of the lower sephiroth of Tiphereth, Yesod, and Malkuth: "In this manner," intones the Acting Usher of the Rite, "The Way of Ascent to the heights is exhibited."[69]

Waite derived the concept of Shekinah's guidance up the middle pillar from a central kabbalistic concern with correspondent erotic relationships between the divine masculine and feminine principles.

---

66. Ibid, 191–92.
67. Waite, "Adeptus Major," 45–46. The Priestess repeats this wisdom in the Adeptus Exemptus ritual: "With those who are in separation I dwell through many exiles, and with them I enter into union. I am that which attains and leads" ("Adeptus Exemptus," 46).
68. *The Pictorial Key to the Tarot; Being Fragments of a Secret Tradition under the Veil of Divination* (London: William Rider & Son, 1911), 13, 79.
69. Waite, "Portal of the Fourth Order," 34.

He termed this the "mystery of sex"—a "mystery of man and God" that explains the correspondence between the material world and the divine realm.[70] This commensuration of kabbalistic eros and mystical attainment was not common among Waite's occultist contemporaries. Lévi, Westcott and Mathers did not comment on Shekinah in their books on kabbalah, focusing largely on the Tree of Life and several related symbolic aspects.[71] Thus, though the sephirotic symbolism that permeates the F.R.C. rituals has a specifically modern occult origin, the erotic mysticism of the Shekinah narrative is closer to the Zoharic roots that Waite claimed for this Secret Tradition concept. However, while Waite builds on the vital structure of correspondent human and divine sexual love he found in the Zohar,[72] his Secret Tradition priorities led him to conflate kabbalistic eros with individual spiritual transformation in a manner more indicative of modern occult self-realization than kabbalistic tradition. The erotic mysticism of traditional Jewish kabbalah has important ramifications for human action: sexually moral and productive marriages can be maintained by mimicking the structure of the divine erotic relationship between masculine and feminine. Further, by following the

---

70. *Secret Doctrine in Israel*, 191, 226; *Holy Kabbalah*, 342, 370. For further scholarship on erotic symbolism in kabbalah, see Scholem, *Major Trends*, 225–29. On the division of the male and female principles, see Scholem, *Major Trends*, 23–31; Tirosh-Samuelson, "Gender in Jewish Mysticism," 197.

71. I refer to Lévi's Zoharic commentary, *Le Livre Des Splendours* (*The Book of Splendours*), Mathers's introduction to *The Kabbalah Unveiled*, and lectures given by Westcott to members of the Theosophical Society between 1888 and 1891, compiled in Westcott, *Kabbalah of the Golden Dawn*. Blavatsky refers to Shekinah in *Isis Unveiled*, vol. 2, 232, but does not pursue the concept in any detail.

72. Contemporary research largely supports Waite's emphasis on kabbalistic eros. See, e.g., Green, "Introduction," lxi; Elliot R. Wolfson, "Murmuring Secrets: Eroticism and Esotericism in Medieval Kabbalah," in *Hidden Intercourse: Eros and Sexuality in the History of Western Esotericism*, ed. Wouter J. Hanegraaff and Jeffrey J. Kripal (Leiden: Brill, 2008), 68; Moshe Idel, *Kabbalah and Eros* (New Haven, CT: Yale University Press, 2005), 69; Beitchman, *Alchemy of the Word*, 44. Others have been less enthusiastic, however, including Scholem. See, e.g., *Major Trends*, 226; *Kabbalah*, 160. Scholem argues that it was only following Isaac Luria that kabbalists began to connect metaphors of divine love to human sex. He accuses Waite of mistranslating eros into the term he transcribed as "mystery of sex," stating that the original Hebrew has no erotic connotation (*Major Trends*, 222–23).

Torah's commandments regarding marriage, sexual behaviour and procreation, the sacred union of man and wife could literally participate in the reunification of the divine male and female principles, a union that would redeem both the upper spiritual realm and the lower material realm from the brokenness of sin.[73] The Zohar and most other forms of Jewish kabbalah tend to describe Shekinah's quest for reunification with the masculine principle as a model for the perfection of the community of Israel and its return from earthly exile.[74] This return from wandering and brokenness can only occur once the actual reunion of Shekinah with her spouse has been effected; thus, much of the prayer, learning, and theurgic/ritualistic praxis pursued by kabbalists has been carried out in order to assist this reunification of male and female principles.[75]

Waite was aware of this history, but this communal aspect of Shekinah symbolism is completely absent from the F.R.C. It might be tempting to read such an interpretation into the ritual for the Adeptus Major grade, where the Priestess instructs the adept that the whole purpose of his F.R.C. involvement has been to "raise the worlds that are below the Throne to the height of those which are above."[76] However, the Priestess quickly clarifies her meaning. She speaks not of unifying the greater cosmos, but of the inner world of the adept: "Restore *your* world to the union, to that supernal state wherein there is no distinction between Shekinah and the Holy One."[77] The F.R.C.'s Shekinah is no symbol of the restitution of fallen humanity or divided divinity to primordial harmony; she acts *only* as

---

73. This idea was particularly emphasized by Isaac Luria and has gained prominence in Kabbalah since. See Dan, *Kabbalah*, 57; Tirosh-Samuelson, "Gender in Jewish Mysticism," 192. As noted above, the re-harmonization of the divine principles is conceived to take place through acts of prayer, meditation, and the following of the whole of the law, not just the parts governing marriage/sexuality (see Scholem, *Major Trends*, 233).
74. Green, "Shekinah," 30; Daniel C. Matt, "Translator's Introduction to the Zohar: Pritzker Edition," in *The Zohar: Pritzker Edition* (Stanford: Stanford University Press, 2004), 36; Tirosh-Samuelson, "Gender in Jewish Mysticism," 192.
75. Dan, *Kabbalah*, 46.
76. Waite, "Adeptus Major," 57.
77. Ibid.

Guide of Paths for the individual. Waite's actualisation of the mystery of sex was thus trained on the goal of transmutation and deification of the self so often preeminent in modern occult systems.[78] His attention to the mystery of sex shows a wider awareness of kabbalistic symbolism than that indicated by the more narrowly sephirotic interests of most fellow occultists,[79] but in most other ways the goals and methods of his deployment of kabbalistic symbolism were in line with the esoteric adaptations of his time. His focus on what Shekinah could do for the mystic, rather than what the mystic could do for Shekinah, is a disembedding similar to his view of the middle pillar as a map for reintegration with the higher self, and his equally adaptive use of the sephiroth to organize symbolic systems for ritual masonic Rosicrucian activities. These taxonomic and imaginative reinterpretations are representative of a modern occult program of syncretism and adaptation, rather than the faithful representation of symbolic elements discovered in the Zohar that Waite claimed.

If anything, Charles Williams's interest in kabbalah was even more closely linked to occultist kabbalah than its Jewish or Christian precursors. Williams seems to have read Westcott's translation of the *Sepher Yetzirah*, but aside from this we do not know of any engagement with Jewish mystical texts. Waite thus represents the central node through which Williams is connected to the vast, intricate network of kabbalistic interpretation, occult or otherwise. Williams, moreover, did not share his Imperator's stated concern for historical rigidity. His playful adaptations of sephirotic symbolism point to a mindset trained on disembedding and adaptation—he drew on kabbalistic symbolism to accomplish purposes ranging from the seriousness of artistic Adeptus Exaltatus expression to the lightness of banal flirtation. In a letter to Olive Speake, another of his young female partners, Williams displayed a capacity to be earnest and

---

78. On modern occult subjectivity and its quest for a "spiritualized understanding" of individuality, see Owen, *Place of Enchantment*, 256–57.

79. On the centrality of the sephiroth to occultist kabbalah see Wouter J. Hanegraaff, "Jewish Influneces V: Occultist Kabbalah," in *Dictionary of Gnosis and Western Esotericism* (Leiden: Brill, 2006), 645–46.

playful at the same time, turning to sephirotic symbolism to profile Speake as a "Path of Light"—a guide equivalent to Shekinah through whom Williams could reach mystical attainment via human sexual desire. Perhaps feeling that his intentions toward Speake were not entirely motivated by the pure desire of Romantic Theology, and therefore represented a movement down the tree as well as up, Williams innovated, adding another pillar to the image: "I will make of you in a ritual the Double Staircase of the Path," Williams told Speake, "Which I have just invented, and yet it is a mystery and a sacrament."[80]

He continued to play with the concepts of Shekinah and the middle pillar in his fiction—again with a productive combination of frivolity and gravitas. Each example of such kabbalistic symbolism that I have found seems to reflect the influence of Waite, while at least one may be a direct reference to Williams's experience in the F.R.C. Knowledge of Waite's adaptations of Shekinah and the middle pillar is, for example, essential to understanding both the characterization of Chloe Burnett and the plot developments through which she progresses toward attainment in *Many Dimensions*. Over the course of the novel she comes to realize herself in the role of Shekinah in a state of desire for union with God.[81] She reaches this realization through interaction with the mysterious stone of Suleiman. The stone is a quintessential example of Williams's multivalent approach to symbolism. It is, at the same time, a science fictional device in dialogue with fourth dimensional time travel theories that were popular in the several decades prior,[82] a clear reference to the Philosophers' Stone of alchemy,[83] and, more importantly for current considerations, an allusion to a stone known as "Schethiya,"[84] a myth which Williams would have stumbled upon in *The Secret Doctrine in*

---

80. Charles Williams to Olive Speake, 10 July 1935, quoted in Lindop, *Charles Williams*, 241–42.
81. See Williams, *Many Dimensions*, 45, 215, 231, 250, 259.
82. See Fleiger, "Time in the Stone of Suleiman," 82.
83. See Chapter Seven, p. xxx.
84. See Dodds, *Charles Williams*, 322.

Israel. Waite attributes its origins to the Talmud and claims that it is further developed in the Zohar,[85] but it seems to be agglomerated from a variety of biblical, Talmudic and kabbalistic references to mystic stones. These include: the *urim* and *thummim*—the mystic stones on the breastplate of the Hebrew High Priest;[86] the stone of Daniel, said in the Zoharic text "The Faithful Shepherd" to be engraved with the Tetragrammaton;[87] and the mystical foundation stone of Freemasonry, which, as Waite describes in his 1911 book on the subject, itself conflates a number of stones of biblical and rabbinic narrative, including a stone lost from the crown of Solomon, the cap-stone of his temple, the stone used by Jacob as a pillow, and Christ, the stone which the builders rejected.[88]

Waite also connects Schethiya to Shekinah. Just as Shekinah, the element of divinity furthest from Ain Soph and closest to materiality, is the aspect of God through which emanative creation occurs,[89] Schethiya was originally a part of the throne of God, in Waite's telling, before being cast by him into the abyss in order to create the world.[90] Schethiya's connection to the stone of Jacob is also important for Waite, as this stone "forms the bond of union between the Divine Essences blessed on the right, blessed on the left, blessed above and below,"[91] just as Shekinah balances divine essences on the right and left of the Tree of Life, while mediating between supernal and material realms. Williams emulates many of the characteristics described by Waite in his construction of the stone of Suleiman. It is also inscribed with the Tetragrammaton, the letters of which "are, in fact,

---

85. Waite, *Secret Doctrine in Israel*, 62.
86. See Paul Carus, "The Oracle of Yahveh: The Urim and Thummin, the Ephod, and the Breastplate of Judgement," *The Monist* 17, no. 3 (1907). Williams also connects his stone to these objects (*Many Dimensions*, 85).
87. Waite, *Secret Doctrine in Israel*, 64n2.
88. *Secret Tradition in Freemasonry*, 1.
89. Scholem, *Kabbalah*, 112.
90. Waite, *Secret Doctrine in Israel*, 62.
91. Ibid, 64n2.

the stone."[92] It is also cubical,[93] and formed of primal matter. The most important aspect of the stone of Suleiman is that like Schethiya it represents a wholeness of divinity and matter, thus representing the divine immanent in the world. From here Williams amplifies the stone's connections to Shekinah, adding in elements of divisibility that represent the sundered feminine principle longing for reunification with the masculine—a symbolic expression of one of the central narratives Williams encountered during his time in the F.R.C. True to the Adeptus Exaltatus technique of achieving secrecy through obscurity, Williams is rarely explicit about "the light of the Shekinah" that is in the stone (242), but the narrative of the estranged Shekinah provides a backdrop to Chloe's quest for mystical attainment all the same. Over the course of the novel she comes to identify herself with the stone's desire for reunification with its divided types and with its divine source, just as adepts in the F.R.C. imagined themselves in the role of Shekinah, their model Guide of Paths. As Chloe becomes more and more aware of the stone's higher nature and begins to respond to its wishes,[94] other characters, particularly Lord Arglay, begin to notice that she and the stone are becoming similar in essence. The link to Shekinah is made clear as Lord Arglay sees Chloe's hand resting next to the stone and "wonder[s] suddenly at the kinship between the two." He then fancies that Chloe's hand is the hand used in early paintings to "image the Power behind creation" (230)—a role ascribed to Shekinah beginning with the Iberian kabbalists.[95]

Williams's portrayal of Chloe's climactic achievement of mystic union closely follows Waite's symbolic Shekinah-middle pillar structure. As the transcendental climax of Chloe's mystical ascent is about to unfold, she and Arglay decide that the stone must be restored to its supernal source—symbolic of Shekinah reuniting with the masculine principle. Lord Arglay, speaking as Solomon—"as if he gave

---

92. Williams, *Many Dimensions*, 7. Cf. 26.
93. Compare Waite, *Secret Doctrine in Israel*, 62.
94. See Williams, *Many Dimensions*, 32, 120–21, 128, 137, 195, 217–18.
95. Scholem, *Kabbalah*, 112.

judgment from his seat in the Court"—channels the middle pillar concept in decreeing "that there is but one Path for the Stone" (257), and asks Chloe if she is ready to be that path. Chloe allows herself to align with Shekinah and become the *linea media* by which the stone can return to its supernatural source. In this conception she acts as Shekinah to guide the stone to union with its divided types, just as the Guide of Paths modelled the way for Williams as an F.R.C. adept. This reunification complete, another process takes place in which Chloe, as though she were another type of the archetype, also becomes united with the stone. Lord Arglay sees her "body receiving the likeness of the Stone...what the Stone had been she now was" (261). Here Williams turns the F.R.C.'s understanding of Shekinah symbolism in both directions: the stone is guided to union by Chloe, but, as it is Shekinah in essence, it guides her back. It is the divinity within the stone with which she identifies that allows her to find "her in herself." The homogenous triad of stone, Chloe and Shekinah complete, all three depart the material world, a transcendence that results in Chloe's spirit eventually leaving her body altogether (267).

Sybil Coningsby of *The Greater Trumps* also references Shekinah and the middle pillar. Like all the novel's characters, she is linked symbolically to several tarot trumps, including the High Priestess. Williams's description of this trump is unique, as is much of his imagined archetypal tarot deck, but it relates closely to other decks such as the one designed by Waite and Pamela Colman Smith in 1909. The High Priestess is "the figure of the hierophantic woman." On the card she has been drawn "sitting on an ancient throne between two heavy pillars,"[96] similar to Waite's design, where the Priestess sits between the pillars of Boaz and Jachin, Mercy and Judgment, just as similar hierophants did in the masonic Rosicrucian settings of the Golden Dawn and F.R.C.[97] Henry Lee senses the connection between Sybil and the High Priestess, enthusing fearfully to Aaron that "she's a woman of great power. She possesses herself entirely...She's like the

---

96. Williams, *Greater Trumps*, 18.
97. Bogdan, *Western Esotericism*, 137.

Woman on the cards, but she doesn't know it—hierophantic, maid and matron at once" (85). This attribution of Sybil to the High Priestess connects her to the F.R.C. figures of the High Priestess, Priestess of the Rite, and Guide of Paths, all connected to Shekinah and the middle pillar in Waite's rituals. In the Theoreticus ritual these figures are also directly associated with the High Priestess of the tarot. Here, in the grade equivalent to the sephira of Yesod, just above Malkuth on the middle pillar, Shekinah is described as "the Great Symbol of the Path," displayed in a diagram on the altar that recalls details from Waite's High Priestess tarot design, which, as we have seen, he also connected to Shekinah.[98] As "maid and matron" at once, Williams may have intended another connection between Sybil and Shekinah, who is a maid in her Malkuth aspect—divided from her lover in Tiphereth—but a mother in her Binah aspect, in union with the fatherly masculine principle, Chokmah.[99]

The connection of Sybil as High Priestess to the middle pillar and thence to Shekinah is made more explicit by Henry's observation that she "possesses herself entirely." Throughout the novel Sybil's demeanour is described as that of the attained mystic who, returning to Moina Mathers's emphasis on balancing the left and right aspects of the Tree of Life, has achieved equanimity between these opposing principles. Henry feels her to have "some sort of a calm, some equanimity in her heart" (86), a sense borne out in Sybil's climactic rebuff of the invasion of the tarot principles in an unbothered, yet absolutely dominant posture. Williams describes this equanimity, maintained even in the face of supernatural terror, as a union between opposing principles: "the elements of that union, which existed separately in others, in her recognized themselves, and something other

---

98. Waite, *Pictorial Key to the Tarot*, 13, 79. See Figure 3 for the Rider-Waite High Priestess card. The F.R.C. diagram is described differently, but has similar characteristics: Both images have the stars of the heptagram arrayed about a seated female figure. A lunar crescent is about the head of Shekinah in the F.R.C. diagram, and at the feet of the High Priestess. Most importantly, both figures balance the opposing forces of creation: "The female figure is at once the equilibrium and the synthesis" (Waite, "Theoreticus," 22–23).

99. Scholem, *Kabbalah*, 111–12.

than themselves, which satisfied them" (189). Given Sybil's expressly stated connection to the High Priestess, and thereby to the middle pillar, Williams is very likely drawing on kabbalistic symbolism here to envision Sybil as a reconciliation of the opposing principles of masculine and feminine, mercy and judgment, light and darkness, eternally vying for reconciliation in a balancing act at once agonistic and harmonious. Thus, where Chloe is symbolically affiliated with Shekinah's desire for unity with the masculine principle, viewed in the occultist terms of the F.R.C. as the desire for the higher self resolved in the Christ-state in Tiphereth, Sybil begins *The Greater Trumps* already in the Christ-state, having long ago established in herself the balance of the attained Fourth Order adept.

THE GREATER TRUMPS

Sybil's allusive connection to Shekinah and the middle pillar via the High Priestess of the tarot trumps is amplified by several connections made in the novel between kabbalah and the tarot. Henry and Aaron are unsure of the origins of the archetypal tarot (of which they perceive themselves to be hereditary guardians) but they see it as something that either originated in Egypt and was later influenced by Jewish mysticism, or something created entirely by "the dreaming rabbis" of the twelfth century, who "whispered in the walled ghetto over fables of unspeakable words."[100] Even more indicative is Henry's explanation of why the cards are magically powerful and metaphysically significant: "The cards are in touch with…well, there aren't any words for it—with the Dance…the Dance that is…everything… Earth, air, fire, water—and the Greater Trumps" (51). The lower suits of the tarot deck communicate with the four elements listed by Henry, but the greater trumps connect to supernatural principles in a cosmic dance, principles that are found manifestly personified inside the Holy of Holies curated by Henry Lee. The cards of the tarot deck

---

100. Ibid, 95. A third option proposed is that the tarot originated in "the hidden covens of doctrine which the Church called witchcraft" (95).

explain the movement of the golden figures dancing in perpetual motion inside this chamber, and gather sympathetic magical power from them (73). Henry calls this "the cabalistic dance" (88), suggesting not just a link between the cosmic waltz of divine principles and the tarot, but also between the golden figures and the dynamic interactions of the Tree of Life.

It is possible that Williams simply intended the term "cabalistic" to indicate inscrutability here, but it is far more likely, given his esoteric inclinations and his ritual experience with kabbalistic symbolism, that he is channeling an occult syncretization of the tarot and the sephiroth that was instigated by Lévi and embraced by most occultists in the modern occult milieu, including Waite. In his *Dogme et rituel de la haute magie* (1856), Lévi innovated a connection between the twenty-two tarot trumps and the twenty-two letters of the Hebrew alphabet, the ten suited numbered cards and the ten sephiroth, and the four suits and the four letters of the Tetragrammaton.[101] Gilbert insists that Waite had "parted with any vestige of belief that Lévi might be a road to enlightenment" by the time he published an English translation of *Dogme et rituel* in 1896 (*Transcendental Magic*),[102] but Waite continued to enthusiastically affirm his predecessor's conflation of tarotic and sephirotic symbolism, one of the French magus's most significant contributions to modern occult adapations of esoteric knowledge. *The Doctrine and Literature of the Kabalah* finds Waite deploying the combination of polemic and aggrandizement that typified his occult/mystical dichotomy: He rejects the historical evidence for Lévi's conflation of the tarot and kabbalah, but at the same time proves unwilling to let go the Secret Tradition value of the idea: "The symbolism of the tarot...is at once disorganised if there be any doubt as to the attribution of its trump cards to the Hebrew alphabet."[103] In a rare public expression of support for occult knowl-

---

101. On Lévi's connection between kabbalah and the tarot see Christopher McIntosh, *Eliphas Lévi and the French Occult Revival* (London: Rider, 1975), 148–49.
102. Gilbert, *A.E. Waite*, 89. Waite had also already included Lévi's ideas on the tarot in a translation of other works assembled as *The Mysteries of Magic* (1886).
103. Waite, *Doctrine and Literature of the Kabalah*, 481–82. Waite maintains his support

edge and society, in 1909 Waite praised the "sephirotic attributions" discovered by conflating the tarot with the Tree of Life: "I offer my assurance, as one who has more to lose than to gain by making the statement, that certain secret schools have developed their scheme of symbolic interpretation to a very high point by the allocation of these cards according to a system which is not known outside them."[104] The tarot and kabbalah thus lent each other additional symbolic importance in Waite's system, a perception shared by most occultists. This esteem for the tarot led Waite to incorporate it into his ritual occult practice. The deck that he designed with Colman Smith, which remains the world's most popular,[105] grew out of his desire to adapt the symbology of the greater trumps for use in the rituals of the I.R.R.[106] We have seen that the F.R.C. continued to use similar "symbols of the paths," painted by John Brahms Trinick, who joined the order when he arrived in England with the ANZAC corps during the Great War.[107]

As with all Secret Tradition knowledge, Waite felt that only "a very few persons" could truly interpret the significance that emerged from syncretizing the tarot with kabbalistic symbolism.[108] He wrote this in 1898, before he had fully developed his concept of the Holy Assembly, but we can assume a link to the small group of Fourth Order adepts that emerged from the complete course of F.R.C. mystical training. Waite's particular interpretations and visual presentations of the tarot thus form an influential part of the toolbox

---

for connecting the tarot to the Tree of Life in his 1938 autobiography, but alters some of Lévi's attributions, suggesting that the French occultist would have made these connections himself had he "understood sephirotic Kabbalism better" (*Shadows*, 192).
104. Arthur Edward Waite, *The Hidden Church of the Holy Graal* (London: Rebman, 1909), 603.
105. See Decker and Dummett, *A History of the Occult Tarot*, 131.
106. Waite, *Shadows*, 184. For more on Waite's approach to the tarot, see "The Great Symbols of the Tarot," *The Occult Review* 43, no. 1 (1926); *Manual of Cartomancy*; *Pictorial Key to the Tarot*; "A French Method of Fortune-Telling by Cards," in *Manual of Cartomancy and Occult Divination* (London: Rider, 1912); *Shadows*, 186–87. See Decker and Dummett, *A History of the Occult Tarot*, 127–41, for a thorough discussion.
107. Gilbert, *A.E. Waite*, 146.
108. Waite, *Doctrine and Literature of the Kabalah*, 482.

of symbolism with which Williams completed his Adeptus Exaltatus task via the production of fiction. *The Greater Trumps* is the only novel where the tarot features, but here it takes on a virtuoso force that, as Lindop argues, suggests Williams's deep familiarity with the material, borne out of experience, as he "could hardly have written all this without deep meditation on the tarot and its symbolism."[109] Aside from the clear influence of Waite,[110] we have very little information as to Williams's other influences or the extent of his tarot knowledge. As Lindop points out, our primary resource for understanding his approach to the tarot, including its connections to his kabbalistic system, is *The Greater Trumps* itself. Knowledge of the occult context in which Williams absorbed kabbalistic imagery is essential to any brave enough to wade into interpretation, or indeed systematization, of the complex tarotic universe imagined into existence in the novel, a project regretfully outside the scope of this book.

The vibrant wave of tarot symbolism that washes through the novel contributed to the ceaseless flux of transformative and adaptive esoteric knowledge in years following. Paul Nagy, a Californian Theosophist, Wiccan and Neo-Pagan, has attempted to analyze and restructure Williams's imagined tarot deck as part of his online "Tarot Hermeneutics" project.[111] Fellow American John Starr Cooke was motivated to explore the tarot in his youth after reading *The Greater Trumps*, a journey that would lead to publication in the 1960s and 70s of three unique tarot decks: the "Book of T," the "Atlantean Tarot," and "Medieval Gypsy."[112] Cooke's discovery of Williams's work and its

---

109. Lindop, *Charles Williams*, 195.
110. In addition to Williams's interaction with tarotic images in the F.R.C, he almost certainly owned the Rider-Waite deck. Along with a deck in the traditional Marseilles design currently held in a private collection, there is a small copy of Waite's "Key to the Tarot," a pamphlet that was normally supplied with purchases of the deck designed by Waite and Colman Smith, suggesting that he probably owned this deck as well (Lindop, *Charles Williams*, 194). At the very least, the pamphlet indicates that he had access to Waite's interpretations in his tarot workings.
111. See Paul Nagy, "Charles Williams, A.E. Waite, and the Secret of *The Greater Trumps*," Tarot Hermeneutics: Exploring how We Create Meaning with the Tarot, http://tarothermeneutics.com/tarotliterature/chaswilliams.html.
112. Decker and Dummett, *A History of the Occult Tarot*, 312–13.

contribution to his own innovative occult practices clearly illustrates the virtue of Granholm's position that artistic works derived from esoteric traditions are not simply derivative cultural products, but contributors to esoteric knowledge in their own right. Williams's tarot vision did not merely play with the image system of a longstanding esoteric tradition—it adapted it and added to it, and in so doing activated a new textual node in the modern occult network.

KABBALISTIC EROS AND ROMANTIC THEOLOGY

The High Priestess is not the only tarot card that connects to kabbalah in the bricolage of Williams's fiction. The Lovers, the sixth trump in the Rider-Waite deck, also connects to kabbalistic eros via the general structure of Romantic Theology. There is no explicit connection to kabbalah in the discovery of the divine within each other by the actual lovers of *The Greater Trumps*, Henry and Nancy, but its symbolism, particularly Waite's concept of the mystery of sex, was a key link in the syncretic chain of literature, Romantic philosophy, mysticism, Christian theology, magical theory, alchemy and sadomasochistic ritual that made up Williams's expression and practice (the two took quite different forms) of Romantic Theology. Waite's mystery of sex, and kabbalistic symbolism in general, are only a part of this philosophical bricolage.[113] Williams's early poetry collection, *The Silver Stair* (1912)—likely written before he discovered kabbalah and certainly before he encountered Waite's Secret Tradition take on the subject—already shows an extant fascination with the mystical possibilities of eros, one that probably owes more to the Romantic connection of the immanent divine to the female form,[114]

---

113. Ashenden argues for a more vital connection, basing Romantic Theology in the "marital theology" of Waite's mystery of sex (Ashenden, *Charles Williams*, 51. Cf. 40, 47–55). Neither Waite nor Williams were concerned with the marital status of Romantic lovers, however, and, as I will show below, Romantic Theology had a number of more influential precursors.

114. Irving Singer illustrates that the Romantics viewed love as a power that enabled the subject to "know and appropriate the universe by means of endless yearning for oneness with another person, or with humanity, or with the cosmos as a whole"

and, more specifically, to the late-Romantic Coventry Patmore, whose poetic depiction of courtly love and marriage suggested that sexual desire could provide a pathway to God.[115]

However, Williams's reading of Waite's texts on kabbalah, compounded with his frequent encounters with the symbolism of the middle pillar and Shekinah in the F.R.C., seem to have clarified his Romantic Theological appreciation for the mysteries of sexual desire. *Outlines of Romantic Theology* is virtually silent on kabbalistic connections. This is quite purposeful—as we have seen, Williams notes that he has not included this school of mystic eros because it is "not part of historic Christian thought," which suggests that he wished to constrain the text to more conventional Christian boundaries, an attempt that failed if we can judge by Bishop Strong's recommendation not to publish this "unorthodox" document. It is crucial, however, to note that he ascended through the F.R.C. grades of Adeptus Major and Adeptus Exemptus, both specifically keyed on the symbolism of Shekinah's union with her divine spouse, in 1923 and 1924, just as he was conceptualizing *Outlines of Romantic Theology*.[116] It is therefore highly likely that Waite's occult/mystical adaptations of kabbalah had a direct result on Williams's formulation of the connection between love and desire in the human and divine spheres, an influence reflected in his observation in *Outlines* that the Zohar, despite its exclusion from the current work, is "extraordinarily valuable" for the study of Romantic Theology.[117]

As usual, the novels tell a story more in keeping with Williams's personal tendency towards syncretization and universalism. Earnest Beaumont has shown that Williams frequently constructs male/female relationships as illustrations of Romantic Theology in his

---

(Singer, *Nature of Love*, 286). On eros in *The Silver Stair* see Hadfield, *Introduction to Charles Williams*, 33; Lindop, *Charles Williams*, 33.

115. Lindop, *Charles Williams*, 33, 110–11. Cf. Ashenden, *Charles Williams*, 40–41.

116. He appears to have written the book throughout most of 1924, finishing in October. See Alice M. Hadfield, "Introduction: The Writing of *Outlines of Romantic Theology*," in *Outlines of Romantic Theology*, ed. Alice M. Hadfield (Berkeley, CA: Apocryphile, 2005), xii–xiii.

117. Williams, *Outlines of Romantic Theology*, 55n.

fiction, particularly those, such as Anthony and Damaris and Henry and Nancy, "in the first pre-marital flush of the Beatrician vision."[118] There are likely shades of kabbalistic eros behind all such mystic couplings, but in *Shadows of Ecstasy* and *Many Dimensions* the connection is more explicit. Rosamond, the object of Philip Travers's desire, is a selfish, materialistic woman who seems to care little for him, but Philip encounters mystical experience through his devotion to her nonetheless, true to the Romantic convention that all occurrences of love are good by virtue of the oneness of self, nature and God.[119] This is achieved through contemplation of her physical form, mirroring Waite's dictate that "the face of a beautiful woman contemplated with eyes open to the Divine Immanence within her is a way of attainment in God."[120] Sitting in Considine's drawing room listening to the melody the magus has prepared in order to direct the consciousness of his guests toward mystical attainment, Philip's senses turn from the sound of the music to the sight of Rosamond, which swells up "subterranean torrents" of masculinity,[121] directed toward the discovery of the divine self within:

> A rush and ripple of sound went through him and in his brain it was not so much sound as Rosamond's visible form, the quivering line of her exquisite side; and the violins swept up more quickly and her round full neck grew up in that beautiful dream and her chin became visible, and they slowed and sighed, and there between her welcoming arms and her breasts was a something of fullness and satisfaction which invited him, but not to her.[122]

But to whom or what then? Williams, as demanded by the secrecy

---

118. Ernest Beaumont, "Charles Williams and the Power of Eros," *Dublin Review*, no. 479 (Spring 1959): 65. Cf. Knight, *Magical World of Charles Williams*, 53; Urang, *Shadows of Heaven*, 63.
119. Singer, *Nature of Love*, 291.
120. Waite, *Divine Union*, 290.
121. Williams, *Shadows of Ecstasy*, 77.
122. Ibid.

of Adeptus Exaltatus communication, is abstruse about the end goal of Philip's erotic vision, but, as Charles A. Huttar notes, the name Rosamond points to a primary association with Shekinah, identified as "the rose of the world" in Waite's *The Secret Doctrine in Israel*.[123] Huttar's observation is supported by an earlier connection in the novel between Rosamond's body and Shekinah, when Philip glimpses Rosamond's arm as she leans over to pass a plate. He realizes the movement of her arm as "something frightfully important" through which "he had looked into incredible space; abysses of intelligence lay beyond it."[124] The frightful geometry of this vision already suggests something of the infinite layers of divinity represented by the sephiroth, but the sublime presence encountered in this Romantic Theological vision is specifically linked to Shekinah, as Philip later reflects that the arm had "lain like a bar of firmamental power across the whole created universe, dividing and reconciling at once."[125] This connects to Shekinah's presence in Malkuth in kabbalistic cosmology—like Rosamond's arm in the microcosm, Shekinah represents a dual relationship in the macrocosm, both divided from the divine along with the natural world and eternally in the process of achieving reconciliation with it. This is the closest Williams comes to defining the principle with which Philip comes into contact through his erotic fascination—his taste for multivalence and his preference for heterodoxy are both indicated by his turn in this passage—one of his primary fictional expansions of Romantic Theology—to the symbolism of kabbalah rather than the specifically Christian imagery used in *Outlines of Romantic Theology*.

Shekinah also connects Philip's Beatrician moment with Williams's own experiences in the F.R.C. In the Adeptus Major ritual, Williams would have encountered Shekinah once again, now as Priestess of the Rite, as he lay upon a litter in a corpse posture

---

123. Charles A. Huttar, "Arms and the Man: The Place of Beatrice in Charles Williams's Romantic Theology," in *Charles Williams: A Celebration*, ed. Brian Horne (Leominster, Herefordshire: Gracewing, 1995), 81.
124. Williams, *Shadows of Ecstasy*, 56.
125. Ibid, 99.

symbolising his mystical death. From this recumbent position, Williams would not have been able to see much of the Priestess as she pressed a rose to his mouth, symbolizing the "kiss of Shekinah," itself perhaps a reference to the divine eros of Shekinah's quest. He could not see her face or body, as the celebrant was covered head to toe in the "veil of Binah," symbolising Shekinah in her supernal state of eternal indivisibility. As the celebrant leaned over him with the kiss of Shekinah, however, he would have experienced the same sense of physicality as Philip, with a glimpse of "the arm of the Priestess and her figure bending over him."[126] It is worth noting that this arm may not have been that of a woman—there is no stipulation recorded in the F.R.C. documents that the celebrant playing these Shekinah roles should be female[127]—however, it seems likely that there was a direct connection between this experience and Williams's imagination of Philip's erotic mystical encounter.

Williams's personal connection of Shekinah to a woman that he himself loved further supports the likelihood that he intended Philip's experience to abstrusely express kabbalistic eros. Williams was fond of parsing the identities of his lovers between their flawed, earthly aspects and idealized deifications performed for both romantic and spiritual purposes. The central example is his creation of the figure of "Celia" to represent the idealized Phyllis Jones,[128] a transmuted form in which Williams glimpsed a personification of the divine feminine principle, specifically identified as Shekinah in a later letter to Lois Lang-Sims.[129] In personal correspondence with Phyllis herself, Williams recalls a meeting between the two on the steps of St Pancras Church: "Celia...you shall be, before angels and men, what you were to me on the steps of St Pancras... So you shall radiate the light out of which God made you; and purify your earthly

---

126. Waite, "Adeptus Major," 46.
127. Williams, however, never played this role, indicating that Waite likely selected female initiates to play the Priestess whenever possible.
128. On Williams's various nicknames for Phyllis, see Hadfield, *Charles Williams: An Exploration*, 74; Lindop, *Charles Williams*, 139.
129. Williams and Lang-Sims, *Letters to Lalage*, 57.

tabernacle till the Shekinah shines through... I saw you in the glory you had with God before the world began."[130] For Williams, the earthly tabernacle of the Phyllis he saw on those steps was a body that, in the words of *Shadows of Ecstasy*, beckoned erotically, "but not to her." It was the divine Celia, Beatrice of the *Paradiso*, the Shekinah within, that summoned Williams to union. The idealization of Phyllis as archetypal woman thus provided him with mystic inspiration that he reproduced in fiction in the vision screened by Philip on the eternal tableau of Rosamond's arm. The meaning of Philip's experience is visible, in an abstract sense, to readers unfamiliar with the symbolism of Shekinah and the correspondent eros of kabbalah, but the passage is yet another striking instance of the intricate contextual matrix of occult knowledge and personal experience behind Williams's characters and symbols, plots and settings.

Indeed, unbeknownst to the reader, Williams intended Chloe Burnett as a fictional projection of Phyllis, deepening the entanglement between Romantic Theology—particularly his lived experience of it—and kabbalah. He completed the novel just after the heartbreak of discovering that she had been seeing another man, even while carrying on an infatuated, though barely physical, relationship with Charles. In letters to Phyllis about the book, he added "Chloe" to her list of nicknames.[131] Given that he had already conflated Phyllis with Shekinah in his mind, Chloe's own relationship to the divine feminine becomes even more symbolically complex. Lord Arglay's character takes on further layers of significance as well. Arglay is not so direct an authorial alter ego as Peter Stanhope or Roger Ingram, but his relationship with Chloe mirrors elements of Charles's connection to Phyllis. Chloe is not romantically entangled with Arglay, but there is great admiration between them, with muted hints of desire as well.[132] Chloe has a relationship with a man her own age, but she finds herself dissatisfied in comparison to the empowerment and

---

130. Charles Williams to Phyllis Jones, n.d, quoted in Lindop, *Charles Williams*, 139.
131. Lindop, *Charles Williams*, 176–77.
132. See, e.g., Williams, *Many Dimensions*, 250.

spiritual fulfilment she gains from her connection to Arglay (50). Indeed, though she may not be physically entangled with the Lord Chief Justice, he still serves as a human reflection of the divine masculine principle. As Chloe grows to identify with the feminine principle represented by Shekinah, she realizes Arglay as the masculine principle. Thinking at one point of the phrase "the End of Desire"—transplanted into the novel, as we have seen, from the rituals of the F.R.C.—Chloe has "a vague feeling that the sentence suggested Lord Arglay himself as the centre" (95). This feeling hints at a potential for interest in erotic union with Arglay the man, but its more significant ramification emerges from the term's connection to mystical attainment. On this level, Arglay as the end of desire functions both microcosmically as Chloe's Romantic Theological object, and macrocosmically as a symbol of the absent masculine principle which Shekinah desires.

Williams cements this relationship by placing the onus for Chloe's middle pillar ascension on Lord Arglay. It is Chloe herself that feels the need for Arglay to will that she become the path for the stone. "'But why will you have me tell you what to do?'" Arglay asks. "'Because you said that the Stone was between us,'" she answers, "'And if that is so how otherwise can I move in the Stone?'" (257) This conversation puts the stone in the place of the middle pillar, sitting between feminine and masculine principles on the left and right that cannot act without the cosmic assistance of their opposite. But Williams continues the conversation in order to connect the cosmic balance of the kabbalistic masculine and feminine to his Romantic Theology:

> "And if I tell you to do it?" he asked.
> "Then I will do what I may," Chloe said.
> "And if I tell you not to do it?" he asked again.
> "Then I will wait till you will have it done, she said, "for without you I cannot go even by myself." (258)

In order to succeed in her mystic quest, Chloe requires the

command of Arglay's masculine will, in the same way that Williams envisioned himself in lifestyle fantasy as the spiritual headmaster of Phyllis and all the young women who came after her. Arglay agrees to command her, but proceeds not with a distant authoritarian manner but with the closeness dictated by Romantic love: "Since this is in your mind I also will be with your mind and I will take upon me what you desire" (262). This statement indicates his awareness of his role in effecting the end of her desire, and also presages his own mystical experience, realized in the course of Chloe's climactic moment of oneness with the stone. Arglay does not reach the point of utter transcendence that Chloe does, but he alone of the people in the room is able to glimpse Chloe's newly attained nature because of his own kinship with the stone. He stands within the "perfection of existence" that flows from her, and views with his "natural eyes" the letters of the Tetragrammaton shining from her forehead (262). Where Philip gains a glimpse of the divine feminine through the arm of Rosamond, Arglay openly contemplates Shekinah in her state of union with the masculine principle through his view of Chloe, just as Williams glimpsed the "glory" Phyllis "had with God before the world began" on the steps of St Pancras.

Williams's personal fondness for kabbalah lies beneath his development of each of these fictionalized Romantic Theological scenarios. The kabbalistic symbolism in his novels is deployed obscurely, but it underpins some of his most decisive portrayals of mystical progression. Waite's application of middle pillar and Shekinah symbolism to the occult ritual materials of the F.R.C. provided Williams with a valuable imagistic experience, an engagement with a kabbalistic structure which he used to connect his experiences of love and desire to his heterodox mystical practices, turning from these points of personal engagement with kabbalah to project their Waitean adaptations into his novels. As his odd relationship with Phyllis Jones began to peter out, Williams was forced to search for the Beatrician function of Shekinah in other women. *Many Dimensions* ends with a suggestion that Williams was aware that he would need other options aside from his real-life Chloe Burnett. Soon after

Chloe's passing, Lord Arglay picks up the phone and dials the Lancaster Typewriting Agency, ready to recruit a new young secretary to assist with his life's work, just as Williams moved onto further extramarital relationships that helped him achieve mystical and artistic attainment. Both of these goals—continuing priorities throughout his life—were also closely tied to his involvement with another esoteric current central to modern occultism: ritual magic.

CHAPTER 5

THE HIGH-PRIESTESS
CHARLES WILLIAMS AND MODERN MAGIC

Charles Williams has rarely, if ever, been described as a magician. Yet, he kept a sword in his office that he deployed as an object of power in his ritualistic sublimation of libido, taught his young devotees the Banishing Ritual of the Pentagram, and sought to elevate his consciousness in the F.R.C. through practices that displayed central characteristics of ceremonial magic. In his poetry and fiction, he frequently turned to magical practices and symbolism to achieve artistic goals ranging from pure entertainment to serious expression of a magical worldview continuous with Romantic Theology and coinherence. In *Witchcraft*, his summary of the history of magic in Western civilization until the seventeenth century, he displays both belief in magical praxis and approbation for many of its workings—a set of theories and practices that he, adopting the words of Apuleius and, probably, the framework of A.E. Waite, termed the "high-priestess of heaven."[1] As I will argue in the next two chapters, magic offered Williams the possibility for Romantic re-enchantment in the face of the sterile vision of the dominant rationalist perspective of his own culture, along with power

---

1. Williams, *Witchcraft*, 35.

and a place of importance denied to him by the reality of personal circumstances, an attraction that I have termed *reanimation*. Though he clearly understood the Church to be polemically set against the set of magical symbols and practices it saw as witchcraft,[2] Williams balanced *theologia* and *magia* together in his belief system, establishing a relatively harmonious balance between the two through an interactive process of experience and interpretation. The result was a Christian, Romantic magic that seems to have been largely consistent in Williams's own perception, though untenably paradoxical in the view of others.

In the last twenty years several critics have undertaken thoughtful analysis of the invigoration magical thought and practice brought to Williams's life, faith, and fiction.[3] As with occultism in general, however, there is a long history of published research that has actively sought to disassociate him from any long-standing, authentic interest in magic.[4] The balance of Williams scholarship is still marked by the discomfort which arises whenever knowledge classified in the "rejected" category of Western esotericism appears in his oeuvre. The problem is the same as with all occult or esoteric materials—most Williams critics simply are not aware of the enormous depth and complexity of the Western magical tradition. There is thus a tendency to lump various magics together, so that Williams's magic, in theory (though not always in practice) focused on mystical attainment and coinherent action, is uncritically conflated with other practices, including the necromancy (invocation of spirits) of medieval grimoires, and devil worship,[5] thus triggering the protective instincts

---

2. Ibid, 307.
3. Particularly good sources for this analysis are Newman, "Companions of the Co-Inherence," 159–60; Dodds, *Charles Williams*, esp. 159–60; "Gavin Ashenden's Charles Williams," esp. 40; Lindop, *Charles Williams*.
4. See, e.g., Hadfield, *Charles Williams: An Exploration*, 30–31, 103–4; Ashenden, *Charles Williams*, 114; George L. Scheper, "The Cessation of Rhetoric," in *The Rhetoric of Vision: Essays on Charles Williams*, ed. Charles Adolph Huttar and Peter J. Schakel (Lewisburg: Bucknell University Press, 1996), 145–46; Cavaliero, "Introduction to *Witchcraft*," xv.
5. See, e.g., George Parker Winship Jr., "This Rough Magic: The Novels of Charles Williams," *Yale Review* 40, no. 2 (1951): 287.

THE HIGH-PRIESTESS

of the cordon sanitaire. It is critically dangerous, however, to reduce "magic" to a single, reified object, or even to a pattern of thought historically specific in its development but conceptually contiguous overall.[6] A great many practices have been described as magic, in different times and in different places, from alchemy to astrology to divination to prestidigitation to animal sacrifice, and each of these in turn are practices with their own variegated histories.[7] People who identify themselves as magicians, or their actions or perceived experiences as magical, thus connect themselves to a vast and complex tradition, and because of this enormity generally find themselves, as we will see in the case of Waite and Williams, selecting aspects of this tradition that appeal to them, while rejecting many others.[8] Groups, individuals and phenomena associated with magic must therefore be analyzed with a very fine historical brush.

MAGIC IN THE WEST

Such caution is required with the elements of most belief systems, but it is particularly applicable to the history of magic because the term has so often been used polemically. Since its origins in the Greek *mageia*, the term has possessed an uneasy balance of positive and negative connotations. The latter, in which magic referenced "sinister or threatening, demon-ridden or simply fraudulent practices," has been dominant, particularly in late antique and early medieval Christian Europe.[9] More positive interpretations have

---

6. See Bernd-Christian Otto, "Historicising 'Western Learned Magic,'" *Aries: Journal for the Study of Western Esotericism* 16 (2016): 162–63; Hanegraaff, *Esotericism and the Academy*, 177; Randall Styers, "Magic and the Play of Power," in *Defining Magic: A Reader*, ed. Michael Stausberg and Bernd-Christian Otto (Sheffield: Equinox, 2012), 258; Egil Asprem, "Patterns of Magicity: A Review of *Defining Magic: A Reader*," *Correspondences* 3 (2015): 136.
7. See Bernd-Christian Otto and Michael Stausberg, *Defining Magic: A Reader* (Sheffield: Equinox, 2013), 2–3.
8. Hanegraaff, *Esotericism and the Academy*, 177.
9. Hanegraaff, *Esotericism and the Academy*, 169. Cf. Styers, *Making Magic*, 32–34; Otto and Stausberg, *Defining Magic*, 2.

always co-existed with such polemics, particularly in the late medieval and Renaissance periods, when magic became associated with the revival of the ancient wisdom narrative that is the background to Waite's Secret Tradition, and with *magia naturalis*, a belief in a "natural magic" specifically opposed by its adherents to *goetia*—magic based in demonic invocation—and therefore more easily tolerated by the Church.[10] Natural magic's concern with discovering the workings of the cosmos so that its elements could be worked via human knowledge and ingenuity would go on to contribute significantly to the rise of modern naturalistic science. Ironically, however, following the Enlightenment the developing forces of scientific rationalism conspired with existing Christian polemics—exacerbated by the Protestant Reformation's urge to exorcise Christianity of vestigial pagan elements—to lump the magia naturalis with other polemical understandings of magic as irrational and superstitious or downright sorcerous, demonic, dangerous and heretical. Thus, despite its weighty complexity, magic joined other such traditions, including kabbalah and alchemy, in the body of knowledge from which a growingly rationalist and empiricist Western culture sought to distance itself.[11] Magic was still explored in some cultural and intellectual spaces, particularly in the Romantic poetry and gothic literature that rose in reaction to the perceived disenchantment and soullessness resultant from Enlightenment rationalism, but overall it was forced into the esoteric, into counter-culture, into hiddenness.[12]

In the nineteenth century another countermovement appeared in the form of the occult revival, in which magical theory and practice saw increased interest in significant sub-sections of various European and North American societies, a fascination paralleled by increased

---

10. Hanegraaff, *Esotericism and the Academy*, 170–76. Styers, *Making Magic*, 35. On the variety of positively presented magical traditions, see Otto, "Historicising," 163–64.
11. See Hanegraaff, *Esotericism and the Academy*, 176; Styers, *Making Magic*, 27–35; Asprem, "Patterns of Magicity," 136.
12. Cf. Bogdan, "Freemasonry and Western Esotericism," 279. Leigh Wilson, *Modernism and Magic: Experiments with Spiritualism, Theosophy and the Occult* (Edinburgh: Edinburgh University Press, 2013), 7–8.

fictional presentations of the subject that spread magical thinking much further than any individual occult movement could. Charles Williams fits into both these categories of renewal—he participated in the network of occultists who reinvigorated magical concepts and adapted them to the intellectual necessities of the modern age, and also joined a significant group of fiction writers that exploited the wonders of a tradition which, because of the high degree of imagination and invention already extant at its epistemological core, proved fertile to the fantastic mode.[13]

Charles Williams's magical worldview displays the imprints of his engagement with fictional presentations of magic such as *Zanoni*, Underhill's *Column of Dust*, and Haggard's *She*.[14] A wide variety of non-fictional sources were likely more influential, however. He held Renaissance and early modern *magi* like Agrippa, Pico and Vaughan in high esteem,[15] and encountered modern adaptations of their Hermetic thought in his personal relationships with his Stella Matutina friends and with Waite—the author of several books on the subject and a conduit, albeit a reluctant one, to the magical theories and practices of the Golden Dawn, the most influential source of magical doctrine in the modern West. The Golden Dawn's magical system—focused on enhancing the power of the individual will and psyche and attaining union with the higher self—was itself a product of centuries of intellectual tradition, highlighted by the Enochian angelic magic derived from Elizabethans John Dee and Edward Kelly,[16] and the use of medieval grimoires such as *Clavicula Salomonis* (*The Key of Solomon the King*), published in a new edition by Mathers in 1889.[17]

Both the grimoires and Enochian magic were used to invoke

---

13. On magic's role in characterizing the twentieth and twenty-first century sublime, see Simon During, *Modern Enchantments: The Cultural Power of Secular Magic* (Cambridge, MA: Harvard University Press, 2002), 39–41.
14. See Chapter Three, p. xxx.
15. Williams, *Witchcraft*, 232.
16. Asprem, *Arguing with Angels*, 46–68.
17. Hanegraaff, "Magic V," 742–43.

intermediary beings—angels, demons and elementals—through ritualistic invocation. The magic of the Golden Dawn would thus seem to be irrelevant to the question of Charles Williams's interest in the subject, but, as discussed below, there is evidence that he participated, in some fashion, in the invocation of spiritual beings in the F.R.C., and also learned to protect himself against malevolent forces of a similar type using the Lesser Banishing Ritual of the Pentagram. Further, modern occult magic was by no means all about invocation. Even when it was, magicians had varying understandings of what was going on. While some envisioned themselves actually engaging with particular entities, or at least with the personifications of divine powers, others understood invocation in a more interior fashion, aiming for contact with higher, archetypal aspects of the magician's own self. Motivated by a need to withstand the skeptical interrogation unleashed by the epistemological forces of scientific naturalism,[18] the aims of modern magic often turned inward, activating the powers of the imagination to traverse imaginal planes, and seeking increased levels of consciousness, the balance of the middle pillar and the higher self within.[19] As we will see at several junctures in this chapter, the effects of this inward turn, which contemporary scholars often refer to as a "psychologization" of magic, are clearly visible in Williams's artistically and mystically motivated magical practice. Some historians have argued that this psychologization represents a secularisation of magic in the modern age.[20] However, Williams is representative of a large group of occultists that deployed magical practice both with a goal of inner spiritual transformation, and with the intent of encountering divine principles that could be personified as deities or intermediaries—as God, Christ, Shekinah or particular

---

18. Hanegraaff, "How Magic Survived," 370.
19. See Hanegraaff, "How Magic Survived," 366–71. Modern magic did not turn entirely inward, as some magicians, including those of the Golden Dawn, maintained an interest in manipulating elements of the natural or divine spheres via the sympathy between objects and/or metaphysical entities. On the balance between interiority and imaginal idealism vs. the perception of interaction with an objective, spiritual reality in modern magic, see Owen, *Place of Enchantment*, 183–84.
20. See, e.g., Hanegraaff, "How Magic Survived," 370–71.

angelic entities in Williams's particularly Waitean case—drawing down power from these principles, or directing consciousness toward union with them.

It should be clear, even from this brief survey of some of the central magical trends that typified the individuals, groups and practices that made up the modern occult network, that there is no such thing as "modern magic" per se; that we can only productively use the term in relation to Williams or anyone else if we maintain awareness of the vagaries of the category.[21] This does not mean that it is impossible to speak of Williams as a magician or examine his magical ideas, but it does indicate that great care is required to accurately place his actions and beliefs in cultural and historical context. The understanding of magic as a monolithic tradition has been the primary culprit in disassociating the author from his personal and aesthetic interest in various magics, resulting in an incomplete picture that has only recently begun to be filled in. The opposite could be true as well, however. Caution must be taken when comparing Williams to other occultists of his day; many of his magical beliefs were quite standard among his peers, but others, such as the mental and physical healing of co-inherent action, were quite unique.

THE "HIGH-PRIESTESS OF HEAVEN"

Williams was well aware of the terminological vagaries of "magic," as he makes clear in *Witchcraft*, introduced as a "history in Christian times of that perverted way of the soul which we call magic."[22] This sentence would seem to be a denunciation of magic understood monolithically through the polemical lenses conventional to a Christian theologian. Williams, however, is merely setting out the boundaries of the book he initially intended to call *Magic* but eventually

---

21. For a brief review of the many uses to which the term magic has been applied, see Otto and Stausberg, *Defining Magic*, 8–10.
22. Williams, *Witchcraft*, xix.

changed to *Witchcraft*,[23] apparently to better reflect his focus on the history of a "lower level" of magic he associates with "witchcraft,"[24] thus setting up a dialectic between rejected forms of magic and higher, more valuable types. He states a belief in the reality behind the claims of those who practiced magic of "the merely vile kind, the night-hags, the potion and poison makers, malefical wizards of the lower sort" (35), but distinguishes these murky figures and practices from a "nobler idea of virtue mingled with power" (xix). For Williams, this higher form of magic was visible both in the *magia naturalis*, which "worked itself out eventually as experimental science," and a secret form which has survived into the present day, "kept carefully secluded in its own Rites," a reference to the secretive esoteric societies that kept magical interest alive following the Enlightenment and which Williams encountered through the mystical and theurgic practices of modern occultism. To be aware of this type of magic, "one would have to share" in these rites (xix), as Williams did in the F.R.C.

In *Witchcraft*, the hero of this secret tradition of magic is Lucius Apuleius, author *Metamorphoses* or *The Golden Ass* (second-century CE), an early precursor of Williams's fictional presentation of magical experimentation and esoteric initiation. Williams draws on the *Apologia* of Apuleius, which pleads innocent of charges of sorcery drawn against him by scheming inlaws. Among other arguments, Apuleius frames magic as a kind of priesthood, "'an art acceptable to the immortal gods, full of all knowledge of worship and prayer, full of piety and wisdom in things divine...high-priestess of the powers of heaven'."[25] For Williams, this concept tops a hierarchy of magical practice, a pyramid with "goetic" forms of magic such as witchcraft and potion-making at its base, the "theurgic" magic of angelic or demonic invocation above, and the *magia naturalis* and a tradition of

---

23. As indicated by a letter to Ursula Grundy (20 September 1939, CWSA I.A.v.3/a), written while working on *Witchcraft*: "I look rather hopelessly at *Magic*. But no doubt something will happen soon."
24. Williams, *Witchcraft*, xix.
25. Ibid, 25. Cf. Apuleius, *Apologia* 25.6–26.

sexual union between humans and spirits above that, the latter of which has been "a great and awful blasphemy" but which "resembled most closely the central dogma of the Church" because of its connections to the incarnation of Christ.

> Besides all these there were, it seems, some few to whom the magical art was indeed 'high-priestess of heaven', who, pushed on by a pure learning, followed in honour and chastity towards a sublime union with the final absolute power; there was a means of doing this, but it was very secret. (35)

This Apuleian vision of magic as the pursuit of mystical attainment is the magic of "the great rituals" of antiquity, of "the mysteries of Isis and the rest," conceived "not so much to control the Divine Ones as to exhibit to the Divine Ones the pure heart, the pious act, the calm yet passionate entreaty."[26] Magic as "high-priestess" is therefore equivalent to, or at least a part of, the ancient wisdom narrative. Building on Apuleius's connection of high-priestess magic to Zoroaster and Persian magic (35), Williams follows esoteric conventions established in the Renaissance, drawing the lineage of the magical wisdom tradition from these early roots to his own time.[27] The Renaissance and early modern periods receive particular attention in a late chapter that departs from the history of witchcraft to look at "The Philosophical and Literary Movement" of magic (221). Williams closely examines Thomas Vaughan's connection of magic to "the wisdom of the Creator" in *Magia Adamica* (1650).[28] Vaughan drew from Renaissance Hermeticists like Agrippa, his teacher Johannes Trithemius and the Christian kabbalist Johannes Reuchlin. Their focus on exploring magic as a "closing of the breach" between spirit and matter inspired Williams; it was "another means" to mystic

---

26. Ibid, 49.
27. Hanegraaff has shown that Renaissance thinkers like Marsilio Ficino and Pico della Mirandola saw the body of ancient wisdom as essentially equivalent to a magical tradition. See Hanegraaff, *Esotericism and the Academy*, 47.
28. *Witchcraft*, 221–22.

union than that offered by the Church, "a means not necessarily opposed, nor even alternative, but perhaps complementary or only auxiliary" (224). Williams's approbation of magical practice blurs into praxis when he notes that these intellectuals sought "the Union" through the "various corollaries of the Union" (224). The phrase is vaguely presented, but the context indicates that these corollaries are lower, microcosmic reflections of the macrocosmic union of spirit and matter indicated by Christ's incarnation. Williams illustrates the concept by describing the magical and alchemical endeavours of another Renaissance magus, John Dee. He connects Dee's experiments, primarily driven by communication with angelic spirits, with Vaughan's alchemy and says that though these pursuits were not typical of magic "in the historical sense of the word," magic as high-priestess lay behind them:

> Both, and perhaps all, might have claimed that this was what lay behind the old kind, and was the only valuable thing in it, as Vaughan clearly did. They would have assented, in faith and hope, if not in knowledge and experience, to Pico della Mirandola's saying that 'No science gives greater proof of the divinity of Christ than magic and the Kabbala.' (228)

Like the Renaissance Hermeticists, Williams connects Christian theology to magical theory *and*, significantly, to magical practice. Practical esoteric pursuits like alchemy are valuable as "lower correspondences" of "the high transmutations" (232)—corollaries through which "the Union" itself can be accessed. His steadfast belief in the reflective correspondence between above and below thus seems to have led him to the same inescapable conclusion as both his modern occult peers and their early modern forebears: the sympathy between macro- and microcosm made magical communication between divine, nature and human not only possible but desirable.

This connection between practical magical experimentation and the idea of magic as a sort of ancient divine wisdom was still influential in Williams's day,[29] so it is difficult to precisely place the influences—beyond Vaughan and Apuleius—of his high-priestess concept. The concept of a "higher magic" was expressed by other occultists, including Lévi and Westcott, who described the "higher magic" as a development of the spiritual nature of the adept with the purpose of coming into contact with the higher self.[30] As usual, however, Waite was likely part of the web of Williams's influences. By the time the two met, Waite had enfolded magic into his polemically constructed dichotomy between mysticism and occultism, rejecting all magical activities as "the path of illusion."[31] Scholars have used this strict dichotomy to distance Williams from magic,[32] but elements of theurgy and ritual magic lingered in Waite's mystical practice, in the same way that his Secret Tradition continued to display the same modern occult elements that he disparaged. As with his mysticism/occultism binary, it is in the tertiary space between dichotomized points that we find Waite's actual approach to magic. As Decker and Dummett conclude, Waite was inconsistent with his exclusion of magical symbol and practice: "He reprobated the practice of magic and poured scorn on its theory; but he could not bear to dispense with any of its symbols or its ritual."[33] This goes a bit far— Waite was quite prepared to discard many of the images and practices of the magical traditions. However, as a number of historians of the modern occult have observed, contrasts between magic and mysticism are quickly reduced to the blurring of historical complexity once the actual beliefs and practices behind stated dichotomies like Waite's are taken into hand.[34] At the same time as he publicly

---

29. Hanegraaff, "Magic V," 738.
30. See William Wynn Westcott (as Frater N.O.M), "Flying Roll No. 19: The Aims and Means of Adeptship," in *Astral Projection, Ritual Magic, and Alchemy: Golden Dawn Material by S.L. Macgregor Mathers and Others*, ed. Francis King (Rochester, VT: Destiny, 1987), 115–16.
31. Waite, *The Book of Ceremonial Magic*, xxv. See p. xxx.
32. See, e.g., McLaren, "Hermeticism and the Metaphysics of Goodness," 1–3; Ashenden, *Charles Williams*, 3n14.
33. Decker and Dummett, *A History of the Occult Tarot*, 141.
34. Henrik Bogdan, "New Perspectives on Western Esotericism," *Nova Religio: The*

scorned all magics he continued to quietly debate the validity of a "Higher Magia" that "justified the original meaning of the term Magic," and was essentially synonymous with what he would soon begin to call the Secret Tradition.[35] As with Williams's high-priestess, the Higher Magia was equivalent to the ancient wisdom "which justified the original meaning of the term Magic...that wisdom which was the issue of experience and knowledge particular to sacred sanctuaries in the years of the Magi";[36] also like Williams, Waite directly attributed this idea to Vaughan,[37] though he would have been aware that connections between magic and the ancient wisdom of sub-mythical figures like Zoroaster were at least as old as late antiquity. Waite rarely described magic positively after this 1906 approbation of the Higher Magia. Yet, in less visible forums his support continued. His 1909 *Manual of Cartomancy*, written pseudonymously as "Grand Orient," replaces the dichotomy between magic and mysticism with a free embrace of the Higher Magia, and even includes a proposal that aspects of practical magic could assist in the exploration of "the inward world of the soul."[38] In addition to valuing the Higher Magia, Grand Orient declares the existence of a centuries-old "priesthood of practical magic" similar in structure to the Holy Assembly, a rare breed of magicians born with "natural, intuitive, psychic and occult gifts."[39] Here Waite displays a perspective similar to Williams's "corollaries of the Union"—magic ultimately has a mystical goal, but this goal can be achieved via a number of occult pathways. Though such activities represent a lower degree of magical function, they are still operative, permissible and valuable: "The work of the soul is the soul's work in all its phases and regions."[40]

Journal of Alternative and Emergent Religions 13, no. 3 (2010): 102; Arthur Versluis, *Magic and Mysticism: An Introduction to Western Esotericism* (Plymouth: Rowman and Littlefield, 2007), 2; Greene, *Magi and Maggidim*, 46.

35. Waite, *Studies in Mysticism*, 54. Cf. *The Book of Ceremonial Magic*, xx.
36. Waite, *The Book of Ceremonial Magic*, xxiii.
37. Waite, "Thomas Vaughan," 71.
38. Waite, *Manual of Cartomancy*, 4.
39. Ibid, 2.
40. Ibid, 5.

THE HIGH-PRIESTESS

The Higher Magia's lingering presence is affirmed again in 1929's *The Holy Kabbalah*. A reference to a "higher sense" of magic from 1898's *Doctrine and Literature of the Kabalah* is changed to a "pretended higher sense,"[41] but in a later footnote Waite still cautions that "it would be unwise to deny altogether that there is such a higher sense."[42] His 1938 autobiography enthusiastically returns to the concept of a higher, mystical category of magic, indicating that it had likely never really gone. After reviewing his movement away from "occult paths" to "a more excellent way," Waite affirms that "there is however, a true Magia, in truth a Higher Magia."[43] These scatterings of continuing support for the concept indicate that Waite likely accentuated a stark division between magic and mysticism not to reject the Higher Magia but to save it from associations with theurgic and goetic practices, the value of which he was far less certain. This strategy of coinciding rejection and restoration is illustrated again by the contrast between his harsh dismissal of all forms of magic in 1915's *The Way of Divine Union* and the lingering importance of ceremonial magic to the ritual activity of the F.R.C.,[44] founded in the same year and dedicated to the elevation of consciousness through ritual incantation and imaginative visualization, using materials derived from the ancient wisdom of the Secret Tradition—an order, in short, that sought mystical attainment with the assistance of the high-priestess of magic.

RITUAL SEMIOTICS AND THE MAGICAL IMAGINATION

F.R.C. initiates pursued their ultimate ineffable goal through a praxis that included ritual interaction with particular images, symbols, words and phrases, engaging with these semiotic elements through acts of visualization and active imagination that owed much to both historical and contemporary magical contexts. The elevation of

---

41. Waite, *Doctrine and Literature of the Kabalah*, 441; *Holy Kabbalah*, 318.
42. Waite, *Holy Kabbalah*, 518n3.
43. Waite, *Shadows*, 26.
44. Waite, *Divine Union*, 25. Cf. 5–6, 23.

consciousness achieved through meditation upon symbols and images was crucial and I will expand on it in a moment, but first I would like to examine the root understanding of the relationship between language and ritual that made this inner magical transmutation possible. Language and magic have a relationship that goes back millennia. The very word "spell" emerges from a linguistic history in which a relationship between between the two seemed natural. Even now, though "spelling" is not seen as a remotely magical process, it denotes, as William Covino observes, "the visible materialization of invisible thought," as does the word "grammar," rooted in an etymology that includes medieval terms for sorcery—*gramarye* and *grimoire*.[45] For the magician, says Covino, "words transform reality, and facility with language makes multiple realities possible."[46]

In the F.R.C., adepts active in a particular ritual spent their time either chant-speaking liturgical phrases or listening to others do the same. Those not acting in the ritual stood to the side, but they too were intended to be entranced by the cadence of ritual language, all focused on the ultimate goal of losing awareness of the conscious self in the discovery of the higher personality within—the aspect of self that is aware of its monistic unity with God and world. It is unsurprising to find Williams, a wordsmith with a flair for magic and ritual, valuing the connection between language and the mystical experience derived through ceremony. Speaking of the ceremonial nature of Milton's poetry, he notes in *The English Poetic Mind* (1932) that "one of the advantages of ceremony, rightly used, is that it gives a place to self-consciousness, and a means whereby self-consciousness may be lost in the consciousness of the office filled or the ritual carried out."[47] Not just the language then, but the movement through the ritual itself is necessary for transmutation of consciousness—for a psychologized magical effect—to occur. An important passage in *Witchcraft* shows that Williams felt that a sense of the magic of ritual

---

45. William A. Covino, *Magic, Rhetoric, and Literacy: An Eccentric History of the Composing Imagination* (Albany: State University of New York Press, 1994), 5.
46. Ibid, 5–6.
47. Charles Williams, *The English Poetic Mind* (Oxford: Clarendon Press, 1932), 116.

THE HIGH-PRIESTESS

—both in and outside of ceremony—could help the self become aware of the cosmic importance of the tiniest word or movement. The "ordered movement" of ritual "maintains and increases that natural sense of the significance of movement. And, of course, of formulae, of words." This observation combines language and movement in affirmation of ritual, an approbation Williiams directly connects to magic: "A finger pointing is quite capable of seeming not only a significant finger, but a ritual finger; an evocative finger; not only a finger of meaning, but a finger of magic." Williams thus ritualizes the mundane, asserting, in a sense similar to the correspondent eros of Romantic Theology, that ceremonial movement and language can help realize maxims inherent in the doctrine of correspondences: "that any phenomenon might alter into another and truer self," and that "a phenomenon, being wholly itself, is laden with universal meaning." For Williams, as for most Hermetic thinkers, "A hand lighting a cigarette is the explanation of everything; a foot stepping from a train is the rock of all existence."[48] This ability of the microcosmic mundane to directly indicate macrocosmic significance is central to the acausal function of magical logic.[49] This correspondent perspective helps explain Williams's attraction to the ritual environment of the F.R.C., and indicates that he likely saw his masonic-Rosicrucian experiences as magical, in the high-priestess sense at the very least.

It is interesting to keep Williams's proverbial finger of magic in mind as we imagine him in the Salvator Mundi temple, watching Imperator Waite or another adept move through the room completing ritual processes of cleansing and initiation. Philip Wellby, an initiate who also spent time in ceremonies led by Waite, described him as a ritual leader who "imparted a living force to the phrase or peroration" of the rites in which he officiated. Wellby recalled times when he infused a "vitality of spirit into the spoken word" in such a way that "he appeared to be a veritable channel of force, dispensing

---

48. Williams, *Witchcraft*, 78–79.
49. Hanegraaff, *A Guide for the Perplexed*, 8, 130–34.

power that was beyond his own disposal in his ordinary daily avocations."[50] In Wellby's perception at least, Waite seems to have succeeded in filling himself with the magical force granted by the inner transmutation of consciousness. Ritual language and movement conspired to effect this transformation. Though some parts of the rituals simply involved listening to a knowledge lecture delivered by the Chief Celebrant, we have seen that others involved more actively ritualistic elements, many of them drawn from Waite's previous experiences in the modern occult ritual environment of the Golden Dawn. These included the reenactments of the crucifixion and rebirth of Christ and entombment of Christian Rosenkreutz in the Adeptus Minor ritual, and the intonation of particular combinations of divine names drawn from kabbalah or the angelic hierarchies, particularly during rituals intended to open and/or cleanse the temple—both the physical ritual space and the temple within—before commencing the ceremony for a particular grade.

The longstanding relationship between magic and semantics is also reflected in the F.R.C.'s infusion of elements of theurgy and invocation into its liturgy, some of these drawn directly from the Golden Dawn. The Fellowship cleansed and purified the temple via a ritual commonly used for such purposes in modern occult societies—the "Lesser Banishing Ritual of the Pentagram." This magical device has undergone a number of permutations and extensions in modern occultism, but it originated with a ritual taught to Neophytes in the Golden Dawn, based upon Lévi's description of a purifying protection spell directed against elemental spirits, called "the conjuration of the four."[51] The Master of the Temple followed the combination of

---

50. Wellby, "Arthur Edward Waite," 103–4. Cf. Gilbert, *A.E. Waite*, 145.
51. There is an interesting circle of occultist influence here, as Lévi's "conjuration of the four" was made more accessible to modern occultists by none other than Waite himself, shortly before the founding of the Golden Dawn. See Éliphas Lévi, *Transcendetal Magic: Its Doctrine and Ritual, Part 2: The Ritual of Transcendental Magic*, trans. Arthur Edward Waite (London: Rider, 1896), 221–23. For Lévi's original conception of "la conjuration des quatre," see *Dogme Et Rituel De La Haute Magie*, 2 vols., vol. 2, *Rituel* (Paris: Germer Bailliere, 1861), 86–89. See Francis King, *Astral Projection, Ritual Magic and Alchemy*, 37, on the extension of Lévi's ideas to the Golden Dawn system.

ritual language and gesture established by the Banishing Ritual when preparing both himself and the temple in the F.R.C.'s "Solemn Ceremony of Opening the Temple in the Light." Turning to the East, the Master performed what occultists, following Lévi, called the "Qabalistic Cross."[52] He touched his forehead and breast and then crossed shoulder to shoulder, pronouncing a Hebraic equivalent to the doxology of the Lord's Prayer, first uttering "*Ateh*" (Thine is/Thou art), and then three kabbalistic divine names: "*Malkuth*" (the kingdom), "*ve-Geburah*" (and the power), "*ve-Gedulah*" (and the glory). Holding his hands before him, wand beneath his arm, the Master then intoned "*Le Olamh. Amen*" (forever, amen). The F.R.C. departed in only one significant measure from the Lesser Banishing Ritual used by other occult societies: Instead of indicating a pentagram in the midst of the ritual, Waite's adepts returned more closely to Lévi's conflation of kabbalah and Catholicism, the Master of the Temple tracing the "Cosmic Cross" in the air with his wand as he "pronounces slowly and distinctly" the "Yod, He, Vau, He" of the Tetragrammaton.[53]

The Lesser Banishing Ritual, which Gilbert identifies as "the nearest thing to a purely magical ritual" encountered by Golden Dawn adepts who had not yet reached the level of the R.R. et A.C., was taught to Neophytes so that they could cleanse and protect themselves in private magical experimentation.[54] It appears that Charles Williams also learned how to use the Banishing Ritual at some point, and was impressed by its magical efficacy. He taught its basics to Joan Wallis in a letter,[55] and did the same to Lois Lang-Sims in another missive, teaching her the magical uses of the device in a manner that suggests a familiarity that goes beyond the F.R.C.'s "cosmic cross" adaptation: "It is a sign in some traditions of any occult Rite," wrote Williams, and drew the shape of the pentagram with arrows included

---

52. See, e.g., Regardie, *Golden Dawn*, 1:107.
53. Waite, "Neophyte," 12–13. Compare with the Golden Dawn's "The Lesser Ritual of the Pentagram," in Regardie, *Golden Dawn*, 1:106–7.
54. See Gilbert, *The Golden Dawn*, 60; King, *Ritual Magic in England*, 57.
55. Charles Williams to Joan Wallis, 4 October 1940.

to indicate the direction in which it must be traced. "Beginning here, you make it in that order, and that is for the Banishment of Evil Spirits or Elementals and the stabilizing of the good." Williams was also aware of the Pentagram's darker uses: "But drawn reversed, which would be upside down and against the sun, it is the very opposite, and magically evil." Williams did not care to "consciously and deliberately" incorporate the pentagram in this way, just as he would not utter the Lord's Prayer backwards or pronounce the Tetragrammaton in reverse "like the Wicked Man in my new novel" (Simon Leclerc of *All Hallows' Eve*).[56] He saw a useful magical tool in what many magicians in the modern Western tradition see as "the foundation of all rituals."[57] We cannot be sure whether he was also taught the Banishing Ritual individually, perhaps by one of his Stella Matutina friends, but knowledge of its basic elements and purposes would have become second nature from the many times he encountered it in the F.R.C., particularly when he himself carried out the ritual as Master of the Temple.[58]

The F.R.C.'s incorporation of the Banishing Ritual also included another element that reflected the magicity of occult ceremonial language: a recitation of the "Angelical Formula,"[59] which invoked the names of the four Archangels connected with the four elements in order to muster protective forces to surround the initiate.[60] In part this invocation represented less an attempt to converse with higher intelligences, and more an attempt at ritual transformation of the psyche. The adept was instructed to "join in this Sacred Working" of the Angelical Formula, "Repeating the words mentally, so that it may have effect upon him."[61] Moreover, the language of the ritual does

---

56. Charles Williams to Lois Lang-Sims, 21 March 1944, in *Letters to Lalage*, 75.
57. Luhrmann, *Persuasions of the Witch's Craft*, 243.
58. For further discussion re: Williams and the Lesser Banishing Ritual, see Lindop, *Charles Williams*, 134; Edward Gauntlett, "Charles Williams and Magic," *The Charles Williams Society Newsletter*, no. 106 (Spring 2003): 17.
59. Waite, "Neophyte," 13.
60. Regardie, *Golden Dawn*, 1:107; Waite, "Neophyte," 13. Cf. King, *Astral Projection, Ritual Magic and Alchemy*, 37.
61. Waite, "Neophyte," 12–13.

THE HIGH-PRIESTESS

not necessarily indicate that an invocation has taken place, though it can be interpreted that way, as the Master states that each angel is (at least figuratively) about him in particular corners of the temple.[62] Other rituals, however, clearly understand an invocation to have occurred. At the grade of Zelator, a similar grouping of incantations is described as "sacred invocations."[63] At Theoreticus the name of Raphael, the angel syncretically associated with the grade, is invoked in order to consecrate Air, the element of the grade.[64] The Adeptus Exemptus ritual features a moment of magical praxis even more directly reminiscent of the occultist desire to draw down divine power for the enrichment of the self. Here the Chief Celebrant prays that "the Great White Light which I invoke upon the soul of this Postulant, who has risen to the life in Thee, may descend also upon myself in the operation of Thy Sacred Mysteries."[65] This light, asserts the Celebrant, will purify him and give him the power to exalt the postulant to the next level of initiation. This drawing down of divine power for the purification and empowerment of the self was, as we have seen, a core element of modern occult magic as practiced by the Golden Dawn and its subsidiaries and imitators.

These blurred lines between ritual semiotics and magical practices ranging from angelic invocation to occultist protection devices undermine understandings of the F.R.C. as "purely mystical." Acknowledging this complexity does not require us to question either the mystic heritage or the ineffable goal of F.R.C. experience. The paradox of achieving an awareness beyond language through intense semiotic engagement has been a central feature of practices deemed mystical by their performers. David Katz describes perceptions of the power of language held by mystics the world over: "Mantras, koans, mystical alphabets and lexicons, ascent texts, prayers, the repetition of scripture, the recitation of religious poetry, and still other linguistic acts…incorporate and encapsulate a

---

62. Ibid, 13.
63. Waite, "Adeptus Exemptus," 11–12.
64. Waite, "Theoreticus," 9.
65. Waite, "Adeptus Exemptus," 29.

dynamic power, the dynamic power, that enlivens the entire cosmic order. By deciphering their meaning, by utilizing their potential, the mystical personality is empowered to alter its own nature and fate, and thereby effect the historical and metahistorical order of things."[66] This deployment of linguistically based meditative practices to alter the inner self and translate the dynamism of (ie. invoke) the divine was exactly the purpose of ritual in the F.R.C., as in the Golden Dawn before it.

The manner in which these orders approached semiotic engagement, however, had aspects more specifically connected to the magical heritage of the esoteric traditions than most other mystical movements that emphasize Katz's dynamic, quasi-magical hermeneutical process. Without sign, symbol and word, these Rosicrucian adepts would not have been able to access the power of imagination, long held to be of supreme importance in esoteric practice.[67] Much of the purpose of ritual in occult secret societies, including the F.R.C., was to offer an environment of symbol and image in which the visualization, concentration and meditation deemed necessary for alteration of consciousness could occur.[68] Imagination was the function that enabled these actions. This was not Coleridgian "fancy" but, as Westcott instructed initiates of the R.R. et A.C., the "Creative Faculty of the human mind, the plastic energy—the Formative Power."[69] This "orderly and intentional mental process" was perceived to tie the ideal to the material,[70] or, in monist perspectives such as that of Williams, to eradicate distinctions between the two in

---

66. Katz, "Mystical Speech and Mystical Meaning," 24.
67. On the importance of imagination in the esoteric traditions see Faivre, *Access to Western Esotericism*, 12–13; Hanegraaff, *A Guide for the Perplexed*, 8–10. On the ramifications of this context for the Golden Dawn see Christopher Plaisance, "Magic Made Modern?: Re-Evaluating the Novelty of the Golden Dawn's Magic," *Correspondences* 2, no. 2 (2014): 165–74.
68. Luhrmann, *Persuasions of the Witch's Craft*, 241; Hanegraaff, *A Guide for the Perplexed*, 45.
69. William Wynn Westcott (as "G. H. Fra. N.O.M."), "Flying Roll No. 5: Supplementary Remarks," in *Astral Projection, Ritual Magic, and Alchemy: Golden Dawn Material by S.L. Macgregor Mathers and Others*, ed. Francis King (Rochester, VT: Destiny, 1987), 51.
70. Ibid.

order to enable "macrocosmic-microcosmic union."[71] Using the example of astrological symbols, Williams argues that though the images of the zodiac "may be but the fables of astronomy," the application of imagination to their symbolism allows the mind to become aware of "the principles at work" in the human and galactic bodies, and through them the "spiritual heavens" to which they correspond. Imagination generates incarnation: by envisioning the images of the zodiac, "they, like the whole universe, exhibit the mystery by which spirit becomes flesh, without losing spirit."[72]

The concept of imagination as a power involved in linking the ideal and material worlds was not new to the modern era. A long, complex history of philosophical speculation preceded the modern esoteric view of imagination as mental power, much of it produced by religious thinkers interested in its capacity to glimpse higher principles via material phenomena.[73] Modern magic, however, elevated the imagination to new heights, influenced by Romantic conceptions of imagination as a creative, active power, even unto the point of Idealism—the belief that existence can be created from the imaginative perspective of the subject.[74] An example of a theory approaching this radical perspective, which we might call the "astral imagination," is seen in Dr. E.W. Berridge's instruction to Second Order initiates of the Golden Dawn: "The imagination is a reality. When a man imagines, he actually creates a form on the Astral or some higher plane; and this form is as real and objective to intelligent beings on that plane, as our earthly surroundings are to us."[75] Imagination thus bridges realities for Berridge, constructing an astral form of the self in an alternate realm of imaginal matter. While the astral self thus

---

71. Williams, "Index of the Body," 83. Cf. Luhrmann, *Persuasions of the Witch's Craft*, 126.
72. Williams, "Index of the Body," 83.
73. See Plaisance, "Magic Made Modern?" 165–74; Egil Asprem, "Esotericism and the Scholastic Imagination," 4–11.
74. On magical imagination in English Romanticism, see Covino, *Magic, Rhetoric, and Literacy*, 74–78.
75. E.W. Berridge (as V. H. Fra. Resurgam), "Flying Roll No. 5: Some Thoughts on the Imagination," in *Astral Projection, Ritual Magic, and Alchemy: Golden Dawn Material by S.L. Macgregor Mathers and Others*, ed. Francis King (Rochester, VT: Destiny, 1987), 51.

created is a product of the imagination in Berridge's conception, his and similar theories saw the "higher plane" thus accessed as pre-existing and actual. Others saw themselves as projecting aspects of the inner self onto an imagined tableau, without creating or interacting with an external real; practitioners of modern psychologized magic imaginatively engaged with mythical forms, narratives and images in order to evoke, subdue or balance forces within.[76] Whether the magical imagination was perceived in this more ephemeral manner or as the tool for real engagement with higher realms that Williams saw it as, the goals of its deployment varied: the psycho-spiritual improvement or alteration of the self or others, the instantiation of dreams or visions, the manipulation of physical forces, some of these also still "occult" to the methods and instruments of the physical sciences, and, more essentially, the elevation of consciousness required to achieve both practical and mystical ends.[77]

All of these targets were achieved through the application of a strong, developed will to the imagination. Leading Golden Dawn adepts like Westcott and Farr taught initiates the basic modern occult magical formula, as summarized by Berridge: "When the Imagination creates an image, and the Will directs and uses that image, marvellous magical effects may be obtained."[78] The faculties of will and imagination were considered to work together in developing the adept's ability to visualize—to expand their vision from a perception of physical objects or symbols into a much grander imaginal space.[79] This visualization could take many forms, but Mathers's instruction

---

76. Alison Butler, *Victorian Occultism and the Making of Modern Magic: Invoking Tradition* (New York: Palgrave Macmillan, 2011), 41. On imagination as a learned, trainable skill that has been used by esoteric practitioners to forge perceptive experiences such as astral travel, see Egil Asprem, "Explaining the Esoteric Imagination: Towards a Theory of Kataphatic Practice," *Aries* 17, no. 1 (2017): 17–50.

77. See Owen, *Place of Enchantment*, 148–52; Luhrmann, *Persuasions of the Witch's Craft*, 126, 297–306; Plaisance, "Magic Made Modern?" 165–68.

78. Berridge, "Flying Roll No. 5," 47. Cf. Butler, *The Making of Modern Magic*, 156–57. Butler argues that this active imagination is largely a modern phenomenon, though Plaisance has identified similar concepts in magical practices dating to the late antique period. See "Magic Made Modern?" 169–73.

79. Luhrmann, *Persuasions of the Witch's Craft*, 207.

in clairvoyance in the Golden Dawn's Flying Roll No. 11 is an indicative example of how the process might work. To use a symbol for clairvoyant divination, the adept should "with the utmost concentration, gaze at it, comprehend it, formulate its meaning and relations."[80] Once the mind had latched upon the image, the adept could transfer their vision to "thought seeing" and "let one form of apprehension glide on with the other—produce the reality of the dream vision, by positive will in the waking state" (77). Once in this elevated frame of mind, the initiate should begin to utter the divine names: "This invocation produces and harmonises currents of spiritual force in sympathy with your object" (77). In the resulting stage of consciousness, the adept could project themselves onto alternate astral planes (80).

We have no evidence that Williams was interested in astral travel, though it is one of the powers given by the stone of Suleiman in *Many Dimensions*. Mathers describes another ritual approach to magical visualization, however, one with "higher aims," that correlates more closely to the Higher Magia of the F.R.C. This magical exercise, called "Rising in the Planes" (80), saw the adept seek mystical attainment by visualizing an ascent in consciousness up the middle pillar of the Tree of Life. As this was the central focus of F.R.C. adepts as well, it is worth citing the whole of Mathers's instruction in order to better conceptualize the modern magical context of the visualization techniques used in the F.R.C.:

> By concentration and contemplation of the Divine, you formulate a Tree of Life passing from you to the spiritual realms above and beyond you. Picture to yourself that you stand in Malkuth—then by

---

80. S.L. MacGregor Mathers (as G.H. Frater D.D.C.F.), "Flying Roll No. 11: Clairvoyance," in *Astral Projection, Ritual Magic, and Alchemy: Golden Dawn Material by S.L. Macgregor Mathers and Others*, ed. Francis King (Rochester, VT: Destiny, 1987), 76. See Owen, *Place of Enchantment*, 149–50, for a summary of Mathers's ideas on visualization, clairvoyance and magic, and Asprem, "Explaining the Esoteric Imagination," 18–23, for an analysis of Mathers's concepts in the context of Golden Dawn perceptions of the role of imagination in astral travel.

the use of the Divine Names and aspirations you strive upward by the Path of Tau toward Yesod, neglecting the crossing rays which attract you as you pass up. Look upwards to the Divine Light shining down from Kether upon you. From Yesod leads up the Path of Temperance, Samekh, the arrow cleaving upward leads the way to Tiphereth, the Great central Sun of Sacred Power. (80)

The adepts of the F.R.C. also used "concentration and contemplation" to travel through the boughs of the Tree of Life. As I illustrated in Chapter 2, the goal of striving to rise from Malkuth to Tiphereth on the middle pillar paths of Tau and Samekh had more diverse purposes in the Golden Dawn—an attainment of occult power as well as a mystic principle—but the magical techniques used to visualize ascent to union with the higher self, the divine Son (or, here, Sun) within, is virtually the same.

In his autobiography, Waite reflected fondly on his long, as yet unfinished journey to self-perfection and attainment via imaginative interaction with sephirotic symbolism: "As one who ascends the Tree of Life, I have passed upwards clothed in Symbols and have dwelt amidst a ministry of images." He saw this mystic life of images as a "good and true leading...great schooling is offered to the mind therein."[81] His ultimate goal for the mystic life was, as we have seen, to "pass beyond the signs," but first the individual must meet with the symbols of the Secret Tradition in the mind, deploying the imagination to create, "a living meaning behind the Symbols and Sacraments." The act of transforming the visual symbol into a greater meaning in the mind reflects Mathers's instruction to pass beyond the symbol into a higher imaginative real, a connection supported by a discussion of the faculty of imagination earlier in *Shadows of Life and Thought*, where Waite identifies a "true Magia" in Shakespeare's famous phrase, "Imagination bodies forth the forms of things unknown."[82] Who has not memorized this line, Waite asks, "And

---

81. Waite, *Shadows*, 277.
82. *A Midsummer Night's Dream*, 5.1.

THE HIGH-PRIESTESS

which of us all has spanned its height and depth of meaning?" His reference to a "true magia" again shows that he had not abandoned the Higher Magia. It also shows that this form of magic, seen as deploying imagination to make the unseen manifest, was not simply a form of ancient wisdom or non-phenomenal mystical practice. Consistent with the magical views of his younger years, Waite continued to value practical engagement with the phenomenal for what it could reveal of the noumenal—"the outward mode of things removes its veils...so that we behold its inward beauty." The higher magical function of imagination that tears away this veil is described as "a lucid mode of mind" that "enlightens some at least who come into this world." Waite includes himself in this group, reflecting that he may never have proceeded along his mystical path without the initial stimulation of imagination in childhood through fantastic tales and the "Magic of Faërie."[83]

Active imagination formed part of the F.R.C.'s Higher Magia as adepts like Williams visualized themselves as Shekinah, ascending the middle pillar to the mystic marriage in Tiphereth or the direct gnosis of Daath. Waite did not produce any knowledge lectures or ritual notes that specifically explain the techniques used to achieve mystical attainment, but from descriptions of the visual layout of the temple and instructions to concentrate on various programmatically arrayed symbols of the Secret Tradition, we can assume an important role for meditation upon the visual, blurring forward into higher vision. At several points the candidate is reminded to move from the sensory visual input provided by a symbol into "the thought-body alone"[84]—language that it is suggestive of the astral imagination propounded by magicians like Berridge and Mathers. A direct astral reference is unlikely, but the action of imagination was certainly designed to transport adepts onto another plane of experience. "It rests with us," Neophytes were instructed, "Whether they [the symbols of the grades] shall remain symbolism, or whether we shall

---

83. Waite, *Shadows*, 26.
84. Waite, "Adeptus Major," 37.

pass in them, and they shall pass in us, into a living region of experience."[85] This expansion from symbolism into infinite inner spaces of consciousness is emphasized again in the grade of Practicus, where the initiate was instructed to let the symbolism they had so far encountered "sink into your heart that you will be penetrated by its active meaning."[86] This instruction suggests the divine gnosis or clairvoyant knowledge that other modern occultists sought through imaginative engagement with material semiotics. The Third Order Portal ritual echoes this while also reflecting the order's programmatic syncretism: the adept was instructed to take up a symbol made up of the four creatures of Ezekiel: representing the four elements, the four aspects of man in the course of transmutation via F.R.C. initiation, and the four lower sephiroth. In the middle of the symbol was the "White Wheel of the Spirit," representing the cosmic Christ and the Emerald Tablet of Hermes Trismegistus. The adept was to place this image onto their forehead,[87] a technique used to gain clairvoyant access to a symbol's correspondent referents in modern occultism.[88]

The F.R.C. thus joined other occult groups in deploying modern adaptations of visual, auditory and kinetic magical interaction in a variety of semiotic contexts, seeking a route from the material to the ideal and back again. Two other related concepts also connect Williams's ritual experiences to the modern occult network. First, though the F.R.C.'s magical practices were certainly more subdued than other orders, its goals were consistent with most other occult actors: the ritual elevation of consciousness and transformation of the self for the ultimate purpose of mystical attainment. It was this goal to which Golden Dawn adepts swore to apply themselves in the Adeptus Minor ritual, and which Westcott identified as the "Higher Magic" that was the "main object" of R.R. et A.C. ritual activity.[89]

---

85. Waite, "Neophyte," 45.
86. Waite, "Practicus," 40. Cf. 37.
87. Waite, "Portal of the Third Order," 32.
88. See, e.g., Mathers, "Flying Roll No. 11," 79.
89. Regardie, *Complete Golden Dawn*, 7:42; Westcott, "Flying Roll No. 19," 115. Cf. Owen, *Place of Enchantment*, 76–77.

Even Aleister Crowley, whose magical practices spanned a goetic and theurgic spectrum that Waite would have rejected out of hand, maintained this central focus on mystical attainment. This was first envisioned more secularly—as union with an elevated, non-divine aspect of the self—but in Crowley's later perception of attainment, magical practice was sometimes directed toward union with a deity called "Aiwass," who he believed he had encountered during a mystical experience in Cairo in 1904.[90] The "single main definition of the object of all magical ritual," he said in his influential *Magick in Theory and Practice*, was the union of microcosm and macrocosm, "or, in the language of Mysticism, union with God."[91] Crowley's conceptions of God and the process of achieving this union were much different than those of Waite or Williams, but this statement represents his awareness of continuity between his own magical goals and the aims of attainment in the Western magical tradition. The application of magical visualization practices to mystical attainment has proved a mainstay in occultism, where, as we saw in Chapter One, most practitioners have viewed the ultimate end of magical experience as ineffable and interior, but have pursued this goal through active interaction with symbol and imagery.

Second, despite Waite's attempt to present the F.R.C. as something entirely removed from the concerns of "phenomenal occultism," the order's turn within to a focus on self-transmutation and the production of altered states of consciousness was entirely consistent with the modern magical trend toward psychologization.[92] This shift is emphasized by Dion Fortune's definition of magic as an

---

90. See Pasi, "Varieties of Magical Experience," 16–28.
91. Aleister Crowley, *Magick in Theory and Practice* (New York: Castle, 1971), 11. Cf. Pasi, "Varieties of Magical Experience," 147.
92. On psychologization in modern magic see Hanegraaff, "How Magic Survived," 366–69; Marco Pasi, "The Modernity of Occultism," in *Hermes in the Academy: Ten Years' Study of Western Esotericism at the University of Amsterdam*, ed. Wouter J. Hanegraaff and Joyce Pijnenburg (Amsterdam: Amsterdam University Press, 2009), 66. Asprem cautions against overextending views of modern magic as internally directed. See Egil Asprem, "Magic Naturalized? Negotiating Science and Occult Experience in Aleister Crowley's Scientific Illuminism," *Aries* 8, no. 2 (2008): 142.

entirely internal, psychological process: "It is my belief, after having worn out two pairs of ceremonial slippers in treading magical circles, that ceremonial magic works exceedingly powerfully upon the subconscious mind, and upon nothing else."[93] Fortune consciously shifted the focus of magical practice away from the manipulation of external phenomena to the transformation of consciousness and the acquisition of "elemental energy" trapped in the recesses of the self.[94] Hanegraaff argues that this mix of magic and psychology, also taken up by influential twentieth-century occultists such as Israel Regardie, is the greatest single outlier of modern magic, a theoretical and discursive shift that increasingly came to see magic "as, essentially, a series of spiritual techniques for 'self-development'."[95] As we have seen, the ways, means and aims of this self-development could differ radically among modern magicians, but the F.R.C.'s aim of elevating consciousness through ritual language and imaginal visualization is congruous with this rapidly adapting psychological focus. Williams's encounter with magic in the F.R.C. constituted a long period of intense, focused engagement with the interwoven semiotics of the esoteric traditions, attempting the alteration of consciousness sought by most other modern occultists.

Charles Williams was a ritualist and an imaginative; in that he was a magician. It would be an error for me to apply the term to him the same way as I might to Crowley or Mathers or Fortune, all of who publicly embraced magic as a corner post of their identities and belief systems. Williams was not nearly so vocal: his ritual activity was carried out in private, and his knowledge of magical practices such as the Banishing Ritual was communicated in letters rather than in published works. We have seen that close friends were largely unaware of his F.R.C. activities; many of these same people were

---

93. Dion Fortune, "The Rationale of Magic," *London Forum (Incorporating The Occult Review)* 60, no. 3 (September 1934): 180. Cf. Miriam Wallraven, *Women Writers and the Occult in Literature and Culture: Female Lucifers, Priestesses, and Witches* (New York: Routledge, 2015), 148.
94. Fortune, "The Rationale of Magic," 180–81.
95. Hanegraaff, "Magic V," 743.

shocked when Williams's sadomasochistic ritual behaviour was revealed by women such as Lois Lang-Sims.[96] Yet, the sources I have surveyed in this chapter clearly indicate that Williams valued magical tradition for its ability to connect the "lower correspondences" of image, word and symbol to the "final absolute power,"[97] joining the microcosmic self to the macrocosmic divine. The magical world offered an acausal, spiritual epistemology that supported his immanent cosmology—had, in fact, historically emerged in tandem with its correspondent tenets. However, though it is clear that Williams incorporated occult magical techniques such as active imagination and psychologized invocation into his practice of the "high-priestess of heaven," biographical materials and non-fictional sources such as *Witchcraft* are not alone enough to get a sense of the importance of magic to his system, how he perceived it to function, and which aspects of magical tradition he valued or rejected. As Gunnar Urang observes, it is in the novels that Williams is most explicit about his preferred methods for magical workings.[98] As with his taste for kabbalistic symbolism and his Rosicrucian experiences, we must turn to his fiction to help broaden our understanding of high-priestess magic and its applications.

---

96. See Williams and Lang-Sims, *Letters to Lalage*, 18–21.
97. Williams, *Witchcraft*, 232, 35.
98. Urang, *Shadows of Heaven*, 51.

CHAPTER 6
A MAGICAL LIFE IN FICTION

Not just magic as high-priestess of heaven but every form of magical theory and practice conceivable can be found in Williams's fiction, from the shamanism of the African forces in *Shadows of Ecstasy* to the black mass conducted by Gregory Persimmons in *War in Heaven*. The coinherent acts performed by Sybil Coningsby, Peter Stanhope and Chloe Burnett have magical implications, while the F.R.C.'s magical elevation of consciousness echoes in Roger's experience of mystical states in ritualistic environments prepared by Considine. The magical power enabled by the correspondence between symbol and ideal in the tarot of *The Greater Trumps*; Berringer's invocation of angelical principles in *The Place of the Lion*; astral travel in *Many Dimensions*; the utterance of reversed divine names by Simon Leclerc—all these indicate the extent of the author's personal research into both modern and historical magical practice. The deployment of magical symbolism and practice varies from novel to novel, as does the type of concept or praxis under consideration. The alchemical magic of Considine blurs into a focus on magical objects—Graal, stone, trumps—in the next three novels, though a number of characters also possess innate thaumaturgical power and explore magical knowledge, while *The Place of the Lion* sees invocation and revocation of angels share centre stage with Anthony's magical deployment of the primordial language of the prelapsarian Adam. Magic is not as prevalent a theme in *Descent into Hell*, though Stanhope's coinherent adetpship splits time with Lawrence Wentworth's creation of a succubus, but it returns to prominence—in a more negative form than in the earlier novels—in *All Hallows' Eve*, where the novel's villainy is driven by the black magic of Simon Leclerc.[1]

The novels do, however, communicate a fairly consistent magical ethic defined by the author's two central priorities: the capability of high-priestess magic to promulgate mystical experience, and coinherence. This ethic usually accords with magical thought common among Christian occultists of the day. Gareth Knight, one of those few who have interpreted Williams's work with an unproblematic awareness of his Christian occultism, has provided us with perhaps the best description of the philosophy of magic that appears in his novels:

> In most areas of life, and in occultism particularly, we find ourselves concerned not so much with the mechanism of techniques, but as to the motivation behind their use. We are likely to understand Williams' intentions in a deeper and more rewarding way in the light of the subject matter of his novels and poems, which are illustrations of the practicalities, pitfalls and potential of magic in most of its forms and phases. Indeed the tenor of his books tends not to a condemnation of a magical view of the world but to the elevation of magic, its redemption in a sense.[2]

As Knight identifies, Williams's presentation of both the "pitfalls" and "potential" of magic is structured around a distinction built on motivation rather than preexisting societal judgments about the

---

1. For a review of the nature and function of magic in the novels see Urang, *Shadows of Heaven*, 51–56.
2. Knight, *Magical World of Charles Williams*, 11.

permissibility of a particular practice. Williams thus does not reject magic out of hand as has been assumed by cordon sanitaire criticism. Rather, he builds a distinction between applications of self-centered and selfless will. Considine's ultimate failure, for example, is not that he seeks to transmute the energies of passion, lust and grief through alchemical and magical "corollaries of the union" in order to explore "all the capacities of man."[3] This process itself might be acceptable, but the magus betrays the spirit of high-priestess magic when he dismisses those who will "tell you to use experience as a way of uniting yourself with God," and lays out a vision that precisely emulates the approach to magic that prompted Waite to dismiss its validity entirely: "I do not turn men to any such remote end; I tell them that they are themselves as gods, if they will, and the ecstasy of that knowledge is their victory."[4] We have seen that the F.R.C. also viewed mystic attainment as a deification, but Considine seeks apotheosis without actual *theos*, the establishment of the self as a god rather than discovery of the higher self that is God. This self-centred approach to magic is repeated by numerous magicians in the novels, from Leclerc to Henry Lee to Persimmons to Manesseh and Dimitri, and represents a sustained critique, carried out over a twenty-year period, of the obsession with self-divinization and self-empowerment often found in the modern magical ethos. The critique is bolstered by a contrasting set of characters—Sybil, Stanhope, Nancy, Arglay and Anthony—coinherent adepts whose will and desire are directed so far from the needs of the self that they are at times scarcely aware of their own actions.

The novels contain far more description as to how Williams may have envisioned the praxis of coinherence than can be found in his letters or other published writings. The most complete description we have is the testimony of Lois Lang-Sims, who was instructed by Williams to offer herself in substitution for Alice Hadfield, later Williams's biographer, then a close friend and companion of "the

---

3. Williams, *Shadows of Ecstasy*, 180.
4. Ibid.

Household." Hadfield was undertaking a sea voyage from Bermuda to England across the war-torn seas of 1944; Williams worried for her safety and psychological well-being. He therefore instructed Lang-Sims, who had never met Hadfield, to offer herself on behalf of "the Company"—the Companions of the Co-inherence. There was little helpful advice to accompany this command, except a note that she may feel nothing in return, or she may be "suddenly inconvenienced." There was no doubt in Williams's mind, however, that "this is a real thing"; any assumption that the function of coinherence might be purely metaphysical was forestalled.[5] Lang-Sims was confused: "*How*, I asked myself, was I to 'present myself shyly to Almighty God in exchange for her'?"[6] She does not seem to have thought to turn to Williams's fiction for support, but she may have found some help in that direction had she done so. The novels are by no means handbooks to Williams's strange practice of "transformative interchange,"[7] but, as both Knight and Newman have shown, they are dotted with characters using magical means to effect coinherent healing, both physical and psychological.[8]

ACTIVE IMAGINATION

One important element of coinherent praxis seems to have been a magical understanding of imagination. In an unpublished paper that provided much of the grist for his later essay on the Romantic poetry of Blake and Wordsworth,[9] Williams described coinherence as "one of the great poetic achievements of the Romantics," directly linking Romantic imagination to coinherent praxis by virtue of Blake's Platonic assertion that "'General Forms have their vitality in Particu-

---

5. Williams and Lang-Sims, *Letters to Lalage*, 53. Cf. Newman, "Companions of the Co-Inherence," 9.
6. Williams and Lang-Sims, *Letters to Lalage*, 54.
7. Knight, *Magical World of Charles Williams*, 11.
8. Newman, "Companions of the Co-Inherence," 11, 21; Knight, *Magical World of Charles Williams*, 67. Cf. Carpenter, *The Inklings*, 105.
9. Williams, "Blake and Wordsworth."

lars'";[10] in other words, that the macrocosm expresses and defines itself in the microcosm. Because of this correspondent relationship, small acts of sacrifice and forgiveness are connected to greater cosmic realities. It is "the profound grasp" of this relationship, Williams wrote, that Blake understood as the "holy Imagination" and Wordsworth meant to indicate, in part, with his concept of the "feeling intellect."[11] Williams rather freely adapts the philosophy of both poets to his coinherent vision in order to emphasize imagination as a central ingredient in achieving the substitution of self for others through the link between the divine principles of sacrifice, forgiveness and love and their lower "particulars."

The imaginal function of coinherence is expanded in the novels, but here it is the modern occult active imagination that seems most at play. When Stanhope attempts to save Pauline from the morbid presence of her doppelgänger, he does so by projecting her person and her struggle onto an imaginative plane, and there offering himself in exchange for her.

> He visualized her going along a road, any road; he visualized another Pauline coming to meet her. And as he did so his mind contemplated not the first but the second Pauline; he took trouble to apprehend the vision, he summoned through all his sensations an approaching fear… He sat on, imagining to himself the long walk with its sinister possibility, the ogreish world lying around, the air with its treachery to all sane appearance. His own eyes began to seek and strain and shrink, his own feet, quiet though actually they were, began to weaken with the necessity of advance upon the road down which the girl was passing. The body of his flesh received her alien terror, his mind carried the burden of her world.[12]

---

10. Charles Williams, untitled, undated, CWSA I.C.64, 11. Williams quotes Blake's *Jerusalem*, 91.29–30. The manuscript is typed and no author is named, but its reference to coinherence and the similarities to "Blake and Wordsworth" indicate Williams's authorship.
11. Ibid.
12. Williams, *Descent into Hell*, 100–1.

A MAGICAL LIFE IN FICTION

As Knight observes, the technique employed by Stanhope here is distinctly magical.[13] It is, moreover, distinctly modern in its entwining of imagination and psychology: there are noticeable typological similarities to occult practices of visualization and even astral imagination. Stanhope uses intense visualization techniques to elevate his imagination to the point where he is able to quite literally experience himself as Pauline in order to take on both the sensory and psychological horror of her encounter, with the strain of his own eyes and the tread of his own feet. Though both body and mind carry her burden, the entire scene takes place on an imaginal plane. This is, in fact, the key to its success, as Stanhope is protected from the full visceral horror of the doppelgänger "because his senses received their communication from within not from without."[14] Stanhope is aware that the doppelgänger may be a manifestation of Pauline's imagination, but "that made no difference to his action." The authorial voice takes over to explain that the imaginal is the real if felt to be so by its perceiver; burdens can be relieved, horrors eradicated on the imaginal plane if the coinherent adept acknowledges this imaginal reality.[15]

We know from the essay on Blake and Wordsworth that Williams saw imagination as an important part of the method of coinherence, but we cannot definitively determine that Williams applied these elements of visualization and astral imagination beyond such fictional presentations. It is important, however, to recall the unusual congruity between the novels and his personal life and philosophy, and to remember that Williams identified closely with Stanhope, to the extent of taking on the character's identity in his own life. The likelihood that Williams is communicating imaginative elements of coinherent praxis that other occultists would have recognized as consistent with astral imagination is reinforced by an event in *Many*

---

13. Knight, *Magical World of Charles Williams*, 67. Knight's book thoroughly examines the magical elements of Williams's novels, from the useful perspective of a practicing magician.
14. Williams, *Descent into Hell*, 101.
15. Williams, *Descent into Hell*, 101–2.

Dimensions. Chloe and Arglay use similar techniques in their attempt to rescue Elijah Pondon, a lab assistant in the employ of Giles Tumulty, who has been trapped in time after experimenting with the application of "etheric vibrations" to the stone in order to enable time travel. Arglay draws what looks "almost like a magical diagram,"[16] with a rectangle in the middle and two or three small sketches representing human figures, intended to "help the mind" concentrate as he and Chloe visualize the laboratory they wish to travel into through time and space (136). Though Chloe "gallantly strove to keep her mind fixed on the diagram at which she was gazing," she is unsuccessful (138); without accuracy of vision, she wanders into an imaginal abyss. Arglay is better able to precisely "shape in his mind the image of the room" and to clearly formulate to himself his desire to help Pondon (140). His intentness of vision, his careful formulation of imagination based upon the diagram, and his clear resolution of "thoughts into lucidity" all contribute to a transformation of the surrounding real (140). Thousands of other planes of time and space swirl around him until "an entirely new plane of things thrust itself in and across various of the appearances" (141). Despite great physical discomfort Arglay is able to grasp this plane in his imagination and, through the unity of all times and places provided by the stone, manages to project to Pondon an image of the same space but in his own time, allowing the lab assistant to step free from the plane of his entrapment.

Arglay does not travel to Pondon in astral form as most occultists likely would have envisioned, but his use of visualization techniques to clairvoyantly envision Pondon's time and space is exactly the method of astral imagination taught by occultists like Mathers and Berridge. The imagination's constructive ability to create realms capable of interacting with material reality enables Arglay's vision of Pondon's future to become the lab assistant's reality, recalling a musing in Williams's Commonplace Book, where he wonders if the "knowledge that time + space are only modes of thought" might not

---

16. Williams, *Many Dimensions*, 136. See 134–43, 196–97 for details of Pondon's rescue.

be "the beginning of all magic."[17] The Romantic Idealism of this astral theory would have been attractive to the radically monistic Williams. By virtue of the unity of all things, what the coinherent adept imagines into being connects to that which already is, with the power to affect it for good or evil. Though Arglay's imagination of Pondon's reality is certainly intended as a fantastic device, it shares the same belief in the power of imagination to shape new realities, both exterior and interior, that is indicated by Stanhope's visualization techniques. Such depictions indicate that Williams had a clear, personal understanding of occult theories of magical imagination; the vivid descriptions of Arglay's pain and nausea, as well as the terror implicit in Chloe's failure to maintain the intense focus required, suggest that this familiarity may have been bred of personal experimentation with astral imagination, in addition to the visualization techniques practiced in the F.R.C.

ACTIVE WILL

The coinherent action described in the novels aligns even more closely with modern magic in its emphasis on the will. We have seen that magicians like Berridge and Crowley saw will as the indispensable partner of imagination in magical practice; Williams's view of coinherence—as illustrated in his fiction anyway—followed along the same lines. Stanhope, for example, must "deliberately" open himself to Pauline's fear, must be "devoted to the action of his spirit."[18] The primacy of the will is one element that differentiates modern magic from earlier forms. The nineteenth century ushered in this change, beginning with Eliphas Lévi,[19] continuing with the teachings of H.P. Blavatsky and the Golden Dawn,[20] and becoming,

---

17. Commonplace Book, 74. The second quotation is taken from Edith Nesbit's *The Story of the Amulet* (1906).
18. Williams, *Descent into Hell*, 100, 102.
19. See Owen, *Place of Enchantment*, 69; Gilbert, *A.E. Waite*, 89.
20. See, e.g., Percy Bullock (as L.O), "Flying Roll No. 27: The Principia of Theurgia or the Higher Magic," in *Astral Projection, Ritual Magic and Alchemy: Golden Dawn Material*

perhaps, most significant in Aleister Crowley's Thelema, which instructed initiates in the development of the will through magical methods. Thus, Crowley's instruction to his followers to "Do what thou wilt" should be read not simply as an anarchic manifesto, but as an encouragement to discover and accomplish the "True Will" of the individual.[21] As Henrik Bogdan illustrates, this view of the will has distinctly religious elements, with the faculty elevated to the status of a "divine or supernatural aspect of man."[22] In this sense, the view of the will that Williams encountered in the F.R.C.—as a human faculty that must undergo transmutation for the purposes of elevation to the level of divine will—is situated squarely in the modern occult context. Williams, however, communicates a magical ethic through his fiction that is predicated on the alignment of human and divine will, one that seems intended as a critique of modern occultists who emphasized the realization of individual will over all else in the manner of Crowley's Thelemic dictate. Appropriate magical action is carried out in alignment with what Williams called the "supernatural Will";[23] illegitimate magic is focused on and driven by the will of the self. Black magic and the invocation of "awful and appalling deities" are, in this framework, "rather under the head of Power than of Will."[24] This is yet another area in which Williams may have been influenced by his F.R.C. Imperator. In the midst of trying to separate his belief system from modern occultism, Waite identified this Nietzschean primacy of the individual will as a central difference between mysticism, which he called a "mystery of the will in union," and "modern occult speculations," branded as "a mystery of the will in separation."[25]

Following a similar dichotomy, the coinherent adepts of

---

by S.L. Macgregor Mathers and Others, ed. Francis King (Rochester, VT: Destiny, 1987); Berridge, "Flying Roll No. 5." For further discussion of the importance of will in modern occultism, see Owen, *Place of Enchantment*, 89–90, 211.
21. Bogdan, *Western Esotericism*, 16–17.
22. Ibid, 16.
23. Williams, *Witchcraft*, 14.
24. Ibid, 15.
25. Waite, *Divine Union*, 26.

Williams's novels must discover the will of the divine and open themselves to it in order to achieve their magical goals. Before Arglay and Chloe can rescue Pondon they must first submit completely to the stone, representative, as we have seen, of various aspects of the divine.[26] In another application of magical imagination, Arglay uses the stone to clairvoyantly view the thoughts of Giles Tumulty in order to learn about his villainous schemes for the stone. Tumulty attempts this same telepathic act, but is foiled because his will is not properly aligned with the supernatural will.[27] *The Greater Trumps* describes cohesion with divine will as an alignment of human and divine consciousness. Sybil Coningsby, an attained adept intuitively aware of the desires of the supernatural will, is able to heal Aaron Lee's ankle using the magic of coinherent interchange, fuelled by divine energy: "Her hand closed round the ankle; her mind went inwards into the consciousness of the Power which contained them both; she loved it and adored it: with her own thought of Aaron in his immediate need, his fear, his pain, she adored. Her own ankle ached and throbbed in sympathy."[28] This coinherent magic works by virtue of the correspondent unity of all figures involved in the act—Sybil is in "the Power" and in Aaron, and they are in her. The coinherence of these three figures allows Sybil to act as a mediative connection between Aaron and a divine source of healing power. Her act thus indicates that in addition to modern techniques of visualization, astral imagination and the application of will, coinherence is rooted in the long tradition of theurgy, wherein the magus invokes or otherwise accesses divine power, sometimes, as in this case, in order to intervene in the natural function of the material world. The sole factor separating Sybil's act from that of a sorcerer or other "malefactor" condemned in *Witchcraft*—aside from the unique physics of coinherence—is intent. Had Sybil approached the healing focused

---

26. Williams, *Many Dimensions*, 134–43.
27. Ibid, 211–12.
28. Williams, *Greater Trumps*, 219. On the magical aspects of Sybil's co-inherent action see Knight, *Magical World of Charles Williams*, 59; Newman, "Companions of the Co-Inherence," 11.

on her own well-being, or even just that of Aaron, Williams's ethical system would have judged her act a failure or perversion.

Newman points out that Sybil's coinherent magic corresponds to the power of prayer and is similar in function. "For Williams, a seamless continuum linked 'ordinary' prayer with Sibyl's magical healing of Aaron and led as far as her ability to still the diabolical storm."[29] Prayer, however, is passive—it waits for the supernatural will to act. Williams's coinherent magic is active. Not only does it require the skill and knowledge of the adept to channel divine power through the imaginative techniques already discussed, it demands individual action as a precursor to supernatural assistance. Though Sybil's healing of Aaron's ankle is effected via adoration of the "Power that contained them both," there is a conscious act of individual will required: "She interceded; she in him and he in her."[30] The coinherent magic performed by adepts like Sybil and Stanhope requires the strong will that occultists saw as vital for magical action. Arglay gives credit to the exercise of his own will, his own strength of precise visualization, in the rescue of Pondon. Chloe questions his claim that it is "we" who have released Pondon, but Arglay firmly replies, "We... By virtue of the Stone, if you like, but after all it was we who determined and tried—determined, dared, and done."[31] Arglay is only following the instructions of the Hajji, who instructs him that in order to channel the stone's magical power, "you need but take it into your hand and will."[32] This group of characters thus exemplifies the application of will to imagination that defined modern occult magical practice, while simultaneously formulating a critique of the use of such techniques for self-empowerment alone.

---

29. Newman, "Companions of the Co-Inherence," 11. Cf. Urang, *Shadows of Heaven*, 53.
30. Williams, *Greater Trumps*, 219.
31. Williams, *Many Dimensions*, 170. The title of the chapter in which Chloe and Arglay save Pondon is, significantly, called "The Action of Lord Arglay."
32. Ibid, 59.

THE WAY OF P'O-LU

The critique of self-centered magic is bolstered by a number of characters who exemplify "the will in separation," sometimes, as with Considine, ambiguously, at other times, as with Leclerc, with clear censure. For Williams, magical action centered on the self is the way of "P'o-lu," a hellish land in the mythos of his Arthurian poetry. P'o-lu is "the terrifying wilderness, the 'upside-down of the world.'"[33] Viewed in this perverted mirror, divine-centered magic becomes the upside down of solipsism. Except for the ambiguous case of Considine, Williams's fiction presents only two possible outcomes for the way of P'o-lu—redemption or damnation. Though Henry and Aaron seek to possess the tarot deck for their own power and knowledge,[34] they eventually encounter redemption because of their respect for the correspondent unity of matter and spirit,[35] just as Gregory Persimmons is redeemed because he "sought the Union" in pursuing Satanic gnosis.[36]

Far more often Williams's P'o-lu magicians experience damnation —usually framed as a drive to achieve the desires of the self that obscures awareness of the divine, both within and without. Giles Tumulty is perhaps the best example. Tumulty seeks scientific knowledge of occult objects and forces through magical experimentation. Unlike the high-priestess magic of coinherence and mystical attainment, Tumulty's experiments are concerned with the natural effects of magic, rather than its supernatural source. As we have seen, his magical abilities are weaker than characters like Arglay as a result. Just as he fails to clairvoyantly access Arglay's thoughts, Tumulty is also unsuccessful in a bid to take over Chloe's mind.[37] Frustrated by

---

33. Williams and Lang-Sims, *Letters to Lalage*, 17.
34. Williams, *Greater Trumps*, 182.
35. See, e.g., Williams, *Greater Trumps*, 87, where Henry demands that the tarot trumps and the golden figurines—representative of micro- and macrocosm—not "be torn apart once more."
36. Williams, *War in Heaven*, 246. See p. xxx.
37. Williams, *Many Dimensions*, 205.

his inability to gain power over the pair, Tumulty curses Chloe, unaware that she is in the process of realizing her identity with Shekinah, and thereby cursing Shekinah herself: "'Damn you,' it was Chloe whom he half-unconsciously apostrophized, 'are you tucked away in it [the stone] as if it was Arglay's bed? I only wish I could get at you.'" In response to his curse, the stone reveals itself to him as the cosmic centre of all things, the source and fabric of everything around him (243–45). But Tumulty has condemned himself to P'o-lu through his solipsism and is unprepared for this glimpse of illumination. He has not, like Williams in the F.R.C., prepared himself for the moment at which a light leaps at him from the stone; he is "dragged down the curving spirals nearer to the illumination into which he was already plunged," stabbed and pierced by the light as he had once stabbed at the stone with his knife to divide it (245). His body is left in tatters on the floor, his spirit, like Chloe's, transcends the material, but only to be "lost in an infinite depth, alone with himself" (246).

A similar fate awaits the necromancer Leclerc, whose magic relies on reversed utterances of the Hebrew "pronouncements" used to create the world, including the Tetragrammaton itself,[38] and is thus literally sourced from the "upside-down" of P'o-lu. Leclerc's central goal in the novel is a perverted form of mystic union—not with the divine self within, but with the "magically multiplied" copies of himself that have been gathering followers in Russia and China (112). At some point, once he and his copies have gained in power in the worlds of the living and dead, Leclerc's intention is to consolidate this power by uniting his multiplied selves, "each known to adoring multitudes...there would be in secret a mystery of reunion, and then all would be in his hand" (114). The end of this self-directed desire is P'o-lu. After failing in his magical attempt to conquer death by enlivening a clay golem with the spirits of Lester and Evelyn, his other selves appear and advance on him. His reaction to this meeting is neither triumph nor the ecstasy of mystic oneness but fear. He tries

---

38. Williams, *All Hallows' Eve*, 107–08. Cf. 63–65.

to banish these looming copies, but everything he does to them is done to himself because of the coinherence of this dark trinity—"What he now said to them, he must say to himself... He hated them, and since they held his hate they hated him" (265). Simon is thus stuck within a "nightmare bubble" of self-obsessed loathing; he descends into the eternal self-absorption of P'o-lu with "his changing and unchanging faces to study" (266). Like Tumulty, he will spend eternity in infinite solitude, separated from the divine by solipsism.

Leclerc is, as Williams admitted after the novel's publication, "an unconvincing magician,"[39] based much more on the sensational magus of the gothic than on occultists Williams encountered in his own life such as Yeats, Waite and Lee. Leclerc is frequently connected to the Antichrist, but his name is probably also a reference to Simon Magus, the notorious magician who tries to buy the power to perform divine miracles from the apostle Peter in the book of Acts.[40] Scholars have also speculated that Leclerc is intended to reference Aleister Crowley.[41] This has only been proposed as a possibility—the most substantial argument presented thus far is Willard's observation that Crowley called himself Simon in *Moonchild*. In addition to this, however, it is worth noting that *All Hallows' Eve* indicates a further connection to Crowley. Leclerc frequently appropriates love as a guiding principle for the messianic philosophy with which he has roused a global following. This is not, however, love as Williams would have it—not love equivalent to the substance of the divine, through which desire enables Romantic Theological experience, but love subverted to a personal lust for power. Williams portrays this appropriation in a manner that recalls one of the two maxims of Thelema revealed in Crowley's *The Book of the Law*. Leclerc's motto, "Love is the fulfilling of the law,"[42] seems to reflect Crowley's famous

---

39. Dodds, *Charles Williams*, 327.
40. See Acts 8:18–24. Williams discusses Simon Magus in *Witchcraft*, 32–34. Cf. Willard, "Acts of the Companions, 291."
41. Duriez and Porter, *The Inklings Handbook*, 86; Willard, "Acts of the Companions," 292.
42. Williams, *All Hallows' Eve*, 198.

dictum, "Love is the law, Love under Will."[43] The authorial voice of *All Hallows' Eve* greets Leclerc's motto with sarcasm, noting that Leclerc intones these words "as if uttering some maxim of great wisdom."[44] His Crowleyite statement is contrasted, moreover, by Lester, who hears it and feels that "the maxim was greater than the speaker"—more, that "you'd be wiser to say that the fulfilling of the law is love" (198), a statement which, considering Williams's heterodox Christian perspective, seems to pit Simon's self-directed purpose against the fulfilment of the law presented by Christ, the "perfect Tetragrammaton" (62), "that other sorcerer...the son of Joseph" (177). Crowley's somewhat playful identification as "the Beast" of Revelation may also present another connection to Leclerc's apocalyptic Antichrist figure.

Williams's sorcerer characters frequently contribute to a consistent critique of self-aggrandizing magical practices, likely channeling internecine conflicts in contemporary occult society in Leclerc's case. This does not, however, extend to a complete repudiation of magic. Williams's valuation of high-priestess magic, his vision via fiction of astral and theurgic elements in coinherent praxis, and his interest in the thaumaturgical potential of the imagination indicate that, like Waite, he was able to clear room under the umbrella of the Higher Magia for a wide variety of magical practices. His ethical distinction between magic aligned with supernatural will and the self-centred way of P'o-lu is rooted in a long tradition in Western magical theory, in which self-seeking and power-hungry forms of practice are rejected, but magical powers are otherwise "welcomed for their utility rather than avoided as stumbling blocks."[45] This view was common in the modern occult context, where, as in Williams's fiction, it was intention more than method that made magic morally tenable. Distinguishing, as is commonly done, between moral categories of "black" and "white" magic, Blavatsky taught that "it is the motive, *and*

---

43. Aleister Crowley, *The Book of the Law: Liber Al Vel Legis* (York Beach, ME: Red Wheel/Weiser, 2009), 157.
44. Williams, *All Hallows' Eve*, 198.
45. Gibbons, *Spirituality and the Occult*, 38–39.

the motive alone, which makes any exercise of power become black, malignant, or white, beneficent."[46] Williams's emphasis on alignment with supernatural will was presaged by Lévi's insistence that magic be practiced "conformably" with the "Supreme Intelligence,"[47] and it is identical to Anna Kingsford's view that in white magic the individual will is united with divine will, while magic based on individual desire is black.[48] Alison Butler argues that Kingsford's ideas informed the approach taken by the Golden Dawn,[49] which dictated that magic could not be used to cause harm, and demanded "purity of aspiration and of life" as the "first and essential qualities" in prospective R.R. et A.C. members who wished to begin the magical education of the Second Order.[50] This requirement was no superficial gloss either; Crowley was denied entry into the R.R. et A.C. because its leadership felt that his character was ill suited.[51] Williams's own magical practice was quite limited in scope compared to occultists like Crowley, Mathers and Yeats, but his ethical system reflects common modern occult convention, which itself grew out of centuries-old perspectives on magics light and dark. Williams's views are even more comfortably situated with occultists such as Kingsford, who approached magic with a similar Christian-occult bent.

ART MAGIC: SEX, POETRY, CONSCIOUSNESS

A magical ethic predicated on self-sacrifice, the willing adoption of the physical and spiritual pain of others, and the prioritization of

---

46. Blavatsky, *Studies in Occultism*, 12.
47. Éliphas Lévi, *The History of Magic*, trans. Arthur Edward Waite (London: William Rider & Son, 1922), 3.
48. Alison Butler, "Magical Beginnings: The Intellectual Origins of the Victorian Occult Revival," *Limina* 9 (2003): 91–92.
49. Ibid. Butler cites Flying Rolls 1, 2, 5 and 6 as evidence of Kingsford's influence.
50. Moina MacGregor Mathers, preface to *Kabbala Denudata: The Kabbalah Unveiled*, by Samuel Macgregor Mathers (Blackmask Online, 2002), 4. http://www.hermetics.org/pdf/Mathers_Kabbalah_Unveiled.pdf. Cf. William Westcott, "The Condition Needed for Entry into the Second Order," quoted in Gilbert, *The Golden Dawn*, 126–29; Owen, *Place of Enchantment*, 74.
51. Owen, *Place of Enchantment*, 79.

divine will over individual desire could only ever exist as an ideal. We can read this utopian ethic in Williams's fiction, but we also can find its antithesis—a tension between Williams's moral standards and the realities of his personal life. This tension helps frame the ethical ambiguity of Considine's magical praxis. Though his magical methods are directed at the empowerment of the self and are thus a moral failure, their portrayal is directly linked to Williams's own pursuit of artistic and mystical ecstasy through the ritualistic excitation of sexual energy. Inkamasi describes the method of Considine's secret group of adepts in *Shadows of Ecstasy*: "Mysteriously, yet by methods which they say are open to all, they have learnt to arouse and restrain and direct the exaltation of love to such purposes as they choose. They have learnt by the contemplation of beauty in man or woman to fill themselves with a wonderful and delighted excitement, and to turn that excitement to deliberate ends."[52] Grevel Lindop has shown that Williams and his friends Lee and Nicholson were fascinated by the idea of transforming libido into individual energy and power. Williams was not the only one of the three to explore the idea of sexual sublimation in fiction; he began *Shadows of Ecstasy* in 1925, hard on the heels of Nicholson's 1924 *The Marriage-Craft*, a fictionalised philosophical discussion of the various purposes of sex, including a form of sexual transmutation very close to that of Considine.[53]

From his discussions with Lee and Nicholson, and likely other sources as well, Williams developed a number of magical practices related to sexual sublimation, usually involving the elevation of desire through repression of libido. In 1930, as Phyllis Jones lay in hospital with a broken leg, Williams attempted to help her recovery by abandoning "an instinct to masturbate."[54] As Lindop observes,

---

52. Williams, *Shadows of Ecstasy*, 108.
53. Lindop, *Charles Williams*, 113–14, 18.
54. Charles Williams to Phyllis Jones, undated, Bodleian MS Res.c. 320/II, letter 39, quoted in Lindop, *Charles Williams*, 178. Lindop relates that in the same letter Williams describes another magical technique employed on Phyllis's behalf. He told his beloved that he had walked around the hospital in the direction of the orbit of the sun in an

"There could be no clearer indication that he viewed sexual energy as a force that could be transmuted for chosen purposes."[55] Just as clear, however, are the accounts of numerous young women with whom Williams engaged in mildly sadomasochistic rituals in order to excite his consciousness and creative potential, which, as David Dodds argues, indicate the need for scholars to admit that "Williams was a practising magician, variously practising, modifying, inventing, and prescribing diverse rituals."[56] Williams may have felt Phyllis Jones to be a beneficiary of his magical experiments, but she paid a corporal price for any gains, suffering raps to the hand from fingers, pencils, rulers and other implements in the course of mini-ritualistic events.[57] Joan Wallis would visit him in his office in Oxford, where he would ask her to go to a cupboard to get a stick, an umbrella, or a more conventionally ritualistic wand or sword.[58] He would make "smooth strokes" over her buttocks with the object while Wallis bent over. At other times he wrote on her arm or drew patterns with the tip of a needle without drawing blood. Olive Speake, a coworker, and Anne Renwick, an undergraduate student, received similar treatment.[59]

Williams's abusive and erratic behaviour does not seem to have turned these women from recognizing his attributes. Despite her strange experiences, Wallis described him as "the most remarkable and good man I've ever met."[60] Lois Lang-Sims, however, reached a more nuanced conclusion. *Letters to Lalage*, her 1989 publication of letters sent to her by Williams between 9 September 1943 and 18 January 1945, undermined the hagiographic vision of Williams that

---

effort to magically assist her healing: "It is good to obey the rituals in small things as in great—when you happen to know the rituals."
55. Ibid.
56. Dodds, "Gavin Ashenden's *Charles Williams*," 36.
57. Lindop, *Charles Williams*, 196.
58. Sources vary as to whether a wand or sword was kept in this cupboard. See Lindop, *Charles Williams*, 334–37; Newman, "Companions of the Co-Inherence," 5; Ashenden, *Charles Williams*, 264–65.
59. On Speake see Lindop, *Charles Williams*, 238–42. On Renwick see ibid, 337–39, 396.
60. Quoted in Ashenden, *Charles Williams*, 264–65. Cf. Lindop, *Charles Williams*, 170–71, 241, 333, 340. For a more condemnatory view of Williams's activities see Frederick and McBride, *Women among the Inklings*, 43–44.

scholars like Hadfield had attempted to build.[61] The letters, accompanied by Lang-Sims's memories of their master/slave relationship, indicate that Williams was not quite so different from a Tumulty or a Leclerc as his magical ethic dictated he should be. As he had done in previous relationships, beginning, apparently, with Phyllis, Charles transformed Lois into the mythical figure of "Lalage"[62]—part schoolgirl, part slave—and coaxed her into playing a submissive role in private, sub-magical rituals. Alone together in his room in Oxford, for example, he instructed her to bend over a chair and lift up her skirt. She did so obediently, at which point he took a ruler, struck her hard on the behind and then began to walk quickly about the room, "talking as if he were agonizedly trying to catch up with ideas that were forever flying beyond his reach." He then stopped suddenly and embraced Lang-Sims, standing in absolute stillness.[63] Lang-Sims theorizes that Williams was "appealing to a traditional methodology concerned with the achievement of power through sexual transcendence."[64] For Lang-Sims, the effect of this ritual was the opposite—she fell ill, and attributed her long sickness to the stress of her relationship with Charles. Upon her recovery she accused him of betraying the Dantean vision of Romantic Theology in objectifying her as a ritual object. Williams, momentarily at least, admitted the charge.[65]

In general, however, he seems to have felt these practices to be justified. In each case his schoolmaster role seems to have partly reflected a feeling that he was contributing to his young partners' self-development. After Olive Speake complained, apparently, that he thought too much of "control and penance," Williams wrote a poem for her excusing his actions and explaining that his treatment of her

---

61. On Williams's relationship with Lang-Sims, see Williams and Lang-Sims, *Letters to Lalage*; Lindop, *Charles Williams*, 381–87; Newman, "Companions of the Co-Inherence," 15–17.
62. Williams and Lang-Sims, *Letters to Lalage*, 60.
63. Ibid, 68.
64. Ibid, 69.
65. Ibid, 79.

was designed for personal renewal, in the hope that "she emerged out of herself, into shape by shade."[66] When Wallis complained that she disliked such treatment, he offered an explanation that appears to have been his primary motivation: his actions were essential to his artistic process: "This is necessary," he said, "For the poem."[67] Lang-Sims theorized that "from some cause hidden deep in his nature, he needed the creative power that he derived from their fulfillment. Without that power he could not work. Essentially, it was a power derived from the consciously directed holding in check of the passions associated with romantic love."[68] Lindop believes that Williams saw Phyllis as a similar conduit to artistic power,[69] and Williams told Olive Speake that as the subject of his ritualistic actions she functioned as his muse. Preparing to write further verse in 1942, he wrote to Speake that were she with him in Oxford, "I should certainly be selfish and use you: how? you very well know; why? because it speeds me to my work."[70] This use of ritual to effect artistic vision and creative power has magical aspects, rooted in the occult understanding of magic as the elevation of consciousness or transformation of the psyche through ritual. In *The English Poetic Mind*, Williams hints that just as the poetic impulse could be aroused in the soul through magical accentuation of visionary faculties, so too could poetry itself function to awaken "'the hiding-places of man's power.'"[71] We find these places, Williams asserts, "in the poetry, and as the poetry fills us, we find them in ourselves. We understand our own architecture; the sense of our capacity for a unity of experience is aroused."[72] Here the boundaries between magic, poetry and imagination blur together. Poetry joins ritual, sexual desire and magical

---

66. Lindop, *Charles Williams*, 240.
67. Newman, "Companions of the Co-Inherence," 5; Hadfield, *Charles Williams: An Exploration*, 106; Williams and Lang-Sims, *Letters to Lalage*, 60.
68. Williams and Lang-Sims, *Letters to Lalage*, 17.
69. Lindop, *Charles Williams*, 130.
70. Charles Williams to Olive Speake, 1942, quoted in Lindop, *Charles Williams*, 241.
71. Williams, *English Poetic Mind*, 208. Williams quotes from Wordsworth's *Prelude*, 12.279.
72. Ibid.

visualization as a tool with which to elevate one's state of consciousness, growing further and further aware of the capacities of the inner self.

It is difficult to trace the sources for this quasi-magical practice of transmuting desire into imagination, which, to borrow Williams's term from a 1944 poem, we might call "art-magic."[73] Certainly the association between poetry and magic was nothing new. In the last chapter I outlined the etymological connections between theurgy and language that lie at the roots of both. In Williams's own time a significant number of writers and poets, including Blackwood, Machen, Crowley, Butts, Yeats, Fortune and Underhill, explored magical theory and practice through the written word. Ashenden explores art magical connections between Williams and Yeats,[74] but limits Williams's interest in "artistic theurgy," arguing that he "remained a practitioner of magic only in the sense that he was a poet."[75] The extension of Williams's art magic into private ritual, however—both with young women and in the F.R.C.—confirms that his thaumaturgical practice went beyond poetry. Lang-Sims thought that Williams's sexual sublimation had roots in medieval practices of repressing sexual desire for ascetic purposes, as well as tantra,[76] of which Lindop believes Williams learned from Lee and Nicholson, in both Western and Eastern forms.[77] In this context, Lee and Nicholson may have offered Williams a window to a wider modern occult fascination with the magical potency of sex. Influential esoteric figures

---

73. "The Queen's Servant," in *Taliessen through Logres, the Region of the Summer Stars and Arthurian Torso* (Grand Rapids, MI: Eerdmans, 1976), 162.
74. Ashenden, *Charles Williams*, 25–26.
75. Ibid, 25, 30.
76. Williams and Lang-Sims, *Letters to Lalage*, 69.
77. Lindop, *Charles Williams*, 241. It should be noted that even supposedly Eastern concepts of Tantra had already been Westernized in the nineteenth century by orientalist scholars, who tended to focus on the sexual aspects of tantric practice (often dismissively), ignoring other elements of a tradition that actually applied to many aspects of daily life. See Hugh Urban, "The Yoga of Sex: Tantra, Orientalism and Sex Magic in the Ordo Templi Orientis," in *Hidden Intercourse: Eros and Sexuality in the History of Western Esotericism*, ed. Wouter J. Hanegraaff and Jeffrey Kripal (Leiden: Brill, 2008), 410–14.

such as Paschal Beverly Randolph, a nineteenth-century American occultist who identified himself with Rosicrucianism, Theodor Reuss, the German founder of the Ordo Templi Orientis (O.T.O.), a magical group which concentrated on the practice of sexual magic, and Aleister Crowley, who became leader of the O.T.O. in 1910, incorporated Eastern tantric practices with Western forms of ritual magic. These practices, particularly in Crowley's case, involved much greater degrees of sexual acitivity and experimentation than Williams's odd celibate rituals, but, as Edward Gauntlett argues, there are a few points of intersection.[78] Randolph echoed Williams's attempt to elevate consciousness through repressed libido in his feeling that the "mystic forces of the soul open to the spaces" at the peak of mutual orgasm.[79] Reuss stated that the "central secret of the O.T.O. was in fact a derivation of the Catholic mass, in which the union of man with God was achieved." This mass featured the eucharistic transubstantiation of semen instead of a wafer,[80] but Reuss's emphasis on the relationship between sex, the incarnation of Christ and mystic union has interesting reflections in Williams's belief that the repressed desire of the male for the female could trigger gnostic awareness of the immanent God.

Williams's rituals of punishment and ecstasy were not equivalent to sex magic—certainly not in the sense of the term understood by occultists like Randolph and Reuss—nor does direct influence by such figures seem at all likely. However, shards of various ideas and impressions may have passed through Lee, Nicholson or other

---

78. Gauntlett, "Charles Williams, Love & Shekinah," 23–24.
79. On Crowley's sexual experimentation, see Urban, "The Yoga of Sex," 432; Owen, *Place of Enchantment*, 215. Randolph's teaching is quoted from an unpublished pamphlet, "The Ansairetic Mystery. A New Revelation Concerning Sex! A Private Letter, Printed, but not Published; It Being Sacred and Confidential" (ca. 1873–1874), quoted in John Patrick Deveney, *Paschal Beverly Randolph* (Albany, NY: State University of New York Press, 1997), 218. For more on Randolph's sexual magic see Godwin, *The Theosophical Enlightenment*, 255-56.
80. Quoted in Urban, "The Yoga of Sex," 424. Cf. Marco Pasi, "The Knight of Spermatophagy: Penetrating the Mysteries of Georges Le Clément De Saint-Marq," in *Hidden Intercourse: Eros and Sexuality in the History of Western Esotericism*, ed. Wouter J. Hanegraaff and Jeffrey Kripal (Leiden: Brill, 2008), 381–82.

unknown nodes, affecting the development of his libidinous ritual practices. And, while there do not seem to have been any direct links to occult sex magic, Lang-Sims's experiences with Williams led her to the conclusion that he was "no dabbler in the occult"; that he had acquired knowledge of magical ritual somewhere and must have "been involved with the practices of ritual magic within a fellowship established for that purpose."[81] So far as we know, this was only partly true. We have seen that the F.R.C. was magical in the sense of its use of ritual language and ceremonial space to elevate consciousness via imaginative engagement, but it certainly never taught magical techniques for sexual exaltation—these were learned and developed elsewhere. The F.R.C. is also an unlikely place for Williams to have developed magical goals that so clearly contravene any concept of a "higher magic." The accounts of Lang-Sims, Wallis and other young women reveal magical acts that are "corollaries of the Union" to some extent: they depend on the correspondent union of human and divine desire and imagination that is the essence of the high-priestess of magic. However, in terms of motivation they are a fractured form of the magical ethic that is communicated in the novels. Williams's rituals of sexual arousal, repression and sublimation were aimed at artistic and mystical attainment, and in that they were acceptable within the mores of his magical system, but their core concern was the development of the potencies of the self, the very pursuit that the novels critique. Williams's personal life indicates the impossibility of the selfless adeptship achieved by characters such as Sybil, Stanhope, Chloe and Arglay. Believing himself to possess the ability to magically enhance his innate creative and relational abilities, Williams was unable to resist deploying this power in the service of desire for artistic achievement, control over others, and, clearly, a vision of woman that was not always as Beatrician as his Romantic Theology demanded.

At the same time as he created an unachievable magical ethic in his fiction, however, he also explored his own failure to live up to it.

---

81. Williams and Lang-Sims, *Letters to Lalage*, 69.

Roger Ingram's departure from his wife to follow Considine may represent such doubts, but no act of characterization seems so closely connected to Williams's ritual objectification of women than the creation of Lawrence Wentworth. A number of critics have identified Stanhope as a proxy of Williams,[82] but Wentworth also seems to be a self-conscious projection, one perhaps intended to balance Stanhope, with whom, as Ashenden notes, Williams comes close to deification.[83] Stanhope is presented as a fully attained adept, a successful playwright worshipped by all who come into contact with him; Wentworth is a man defined by central flaws of self-absorption that lead him into madness. He begins the novel as a successful historian who leads bi-weekly groups of young people in discussions of "military history and the principles of art and the nature of the gods,"[84] a role which seems to mirror Williams's many mentoring relationships, particularly with younger women. Wentworth is destroyed, however, by his unrequited love for one of this group, Adela Hunt, a beautiful young woman whose affections are distracted by a much younger man, a misfortune Williams also experienced at the hands of Phyllis Jones.[85] Wentworth's jealousy destroys his emotional balance, creating "chaos within"[86]—he first tries to alleviate his disordered obsession by going for a walk in the village, waiting casually by the train station, hoping for, yet against, a chance encounter with Adela and his young rival.[87] Lindop notes clear parallels between these odd vigils and Phyllis Jones's account of Williams following her through the streets—"just sort of talking to himself"—after she ended her romantic entanglement with him.[88]

To alleviate his frustration, Wentworth fashions a magical

---

82. See, e.g., Newman, "Companions of the Co-Inherence," 11; Ashenden, *Charles Williams*, 155–56; Frederick and McBride, *Women among the Inklings*, 41–42.
83. Ashenden, *Charles Williams*, 156. Lindop also argues that Wentworth and Stanhope are "polarized self-portraits of Williams" (Lindop, *Charles Williams*, 277).
84. Williams, *Descent into Hell*, 40.
85. Lindop, *Charles Williams*, 146.
86. Williams, *Descent into Hell*, 49.
87. Ibid, 51.
88. Lindop, *Charles Williams*, 146.

succubus, one that has all the physical trappings of the real Adela but has no existence independent of its creator's imagination. As a "magical apparition of its father's desires,"[89] the succubus, like Pauline's doppelgänger, is a conjuration of the imagination in a perverted state. As such, it is more Wentworth than Adela, which initially delights the accidental sorcerer as it has none of the characteristics "that troubled him in the incarnation of the beloved."[90] Urang points out that the succubus, as a projection of Wentworth's desires rather than the actual object, is a rejection of coinherence.[91] It also subverts Romantic Theology: because this Adela is a projection of Wentworth's self-directed desire, both the lust and emotion aroused by her are an "idolatry of self" rather than elements of a sacramental experience that points the way to mystical attainment.[92] Wentworth turns inward, but remains blind to the divine that awaits him there. As Earnest Beaumont illustrates, this is Williams's "one way of damnation,"[93] the spiral into an eternity of solipsism also experienced by Tumulty and Leclerc. These latter two characters, however, are not designed in the spirit of self-conscious critique that Wentworth seems to represent. Lang-Sims eventually realized that she and "certain other women" were, in Williams's eyes, "'types' of his Lady"[94]—proxies for Phyllis Jones. Her account shows that to varying degrees Williams's relationships after Jones were attempts to maintain the magical injection of vitality which that relationship had given to his artistic praxis, and to continue to glimpse Phyllis, fractally, in the mirror of other partners, imaginatively projecting her shade just as Wentworth casts a spell of illusion out of his desire for Adela. Stanhope and Wentworth thus represent an ethical tension in their creator's mind as to the suitability of his own magical acts—Stanhope the coinherent adept in alignment with supernatural will; Wentworth

---

89. Williams, *Descent into Hell*, 126.
90. Ibid, 127.
91. Urang, *Shadows of Heaven*, 65–67.
92. Williams, *Descent into Hell*, 127.
93. Beaumont, "Charles Williams and the Power of Eros," 63.
94. Williams and Lang-Sims, *Letters to Lalage*, 17.

the self-absorbed amateur occultist, unwittingly following the way down to P'o-lu.

REANIMATION: ENCHANTMENT AND EMPOWERMENT

Despite probable misgivings about the ethics of his ritualistic encounters, Williams persisted in his practice of art magic, stimulating and repressing desire through ceremonial movement and the Shekinah image of the objectified female in order to stimulate higher levels of poetic sensibility and mystical knowledge. As he explained to Wallis and Speake, he saw these rituals as vital creative sources. Artistic inspiration, however, does not explain the full gamut of his magical interests, which also included the high-priestess magic of the F.R.C., the Banishing Ritual, and the potential of imagination to create alternative, astral forms of reality. I would like to conclude my discussion of this aspect of Williams's occultism by analyzing his magical activities in terms of "reanimation." I intend this term to communicate two central meanings: In the first, reanimation suggests a reinvigoration not just of lifeless bodies, but of the whole of material existence. Thus, magic reanimates by reintroducing the *anima*, or soul, into a world perceived to be rendered sterile by materialism, industrialization and empiricism. In the second sense of the term, reanimation indicates a socio-political awakening—an idealization of power by individuals who are rendered powerless because they are disadvantaged by class, income, education, race, gender, etc.

In the first sense of reanimation, magic has been a tool of reinvigoration for modern occultists concerned with resisting what Max Weber famously called "the disenchantment of the world"—the dismissal of "mysterious incalculable forces" by the rise of Enlightenment rationalism.[95] It is hardly surprising that magic should be enlisted against the strictures of post-Enlightenment materialism,

---

95. Max Weber, "Science as a Vocation," in *Max Weber: Essays in Sociology*, ed. H.H. Gerth and C. Wright Mills (New York: Oxford University Press, 1949), 155. For the history of the disenchantment thesis see Michael Saler, "Modernity and Enchantment: A Historiographic Review," *American Historical Review* III, no. 3 (June 2006): 695–99.

given that it was a central target of the polemicized accusations of irrationality and superstition that typified post-Enlightenment empiricist responses to the esoteric traditions. Magic's central function as the rejected other of Enlightenment rationalism is reflected in the very etymology of the term dis*enchant*ment, and even more literally visible in Weber's German *entzauberung* or "removal of magic."[96] Recent scholarship has convincingly shown, however, that post-Enlightenment culture has been marked not by a dichotomy between a primordial enchanted perspective and a triumphantly dominant disenchantment, but by a symbiotic antinomy, a productive tension between "seemingly irreconcilable forces and ideas" that fruitfully contributes to the identities and priorities of all parties.[97] Michael Saler argues that cultural movements broadly seen as forms of modern enchantment (imagination, fantasy, popular culture, the occult) are "compatible with, and even dependent on, those tenets of modernity usually seen as disenchanting the world, such as rationality and self-reflexivity."[98] In this framework, the challenges posed by rationalism, empiricism and naturalism to magical theory have catalysed further invention in an already innovative tradition. We have seen, for example, that Williams's magic reflected a modern occult inward turn, performing on an imaginal plane and achieving on a psychological one, thus creating a space for magical praxis in which "processes of secularisation and disenchantment in the everyday world simply *have no bearing*."[99] Saler describes the enchantment produced by this imaginal engagement as equivalent to a secularized experience of the sublime,[100] while Hanegraaff argues that modern magic is itself disenchanted because of its adaptation to

---

96. Saler, "Rethinking Secularism: Modernity, Enchantment, and Fictionalism," n.p.
97. Saler, "Modernity and Enchantment," 700.
98. Ibid, 702. Asprem argues that the concept of disenchantment is less a totalizing social process and more of a series of "intellectual *problems*" encountered in various historical, social and cultural contexts. See *The Problem of Disenchantment: Scientific Naturalism and Esoteric Discourse, 1900–1939* (Leiden: Brill, 2014), esp. 4–5.
99. Hanegraaff, "How Magic Survived," 370.
100. See, e.g., Saler, "Modernity and Enchantment," 714.

empiricist frameworks,[101] but the scope of enchantment in modern occultism had wider aims. The motive of enchantment is often mixed with spiritual goals that target a form of transcendence that crosses the boundaries of the secular, as seen in the fantastic literature of the Inklings. The spiritual occultism of figures like Waite, Williams, and Kingsford was directed at the sublime in the sense of Burke's intention of the term—as an encounter with divinity.[102]

Even adherents of the cordon sanitaire approach to Williams's work would agree with Gavin Ashenden's assertion that though Williams rejected "the theurgic and goetic," he embraced the magical possibilities of "artistic 'enchantment'."[103] As I have already argued, however, the degree of reanimation that Williams sought in magic goes beyond its exploration in poetry or fiction. His imaginative alteration of consciousness in the F.R.C., his interest in the potential for magical imagination to form and reform time and space, his ritualistic sublimation of sexual desire, and even his correspondent vision of a human finger as simultaneously a mundane pointer and a tool of evocation, indicate a much more personal and experiential engagement. Magic was "necessary for the poem," but the poem could be lived as much as written out on the page. Magical theory and practice were a central part of the lifestyle fantasy pursued by Williams and other modern occultists. Magic joined Silvania, the worlds of Arthurian mysticism, and the adoption of mythical personalities like Stanhope and Taliessen in a series of methods Williams deployed in order to reanimate—or at least further animate—his view of the world.[104]

Williams's novels are an extension of this lifestyle fantasy. Magic and fiction have long functioned together to produce enchantment; the fantastic was, to a degree, actually forged in what Saler calls a "ghetto of popular culture" into which magic and the supernatural

---

101. Hanegraaff, "How Magic Survived," 360.
102. Burke, *The Sublime and the Beautiful*, 65–67.
103. Ashenden, *Charles Williams*, 33.
104. Williams mythopoeically identified with the Arthurian poet Taliessen while writing his later poetry. See Williams and Lang-Sims, *Letters to Lalage*, 17.

were herded by the forces of Enlightenment rationalism.[105] Given this shared history, it is no surprise that so many occultists have explored and translated their experiences via fantastic fiction, as described in Chapter Three. This enchantment via fiction is multidirectional; occult fiction is frequently born out of lives purposefully lived on the liminal bounds of the fictional to start with. In her research among London-based occultists of the 1980s, Luhrmann found that many of her subjects treated magical claims as simultaneously serious and true *and* playfully fictional, thus avoiding the strictures of traditional reality claims. The modern magician "plays at magic and understands the play as serious, and the truth of magical theory hovers in limbo between reality and fantasy. Magic is a modernist religion: it challenges the validity of religious dogmatism, authoritative symbology, and intellectual analysis."[106] The lure of magic for Luhrmann's subjects was thus its offer of a modern day otherworld, a land of alterity separate from, but lying just beside, the real—still populated, as for millennia prior, by mythical denizens like elemental spirits and planetary intelligences, still enabling events and logics that defied the dictates of most naturalistic structures, but doing so with a conscious, self-reflexive "let's-pretend" ethos. To degrees that depended very much on individual magical perspectives, this otherworld could be entirely fictional, entirely real, or, most often, a productive mix of both.

We must be careful when transplanting the findings of Luhrmann's research—carried out among magicians with clear postmodern affinities for relativism and subjectivity—onto occultists of

---

105. Saler, "Modernity and Enchantment," 696.
106. Luhrmann, *Persuasions of the Witch's Craft*, 367. Research similar to Luhrmann's social anthropological approach from Williams's own time would be more directly valuable to our understanding of his modern occult context, but as this is not available we can still benefit from Luhrmann's findings, given that many of the cultural conditions that affected modern occultists remain the same for magicians today. Moreover, the groups that Luhrmann studied have much the same focus as societies such as the Golden Dawn and the F.R.C.—they are, in fact, descended in a complicated genealogical line from the Golden Dawn and its offshoots, and utilize its rituals and knowledge in the formation of their own magical practices and philosophies.

Williams's period. Yet, this playful, self-reflexive seriousness did not appear out of nowhere; it has clear roots in the lifestyle fantasy and fictional projection of late nineteenth- and early twentieth-century occultism. As we have seen, magicians like Williams continued to believe strongly in external, supernatural realities, even as they accentuated the role of interior transmutation and active imagination in their magical practice. Despite this continued focus on an external, non-subjective real, however, the complex interaction between life and fiction exemplified in Williams's novels indicates that *homo ludens* constituted an important part of his magus identity. Not all his presentations of magic are rooted in serious exploration or personal experience—we have seen that figures like Leclerc are "unconvincing" and drawn largely from pre-existing fictional tropes. Other concepts are scarcely playful: magical concepts he held dear—coinherence, the image-driven elevation of consciousness—are explored with seriousness, despite their fictional setting. In general, however, magical theory, practice and symbol take up the liminal space between play and reality that is characteristic of modern magic. Actual interest in visualization and astral imagination lies behind Arglay's rescue of Pondon, for example, but even the Chief Justice treats his achievement with some of the scepticism and irony required to produce the hesitation of the fantastic; the reanimation of modern magic.

Aside from such enchantment, another motivation has commonly inspired both modern and pre-modern magicians to take up the occult arts—the pursuit of power. From a combination of interviews with contemporary practitioners, surveys of occult magical texts, and readings of novels constructed using elements of modern magic, Luhrmann concludes that the themes which emerge "from this creative amalgam of different myths, stories and symbols are about the nature of power: of the value of losing it to regain it, of the knowledge to control it."[107] We have seen that Williams's novels also centrally revolve around the notion of power—of surrendering the

---

107. Luhrmann, *Persuasions of the Witch's Craft*, 94.

will to the divine in order to participate in the action of a greater power; of failing this test of selflessness and descending the way of P'o-Lu; and of an ambiguous path between these poles exemplified by characters such as Considine and Persimmons. Luhrmann discovered that magicians are compelled by such fictional portrayals: "Conflicted by their desire to have an impact within the larger social world...the romantic fantasy constitutes for them some sort of resolution, perhaps as therapy, perhaps as escape."[108] Thus, even in consciously fictional forums like the imaginal experience of fiction, magic offers a subsection of society an elevated sense of self, a reanimation in the sense of the reinvigoration of the *anima*—the spirit or soul—in the dead or dying. Like Frankenstein energizes his monster, magical reanimation offers the modern self a rising from existential death—a crypt of insignificance, dissonance, nihilism—either through the mythopoeic enhancement of the place of the self in the world, or the perception of ability to transcend the limitations of material causality, whether solely on an imaginal plane or not. Research has shown a correlation between the feelings of powerlessness that result from abuse or trauma and involvement with new religious movements, such as Paganism and Wicca, which emphasize magical practice. Modern magic's emphasis on the will inspires those who believe themselves incapable of influencing the course of their own lives, let alone society in general. Siân Reid has surveyed case studies that indicate this relationship between magic and the reacquisition of power, and concludes that despite magic's unorthodoxy it appeals to those in need of change and influence as "a belief that one is capable of causing change (that one is powerful) and that the change will occur according to one's Will (that one is in control)."[109]

---

108. Ibid.
109. Sian Reid, "As I Do Will, So Mote It Be: Magic as Metaphor in Neo-Pagan Witchcraft," *Magical Religion and Modern Witchcraft* (1996): 150. Cf. 147–49, 161; Greenwood, "Gender and Power in Magical Practices," 149–50. Magic's will to empower is not always seen as positive. Rodney Stark and William Bainbridge, for example, describe magic as a Marxist opiate, arguing that it plays a compensatory role similar to the promise of afterlife, offering—but never providing—material benefits in place of those that are unavailable because of the believer's socio-economic position (Rodney Stark

Along with this empowerment in the face of trauma, Susan Greenwood has shown that magical spaces such as the environment of ritual can allow for a realignment of gender dynamics.[110]

While Williams did not suffer from gender discrimination and there is no evidence of his experiencing abuse, feelings of powerlessness seem quite likely, particularly in his publishing career. Like most artists, Williams frequently faced rejection. He seems to have been quite sensitive to it, particularly early on. George Robinson relates that his blunt review of one of Charles's poems as "completely obscure" may have ended their boyhood friendship. Williams said nothing in reply to the critique, but years later Robinson could still feel "that sensation of a gate shutting between us."[111] The artist life also posed financial obstacles: Charles struggled with money all his life while he watched friends like Eliot and Lewis, higher on the socio-economic ladder despite similar professions, living much more comfortable lives. While those who find themselves powerless because of abuse, gender inequality or actual poverty may not sympathize with the predicament of a relatively successful white male, the attraction of magical theory and practice to the powerless can also be extrapolated to this perception of disempowerment via class and socio-economic status. Whatever the reason for feeling disempowerment or loss of control, the urge to mastery seen in Williams's relationships with young women suggests that these sensations were operative in his life. Though he was not the only person to find a productive tool for the elevation of consciousness in the combination of sadomasochism and ritual magic,[112] he could

---

and William Sims Bainbridge, *A Theory of Religion* (New Brunswick, NJ: Rutgers University Press, 1996), 36–42.
110. Greenwood, "Gender and Power in Magical Practices," 150.
111. George Robinson, untitled reminscences of Charles Williams, 28 November 1954, CWSA II.A.4.
112. Greenwood cites an article from an American pagan magazine, in which two pagans describe the mystical benefits of conflating magic and sadomasochism: "When we add ritual to our S/M, performing it with spiritual intention, we can travel deeper yet...beyond the personal unconscious mind and into universal consciousness, or spiritual awareness." See Greenwood, "Gender and Power in Magical Practices," 150,

have achieved altered states of ecstatic and creative consciousness without domination and without causing his magical partners physical and psychological pain. The desire to inflict punishment, to dominate another, indicates a clear desire for the elevation of position and perception of the self that is indicative of the urge to reanimation.

Williams's portrayal of magical action in his fiction suggests that he was also attracted to its mostly commonly sought form of power: mastery over nature. This is what Lévi found in the "absolute science" of magic: "The adept becomes king of the elements, transmuter of metals, interpreter of visions, controller of oracles, master of life in fine, according to the mathematical order of Nature and conformably to the will of the Supreme Intelligence. This is Magic in all its glory."[113] Anthony Durrant's conquest of the angelical principles is written along exactly these lines. When he proposes to the occultist Foster that the breach between natural and supernatural opened by Berringer could perhaps be closed, Foster only laughs at him: "Are we to govern the principles of creation?" Anthony retorts that "we don't know till we try," and articulates a theory of magical power based entirely on the correspondence between himself and the divine within: "If [the principles] are part of me...then perhaps the authority which is in me over me shall be in me over them."[114] If, in other words, Anthony can become aware of the supernatural will within, then he should also be able to rule over the principles of nature by virtue of this correspondent connection, becoming Lévi's "king of the elements." Contrasted to Richardson, the ascetic mystic of *The Place of the Lion*, Anthony is a man of action, an exemplar of the way of affirmation. Richardson believes Anthony is "wasting time on images," but it is Anthony who drives the supernals back into the supernatural. He doubts himself at first—"It was hopeless, it was insane" (74)—but concludes in the end that an attempt must be

---

quoting Dossie Easton and Catherine Liszt, "Sex, Spirit & S/M," *Green Egg* 29, no. 110 (May–June 1997): 16–10.
113. Lévi, *History of Magic*, 3.
114. Williams, *Place of the Lion*, 55–57.

made. "I feel a trifle macrocosmic," he sighs to himself before attempting to control the occult forces of the macrocosm, "But if the proportion is in me let these others know it. Let me take the dominion over them" (75). He battles the angelicals, strength for strength. He and Damaris are threatened by the thunderous roar of the principle manifest as a lion, but Anthony silences it with his own magical cry: "It was a sound as of a single word, but not English, nor Latin, nor Greek. Hebrew it might have been or something older than Hebrew, some incantation whereby the prediluvian magicians had controlled contentions among spirits or the language in which our father Adam named the beasts of the garden" (200-1). Striding on, Damaris witnesses him governing creation like that same Adam: "He called and he commanded; nature lay expectant about him" (202). Not just nature, but the cherubim and seraphim manifested in animal form come to Anthony's summons. Elevated above the angels, he is a god of imagination.

A good deal of ludic exploration of magic is taking place here. There is no evidence that Williams perceived himself in such a vaunted Adamic role, but Anthony's epic achievement represents the author's own magical theory nonetheless. The cosmology according to which Anthony justifies his magical redemption is Williams's correspondent monism; his choice to prevent the natural from being overcome by the supernatural exemplifies the way of affirmation. As with Considine, Arglay, Sybil and Stanhope, there is a good deal of intent seriousness beneath the playful surface of Anthony's magical actions. Interpretation of such fictional presentations of magical power thus supports biographical evidence that Williams was attracted to the reanimation of magical theory and practice. This lure operated in both senses of the term that I have highlighted: It brought the supernatural together with the natural to re-enchant the world, and it provided feelings of social and relational mastery—achieved in the hieratic leadership roles Williams held in the F.R.C., and in his master/slave relationships.

INTERPRETIVE DRIFT: THE DEVELOPMENT OF A MODERN CHRISTIAN MAGIC

It is not clear when Williams first began to embrace this reanimation of his perspective of self and world. Perhaps he initially resisted the promise of adeptship, deterred by allegations of superstition heard at school or heresy learned in church. Even if he was reluctant initially —and there is no evidence that he was—he clearly began to attend to magic's exotic call at some point, regardless of any countering instincts developed for reasons of intellect or faith. Luhrmann's research has shown that any process of incorporating magical concepts would not have been so difficult as might be assumed. Her anthropological work with contemporary magicians asked a simple question regarding their processes of rationalization and meaning making: what would lead "ordinary, well-educated, usually middle-class people" to find magic persuasive?[115] She concludes that magicians come to this epistemological stage via a long-term process of interaction with magical practice, symbol and philosophy that she calls "interpretive drift."[116] Luhrmann notes a tendency to interpret human behaviour as though it were based on the rational, progressive evolution of belief on behalf of a unitary self,[117] as seen, for example, in the case of Williams scholars who have assumed that he could only be a Christian *or* a magician, a "secret hermeticist" *or* a "companionable spiritual exemplar."[118] The wide range of critical opinions about Williams's valuation of magic (and the occult in general) may stem in part from this either/or assumption that he would, young or old, have possessed a rationally consistent approach to the subject. However, as Luhrmann observes, "One could argue that many beliefs are logically inconsistent, that people manipulate their own beliefs, and that the manipulation and inconsistency may be useful." She gives the example of a person faced with the

---

115. Luhrmann, *Persuasions of the Witch's Craft*, 7.
116. Ibid, 335–52.
117. Ibid, 336.
118. Cavaliero, review of *Alchemy and Integration*, 51.

contrasting beliefs that a project should be finished quickly, but also that it should take a great deal of time. This person's success is assured: if they do well in a short period of time they succeed, if they do not then it is simply the small window afforded to them that is to blame. A similar example is a person who tries to be more spontaneous—simply acting on this value puts the individual into a position where true spontaneity becomes impossible. Still, the individual juggles the value of spontaneity successfully, without awareness of the irrational relationship between ideal and action.[119] Luhrmann emphasizes that magicians are no different than anyone else when it comes to belief formation. They require apparently cohesive concepts and ideals, but these will not necessarily be logically ordered: "Magicians argue in different ways at different times; some of them claim to believe one thing when practising magic, and another thing when not practising magic; others seem to be firmly committed to their practice, and produce arguments about relativism which do not seem entirely plausible in the face of their behaviour."[120]

Luhrmann observed this process to be more experiential than intellectual. Her proto-magician subjects did not deliberately set out to change their perception of the world, but after learning magical concepts, symbols and practices in various textual, ritual and social forums, they displayed new patterns in logic and meaning attribution, "new ways of identifying events as significant, of drawing connections between events, with new, complex knowledge in which events could be put into context." Having reached this point, neophyte adepts encountered magical experiences, usually of an imaginal, interior and/or psychological nature. "Hard to abstract, hard to verbalize, these dynamic experiences became part of the business of engaging in magic, and they made the magic real for its participants, because they gave content to its ideas." The central processes of interpretive drift seemed to occure following these experiences. Both the magical knowledge that preceded the encounter

---

119. Luhrmann, *Persuasions of the Witch's Craft*, 336–37.
120. Ibid, 337.

and the event itself had to be framed within the pre-existing worldview of the experiencer. These processes were *ad hoc* and not necessarily rational, but they served the purpose of justifying and reinforcing involvement with the magical practices that had stimulated the experience.[121] It may be productive to think of Williams's magical experiences in this light: his ritual elevation of consciousness through magical visualization and ceremonial interaction with language brought him experiences of mystical insight; he perceived his sadomasochistic sessions as vital to the function of his poetic imagination; and he felt himself to have successfully substituted his own body and psyche in order to coinherently take on the pain of others. In all these cases, Williams would have been faced with a choice—rejection of the reality and value of his experiences, or a natural drift toward the integration of a magical episteme.

The view of the history of magic expressed in *Witchcraft* suggests that he had gone through much of this process of interpretive drift by the late thirties. We have seen that some of the magical experiences he pursued at the time remained untenable with Romantic Theology or coinherent magic, but *Witchcraft* indicates that if Williams had ever struggled to justify magical thinking with Christian aspects of his belief system, harmony had now been achieved. High-priestess magic was found to be equivalent to ritual behaviour valued in the early and medieval Church. These were times, in Williams's conception, where "ritual maintain[ed] and increase[ed] that natural sense of the significance of movement. And, of course, of formulae, of words." Such an environment allowed invocation of the divine via these magical formulae: "He sent his graces, He came Himself, according to ritual movements and ritual formulae. Words controlled the God... The sense of alteration, the sense of meaning, the evocation of power, the expectation of the God, lay all about the world." The rituals and processes used for this invocation were those of the pagan traditions that preceded Christianity, which had, in Williams's opinion, either adopted the magical traditions of its forebears or

---

121. Ibid, 12–13.

A MAGICAL LIFE IN FICTION

systematically rejected them.[122] *Witchcraft* mirrors much of this rejection, reflecting the negative image of goetic magic seen in the novels, but this construction of a magical ethic out of both personal experience and intellectual engagement with preexisting magical theory also shows evidence of a process of interpretive drift. The articulation of the high-priestess concept exemplifies this. Like Waite, Williams folded the elements of magical theory and practice he valued into the protective shell of a higher magic, distancing himself, whether consciously or unconsciously, from goetic practices that had been condemned throughout the history of Christian polemics. This was not, however, a rejection of magic but a drift toward it. By dispelling elements of magical practice that could not be intellectually or psychologically harmonized, Williams enabled himself to continue to value all other aspects of magical theory and thus maintain the validity of the experiences that had sprung from this knowledge.

This selective approach to the development of a magical paradigm supports Hanegraaff's observation that in the history of magic since antiquity, "the term could mean very different things to different parties, and each participant in the discourse had a wide choice of connotations to highlight or play down at will, according to his particular religious, scientific, or philosophical agenda."[123] Williams highlighted a number of significant elements of magical practice past and present. He attributed magicity to early Christian concepts, highlighted the vestigial pagan elements of both antique and medieval Christian sacraments, valued the magia naturalis of the Renaissance and early modern periods, and incorporated aspects of modern occult practice that he perceived valuable for his system, including visualization, magical imagination, the development of the personal will, the protection of the Banishing Ritual, and the sublimation of libido. Just as important for his ongoing process of drift was the choice of magical phenomena to "play down." His rejection of self-motivated magical action was consistent with other occult

---

122. Williams, *Witchcraft*, 79–80.
123. Hanegraaff, *Esotericism and the Academy*, 177.

ethical systems, but his pattern of disassociation tended, like Waite's, to be more rigid. Williams's magical ethic mirrored distinctions such as Mathers's contrast between the "black magic of pact and devil-worship" and "Qabalistic Magic" designed to help the adept achieve union with the higher self, but Williams did not share Mathers's goal of gaining power over angelical, demonic and elemental forces.[124] Always the "true romantic,"[125] Williams was also completely disinterested by another trend commonly seen in modern occultism—the urge to naturalize magical theory in order to legitimate it scientifically, as seen, for example, in Crowley's attempt to establish his magical claims through repeated, well-documented experimentation, while also thoroughly systematizing a vast, syncretized body of occult knowledge in a thoroughly Linnaean manner.[126]

Given the turbulent, sometimes paradoxical nature of modern magical belief, any conclusion as to Williams's magus identity must rest ultimately on discourse: if, in addressing the question of whether he had a deep, abiding interest in magic, we call to mind the demonic necromancer created by historical polemics and magnified in the fictional forums of the gothic, then we can most certainly say that he was not a magician. If, however, we analyze the question in light of the complex approach to magic taken by other occultists, then he must undoubtedly be included with William Westcott, A.E. Waite, Dion Fortune, and the late twentieth-century Londoners of Luhrmann's research in the fascinating and culturally important network of modern magic. Though he frequently failed to live up to his own magical ideals, a picture of the godly magus emerges from Williams's life and work—a devotee of art-magic, vitally aware of correspondences between matter and spirit, aligned with the supernatural will, and called to the realm of imagination for magical action.

---

124. S.L. MacGregor Mathers, introduction to *The Book of Abramelin the Mage* (London: John M. Watkins, 1900), xxxv.
125. Williams, "Blake and Wordsworth," 60.
126. See Asprem, "Magic Naturalized?" 142–54.

CHAPTER 7

THE TRANSMUTATION OF CHARLES WILLIAMS
SPIRITUAL AND LITERARY ALCHEMY

On 20 and 27 October 2015, Charles Williams lurched suddenly from obscurity to mass exposure as his name, his fiction, and his concept of coinherence streamed out to millions of viewers of *Lewis*,[1] a long running British detective series based in Oxford. In a two-part episode called "Magnum Opus," Detective Inspector Robert Lewis and his partner DI James Hathaway discover that the Companions of the Co-inherence has been revived in Oxford by a small group intent on absolving themselves of their sins through a process intended to resemble Williams's methods of substitution. As they do so, however, a mysterious alchemist is killing them, one by one, according to a scheme of murder that follows the broad outlines of alchemy's *magnum opus*, or "Great Work"—the transformation of a base substance into a higher form. Strangely, the writer of "Magnum Opus," Chris Murray, takes steps to dissociate the two central strands that drive the episode—alchemy and coinherence. Lewis asks Hathaway, a man versed in knowledges obscure and arcane, "Did Charles Williams write about alchemy?" "No," Hath-

---

1. Each episode was viewed by over four million people in the UK alone (source: http://www.barb.co.uk/viewing-data/weekly-top-30/).

away responds, "Theology, supernatural novels and he was a bit of a mystic." The statement is so definitive that one suspects a red herring—surely a connection between Williams and alchemy will be revealed later in the action. But we are disappointed. Lewis and Hathaway double-check the possibility of a connection with an Oxford professor of religious history. He is just as emphatic: "There isn't one."[2] The inclusion of alchemy with the philosophy of Charles Williams thus appears to have been coincidental. However, while Detectives Lewis and Hathaway manage, as usual, to solve their case, on this occasion they could not have been more misled. Charles Williams had everything to do with alchemy.

It is difficult to miss the alchemical symbolism in Williams's novels, plays and poetry, though one must be suitably familiar with the symbols and concepts of this vast tradition. Williams acquired this familiarity from personal experience in the F.R.C. with symbols such as the Philosophers' Stone and chemical wedding, concepts which this chapter will help illustrate and then relate to his fiction. Even more important was the basic narrative of the Great Work, or "great experiment"—the transmutation of base materials into nobler ones through a process of death and rebirth, in which a substance—usually metal—would undergo a stage of decay and putrefaction, emerging revivified and more potent than before. The procedures used were often simple and repetitive, summarized by the imperative *solve et coagula* (dissolve and coagulate). Historically, these processes were usually applied to transmutation of matter, but the F.R.C. followed modern occult trends in structuring the initiatory experience of its adepts around a process of inner transformation—a disintegration and reconstruction of soul and/or psyche known as spiritual alchemy. Influenced by A.E. Waite and by A.H.E. Lee, who was interested in modern occult alchemical theories and their application to the transmutation of sexual energies, Williams incorporated this modern spiritual alchemy into his belief system. From this point, like many alchemists before him, he blended alchemical terms and

---

2. Matthew Evans, "Magnum Opus," *Lewis: Season 9* (2015).

images together with elements from other esoteric systems in the symbolic tapestry of his novels. This integration formed a veil intended to reveal rather than conceal the mystic message of the Secret Tradition, though it has proved largely opaque to most readers.

Spiritual alchemy was central to Williams's occult experiences, his goal of mystical attainment, and even, despite Murray's dissociation, his doctrine of coinherence. Yet, as with kabbalah, the subject has received very little critical attention. One exception is Gavin Ashenden, who explores an interest in alchemy he ascribes to Williams's early career. Ashenden's attention to alchemy is to be commended, and his book is helpful for understanding the alchemical metaphysics behind the transmutative magic of Nigel Considine, but he maintains the walls of the cordon sanitaire, arguing that Williams discovered alchemy in a form "deliberately Christianized" by Waite,[3] and proceeded to develop "the language of alchemical transmutation" into "the universal language of Christendom."[4] I would argue a much different view: There would have been very little need to "Christianize" alchemy as its central themes, concepts and practices had, from its point of transfer from the Arab world into twelfth- and thirteenth-century Europe, been consistently infused with Christian myth and symbol. Perhaps because of this shared history, but also as a natural result of his heterodox tendencies, Williams does not seem to have been all that concerned with the degree of alchemy's consanguinity with Christianity. He found it attractive, historically, as one of the "corollaries of the Union,"[5] and in his own time he was heavily influenced by spiritual applications of alchemical thought which were all the rage in modern occultism. By understanding Williams as both alchemist and alchemized, we can

---

3. Ashenden, *Charles Williams*, 71. Ashenden later takes a different view, arguing that it was Williams, not Waite, who fully Christianized the F.R.C. system (95). Lindop also traces Considine's magical theory to alchemy (*Charles Williams*, 118), but otherwise does not discuss alchemical influences in detail.
4. Ashenden, *Charles Williams*, 71, 79. Cf. 95–96, 119.
5. Williams, *Witchcraft*, 224.

much better understand the narratives of transmutation in his novels: the death and rebirth of the self experienced by characters from Considine to Chloe.

FROM METALLURGY TO PARTICLE PHYSICS: A BRIEF HISTORY OF ALCHEMY

Alchemy emerged c. 100–300 CE in Hellenistic Egypt from a conflation of Aristotelian physics, the Gnostic view of matter as impure in comparison to spirit, Hermetic and neo-Platonic beliefs in a correspondent, unified universe, and the Stoic concept of the *pneuma* or "seminal principle" which shaped the originally formless nature of matter into specific elements and materials.[6] Alchemists of this early period, such as Zosimos of Panopolis and Maria the Jewess, applied these philosophical traditions to pre-existing metallurgical techniques used to feign the appearance of precious metals, though the alchemists were focused on creation rather than imitation.[7] Alchemy made its way to Byzantium, but really gathered steam in the Arab world, where innovative philosophers such as Jabir (ca. 700–800) and Rhazes (865–925) developed many of the concepts and practices that would be used by later European alchemists.[8] This transference to Christendom began in the twelfth century and reached its apogee in early modern Europe, where influential thinkers like Elias Ashmole, Robert Boyle and Isaac Newton devoted much of their time to ques-

---

6. On alchemy's Alexandrian origins see Principe, *Secrets of Alchemy*, 9–14; Claudia Kren, *Alchemy in Europe: A Guide to Research* (London: Garland, 1990), viii; Allison P. Coudert, "Alchemy IV: 16th–18th Century," in *Dictionary of Gnosis and Western Esotericism*, ed. Wouter J. Hanegraaff (Leiden: Brill, 2006), 43.

7. For a brief historical outline of alchemy's development, see Morrisson, *Modern Alchemy*, 3–4. For a more detailed survey see Principe, *Secrets of Alchemy*, 9–136. The entries on alchemy in Wouter J. Hanegraaff, *Dictionary of Gnosis and Western Esotericism* (Leiden: Brill, 2006) are very helpful for getting a sense of the historical progression (and enormous diversity) of the alchemical tradition. See especially Bernard D. Haage, "Alchemy II: Antiquity-12th-Century," 22–31; Herwig Buntz, "Alchemy III: 12th/13th–15th Century," 34–38; Allison P. Coudert, "Alchemy IV: 16th–18th Century," 42–47; Richard Caron, "Alchemy V: 19th–20th Century," 51–56.

8. See Haage, "Alchemy II," 26–29.

tions concerning the nature of the elements and methods by which they might be transmuted. However, although alchemy was respected by many intellectuals, it never reached the degree of cultural acceptability achieved by other natural philosophical endeavours of the period. Already associated with magic, kabbalah and, more polemically, witchcraft and demonic practices in the High Middle Ages and the Renaissance, alchemy was pushed entirely into the circle of rejected knowledge occupied by the esoteric traditions during and following the Enlightenment.[9] By the second quarter of the eighteenth century, alchemy was primarily seen as a practice of goldmaking—dubious at best, fraudulent at worst—or as a spiritual practice diametrically opposed to its naturalistic cousin chemistry, a dichotomy that had become largely ingrained by the late nineteenth century, despite the virtual synonymity of alchemy with chemistry only two centuries earlier.[10]

The alchemical tradition that emerged over the course of this long period of development produced a wide range of beliefs and practices, methods and conclusions. This scope included laboratory experimentation intended to discover the properties of physical substances, attempts to transmute metals such as lead and mercury into more valuable materials, medical research, the use of alchemical narrative and symbol to illustrate theological and/or mystical belief systems, and the application of alchemical lore for spiritual purposes, sometimes in concert with laboratory-based practices.[11] Some alchemists pursued only one of these lines of inquiry, most linked

---

9. See Lawrence M. Principe, "Alchemy I: Introduction," in *Dictionary of Gnosis and Western Esotericism*, ed. Wouter J. Hanegraaff (Leiden: Brill, 2006), 14–15; Brian Vickers, "The 'New Historiography' and the Limits of Alchemy," *Annals of Science* 65, no. 1 (2008): 130.

10. On alchemy's post-Enlightenment decline, see Principe, *Secrets of Alchemy*, 84–92; William R. Newman and Lawrence M. Principe, "Alchemy vs. Chemistry: The Etymological Origins of a Historiographic Mistake," *Early Science and Medicine* 3, no. 1 (1998); Morrisson, *Modern Alchemy*, 4.

11. On the diverse concerns of alchemical practice see Stanton J. Linden, ed., *The Alchemy Reader: From Hermes Trismegistus to Isaac Newton* (Cambridge: Cambridge University Press, 2003), 4; Principe, "Alchemy I," 12–13; Morrisson, *Modern Alchemy*, 3–4.

two or more together. Very few generalizations can be drawn from this diversity, but broadly speaking alchemists followed the process of *solve et coagula*. First, they sought to strip base substances of their impurities and/or the characteristics that defined their current essence, through processes such as dissolution, distillation, combustion, or putrefaction, reducing the substance to a state that was often recognized as the *prima materia*—a single, uniform substance out of which alchemists believed all things were made and to which all things could therefore return. Once the base substance's original, flawed nature had been eliminated, it could be enobled through transmutation: tincturing agents—the most potent of which was described as the Philosophers' Stone—communicated the soul or essence of a nobler metal (usually gold or silver) to the undifferentiated metallic matter.[12] The means of attaining the Philosophers' Stone varied widely, but most alchemists agreed that a sequence of colour changes in the substances under transformation could guide the process. In the most basic formulation of this colour symbolism, the *nigredo* (black) first seen in the stages of putrefaction was followed by the *albedo* (white), an intermediate stage connected to the production of silver, and the *rubedo* (red), symbolizing the successful creation of the Philosophers' Stone.[13] Along with the creation of gold, the discovery of the Stone was the central motivation of all these centuries of alchemical practice. The Stone was conceived as a necessary ingredient in the Great Work, or as a healing product equivalent to another legendary aim of alchemy: the elixir of life. Most commonly, it was believed to be a tool with which, upon its successful creation, one would be able to transmute large quantities of lesser metals to gold.[14]

---

12. On the stages of the alchemical process, see Morrisson, *Modern Alchemy*, 3–4; Haage, "Alchemy II," 17–18; Buntz, "Alchemy III," 35–36; Linden, *The Alchemy Reader*, 13, 17–19.
13. Coudert, "Alchemy IV," 43; Linden, *The Alchemy Reader*, 16. Other colours were posited as well, representing further intermediate stages.
14. On the Philosophers' Stone see Linden, *The Alchemy Reader*, 16; Coudert, "Alchemy IV," 43. Haage, "Alchemy II," 18; Buntz, "Alchemy III," 17.

Alchemy never fully disappeared following its eighteenth-century fall from grace, but it maintained a low profile until it enjoyed a resurgence in the occult revival, albeit in an adapted spiritual and psychological form. The genesis of such modern interpretations was the 1850 publication of *A Suggestive Inquiry into the Hermetic Mystery* by Mary Anne Atwood (née South) in conceptual collaboration with her father, Thomas South.[15] Influenced by Jacob Boehme, Atwood portrayed alchemy as an ancient wisdom tradition concerned not with the transmutation of metals but with spiritual transformation. The human self, rather than a metallurgical workshop, was "the true laboratory of the Hermetic Art."[16] She also interpreted the *prima materia*, the quintessence and other elevated forms of matter proposed by alchemists as equivalent to the ether, a subtle force or fluid commonly believed by physicists of the period to permeate all matter, acting as a causal agent for phenomena such as light, magnetism and electricity.[17] In mesmerism, another theory popular in nineteenth-century science, though one that was losing credence in the scientific community of Atwood's time, it was believed that this ether was also equivalent to an animal magnetic force, which, when manipulated through the application of the mesmerizer's will, could (among other effects) cause a somnambulic trance state in more sensitive subjects.[18] Atwood merged these concepts to reinterpret the history of alchemy, suggesting that those alchemists who truly understood their art were essentially mesmerists *avant la lettre*, manipulating the ether in order to effect a trance state in which they could

---

15. Mary Anne Atwood, *A Suggestive Inquiry into the Hermetic Mystery; with a Dissertation on the More Celebrated of the Alchemical Philosophers; Being an Attempt toward the Recovery of the Ancient Experiment of Nature* (London: Trelawney Saunders, 1850).
16. Ibid, 153. On Atwood's debt to Boehme, see Zuber, *Spiritual Alchemy*, 477–84. For a detailed exploration of Atwood's spiritual alchemy see Ibid, 462–508. Cf. Principe and Newman, "Historiography of Alchemy," 389–91; Principe, *Secrets of Alchemy*, 94–98; Gilbert, *A.E. Waite*, 93; Morrisson, *Modern Alchemy*, 36–37.
17. Asprem, "Parapsychology," 142–44.
18. An excellent resource on mesmerism, particularly its British context, is Alison Winter, *Mesmerized: Powers of Mind in Victorian Britain* (Chicago: University of Chicago Press, 1998). For brief summaries of the practice see Godwin, *Theosophical Enlightenment*, 151–61; Oppenheim, *The Other World*, 210–17.

literally fabricate an incorporeal Philosophers' Stone within themselves, an interior transformation that would, in turn, allow them to transmute the elements of the material world.[19] Crucially, Atwood believed that mystic union could be achieved once the transmutation of the human subject was complete.[20]

This spiritualized conception of alchemy was taken up by a number of other thinkers. Seven years after Atwood's publication, American General Ethan Allen Hitchcock produced a specifically Christian interpretation of alchemy in *Remarks upon Alchemy and the Alchemists*. Hitchcock, like Atwood, believed that "the subject of Alchemy was Man; while the object was the perfection of Man," and could find no evidence that the "genuine Alchemists" were interested in "mere mechanical theories."[21] Most famously, the concept of alchemy as a process of inner transmutation played a central role in Carl Jung's conceptualization of a framework of basic stages of human psychological development.[22] Jung's concept of alchemy as psychic transmutation, which was, like Williams's alchemical perception, influenced by Waite,[23] was the window into the science of transmutation for a number of other widely read voices, including Joseph Campbell and Northrop Frye, thus propelling the concept of alchemy as primarily spiritual into the mainstream.[24]

---

19. On Atwood's fusion of mesmerism with spiritual alchemy, see Atwood, *Suggestive Inquiry*, 85, 175–76, 185, 257–58. Cf. Zuber, "Spiritual Alchemy," 475–84; Principe and Newman, "Historiography of Alchemy," 391; Principe, *Secrets of Alchemy*, 94–98.
20. See Zuber, "Spiritual Alchemy," 433. Cf. Gilbert, *A.E. Waite*, 93.
21. Ethan Allen Hitchcock, *Remarks Upon Alchemy and the Alchemists* (Boston: Crosby, Nichols, 1857), 22, 295. Hitchcock had already published some of his ideas in a shorter tract two years earlier. See Principe and Newman, "Historiography of Alchemy," 392; Principe, *Secrets of Alchemy*, 98–99. For a summary of the development of occultist spiritual alchemy in the nineteenth and twentieth centuries, see Caron, "Alchemy V," 52–53.
22. Daniel Merkur, "The Study of Spiritual Alchemy: Mysticism, Gold-Making, and Esoteric Hermeneutics," *Ambix* 37, no. 1 (March 1990): 38–39; Principe, *Secrets of Alchemy*, 102–4.
23. Owen, *Place of Enchantment*, 143; Principe, *Secrets of Alchemy*, 103. Principe attributes the similarities between occult and Jungian alchemy partly to Waite, noting that Waite's early writings on alchemy were passed around Jung's Zurich Psychological Club in the 1910s.
24. See Principe and Newman, "Historiography of Alchemy," 401–4; George-Florin

William R. Newman and Lawrence M. Principe, both historians of science, have bemoaned this esoteric and psychological alchemical resurgence, arguing that modern alchemy's emphasis on inner, spiritual transmutation has discoloured the historiography of a largely physical, proto-empiricist tradition. They do not deny that alchemists throughout history attached religious and/or spiritual motives to their practice,[25] but they see nineteenth-century spiritual alchemy as as the first non-laboratory-based form of the tradition, asserting that the contemporary "chasm between 'alchemy' and 'chemistry'" is an "artifact" forged by modern spiritual interpretations.[26] Newman and Principe's "new historiography" of alchemy has been enormously valuable in restoring the centrality of physical transmutation to our perspective of historical alchemical practice, especially prior to the nineteenth century.[27] However, in seeking to show that alchemy is not simply a spiritual or religious form of chemistry, they end up throwing the homunculus out with the bathwater, downplaying alchemy's historic connections to esoteric traditions such as magic, kabbalah and astrology in order to solidify its identity as a protoscience. More scholars of alchemy than not, however, continue to emphasize the existence of a differentiation between spiritual and material intentions behind alchemical practice since at least the point of Roger Bacon's distinction between *"alkimie operativa et practica"*—practical knowledge such as the method of gold-making—and

---

Calian, "*Alkimia Operativa* and *Alkimia Speculativa*: Some Modern Controversies on the Historiography of Alchemy," in *Annual of Medieval Studies at Ceu*, ed. Katalin Szende and Judith A. Rasson (Budapest: Archaeolingua Foundation and Publishing House, 2010), 167–72; Kren, *Alchemy in Europe*, ix; Owen, *Place of Enchantment*, 143–44.

25. See Principe and Newman, "Historiography of Alchemy," 398; Principe, *Secrets of Alchemy*, 194.

26. Principe and Newman, "Historiography of Alchemy," 418; Principe, *Secrets of Alchemy*, 94.

27. For a selection of publications that contribute to the "new historiography" project, see Principe and Newman, "Historiography of Alchemy"; "Alchemy vs. Chemistry"; Principe, "Alchemy I," 13–14; *Secrets of Alchemy*, esp. 94, 194, 205; William R. Newman, "Brian Vickers on Alchemy and the Occult: A Response," *Perspectives on Science* 17, no. 4 (Winter 2009).

"*alkimia speculativa*"—metaphysical knowledge[28]—though Principe correctly points out that only moderns would interpret such a binary as a rigid distinction between naturalistic and spiritual approaches.[29]

More crucially, the "new historiography" ignores the need to see post-nineteenth-century spiritual and psychological interpretations as serious alchemical traditions in their own right, and, perhaps most glaringly, elides an extant tradition of inner transmutation that has existed since at least the time of Boehme.[30] Atwood was not formulating a spiritual alchemy *sui generis* in adopting the ideas of this German theosopher. Boehme never questioned that alchemy was largely a practice of physical transmutation, but he deployed its symbols and terminology both to inform his unique cosmology and, more importantly for our current purposes, to propose an alchemical theory of interior transformation.[31] As Principe and Newman note, Boehme in no way represents "the mainstream" of alchemical thought in his period,[32] but his ideas contributed to the development of a predominantly spiritual alchemy focused largely on transmutation of the self, often with a final goal of mystical attainment. This thread runs through important early modern esoteric thinkers including Thomas Vaughan, Michael Maier and Robert Fludd to later developments in magic, kabbalah, astrology and alchemy.[33] Boehme's mystical approach to alchemical symbolism was also taken

---

28. Calian, "*Alkimia Operativa* and *Alkimia Speculativa*," 178. Bacon makes the distinction in Chapter Twelve of his *Opus tertium* (1267). Cf. Linden, *The Alchemy Reader*, 50; Merkur, "Study of Spiritual Alchemy," 43.

29. See Principe, *Secrets of Alchemy*, 194.

30. A number of scholars have criticized Newman and Principe for what George-Florin Calian calls a "dramatically inflexible" rejection of spiritual and esoteric aspects of alchemical history ("*Alkimia Operativa* and *Alkimia Speculativa*," 170, 174, 177–78). Cf. Vickers, "The 'New Historiography'."

31. See Zuber, "Spiritual Alchemy," 154–93; Calian, "*Alkimia Operativa* and *Alkimia Speculativa*," 170, 174, 177–78; Merkur, "Study of Spiritual Alchemy," 35–36.

32. Principe and Newman, "Historiography of Alchemy," 399.

33. On the varying approaches to "spiritual alchemy" from the Renaissance forwards, and their incorporation with physical alchemical practices, see Hereward Tilton, "Alchymia Archetypica: Theurgy, Inner Transformation and the Historiography of Alchemy," *Quaderni di Studi Indo-Mediterranei* 5 (2012): 179–215; Calian, "*Alkimia Operativa* and *Alkimia Speculativa*," 166–67; Zuber, "Spiritual Alchemy," 46–49.

up by the mysterious authors of the Rosicrucian manifestoes; one of their number, Johann Valentin Andreae, also probably wrote one of the most well known alchemical allegories, *Die Chymische Hochzeit Christiani Rosenkreutz* (*The Chemical Wedding of Christian Rosenkreutz*), published in 1616 only one year after the *Confessio Fraternitatis*. From this point of origin, alchemical symbolism was enfolded into the rituals of the earliest known Rosicrucian groups in Germany and was still a vital part of Williams's own Rosicrucian experience of inner transmutation in the F.R.C. All these formulations of spiritual transformation—from Boehme to Rosicrucianism to Atwood to Jung—vary in nature and intent, but all fall under the aegis of "spiritual alchemy" because of their focus on interior rather than exterior transmutation. This is not to say that these spiritual interpretations have existed in a vacuum. As Tara E. Nummedal argues, alchemy has been, particularly since the early modern period, a practice much more multifarious than something that can be encapsulated in the image of the proto-scientific alchemist crouched over his athanor.[34] Alchemy has been practiced in a variety of philosophical, textual, experimental, metallurgical, medical, psychological, mystical and magical modes, almost always with more than one of these ongoing at any particular time. Spiritual alchemy was no different—though it pursued interior spiritual or psychological transformation, it was based in alchemy's rich textual and philosophical tradition, much of which was produced in tandem with laboratory-based experimentation.

This principle of diversity also applies to modern occult alchemy, which was far from purely spiritual. In the nineteenth century Atwood's spiritual focus was dominant and, indeed, in large part responsible for the resurgence in interest in alchemy. By the turn of the twentieth century, however, discoveries in modern physics returned the alchemy of the laboratory to the forefront, both in- and outside of the occult milieu. In 1901 chemist Frederick Soddy and

---

34. Tara E. Nummedal, "Words and Works in the History of Alchemy," *Isis* 102, no. 2 (June 2011): 331.

physicist Earnest Rutherford discovered that radioactive elements actually *could* be transmuted from one to another.[35] By 1919 Rutherford had successfully transmuted nitrogen into oxygen, leading to an alchemical revival in which atomic physics was frequently referred to as "modern alchemy" in textbooks, scientific accounts and the press.[36] Unsurprisingly, these developments rekindled interest in a tradition that had been claiming the reality of such material transmutations for centuries. This manifested among professional scientists —Rutherford's last book was titled *The Newer Alchemy* (1937)—but also among some occultists. Crowley took chemistry courses in the 1890s under the instruction of Nobel Prize winning chemist William Ramsay, who described the transmutation of radioactive elements in alchemical terms, an experience which seems to have been a part of Crowley's motivation for combining ancient esoteric wisdom with the methods and discoveries of modern science.[37] Even Waite, whose view of "the sublime dream of psycho-chemistry" was largely synonymous with Atwood's in the late 1880s and early 90s,[38] was ready to denounce her elision of physical alchemy by the time he was appointed Honorary Vice-President of London's short-lived Alchemical Society in 1912,[39] an organization which researched alchemy in a context "embedded in mainstream scientific structures."[40] To a degree, this appreciation for alchemy's empirical heritage had already been ongoing among occultists. Florence Farr and Edward

---

35. Morrisson, *Modern Alchemy*, 5–9.
36. Ibid, 64. Morrisson notes that with the advent of the nuclear bomb, society's view of atomic physics moved away from interest in transmutation (29).
37. Ibid, 44–47. On interactions between modern chemistry and occult alchemical understandings see also Stockhammer, "Rosicrucian Radioactivity," 134–36.
38. Arthur Edward Waite, *Lives of Alchemystical Philosophers* (London: George Redway, 1888), 37. Even at this early stage, Waite did not follow Atwood's view that alchemists had not historically been interested in actual physical transmutation (see 26–27). Cf. Gilbert, *A.E. Waite*, 93.
39. Gilbert, *A.E. Waite*, 151; Morrisson, *Modern Alchemy*, 58.
40. Asprem, *The Problem of Disenchantment*, 249. Cf. 247–59 for a wider discussion of the varying physical and/or spiritual approaches that intermingled within the context of the Alchemical Society.

Berridge explored medicinal aspects of the alchemical tradition,[41] while William Alexander (W.A.) Ayton led a subgroup of the Golden Dawn dedicated to alchemical instruction. Ayton valued spiritual alchemical interpretations but he was also a source of knowledge for those adepts who wished to experiment with physical materials in addition to the inner transmutation pursued within the ritual environment of the Golden Dawn.[42] Yeats reports that Ayton claimed to have an alchemical laboratory in his cellar and to have successfully prepared the elixir of life.[43]

Even Ayton, however, continued to recommend the value of Atwood's *Suggestive Inquiry*,[44] and, like the alchemists of old, emphasized that laboratory success could not be had without a prior process of self-purification. He instructed Frederick Leigh Gardner, a student in his alchemical subgroup, that the achievement of these "necessary personal conditions" was of "immense and inconceivable" difficulty for those without knowledge of the process—an esoteric knowledge so latent with potential that Ayton dared not communicate it to Gardner "except under the most inviolable secrecy."[45] Indeed, most occultists interested in alchemy continued to value its symbol and narrative on the largely spiritual or psychical level of inner transmutation. Isabelle de Steiger, a central figure in the modern occult network, disseminated the theories of Atwood, a close friend, in the context of her involvement with the Theosophical Society, Kingsford's Hermetic Society, the Golden Dawn, Waite's I.R.R., and the English branch of the Anthroposophical Society. De Steiger maintained her staunch defense of Atwood's thesis even after she joined Waite, another close friend, as Honorary Vice-President of the

---

41. Owen, *Place of Enchantment*, 124.
42. Morrisson, *Modern Alchemy*, 35, 41–42.
43. W. B. Yeats, *The Trembling of the Veil* (London: T. Werner Laurie, 1922), 70. Cf. Ellic Howe, ed., *The Alchemist of the Golden Dawn: The Letters of the Revd W.A. Ayton to F.L. Gardner and Others, 1886–1905* (Wellingborough, Northamptonshire: Aquarian Press, 1985), 9–10.
44. Ibid, 50–51.
45. Ibid, 53. On Ayton and his series of letters to Gardner, see Howe, *The Magicians of the Golden Dawn*, 145–48.

Alchemical Society.[46] More contemporary to Williams, Israel Regardie also acknowledged the validity of alchemy's physical tradition, but was more interested, unsurprisingly given his background as an occultist and practicing psychologist, in its psychological and spiritual implications.[47] In addition to her interest in potential medical applications of alchemy, Florence Farr espoused its analogical and metaphorical implications for the discovery of the higher self.[48] As Alex Owen argues in the course of her explication of the modern occult "pursuit of a complete understanding of self," adepts like Farr were primarily interested in alchemy as a transmutation of the essence of the human subject.[49]

INFLUENCES: LEE, WAITE, ATWOOD

Influences from virtually every aspect of this diverse history of alchemy are visible in Charles Williams's work, particularly once his fiction is added to the evidence under analysis. When expressing admiration for Renaissance and early modern Hermetic thinkers like Pico, Agrippa, Dee, and Vaughan who "sought the Union" through "the various corollaries of the Union,"[50] he seems to understand them primarily as alchemists. It was common in Williams's time (as it had been since the early modern period) to use alchemy as a descriptor for Hermeticism in general—Regardie, for example, saw both terms as synonymous with the "Wisdom and Magic" traditions[51]—but Williams uses allusive alchemical terms and *decknamen*

---

46. See Isabelle de Steiger, "The Hermetic Mystery 2," *The Journal of the Alchemical Society* 2, no. 7 (Nov 1913): 21–22. On de Steiger's alchemy see Asprem, *The Problem of Disenchantment*, 155–57.
47. See Israel Regardie, *The Philosopher's Stone* (London: Rider, 1938), 15, 18. Cf. Principe, *Secrets of Alchemy*, 104; Morrisson, *Modern Alchemy*, 188–89, 191.
48. Florence Farr (as S.S.D.D), "An Introduction to Alchemy and Notes," in *A Short Enquiry Concerning the Hermetic Art, by a Lover of Philalethes*, Collectanea Hermetica (London: Theosophical Publishing Society, 1894), 9–10. Cf. Owen, *Place of Enchantment*, 125, 131.
49. Owen, *Place of Enchantment*, 123.
50. Williams, *Witchcraft*, 224. See previous discussion, p. xxx.
51. Regardie, *Philosopher's Stone*, 13.

—coded names used to refer to particular elements and substances in alchemical recipes and texts—to describe the "praxis" behind the "corollaries": "The very language they used needs an encyclopedia to explain it—the Salts and the Vitriols, the Sulphurs and the Stones, the Eagles and the Dragons, the Ternary and the Septenary, the Dissolutions and the Coagulations, the Males and the Females."[52] Thus, typical of spiritual alchemists from Boehme to Jung, Williams seems to have been fascinated by the alchemical imagery that resulted from centuries of laboratory experimentation and protective, obscurantist communication of its results, physical practices that he validated as some of the "lower correspondences" of the "high transmutations."[53] Despite this interest in pre-modern alchemical theory and practice, however, Williams's life and fiction reveal an alchemist much more in tune with Boehme, Rosicrucianism and occult spiritual alchemy.

Not coincidentally, the two individuals through whom Williams seems to have gained most of his exposure to alchemy were also spiritual alchemists. The first of these was A.E. Waite, whose F.R.C. rituals seem to have done much to define Williams's understanding of interior transformation. The second was A.H.E. Lee. A lack of records makes it difficult to ascertain how much influence Lee had on Williams in general, let alone in the development of his alchemical vision. We can assume, however, as Grevel Lindop does, that Williams's meetings at Lee's vicarage in North London were influential.[54] Lindop reveals that a private notebook belonging to Lee, held in the Warburg in London,[55] contains notes on the Golden Dawn's Flying Roll No. 7, an exposition of alchemical symbols and their relation to other, primarily kabbalistic, esoteric systems, delivered to Golden Dawn members by Westcott in 1890.[56] Notes on the *Suggestive Inquiry* in the same notebook show Lee's interest in Atwood, whose

---

52. Williams, *Witchcraft*, 224.
53. Ibid, 232.
54. Lindop, *Charles Williams*, 64, 78.
55. Warburg Institute Library, Yorke Collection, NS 32 (restricted).
56. Lindop, *Charles Williams*, 64. Cf. King, *Astral Projection, Ritual Magic and Alchemy*, 177.

work combined two of his interests: alchemy and mesmerism, the latter a subject with which he was so engaged that he translated Baron du Potet de Sennevoy's 1852 treatise on magic and animal magnetism, *La Magie Dévoilée*, published as *Magnetism and Magic* in 1927. Lindop believes that given Lee's interest in Atwood, Williams would almost certainly have been exposed to her alchemical mysticism.[57] However, Lee's notes were taken at least a year before he met Williams, and Atwood's thought would have been readily available for Williams to encounter and read on his own, as it was ubiquitous in occult circles, particularly following the republication of *A Suggestive Inquiry* under de Steiger's guidance in 1918, with a third printing in 1920. Even if he did not himself read Atwood, we know that he was interested in her ideas. A page of his Commonplace Book is filled with notes taken after reading W.L. Wilmshurst's, "The Later Mysticism of Mrs. Atwood," in *The Quest*.[58] Here Williams's fiction offers, as usual, a helpful tool for understanding his esoteric interests. As I will discuss shortly, his portrayal of the alchemical magic of Considine seems to reflect Atwood's connection of the mesmerist trance to interior transmutation.

Waite is even more likely to been an impactful influence, particularly via the alchemical symbolism and broad narrative of interior transmutation that were communicated to Williams in the F.R.C. As with magic, kabbalah and the tarot, Waite played a leading role in defining the perception of alchemy among his contemporaries. This influence was promulgated through a number of translations of alchemical texts, including works by Basil Valentine, Paracelsus and Edward Kelley,[59] along with articles, the rituals of the I.R.R. and F.R.C., and books, particularly his 1926 *The Secret Tradition in Alchemy*.[60] In these texts Waite presented a vision of the central

---

57. Lindop, *Charles Williams*, 78.
58. W.L. Wilmshurst, "The Later Mysticism of Mrs. Atwood," *Quest* 1, no. 4 (July 1919): 487–507; 2, no. 1 (Oct 1919), 31–53.
59. On Waite's translation of alchemical texts, see Waite, *Shadows*, 130–31. Cf. Morrisson, *Modern Alchemy*, 43; Gilbert, *A.E. Waite*, 81, 95; Caron, "Alchemy V," 53.
60. Waite also produced *Azoth: Or, the Star in the East* (London: The Theosophical

themes and historical strands of alchemy that was well-argued enough to get him appointed to his position in the Alchemical Society, and compelling enough to function as one of the most influential brands of spiritual alchemy available in the early twentieth-century occult world. Initially this vision was largely organized around Atwood's emphasis on the transformative power of inner transmutation, both on individual and wider social levels. Though he acknowledged the importance of laboratory work even at this early juncture, and criticized both Atwood and Hitchcock for ignoring this aspect of alchemical history,[61] he saw in mesmerism, clairvoyance, magic and Spiritualism "the *raison d'être* of the sublime dream of psycho-chemistry [alchemy]—that, namely, there is a change, a transmutation, or a new birth, possible to embodied man which shall manifestly develop the esoteric potencies of his spiritual being."[62] Interestingly enough, however, in the same years that Waite began to advocate a complete rejection of "phenomenal occultism," he moved away from Atwood's enthusiastic spiritual interpretation of alchemy, dismissing the possibility of a specific spiritual trend before the time of the Protestant Reformation.[63] This shift leads Newman and Principe to proclaim that Waite had finally "transmuted himself into a positivist"[64]—had, in their view, come to his senses and recognized the proto-scientific history of alchemy.

Waite, however, had done nothing of the sort. He does seem to have become more and more convinced that, as he had already stated in 1890, "The testimony of the alchemists themselves to the physical

---

Publishing Society, 1893), a study of "the alchemical transfiguration of humanity" written with the syncretic enthusiasm of the occultist's youth, *Lives of Alchemystical Philosophers*, and "What Is Alchemy?," *The Unknown World* 1, no. 1 (15 August 1894).
61. See Waite, *Lives of Alchemystical Philosophers*, 26–34.
62. Ibid, 36–37. A similar view is expressed in an article published in *Light* in the same period. See "New Light of Mysticism." Cf. Gilbert, *A.E. Waite*, 92–93.
63. Waite, *Secret Tradition in Alchemy*, 26–30, 366. Waite had already made this move away from Atwood's thought by 1911, in *The Secret Tradition in Freemasonry*. See Gilbert, *A.E. Waite*, 151.
64. Principe and Newman, "Historiography of Alchemy," 395. Cf. Principe, *Secrets of Alchemy*, 100. Morrisson takes a similar, though more nuanced tack. See *Modern Alchemy*, 57–58.

nature of their object is quite unequivocal and conclusive."[65] However, Newman and Principe seem to have dubbed Waite a positivist without actually reading *A Secret Tradition in Alchemy*, which is centrally oriented, like most of his books, toward discovering the ancient wisdom of the Secret Tradition. As a historian, Waite dutifully identifies the inadequacy of Atwood's synthesis, in much the same manner as he ridiculed occultists for their muddled views on magic and kabbalah, but as an occultist mystic—the role which ultimately defined his priorities—he maintains his focus on spiritual alchemy: "The great work in its proper and plenary understanding is spiritual, and it is this only which matters for those who are on the quest of reality—transmutation performed in the spirit rather than that of physics."[66] The goal of his present work, Waite states clearly, is to "collect and estimate" evidence of "great secrets of the soul" hidden within alchemy's "scheme of cryptology,"[67] a goal "based upon considerations which are of no physical kind."[68] Waite differs from Atwood in limiting the origins of a specific spiritual lineage to post-Reformational alchemy, but he too places Boehme, "a luminary of the first magnitude,"[69] at the center of a tradition of "Higher Alchemy," drawing a line onwards through Fludd, Vaughan and Rosicrucianism to the present day.[70] Those who practiced physical alchemy were not necessarily disassociated from this tradition, but as far as Waite is concerned, "We can leave to the physical alchemists those things of Caesar which belong to them, retaining the things which concern the mysteries of divine symbolism."[71] Waite's personal focus thus remained as spiritual as Atwood's—more so if we take into consideration that he did not share her belief that manipulation of subtle, etheric fluids was part of the process of inner transmutation. He also

---

65. Waite, *Lives of Alchemystical Philosophers*, 27.
66. Waite, *Secret Tradition in Alchemy*, 360.
67. Ibid, xxi. Cf. 5.
68. Ibid, 2.
69. Ibid, 35. Cf. 344–47.
70. Ibid, 9n1. Cf. 16–17, 336–47, 359–67.
71. Waite, *Hidden Church of the Holy Graal*, 537.

maintained another central premise of Atwood's thesis—that alchemical language was used to veil the praxis of self-transmutation in which "the mind and soul of the searcher passed beyond the the region of speculation into that of demonstrative experience."[72] Alchemy thus joined kabbalah, magic and Freemasonry in a group of intellectual, philosophical and religious traditions in which Waite found Secret Tradition knowledge hidden from the "specific condemnation" of orthodox religious powers by "the adoption of symbolic veils."[73]

ROSICRUCIAN ALCHEMY

Another of these traditions was Rosicrucianism, and it was likely in this context that Waite's personal or authorial influence most guided Williams's own knowledge of alchemy. Alchemical symbolism had been a part of the masonic Rosicrucian heritage of the F.R.C. since its genesis in the Rosicrucian manifestoes of the early seventeenth century. Although the manifestoes specifically spoke out against the transmutation of metals to gold, Rosicrucianism was quickly connected to alchemy by early Rosicrucian apologists like Maier and Fludd.[74] Indeed, the manifestoes' message of a coming spiritual, moral and political transformation of society likely emerged, in part, from the popularity of both philosophical and practical approaches to alchemy in the Tübingen context in which the manifestoes appeared.[75] The eighteenth-century Gold- und Rosenkreuzer took up this alchemical heritage. Members were encouraged to pursue both material alchemy and its more philosophical/theoretical aspects, and

---

72. Waite, "The Canon of Criticism in Respect of Alchemical Literature," *The Journal of the Alchemical Society* I, no. 2 (February 1913): 24.
73. Ibid.
74. On Maier, alchemy and Rosicrucianism see Hereward Tilton, *The Quest for the Phoenix: Spiritual Alchemy and Rosicrucianism in the Work of Count Michael Maier (1569–1622)* (Berlin: Walter de Gruyter, 2003); on Fludd, see Tilton, "Alchymia Archetypica," 194–95; Coudert, "Alchemy IV," 46. On the significance of the Rosicrucian manifestoes and resulting "furore" to the development of spiritual alchemy, see ibid, 44.
75. See McIntosh, *The Rosy Cross Unveiled*, 42–46.

alchemical symbolism informed both the society's initiatory rituals and its central narrative of spiritual transformation.[76] Also incorporated into masonic grades not specifically linked to Rosicrucianism,[77] alchemy continued to play a role in esoteric secret societies right up until Waite discovered them through his own involvement, beginning with the Hermetic Order of the Golden Dawn.

This masonic Rosicrucian order actually did not focus as much on alchemical symbolism as some of the societies that went before it. Its rituals taught the adept the alignment of the alchemical elements with the sephiroth and the planets,[78] but the images of the Great Work do not stand out among the blur of astrological, geomantic, Enochian, Egyptian and Freemasonic material that swirls chaotically together, programmatically organized around the Tree of Life. In addition to the rituals, two documents related to alchemy circulated among members of the order. Flying Roll No. 7, a treatise on alchemy delivered in 1889 by Westcott, explains various terms and symbols and their connection to other semiotic systems such as that of kabbalah. The text is largely focused on the visual history of physical alchemy, and thus takes very little time to connect alchemy to the transmutation of self that was one of the central preoccupations of the order. However, Westcott does note that there also exists a spiritual alchemy "upon the *Highest Plane*."[79] A second document, "The Formulae of the Magic of Light: An Introduction to the Practical Working of the Z-2 Formulae," was circulated only among R.R. et A.C. initiates. Part Five of the Z-2 document interprets the symbolism of the Neophyte ritual in alchemical terms.[80] Z-2 is neither easily

---

76. McIntosh, *The Rose Cross and the Age of Reason*, 75–90; Tilton, "Alchymia Archetypica," 185–88.
77. See Tilton, "Alchymia Archetypica," 182–85.
78. See, e.g., in the Theoricus ritual (Regardie, *Complete Golden Dawn*, 6:114) and Practicus ritual (ibid, 128, 148).
79. William Wynn Westcott [as S.A.], "Flying Roll No. 7: Alchemy," in *Astral Projection, Ritual Magic, and Alchemy: Golden Dawn Material by S.L. Macgregor Mathers and Others*, ed. Francis King (Rochester, VT: Destiny Books, 1987), 181.
80. The document is reprinted in Regardie, *Complete Golden Dawn*, 6:32–52. See 48–52 for the section on alchemy. Crowley reprinted Z-2 in *The Equinox* ("The Temple of

comprehensible nor to be interpreted literally, but it clearly instructs adepts to consider the Neophyte ritual as a recipe for individual spiritual transformation. The ceremony is described as the "alembic" in which the operation takes place, the Hierophant is the alchemist, the officers conducting the ritual are the alchemical "processes and forces employed," and the candidate, of course, is "the matter to be transmuted."[81] The actual Neophyte ritual involved very little in the way of alchemical symbolism, but, as described in Z-2, the entire ritual followed the basic narrative of alchemy, a procession through "the path of darkness," purified by water and fire, to a state of "living beauty" and "gentle light."[82] The Adeptus Minor ritual was also not explicitly alchemical, but it too follows the process of symbolic death and rebirth symbolized by the life of Christ. As part of the adept's "obligation" they swore to actualize a similar transmutation within themselves, committing to "the Great Work, which is, to purify and exalt my Spiritual Nature so that with the Divine Aid I may at length attain to be more than human."[83]

Waite was clearly energized by this ritual experience with transmutative symbol and process. Recognizing the importance of the eighteenth-century German masonic context for the development of spiritual alchemy,[84] he seems to have adapted the original Golden Dawn materials for the F.R.C. partly in order to return to a stronger emphasis on alchemical symbolism. Charles Williams began his initiatory engagement with this symbolism in his very first ritual, as the Lucifer removed the coarse black robe—representative of "the unpurified life of earth"[85]—in which he had entered the tomb in darkness, and clothed him in the ritual garb of the Neophyte: a black robe with a collar of white silk, wrapped about the waist with a cord

---

Solomon the King (Book II—Continued)," *The Equinox* I, no. 3 (March 1910)), attributed to G.H. Frater I.A. (Allan Bennett).
81. Regardie, *Complete Golden Dawn*, 6:48. An alembic is a two-part vessel used to distill substances.
82. Ibid, 6:15.
83. Ibid, 7:42.
84. Waite, *Secret Tradition in Alchemy*, 359–67. Cf. "Thomas Vaughan," 73–74.
85. Waite, "Neophyte," 35.

of brown and red, representative of the alchemical stages of the *nigredo*, *albedo*, and *rubedo*. This colour symbolism foretold the process of transmutation and purification he had to undergo in the rituals of the lower orders: In the Grade of Zelator, the initiate sought to purify the body; in Theoreticus, the mind. In the Grade of Practicus the heart was "restored in purity," while a Philosophus focused on consecrating the will.[86] In the Third Order, Williams followed the transformative path symbolized by the death and rebirth of Christ in the Adeptus Minor ritual. As he was taken down from his bound position on the cross, the black robes he had worn in the lower order were removed and replaced with new, white garments. This represented his regeneration via putrefaction to a purified state in which his soul was considered ready for a spiritual *coagula*, the mystical marriage between his lower and higher selves through which he would achieve the "Christ-State."[87] This marriage took place, as I described in Chapter Two, in the Grade of Adeptus Major, where the adept met "the day of your Bridal, the end to a life of separation and the death of all that hinders the joy of ineffable union."[88] This coagulation of "Soul" and "Spouse"—the individual self and the Christ-spirit within—was perceived as the ultimate stage of the "Great Work."[89] This mystical marriage thus channels the alchemical tradition of the "chemical wedding," in which a king and queen or brother and sister were united to form a hermaphroditic offspring that represented the successful conclusion of the Great Work. These sexually differentiated pairings represent the combination of binary principles in which many alchemists saw the key to their success in the laboratory. The most common physical expression of this process was the coagulation of sulphur—a masculine,

---

86. Waite, "Zelator," 9; "Theoreticus," 17; "Practicus," 7; "Philosophus," 7; "Portal of the Third Order," 21, 29. For a summary of this process see"Adeptus Major," 33–34.
87. Waite, "Adeptus Minor," 13, 34–35. This colour symbolism is reiterated in "On the Threshold of Sacred Mystery," 26. Waite's formulation in this ritual is drawn almost verbatim from a passage in *Divine Union*, 313–14.
88. Waite, "Adeptus Major," 35.
89. Ibid, 51.

hot, dry and volatile principle—and mercury—feminine, wet, cold and fixed.[90] Following this mystical marriage, Williams would have been perceived to have achieved, though only in glimpses, the state of *rubedo*, "that of the spirit in its splendour...the Christ-Spirit,"[91] or at least been given the opportunity for such an experience via ritual.

As a Rosicrucian adept Williams was thus both alchemist—assisting in the purification of others via his role as Master of the Temple—and alchemized—the subject of a spiritual transformation that sought, as with other modern occultists including Farr, de Steiger and Regardie, to effect the disintegration of individual impurities and material illusions at the *solve* stage in order to create a purified adept ready for *coagula*. The symbolism and basic concepts used to effect this alchemical transmutation were drawn from a long tradition that reached back to antiquity, and the mystical interpretations of these materials owed much to the theosophy of Jacob Boehme and early Rosicrucianism, but Williams's alchemical experiences took place in a context indelibly tinctured by occultist interpretations and priorities spooled off from Atwood. Entirely removed from the natural and empirical concerns that dominated alchemy up to and including the early modern era, the F.R.C. followed the Golden Dawn in seeking the Great Work within the self via ritual. Williams and his fellow adepts transmuted impure qualities of body, mind, heart and will in order to prepare for higher levels of initiation, incorporating alchemical symbolism in the bricolage of image and word with which the magical imagination could be prompted toward an experience of inner attainment.

---

90. Linden, *The Alchemy Reader*, 16; Haage, "Alchemy II," 19–20; Karen-Claire Voss, "Spiritual Alchemy: Interpreting Representative Texts and Images," in *Gnosis and Hermeticism: From Antiquity to Modern Times*, ed. Roelof Van den Broek and Wouter J. Hanegraaff (Albany, NY: State University of New York Press, 1998), 157; Buntz, "Alchemy III," 36.
91. Waite, "On the Threshold of Sacred Mystery," 26.

THE GREAT WORK IN FICTION

Alchemical transmutation—physical, spiritual and everything in between—operated upon the central assumption that all things are reducible to a single essence. Waite, like many alchemists before him, was fond of illustrating this concept by quoting the *Tabula Smaragdina*, or "Emerald Tablet," a text dating back to late antiquity and pseudonymously attributed to Hermes Trismegistus: "*Est una sola Res*," which translates to "there is only one thing," a Hermetic statement of cosmic unity.[92] Writing to Phyllis Jones, Williams expanded this maxim to the Great Work of mystical alchemy that he encountered in Waite's order: "There is (it is said) only one work which is pursued everywhere and at all times, from which nothing is alien and to which all things are directed (otherwise they are null and void). And that is the re-union of man and God."[93] If all microcosmic phenomena should be considered as but reflections of a greater cosmic whole, then surely, Williams seems to suggest, all actions are but shadows of one action, all moments repetitions of the one moment of mystical attainment wherein the adept was supposed to gain a glimpse of the "one thing" in its unified totality. As we have seen, the Hermetic monism of the Emerald Tablet was the *sine qua non* of Williams's philosophy, particularly his concepts of Romantic Theology, the way of affirmation and coinherence. It underpinned his initiatory activity in the F.R.C., made possible his magical and poetic exercises of imagination, and provides the cosmological framework for the interaction of natural and supernatural in his fiction. There are also more specific references to the symbolism of transmutation

---

92. Waite, *Shadows*, 132. Cf. "On the Threshold of Sacred Mystery," 31. On the Tabula Smaragdina see William R. Newman and Anthony Grafton, "Introduction: The Problematic Status of Astrology and Alchemy in Premodern Europe," in *Secrets of Nature: Astrology and Alchemy in Early Modern Europe*, ed. William R. Newman and Anthony Grafton (Cambridge, MA: MIT Press, 2001), 25; Julius Ruska, *Tabula Smaragdina: Ein Beitrag zur Geschichte der hermetischen Literatur* (Heidelberg: Carl Winter, 1926).
93. Charles Williams to Phyllis Jones, January 1929, Bodleian MS REs. c. 320/I, letter 34, quoted in Lindop, *Charles Williams*, 153.

in his fiction, as in his plays, poetry and non-fiction as well.[94] Spiritual alchemy stands out in two novels in particular: *Many Dimensions*, which imagines the Philosophers' Stone released into modern England, and *Shadows of Ecstasy*, where the transmutative magic of Considine suggests both modern and pre-modern alchemical influences.

As already discussed, the magical stone of *Many Dimensions* references several kabbalistic concepts, particularly Shekinah and her desire to reunite with the masculine principle. True to Williams's multivalent style, however, the stone also possesses alchemical implications, serving as a rich symbol of the monistic cohesion of spirit and matter indicated by *Est una sola Res*. As the Hajji Ibrahim explains, the stone is the "First Matter...from which all things are made"[95]—the *prima materia*, the "one thing." By virtue of this primal essence, it connects "matter to matter" and "perhaps mind to mind, and soul to soul,"[96] and thus makes possible the movement of both itself and the novel's characters between different spatial, temporal, imaginal and mystical planes. This monism allows the teleportation and time travel beginning to be explored in science fiction texts of the period: "You go into it and come out again where you have desired because everything is in it."[97] Because mind is in the stone it enables many of the psychic powers pursued by occult groups in Williams's day, including astral travel, telepathy, and clairvoyance.[98] It is significant to note the connection of these abilities to the stone's alchemical roots, as all three sprang, in different ways, from nineteenth-century theories proposed by mesmerists to explain phenomena witnessed in subjects under mesmeric trance.[99] This connection poses a possible connection between Williams's conception of the stone of Suleiman and Atwood's conflation of alchemy and mesmerism.

---

94. See Ashenden, *Charles Williams*, 82–83.
95. Williams, *Many Dimensions*, 56.
96. Ibid.
97. Ibid, 192.
98. Ibid, 20, 24, 101.
99. See Oppenheim, *The Other World*, 218–20.

More primarily than the *prima materia*, the stone of *Many Dimensions* enfolds a complex reference to the Philosophers' Stone.[100] As Waite noted in *The Hidden Church of the Holy Graal*, the Philosophers' Stone has been "described in numberless ways and seldom after the same manner."[101] This multiplicity is reflected in Williams's construction of the stone of Suleiman. The stone has important modern reference points and implications, but it also refers to conceptions of the Philosophers' Stone developed in the medieval and early modern periods. Its magical authority over the material world recalls the traditional view of the Stone as a tool with which to manipulate all other forms of matter, and it displays the healing properties of the panacea or elixir of life pursued by Arab alchemists such as Jabir, and in the early modern West by the Paracelsians.[102] Williams may also have intended a more specific reference to the theories of Elias Ashmole, an English Freemason, would-be Rosicrucian and co-founder of the Royal Society. Working in a little recognized seventeenth-century tradition which Principe calls "supernatural alchemy,"[103] Ashmole posited four types of Stone: the "Minerall" stone commonly sought by the alchemists in order to transmute metals, and three others, "Vegitable" "Magicall," and "Angelicall," of a more "marvelously subtle" nature.[104] The latter two Stones seem visible on the pages of *Many Dimensions*. The magical stone makes "it

---

100. With the exception of Thomas Willard (*Acts of the Companions*, 284), scholars have largely missed this connection. McLaren and Cavaliero identify the influence of Jewish and Islamic mysticism on the stone's construction but do not address its alchemical significance ("Hermeticism and the Metaphysics of Goodness," 17–18; "Poet of Theology, 70), while Ashenden (*Charles Williams*) discusses the importance of alchemy to Williams's system and analyzes transmutative symbolism in *Shadows of Ecstasy* and *War in Heaven*, but does not touch on *Many Dimensions*.
101. Waite, *Hidden Church of the Holy Graal*, 11.
102. Haage, "Alchemy II," 16. On the stone's healing powers see Williams, *Many Dimensions*, 104, 67.
103. Lawrence M. Principe, *The Aspiring Adept: Robert Boyle and His Alchemical Quest* (Princeton: Princeton University Press, 2000), 197. Zuber criticizes the use of "supernatural" in this context. See Zuber, "Spiritual Alchemy," 47.
104. See Elias Ashmole, "Prolegomena," in *Theatrum Chemicum Brittanicum* (London: Grismond, 1652), n.p. Cf. Principe, *Aspiring Adept*, 197–98. For Waite on Ashmole and his four stones, see *Secret Tradition in Alchemy*, 336.

possible to discover any Person in what part of the World soever," as Chloe and Arglay do when they search for the stranded lab assistant Pondon in the fabric of space-time. It also anticipates, in early modern fashion, Lord Arglay's astral travel to Chloe's flat and Pondon's lab, in that it "fairly presents to your view even the *whole World*, wherein to *behold, heare*, or *see* your *Desire*."[105] The angelical stone has functions that are clearly less related, such as "the Apparition of Angells," but it seems more than coincidental that Solomon, along with Moses and Hermes, was one of only three who could wield it. Ashmole's conjecture that "nor dare Evill Spirit approach the place where it *lodgeth*"[106] calls to mind the protection the stone offers to Chloe when Prince Ali comes to steal it and ends, for his efforts, dead outside Chloe's window, "burnt as if by lightning and broken as if cast from an immense distance" by the power that is within the stone.[107] The angelical stone also has a "Divine Power, Celestiall, *and* Invisible," and "*endowes* the possessor with Divine Gifts."[108] There is no way of knowing whether Ashmole's "supernatural alchemy" did indeed seep through to Williams in some way, but here may be a source of his novel decision to place the invisible, supernatural power of Shekinah within an object that very much reflects the Philosophers' Stone.

Pre-modern reference points thus contributed significantly to Williams's construction of the stone of Suleiman, but the most vital symbolic connections to the Philosophers' Stone are distinctly modern. The function of the stone of Suleiman that is most important to the plot and themes of *Many Dimensions* is its ability to move "soul to soul," thus enabling the mystical marriage Chloe achieves both with Shekinah and as Shekinah in the climactic scene. On this level, references to the Philosophers' Stone turn from playful science fiction to a serious exploration of the alchemical symbolism used to illustrate spiritual transmutation in the F.R.C. Chloe's achievement of

---

105. Ashmole, "Prolegomena," n.p.
106. Ibid.
107. Williams, *Many Dimensions*, 220.
108. Ashmole, "Prolegomena," n.p.

the end of desire recalls two symbolic applications of the Philosophers' Stone in the F.R.C. rituals. In the first, the Adeptus Exemptus officiating in the Adeptus Major ritual illustrates inner transmutation as a chemical wedding. Equating mind to the alchemically significant element of mercury, desire to sulphur, and will to salt—the three elements commonly considered to be most significant in the Great Work following Paracelsus[109]—the Exemptus frames the initiatory journey as one from "native Mercury, Sulphur and Salt" to higher "Philosophical" forms of the same elements, recalling the transmutation of mind, desire and will that had occurred in the Theoreticus, Practicus and Philosophus grades. Once this transformation is complete, "the transmutation of Desire fixes Mind, and hence Mercury is said to be coagulated by Sulphur, while transmuted Will and its Purpose direct all the principles of love and understanding to that Divine World which is first in the Tree of Life [the supernals]."[110] The divided parts of the self thus join in mystical marriage: "The triad becomes a unity, which is the state of the Mystical Stone."[111] Waite thus merges the symbolism of alchemy and kabbalah to frame the successful completion of the spiritually transmutative process as a coming together of different aspects of the self, a coagulation completed by union with one's higher being. This united self is equivalent to the Philosophers' Stone, also seen as a unity of initially divided, opposing principles.

Chloe must undergo a similar process of dissolution and coagulation. She begins with only an intuitive understanding of the nature of the stone and its significance. As with the Second Order F.R.C. initiate, this is because her mind, will and desire have not yet been transmuted to the state necessary for the mystic marriage of the Third Order to take place. Before this transmutation she has "not made herself a path for the Will of the Stone,"[112] but at the point where she and the stone unite, "her will abolished itself before its own" (261).

---

109. Coudert, "Alchemy IV," 43.
110. Waite, "Adeptus Major," 39.
111. Ibid.
112. Williams, *Many Dimensions*, 247.

The same holds true for mind: by the concluding chapters "the stone and her mind were finding their union" (249). Desire, most of all, is the subject of transmutation. Over the course of the novel she loses interest in the prosaic sexual partnerships that had once satisfied her. After a date with her boyfriend Frank, she feels starkly that he has "no answer for the desires that thrilled her" (50). Both the stone and Lord Arglay appear as better aims (50), but she feels confused and unfulfilled on the whole. After she comes to identify more closely with the stone, however, symbolic of becoming more aware of the unity of herself with divinity and the rest of creation, she is at the point where "with her body and mind and everything else, she desired the End of Desire" (216).

Chloe's mystical narrative arc also connects to a concept Waite expressed exoterically in *The Way of Divine Union*, where the adept is described as concomitant to "the tingeing stone in alchemy."[113] Williams may have encountered this interpretation of the Philosophers' Stone here or in *The Secret Tradition in Alchemy*,[114] but he definitely discovered it more esoterically in "The Ceremony of Consecration on the Threshold of a Sacred Mystery," where, acting as "Second Spokesman," he took part in a conversation between three adepts—a scripted encapsulation of Waite's vision of spiritual alchemy. The "Spokesman of the Rite" reminded the other initiates that "transmutation is from within in Spiritual Alchemy, unlike the work in the crucible, as dreamed of old." Williams then intoned: "The Mystic Stone is within us and transmutes all things. The authentic affirmation is therefore: Behold I make all things new." This, said a third adept, was "the work of Divine Alchemy."[115] The quotation from the enthroned Jesus of Revelation 21:5—"Behold I make all things new"—connects Christ to the Philosophers' Stone, building on a long tradition of associating the stone with both the incarnate Christ (a merging of microcosmic and macrocosmic principles), and

---

113. Waite, *Divine Union*, 195.
114. See Waite, *Secret Tradition in Alchemy*, 342–46.
115. Waite, "On the Threshold of Sacred Mystery," 26.

the regenerative narrative of his death and resurrection.[116] The F.R.C. thus perceived the Philosophers' Stone as a useful symbol of both the attained adept—the initiate who has become the "tingeing stone"— and the Christ-spirit, which the adept sought within. Williams's description of Chloe's moment of standing "her in herself" follows this same pattern of finding the stone within to become the stone. After she has helped the stone of Suleiman unify with its divided types, Lord Arglay watches as the stone melts into her hands as "finally it took its place Within her—what the Stone had been she now was."[117] The attained Chloe has become one with the stone, one with Shekinah, one with the Christ-spirit—all representations of union with the higher self derived directly from Williams's occult Rosicrucian ritual experiences.

Allusions to the Philosophers' Stone in this climactic scene of *Many Dimensions* also reflect the the bricolage of programmatic syncretism that Williams experienced in the F.R.C. Chloe's attainment is described with the very same mix of symbolism Waite uses in his autobiography to describe his own spiritual transmutation: Chloe has made the journey from "the First Matter" to "the last operation which results in Philosophical Gold," effected by visualizing movement along "the Paths of the Tree of Life," with awareness of the correspondent, reflective unity of the "one thing."[118] Williams thus joins kabbalistic, alchemical and Hermetic terminology with the mystico-magical praxis of modern spiritual alchemy, creating, in Chloe, a fictionalized Guide of Paths. His Adeptus Exaltatus motivations propel her from secret ritual into published narrative, for the mystic benefit of any reader motivated to follow his obscure signposting.

Alchemical symbolism takes on a similar combination of serious and playful function in *Shadows of Ecstasy*. It informs the moment of

---

116. See Principe, *Secrets*, 200–1; Crisciani, "Conception of Alchemy," 173. Cf. Calian, *Alkimia Operativa* and *Alkimia Speculativa*, 181; Coudert, "Alchemy IV," 46. Zuber, "Spiritual Alchemy," 138–39.
117. Williams, *Many Dimensions*, 261.
118. Waite, *Shadows*, 132.

gnosis Roger experiences beneath Considine's mesmerist gaze. In his trance state, Ingram drowns, imaginally, in the ocean, becoming aware of his oneness with it until "he was himself the sea."[119] Considering Williams's alchemical interests, it is tempting to interpret Roger's thalassic immersion in terms of the tinctering and/or combination of substances that takes place at the alchemical stages of *coagula*. Williams's language reinforces this line of interpretation: "Could a man's body always be impregnated with this salt...and infiltrated with this sea, he might always know." This description calls forth the mercury—usually associated with water and sometimes directly with the sea—and salt of Paracelsian alchemical symbolism, in which sulphur, mercury and salt were seen, in a series of widely varying interpretations, as representative of a triad of body, spirit and soul; when unified these three reproduced the unified state of the Philosophers' Stone.[120] Here Roger's material body and perception—his sulphur—can be seen as tinctured ("impregnated," "infiltrated") with the nobler essences of spirit and soul—mercury and salt—thus elevating his perception so that he has full knowledge of the "one thing." In this coagulated state "experience would always be new," a quality, says the novel, of "everlasting and universal life."[121] Following Considine's death a short time later, Roger imagines his body carried back to Africa by his devotees, encased in a submarine below the sea. This vision can also be interpreted alchemically. The submarine is described as a "vessel," within which Roger imagines Considine's body changing as life "was re-animating the willing flesh." As in Roger's previous vision, "the waters flowed into it and became the man who moved in them" (223). The two passages are clearly related —both men are reinvigorated by salt and sea, and both are treated as base substances tinctured in an alchemical vessel.

Roger is not the first of Considine's adepts to pursue alchemical regeneration. The essence of the F.R.C.'s focus on mystical death and

---

119. Williams, *Shadows of Ecstasy*, 205.
120. Buntz, "Alchemy III," 37; Coudert, "Alchemy IV," 43.
121. Williams, *Shadows of Ecstasy*, 205.

rebirth lies at the root of Considine's instruction to his adepts to embrace rather than fear death, transmuting it within the self in order to gain life. Herr Nielsen's attempt to conquer death through suicide channels Williams's initiatory experience of mystical death in the Adeptus Minor ritual. Having followed Considine for fifty years, Nielsen has perfected the technique of elongating life through the transmutation of passion, but he desires to go further and conquer death entirely by passing through it to immortality. As Phillip, Roger and Sir Bernard watch, the suicide of Nielsen—"the neophyte of death" (178)—is enacted before the sapphire-blue curtain of Considine's apartments in a ritual environment not unlike that of Williams's Rosicrucian initiation:

> Behind the two exalted figures the deep blue of the curtains seemed to be troubled as if distance itself were shaken with the cry and the command. The splendour of colour quivered with the neighbourhood of the ecstasy of man imagining the truth of his being… All that mingled intensity swept through and filled the room, so that the imaginations of Roger and Phillip felt and moved in it…before them Considine cried again to the ardent postulant of transmuted energy: "Die then, die, exult and live." (84–85)

This was the command that the hierophants of the F.R.C. gave to Williams, and the core of the message which he was expected to communicate once he took on the role of Adeptus Exaltatus. Here, however, Williams introduces a narrative of alchemical transmutation only to subvert the self-centred motive behind Nielsen's death and affirm the ethic of his own spiritual alchemy, aimed at discovering the divine within. Nielsen's "great experiment"[122] is initially putatively successful, as his body lives on in a coma and displays tremors of a lingering vitalism. After a week, however, he dies despite Considine's efforts to assist his resurrection. Like his master, Nielsen

---

122. The term is used twice in the novel to describe Considine's attempt to transmute death into immortality. See 154, 214.

fails to adhere to Williams's ultimate criterion for successful occult practice. His attempt to transmute death reflects the Great Work of "the union of man and God," of which Williams spoke to Phyllis Jones, yet it is but a "shadow" of this ecstasy—it seeks transmutation in order to achieve immortality for the lower self, rather than discover the already eternal higher self within. However, in a novel that thrives on multiplicity of meaning and ethic, Considine's techniques retain much value for the reinvigoration and transmutation of spirit and psyche. The magician outlines two possible outcomes for his techniques: "Living for ever or dying and living again" (71). The former goal is incompatible with Williams's ethic, but the latter carries two opposing yet paradoxically reflexive meanings: one, Nielsen's attempt to conquer death, the other, spiritual rebirth. Considine links both senses to poetry and challenges Roger to deny that he has felt this call to death and rebirth in his poetry. Roger is forced to admit the connection: "'No, no; you're right. One dies and lives in it, but I can't tell how" (72).

Roger's inability to glimpse the praxis behind Considine's transmutative process is mirrored by the novel itself, which is never very specific. The list of potential alterations sent to Victor Gollancz indicates that this abstraction was purposeful, as Williams proposed to "cut out all Mrs. Considine...and leave to the imagination the whole question of how Considine does it."[123] We are thus left to infer Considine's methods from a mix of contextual information and the scraps the novel does give us. We know that ritual is important—Considine is ever hieratic, but especially so as he presides over Nielsen's experiment, or as he encourages his adepts to transform the grotesque experience of Inkamasi's forced suicide into higher forms of emotion, power and experience. Considine himself connects his method to medieval "alchemy, sorcery, fountains of youth" (73), but there is little —except for a shared interest in extending the human lifespan—to connect his techniques to such pre-modern pursuits. Two other

---

123. Charles Williams to Victor Gollancz, 18 June 1930, "Shadow of Ecstasy: Alterations," CWSA I.F.xiii/a.

sources, both occultist and both indicative of the turn inward taken by modern magic and alchemy, seem to have been more at play behind Williams's invention of Considine's strange methods. First, Williams's initial inclusion of a scene with Mrs. Considine indicates that he conceived of her husband's transmutative practice as some form of applied Romantic Theology. In this sense, we can guess that earlier drafts featured a scene that reflected the experiments with sublimated sexual desire which Williams had begun to carry out with Phyllis Jones and would continue to practice with other young women for the remainder of his life. As discussed in Chapter Six, these methods were based within the broader context of occult interest in fusing magic with sexual desire, and specifically influenced by Lee and Nicholson, who seem to have shared with Williams their exuberance for the transmutation of sexual energy into personal power and artistic vision.[124] Though this transformation reflects the alchemical process, however, it is not so specific to that tradition as a second modern current that probably influenced Williams's development of Considine's techniques: the spiritual alchemy of Mary Anne Atwood.

Considine recalls that he, like "true adepts" since the time of Caesar, had long searched for a way to transmute love and desire into "communion with ecstasy," but did not discover the technique for doing so until he attempted to complete this Great Work in an altered state of consciousness: "I beheld in a trance the making of sex, I went down to where in history and in the individual being—which are one, as all the mystics know...—to where those high laboratories lie. And there, in trance or in waking I do not know, I myself carried out the great experiment" (153–54). This trance state could refer to a variety of techniques and traditions, but given Williams's interest in Atwood it is very likely that he intended a connection to the mesmerist aspects of Considine's magical control over others: To thrust Roger into mystic reverie, he uses the hypnotic gaze sometimes used by mesmerist somnambulizers, and he controls Inkamasi with a

---

124. Lindop, *Charles Williams*, 118.

similar gaze enforced by will, often seen as a vital element of mesmerist practice.[125] The connection to mesmerism is solidified when Inkamasi initially resists but then succumbs to Considine's instructions—"almost as if moving in his sleep" (67). It is most likely then, that Considine's successful achievement of the great experiment is rooted in Atwood's proposition that alchemists throughout history had manipulated the etheric *prima materia* to put themselves in a trance state in which they could create an incorporeal Philosophers' Stone within themselves.

Once the alchemist had reached this point, Atwood theorized that they would attain power over the "Universal Subject"—the etheric divine substance that permeated all matter. In manipulating the ether to form the Philosophers' Stone within, the alchemist would, "find the Divine Nature not only, but [also] effect it."[126] *The Suggestive Inquiry* is a confused mass of quotations, alchemical allusions and contemporary scientific terminology, but this and other passages in the text suggest that Atwood saw the divine as a substance—not a strictly physical force but not a transcendent spiritual entity either. Her spiritual alchemy thus ties in to a nineteenth-century scientific context in which many different theorists—from occultists to established physicists—sought to explain phenomena once considered spiritual with reference to invisible fluids and forces like the ether and the animal magnetic fluid.[127] Williams's notes on Wilmshurst's article on the "Later Mysticism" of Atwood are relatively sparse but the body of his interest seems to be taken up with Wilmhurst's summary of Atwood's conception of the physical qualities of faith, which was, Williams summarized, "introduced into our planet" after the Advent, creating "a concrete metaphysical substantia, [the] appropriation of which by the wind and the will effects as it were a chemical change, making for regeneration."[128] Williams was clearly

---

125. See Robert Darnton, *Mesmerism and the End of Enlightenment in France* (Cambridge, MA: Harvard University Press, 1968), 163–64.
126. Atwood, *Suggestive Inquiry*, 516.
127. Asprem, "Parapsychology," 137–53.
128. Commonplace Book, 172.

attracted to this idea. Years later, in *Witchcraft*, he identified both divine love and the supernatural will as "part of and reposed on a *substance* which was invisible and which operated by laws greater than, if not in opposition to, those which were apparent in the visible world."[129] As the last part of this statement shows, the "true Romantic" Williams was not ready to extend the reach of natural law to the higher realms, as many contemporary Theosophists, Spiritualists and magicians sought to do.[130] However, his monism prompted him to conclude, like Atwood, that the two must interact. The alchemical vision in his novels displays aspects of Atwood's blend of spiritual and material: In addition to the combination of mesmerism and alchemy in Considine's method, the previous four novels each present divinity manifest in the world as substance. Only the stone of Suleiman is a direct symbol of the correspondent, monist cosmology of alchemy, but the Graal, trumps and angelical principles are also instances of the divine revealing itself as manifest in the world, recalling the metaphysical laws established, in Williams's eyes, by the incarnation.

This reflexivity of natural and supernatural, very likely informed by the attention paid to Hermetic unity by both spiritual alchemy and its physical precursors, underpinned Williams's concept of coinherence. Ashenden has argued that Charles's interest in "a simplistic notion of transmutation" peaked at the time he was writing *Shadows of Ecstasy* and was eventually replaced by the "more developed concept of change and exchange" represented by coinherence.[131] As we have seen, coinherence certainly became dominant in Williams's work from the mid-1930s forward. However, just as coinherence continued to deploy important magical elements, its radical physics

---

129. Williams, *Witchcraft*, 14.
130. See Oppenheim, *The Other World*, 191; Shane McCorristine, "General Introduction," in *Spiritualism, Mesmerism and the Occult, 1800-1920—Apparitions, Spectral Illusions and Hallucinations*, ed. Shane McCorristine (London: Pickering and Chatto, 2012), 10; Nicola Bown, Carolyn Burdett, and Pamela Thurschwell, introduction to *The Victorian Supernatural* (Cambridge: Cambridge University Press, 2004), 1-13.
131. Ashenden, *Charles Williams*, 79, 114. Cf. 95-96.

and metaphysics remained rooted in an alchemical worldview. Its assumption that body can be connected to body via a mental and/or spiritual link, forged in concert with supernatural will, is built out of two of alchemy's most central principles: the Hermetic unity of *Est una sola Res*, and transmutation. Sybil heals Aaron's ankle via the correspondent alignment of her will and the supernatural will—a spiritual link—and between Aaron's body and her body—a physical one. Coinherence is thus established on the basis of correspondence, made possible by the unity of nature, God and humanity, represented in *Many Dimensions* by the *prima materia* and the Philosophers' Stone.

In addition to maintaining a fundamental reliance on the "one thing" of the alchemical tradition, Williams did not turn from transmutation in his theorization of coinherence; rather, he expanded its scope so that any number of alchemists could participate. Substitution was transmutation performed within the self so that it might also be effected within another. Peter Stanhope takes on Pauline Anstruther's fear in order to effect just such a transaction: "The body of his flesh received her alien terror, his mind carried the burden of her world."[132] As a powerful, balanced adept, Stanhope is able to rid himself of these base emotions—expose himself to psychological and spiritual putrefaction—where Pauline cannot, thus allowing her to pass through the darkness of the *nigredo* stage and become a more ennobled self. This transformation complete, it is Pauline's turn, to use Atwood's terms, to "effect" the "Divine Nature." Now herself a coinherent adept, she uses Stanhope's methods to assist in the spiritual transformation of a long-dead ancestor. This substitution takes place backwards through time, indicating the radical cosmology that Williams's monism had led him to. Even outside the flexible boundaries of fantastic fiction, Williams concluded that physical dimensions like time could not be obstacles to the coinherent transmutation of past sufferings: "The past and future are subject to interchange, as the present with both, the dead with the living, the

---

132. Williams, *Descent into Hell*, 23.

living with the dead."[133] Even the difference between subject and object is reduced by this correspondent outlook—"'oneself' and 'others' are only the specialized terms of its technique,"[134] rather than realities of spatial or temporal differentiation. This, for Williams, was the logical outcome of the Hermetic cosmology cherished by the alchemical tradition.

A LITERARY ALCHEMIST

In the history of alchemy there have been many who have turned from their experiments—whether performed among beakers and vials or in the laboratory of the self—to communicate their results to others. From its roots in the pages of the dream-like allegories of Zosimos of Panopolis,[135] alchemy has been, as Nummedal identifies, "simultaneously bookish, experiential, and experimental."[136] It thus "stubbornly resists any attempt to separate out the histories of reading, writing, making, and doing"[137]—rare was the alchemist who practiced the Great Work without a good degree of textual interaction, either reading or writing alchemical treatises, recipes, or notebooks, many of which were also illustrated. Both image and word were deployed allegorically, using decknamen and other allusive terminology and imagery in order to communicate alchemical secrets only among those already familiar with the tradition.[138] Perhaps because of this symbolic heritage, the esoteric knowledge of alchemy has long been interwoven with poetry and, later on, with fiction. From the approbatory approaches of Shakespeare and Spenser, to more critical references in Dante's *Inferno* and Ben Jonson's *The Alchemist*,[139] alchemy had been of interest to literary figures who had

---

133. Williams, *He Came Down*, 130.
134. Williams, *Descent of the Dove*, 236.
135. On the "Dream" or "Vision" of Zosimos, see Haage, "Alchemy II," 25.
136. Nummedal, "Words and Works," 331.
137. Ibid. Cf. 335–36.
138. Ibid, 333; Buntz, "Alchemy III," 38.
139. For examples of alchemy in literature see Principe, *Secrets of Alchemy*, 182, 186–87;

little else to do with transmutation long before J.K. Rowling re-introduced the Philosophers' Stone to *Harry Potter* fandom. For some, however, the written word could be incorporated with other elements of alchemical practice, as was the case in the modern period with occultists who practiced spiritual alchemy and incorporated its symbolism into their fiction, such as W.B. Yeats and Arthur Machen.[140] Charles Williams has not previously been identified as a contributor to this tradition. Yet, he turned readily to alchemical symbolism as part of his Adeptus Exaltatus commitment to be a "tingeing stone"—to communicate the Secret Tradition through veiled language that maintained its esoteric nature. He wove alchemical strands into his fiction, creating symbolic and allegorical passages that rival most other examples in history in their poetic depth and productive obscurity. The clearest example is *Many Dimensions*, an alchemical allegory that describes the quest for spiritual regeneration with reference to the Philosophers' Stone. It is far from the first text to turn to fiction to tell this story. As alchemical allegory, *Many Dimensions* relates dialogically to a generic tradition exemplified by a sixteenth-century work of fiction written by another Rosicrucian—probably the first Rosicrucian—Johann Valentin Andreae.

Andreae is thought to have been a central figure in the Tübingen circle of reformists responsible for the Rosicrucian manifestoes, though he never admitted to his part in their authorship.[141] Part of the justification for associating him with the manifestoes is his admission, late in life, that he was the author of *The Chemical Wedding*, which Andreae wrote as a student sometime between 1603 and 1605, and published anonymously in 1616.[142] Possibly a coded

---

Eugene Webb, "The Alchemy of Man and the Alchemy of God: The Alchemist as Cultural Symbol in Modern Thought," *Religion and Literature* 17, no. 1 (Spring 1985): 48.
140. See William T. Gorski, *Yeats and Alchemy* (New York: SUNY Press, 1996); Jake Poller, "The Transmutations of Arthur Machen: Alchemy in 'The Great God Pan' and 'The Three Impostors'," *Literature and Theology* 29, no. 1 (2015). Yeats's *Rosa Alchemica* (1896) and Machen's "The White People" (1904) are examples of occult fiction replete with alchemical symbolism.
141. For a brief bibliographical sketch, see Edighoffer, "Andreae, Johann Valentin."
142. Ibid, 74; McIntosh, *The Rosy Cross Unveiled*, 19–20.

representation of physical alchemical processes, as is the case with many alchemical manuscripts, the narrative describes a journey undertaken by Christian Rosenkreutz, who accepts an angelic summons to attend a chemical wedding. Over the course of seven days Christian is filtered out from among a large group of other alchemists, until he is one of the select few able to successfully accomplish the last of a number of operations necessary to effect the resurrection of six royals—three kings and three queens—who have been beheaded by a coal-black figure—symbolic of the *nigredo* process—who proceeds to behead itself. Christian and the other alchemists are upset by this bloody result, but a virgin named Alchimia appears and tasks them with the resurrection of the royals. This is effected, after a series of experiments, by mixing the broken-down essence of the putrefacted bodies of the kings and queens with their spirits, which have been hovering above their coffins and about the castle in which the alchemical operations have been taking place. The final product of this Great Work is a single royal couple whose wedding feast Christian attends on the seventh day.[143]

On a surface level, there is not much to suggest similitude between Andreae's youthful work and *Many Dimensions*. Throughout *The Chemical Wedding*, however, there is a strong emphasis on the purification and transmutation of the alchemist himself, without which physical operations cannot be successful. This is mirrored by Chloe's transformation of mind, desire and will. Christian is one of very few alchemists in Andreae's novel who are found worthy to complete the latter stages of the Great Work, just as Chloe and Arglay emerge as the only characters in a cast of greedy dozens with sufficient mettle to understand the stone and reunite its material aspects with their supernal source. We have seen that Chloe becomes a human embodiment of the Philosophers' Stone in achieving the mystic marriage of her lower and higher selves. *The Chemical Wedding*

---

143. See Johann Valentin Andreae, *The Chemical Wedding of Christian Rosenkreutz*, trans. Joscelyn Godwin (Grand Rapids, MI: Phanes Press, 1991). Cf. Faivre, *Access to Western Esotericism*, 163–75; Everett F. Bleiler, "Johann Valentin Andreae, Fantasist and Utopist," *Science Fiction Studies* 35, no. 1 (Mar 2009): 1–30.

is open to an interpretation of a similar spiritual alchemical sense, in which the nuptials to which Christian Rosenkreutz has been invited are his own. Just as with *Many Dimensions*, possible interpretations of Andreae's narrative are manifold, but I am in agreement with Antoine Faivre's conclusion that the story is ultimately a mystical allegory, rooted in the symbolism of alchemical transmutation: "This *Chemical Wedding* is above all an alchemical and mystical wedding; under the enlightening cloak of the symbol, it describes the process of the ascent of the soul toward God."[144] Chloe and Arglay illustrate this chemical wedding with the gender-based symbolism Andreae and countless other alchemists used to illustrate the union of opposing principles at the stage of *coagula*. Before Chloe can realize her own mystic marriage, and before Arglay has a similar experience in coming to awareness of the unity of all existence, they must understand *coagula* on a symbolic level in the image of each other. Chloe, in particular, sees the end of her desire in Arglay, abandoning Frank to seek the likeness of the divine in her unrequited love for her boss. Williams thus merges the chemical wedding of alchemical allegory with kabbalistic symbolism in order to illustrate Romantic Theology through fiction. Elsewhere, he describes Romantic Theology as a "great experiment," with Adam and Eve as its "first matter,"[145] reinforcing the likelihood that he considered the alchemical tradition of the chemical wedding along with the Philosophers' Stone in the writing of *Many Dimensions*.

It is thus quite plausible that Williams consciously wrote the novel into the tradition of alchemical allegory. He may or may not have been specifically influenced by *The Chemical Wedding*, but if he did not actually read Andreae's text, he certainly would have known of its existence and the general run of its narrative. Either way, the text stands as an important node in the network of Rosicrucian and alchemical influence that led Williams to produce his own allegory of transmutation. Had Williams never read any alchemical texts at all,

---

144. Faivre, *Access to Western Esotericism*, 166.
145. Williams, *He Came Down*, 89.

he would still have encountered a spiritualized conception of the chemical wedding in the F.R.C. ceremonies for the grades of Adeptus Minor and Major, both of which invited adepts to achieve the mystical marriage within the self by imagining themselves to be, like Roger Ingram, base metals thrust into the vessel of the alchemist for the purposes of transmutation.

One further important element of *The Chemical Wedding* differs from Williams's alchemical allegory, but broadly informs his fiction as a whole. While Chloe's transmutation results in complete transcendence of the material world, Christian gets only so far as the threshold. He is knighted by the newly coagulated King and Queen for his alchemical efforts, but in the end he is banished back outside the outer gates of the castle, forced to begin his journey all over again as a result of accidentally opening the sepulchre of Venus and glimpsing her naked. Like Andreae's tale as a whole, this mysterious demotion can be read in a number of ways, but if *The Chemical Wedding* is read as spiritual allegory, Christian's punishment seems to indicate that he must undergo the process of inner transmutation once more before he can be fully purified. It may also, as Edighoffer notes, represent the descent that the adept must make from the heights of mystical attainment to become a guide for others who would follow.[146] Though Williams designates a different fate for Chloe, Rosenkreutz's return from the castle ramparts represents his own turn away from experience toward expression as Adeptus Exaltatus. Thus, his abstruse communication of the tenets of spiritual alchemy in *Many Dimensions* resonates with Faivre's observation that Andreae's text, in addition to profiling the transformation of Christian Rosenkreutz, "invites us to descend within ourselves, while being transformed."[147] Transformation as a result of reader experience was a goal of all Williams's fiction—his call to rebirth and/or coinherent interchange of the body, soul and mind ties him to the rich tradition of image and allegory that has made alchemy so attractive to writers,

---

146. Edighoffer, "Andreae, Johann Valentin," 74.
147. Faivre, *Access to Western Esotericism*, 169.

artists and spiritual seekers, in addition to those exploring the secrets of nature. Like most other authors of alchemical fiction, Williams never spent a moment distilling material substances in the laboratory, but he saw enormous value in the rich symbolic heritage of alchemy and even more in its founding narrative of putrefaction and reconstitution.

In addition to mirroring the goal of narratives like *The Chemical Wedding*, Williams's fiction stays true to the core stylistic principles of textual alchemy. Its symbolism is multivalent, its referents sometimes confused and obscurantist, its allegory unclear without direct access to particular esoteric knowledge, specifically that derived from the F.R.C. rituals, the Lee circle and other modern occult interactions. Most of the esoteric symbolism deployed in the novels is, unlike the stone of Suleiman, not alchemical in itself. However, images and terms from any particular heritage can still prove valuable to a literary alchemist in search of decknamen. The animal symbolism of *The Place of the Lion*, for example, does not seem to relate to any one specific tradition and continues to perplex his critics.[148] Only one of the animalian forms taken by the angelical principles—the phoenix, popular in alchemical writings as a symbol of death and rebirth, "momently consumed, momently reborn"[149]—seems to specifically channel the imagery of the Great Work. However, the other animals —eagle, serpent, lion, unicorn, pterodactyl, butterfly, horse and lamb —function as decknamen. They are, like their alchemical precursors, purposefully multivalent and obscure. Behind them lies a cosmology that the reader is intended to grasp on an intellectual level at once more tenuous and more substantial than is possible via clearer signifiers. This is not, of course, a semiotic strategy unique to alchemy. It is probably not coincidental that another likely source of inspiration for the novel, *The Celestial Hierarchy* (c. fifth century CE) of Pseudo-Dionysius, opines that the principles of the "invisible and infinite and incomprehensible" divine are better expressed using symbols that are

---

148. See, e.g., Medcalf, "Athanasian Principle," 29–30.
149. Williams, *Place of the Lion*, 185.

most dissimilar to it, such as the winged ox, eagle, lion and man of Ezekiel,[150] the last three of which are prominent symbols in *The Place of the Lion*. The use of symbol, image and illusive terminology to both protect secret wisdom from those not worthy to consume it and, in Dionysius's words, to "elevate our mind"[151] toward awareness of the ineffable divine, is a feature in many esoteric texts besides those specifically produced in the alchemical tradition. However, when Williams's use of tropes such as the Philosophers' Stone, the phoenix, and the Great Work is taken into account, along with his contribution to the genre of alchemical allegory in *Many Dimensions*, it is no stretch to view him as a literary alchemist working to perpetuate the spiritual alchemy of the F.R.C.

Williams therefore encountered modern spiritual alchemy as both the subject of transmutation and as an alchemist himself, following Waite's statement that once the adept becomes the "tingeing stone in alchemy" they have stepped into the role of "communicating life to others."[152] As a literary alchemist, he deployed the symbolism of kabbalah, various magical traditions, the tarot and alchemy itself in order to express a consistent doctrine of attainment through personal transformation. Having been transmuted into a human "tingeing stone," Williams communicated esoteric theory and practice through his fiction, usually in the adapted forms he encountered in the modern occult network, in order to meld the natural and supernatural, to share his unified theory of spirit and matter, to point the way to the discovery of the higher self within. As a literary alchemist, Williams stood like Christian Rosenkreutz before the gates that bar the path to the chemical wedding, pointing the way onward via semiotics occulted to the uninitiated, but capable, he believed, of evoking flashes of insight that could provoke the transmutative moments he himself had experienced. As his priorities shifted from attainment to coinherence, he continued to use fiction as the forum

---

150. Dionysius the Aeropagite, *The Celestial and Ecclesiastical Hiearchy*, trans. Rev. John Parker (London: Skeffington, 1984), 16–18.
151. Ibid, 19.
152. Waite, *Divine Union*, 195.

in which he most clearly communicated the tenets of this esoteric practice; several such passages show the continued importance of alchemical transmutation to coinherent substitution. Perhaps it is this philosophical debt to alchemy that drew Chris Murray, the screenwriter of "Magnum Opus," to link alchemy and coinherence together, despite the probability that, as the script suggests, he was not aware of Williams's spiritual alchemical activities. Regardless, the conflation is certainly a happy stumble towards historical accuracy: despite the denials of DI Hathaway and the Oxford don, there were many connections between Charles Williams and alchemy.

EPILOGUE:
THE COAGULATION OF BELIEF

Williams's fiction seeks to provoke spiritual transformation in its readers by transmuting word and symbol into awareness of the cosmic unity that made both coinherence and mystical attainment possible. Consciously aware of himself as "tingeing stone," Williams engaged in a literary alchemy of *solve et coagula*, disembedding semiotics from the original context of traditions from kabbalah to Christianity to Arthurian legend, then combining them in a coagulated brew of symbolism that could point the way to the all-encompassing experience of "the reunion of man and God," an event made possible, for Williams as for many other occult mystics, by the "one thing" of Hermetic cosmology. This process of disembedding and coagulating was emblematic of modern occult programmatic syncretism, a streamlined agglomeration of symbolism intended to better communicate the universal message of the ancient wisdom tradition. In this book I have illustrated Williams's interaction with several symbolic systems that were central to this syncretic project, both in his occult life and in his fiction. There are other movements and traditions that have been associated with modern occultism to which Williams might also be productively connected. We have seen that Owen Barfield greeted

EPILOGUE: THE COAGULATION OF BELIEF

him as a virtual Anthroposophist, and that he was interested in the potential for astrological symbolism to prompt awareness of the connections between micro- and macrocosm. In *Witchcraft* he lends credence to the possibilities of "clairvoyance, clairaudience, foresight, and telepathy,"[1] about which occultists tended to be much more enthusiastic than most.

These phenomena were also of much interest to psychical researchers and devotees of Spiritualism, another movement which may have attracted Williams's interest. Spiritualism is commonly held to have begun with the Fox sisters of Hydesville, New York, who claimed to have used a system of knocks to communicate with the spirit of a peddler. By late 1849, the sisters's claims had produced an American furore regarding the possibility of talking with the spirits of the departed.[2] Hundreds of other mediums soon appeared around the country, relating messages from the dead to audiences in private séances or public galleries. The spirits contacted at such séances ranged from loved ones to past sages in human history—an influential and much respected British medium, the Reverend Stainton Moses, was in contact with no less than eighty such eminent personages, among them Elijah, John the Baptist, Plato, Aristotle, Benjamin Franklin and Beethoven.[3] As Spiritualism grew into a global phenomenon, it expanded its range of observable phenomena. By Williams's time it had become an extremely diverse movement, often interconnected with the modern occult network, which featured many individuals who shared Spiritualism's interest in mediumship and its belief in alternate realms of existence accessible from the material world.[4]

---

1. Williams, *Witchcraft*, 80.
2. On the Fox sisters and their "Rochester rappings," see Howard Kerr, *Mediums, and Spirit-Rappers, and Roaring Radicals* (London: University of Illinois Press, 1972), 4–8; R. Laurence Moore, *In Search of White Crows: Spiritualism, Parapsychology, and American Culture* (New York: Oxford University Press, 1977), 7–8.
3. Oppenheim, *The Other World*, 78.
4. Scholars have tended to see Spiritualism and occultism as largely separate movements (see, e.g., Oppenheim, *The Other World*, 159; Godwin, *Theosophical Enlightenment*, 292), but the two movements shared roots in mesmerism, magical theory and practice

The otherworlds of *All Hallows' Eve* and *Descent into Hell*, spirit planes that lie just beside, around and beneath the boundaries of the perceptible world, seem to emerge from this context and may reflect a personal interest on Williams's part. His suggestion that coinherent interchange acts across time and space does not mark him as a Spiritualist per se, but it does suggest a perception of the spiritual and natural worlds as subject to a set of shared laws that would allow interchange similar to spirit communication. A letter to Gollancz in 1932 supports this interpretation. Already thinking about his "ghost-theme," Williams told Gollancz that he wished to try it because "the Merciful One *is*."[5] The statement is vague, but it suggests that he was willing to give credence to the concept of an accessible spirit world near at hand, based, like most of his esoteric beliefs, on the Hermetic assumption that because all things are "the Merciful One," then all aspects of existence must interact with each other. Thus, while Pauline Anstruther does not directly contact her long-dead ancestor, she is aware of the crisis state of his spirit and is able to save him through coinherent action. Lester's manifestation in the material world in *All Hallows' Eve* refers directly to physical manifestations of spirits witnessed at séances, while Betty's ability to actually travel into the spirit realm reflects the wildest hopes of Spiritualism, blended with the astral travel explored by Theosophists and occultists. These fictional echoes of an interest in Spiritualism are supported by a passage in the Commonplace Book, where Williams theorizes that Spiritualist mediumship might be made possible by "temporary possession by the god,"[6] suggesting that he believed mediums to be

---

and Swedenborgianism, tended to attract people with corresponding aims and interests, and displayed similar beliefs and practices (See Moore, *In Search of White Crows*, 6; Wilson, *Modernism and Magic*, 8–9; McCorristine, "General Introduction," xxii). By Williams's time, distinctions between the two movements had become quite blurred, particularly as Spiritualists had become more interested in synthesising occult concepts (John Patrick Deveney, "Spiritualism," in *Dictionary of Gnosis and Western Esotericism*, ed. Wouter J. Hanegraaff (Leiden: Brill, 2006), 1079).
5. Charles Williams to Victor Gollancz, 28 July 1932, CWSA I.F.xiii/c (emphasis Williams).
6. Commonplace Book, 101.

in contact with some aspect of divinity, though not necessarily human spirits. There is no way of knowing for certain what his true feeling on the issue was, but his monist cosmology seems to have caused him to see something consanguineous, and therefore artistically useful, in the basic assumptions of Spiritualism. His exposure to the movement may have come, in part, from his F.R.C. connections. In *Shadows of Life and Thought*, Waite relates an experience in which the spirit of a Native American was channelled by another member of the F.R.C. in his presence. The spirit told Waite that his daughter had recovered from an illness, a claim that Waite verified on returning home.[7] This seems to have helped vindicate his own lifelong interest in Spiritualism.

Tracing a Spiritualist influence from Waite to Williams is tenuous, as is establishing a personal interest in Spiritualism on Williams's part, though the evidence described above suggests that the latter possibility is quite likely. However, the countless points of comparison between Waite's rituals and esoteric books and Williams's life and fiction indicate significant influence overall. From kabbalah to the tarot to alchemy, the ink from Waite's pen seems to have seeped onto the pages of Williams's novels and poetry in an osmosis of narrative. Unfortunately, as we have seen, this influence has often been framed as a "Christianization" of esoteric materials: Waite's superficial rejection of occultism has been exploited to dissociate Williams from a movement considered to be the stygian antithesis of Christianity by cordon sanitaire interpretations. Such acts of dichotomous boundary formation show the inherent danger of working with monolithic terms like "occultism," "magic," "mysticism," and "Christianity." These categories are necessary for communication, categorization and conceptualization, but should not pass unqualified beyond the introductory stages of a work of scholarship. The stark distinctions between occultism and Christianity that have been nurtured by researchers of Waite and Williams indicate the need for continued research of esoteric movements, figures and ideas

---

7. Waite, *Shadows*, 205.

in order to provide more nuanced pictures of historical fractals like occultism. Such a maturation of research approaches would also help avoid cordon sanitaire thinking that derives from a direction opposite that usually seen in Williams criticism, wherein scholars of occultism tend to skim over the important Christian context of modern esoteric movements, including that derived from traditions like Freemasonry, Rosicrucianism, alchemy and even kabbalah, which have important roots in Christian theology and symbolism. The reasons behind the underappreciation of Christian currents in occult theory and practice are unclear. One possibility may be the influence of what Jay Johnston has called a "hierarchy of deviance," referring to the tendency of scholars of esotericism to pay more attention to particular traditions because they possess a quality of trangressional otherness—violate more taboos, or possess more alterity in the perspective of researchers themselves. Given their relatively high percentage of specifically Christian content, the esoteric thought systems of figures like Waite and Williams may attract less attention because they are, in Johnston's words, more "dowdy esotericisms."[8] Whatever the case, evaluation of modern occult phenomena often requires consideration of Christian influences and contexts. Hanegraaff argues that this milieu is even important for understanding Crowley, an exemplar of anti-Christian occultism, because the "profoundly biblical language" of some of his narratives of mystico-magical experience connect him to Christianity to the degree that "it could even be claimed...that in his very rejection of established Christianity he was a heretical Christian."[9] Williams, like many other occultists including Lévi, Kingsford and Waite, far more clearly blended various modern adaptations of esoteric thought with his mystical Christianity, indicative of a modern occult enthusiasm for ecumenical, non-doctrinal forms of the reli-

---

8. Jay Johnston, keynote lecture for the Sixth International Conference of the European Society for the Study of Western Esotericism: Western Esotericism and Deviance, University of Erfurt, 1–3 June 2017.
9. Wouter J. Hanegraaff, foreword to *Aleister Crowley and Western Esotericism*, ed. Henrik Bogdan and Martin Starr (Oxford: Oxford University Press, 2012), ix.

EPILOGUE: THE COAGULATION OF BELIEF

gion that balanced the rejection of figures like Blavatsky and Crowley.

I hope that this book has shown the value of literary analysis for sussing out the complex entanglements of influence and allusion usually found in the heterodox religious systems of alternative religious thinkers like Waite and Williams. As a relatively prolific author of poetry and fiction who clearly sought to enhance rather than dilute his personal perspective in his authorial role, Williams is a striking example of the research efficacy that can be achieved by combining historical research methods with complementary literary analysis. This combined method is particularly helpful in addressing the difficult question of the balance Williams struck between occult and Christian elements of his belief structure. His novels portray occultists informed by several contrasting valuations of esoteric knowledge: the goetic sorcerer Leclerc is a foil to coinherent adepts like Stanhope, while the murderous Satanist Persimmons, damnable yet redeemed by the intensity of his mystic quest, lies somewhere in between. Nowhere is the magician of modern occultism better represented, however, than in Nigel Considine, who seems to encapsulate a variety of stances toward modern occult theory and practice, both positive and negative. His characterization, particularly when framed by the reactions of both enemies and followers to him and his message, provides a helpful window to Williams's own complex range of approaches to modern occultism.

We have already encountered many congruities between Williams's occultism and Considine's magico-alchemical practices in the course of this book. The author's ritualistic sublimation of repressed libido reflects his character's transmutation of various passions into physical longevity and psychic power; Considine's ability to reveal the true meaning of poetry reflects Williams's valuation of imagination and poetic ecstasy; Williams's view of mystical attainment as awareness of the correspondent unity of human, God and nature relates to Considine's quest for "the ending in his own person of all the accidents of place and time."[10] At various other points I have also shown how the portrayal of Considine seems to be informed by an idealized perception of the modern occult hierophant. As Imperator Waite stood before the symbol-embossed drapes of the Salvator Mundi temple, so Considine towers hieratically before the curtains of his drawing room. In the same way that hundreds of modern occultists gathered into secret societies, drawn by the magnetic personalities of figures like Crowley, Fortune and Mathers, so the "Devotees" of Considine's global occult circle kneel before him (110). Considine seeks to transmute base emotions such as love, hate, and sorrow into a higher state of strength and will, and "that passionate strength and will into the exploration of all the capacities of man" (180), just as modern occultists sought to enhance the hidden potential of will and mind through magical ritual and experimentation, many awaiting a new age or phase of human mental and spiritual development, an epoch which Considine calls "The Second Evolution of Man."[11]

Considine is the protagonist of a visionary occult Romantic revolution that would have found Williams marching at its head were it ever to descend from the realm of fantasy. Yet, Williams's stance toward the occult cannot be easily extrapolated from this character. While there frequently seems to be a mimetic relationship between Considine and leading modern occultists, at other points in the novel he wears the black cloak of the gothic sorcerer antagonist, quite divorced from any sort of realist perspective—killing missionaries in Africa, overpowering the self-will of his devotees with his dark mesmeric gaze, and encouraging Inkamasi to commit suicide so that he and his followers can feed off the emotions that result from witnessing his death. These actions go quite beyond any connection to modern occultism, but two further characteristics seem to be direct critiques of common attributes of modern occultism. First, while Considine shows a deep knowledge of Christianity, he ultimately

---

10. See Williams, *Shadows of Ecstasy*, 207.
11. Ibid, 53. Cf. Hammer, *Claiming Knowledge*, 248–50.

EPILOGUE: THE COAGULATION OF BELIEF

rejects it in favour of his own Romantic vision and quest for magical power, a representation of the anti-Christian rhetoric deployed by occultists such as Crowley. His further failing, as we have seen, is the misdirected aim of his magical practice. Though he acknowledges that his methods can be used to achieve the chemical wedding with the divine self within, his own goal is the uniting of the self with its own hidden sources of power.[12]

The relationship between Considine and the perspective of his creator is thus deeply ambiguous.[13] He is both protagonist and antagonist, exemplar and murderer, Christ and Antichrist.[14] A clearer sense of the occultist elements in Williams's valuations of imagination, magical potency, and correspondent unity can be gained by observing the reactions of the other characters to the occultist messiah that has fractured the permeable seal between realist and fantastical perspective. Scott McLaren argues convincingly that Considine is a protagonist tragically defeated by characters that represent viewpoints which Williams detested. These include Caithness (dogmatic Christianity), Mottreux (self-directed occultism), and Rosamond (superficiality/materialism). It is clear, as McLaren notes, that Considine's ethic is closer to Williams's own than these characters.[15] However, the reaction of the novel's three other main characters, all more clearly protagonistic than Considine, is more complex.

---

12. See Williams, *Shadows of Ecstasy*, 180.
13. As also illustrated by Ashenden, *Charles Williams*, 87; McLaren, "A Problem of Morality," 109–10, 121–24.
14. For comparisons of Considine with Christ see Williams, *Shadows of Ecstasy*, 75, 129, 155, 193–94, 219. For Antichrist see 92, 190, 208.
15. McLaren, "A Problem of Morality," 121–24. Strangely, McLaren concludes his discussion by arguing that in light of Williams and Considine's shared emphasis on correspondent unity "it is difficult to argue credibly that Considine's ultimate aim is anything but wholly good and wholly Christian" (123). This is a reverse application of the cordon sanitaire thinking that has prevented effective analysis of Williams's place within the modern occult network. McLaren assumes that Considine's emphasis on the unity of matter and spirit is Christian because it is congruous to Williams's own viewpoint. Considine's monism, however, emerges from Williams's Hermetic beliefs and is here specifically meant to contrast the Manichean perspective of the dogmatic Caithness, pointing to a more heterodox Christian interpretation Williams saw as contiguous with the concept of incarnation.

Sir Bernard's embodiment of reason ultimately seems to lose out to Considine's valorization of passion and ecstasy, but this victory is achieved primarily in comparison to Roger rather then to Considine himself. The perspectives of Philip, representative of Romantic love, and Roger engage in a more meaningful way with Considine's soteriology of transmutation. Philip's mystical experience is engendered, as we saw in Chapter Three, by Considine's techniques, and he has "a curiously empty feeling somewhere when he thought of denying them,"[16] but ultimately his Romantic Theological vision rises to a point higher than that which Considine offers him—a glimpse of the divine as Shekinah via imaginative focalization on the body of his beloved.

In the end, it is only Roger Ingram who considers Considine in all his complexity. Grevel Lindop, noting that Considine "represents many things which were truly important to Williams," proposes that the magus might represent "a question that must have preoccupied Williams at this time—the question of whether some form of inner work (meditation, alchemy, or ritual) could render life more profound and intense as well as more long-lasting, and if so whether such work was ethically right. Williams...was asking how far he could, and should, go on the path of adeptship. And he was leaving the question unanswered."[17] It is Roger to whom this question is ultimately posed, Roger who most closely represents Williams's occultist motivations and best models the gains he took from modern esoteric involvement. Far more than any other character in *Shadows of Ecstasy*, Roger, like Peter Stanhope, closely reflects Williams's own perspective.[18] In addition to sharing his creator's line of work as a poet and literary critic, this "Professor of Applied Literature" also lives in Hampstead,[19] where Williams lived for most of his decades in London. Faced with a figure who offers the path to self-empowerment, reenchantment, magic and mystery laid before potential adepts

---

16. Williams, *Shadows of Ecstasy*, 115.
17. Lindop, *Charles Williams*, 118–19.
18. As argued by Willard, "Acts of the Companions," 290; Carpenter, *The Inklings*, 93.
19. Williams, *Shadows of Ecstasy*, 7.

EPILOGUE: THE COAGULATION OF BELIEF

by occultists from Mathers to Waite, Ingram also represents Williams's deep yearning to follow this path, a desire that is not resolved with Considine's apparent death. Roger maintains a skepticism toward Considine through much of the novel. When he hears the magus speak on behalf of the Allied Supremacies of Africa, he connects his Romantic message with three cataclysmic figures: Milton's Christ—the "Filial Godhead" on the verge of accepting the task of ending the eternal battle between good and evil by incarnating into the world; the ambiguous figure of Milton's Satan—the "superior fiend...moving towards the shore" as the African forces move toward the cliffs of England;[20] and Yeats's "rough beast" that "slouches toward Bethlehem to be born" in "The Second Coming" (1919),[21] an image that, like Considine, channels the apocalypticism of both Christ and Antichrist, heralding the arrival of a cataclysm poorly understood but long expected. This group of associations indicates that Roger is keenly aware that Considine represents a turn in the course of history, but does not quite know where to place him —ethically, politically or metaphysically.

As we have seen, however, Roger comes to see that there is a way to a higher ecstasy in Considine's practices, one he had already felt in poetry, but could not discover without Nigel's assistance. Ingram commits after the magus evokes his first mystical experience, now saying, "I believe he knows what poetry is, and I've never met a man before who did" (86). It is Considine's gaze that casts Roger into reverie in his second mystical experience at the seaside, but it is a line of poetry—"thus the Filial Godhead answering spake"—that elevates his consciousness into vision. Through such experiences, Roger gains both mystic awareness and the reanimation of art-magic. In brief

---

20. Ibid, 44. Cf. *Paradise Lost* 1.283–84. In the context of *Shadows of Ecstasy*, the reference to Milton's Satan is most likely one filtered through Romantic interpretations of Milton's anti-hero as a redemptive, liberating force—a foil to the dogmas of institutional Christianity mirrored by Considine himself. See Asbjørn Dyrendal, James R. Lewis, and Jesper Aa. Petersen, *The Invention of Satanism* (New York: Oxford University Press, 2016), 30–31.
21. Williams, *Shadows of Ecstasy*, 45.

moments during his mystical drowning he is vitally aware of the intensity of the experience, a knowledge that grants him the controlled attainment sought by the magician: "He knew, and then what power was his!...He rejoiced in an ecstasy that controlled itself in great tidal breaths." Ultimately, however, the "great passions" which he had sought in poetry and now been instructed to transmute, "swept through him unrecognized until far off he saw the glory of their departure" (205). At this point Roger moves toward something beyond poetry, beyond art, beyond magic, just as Williams sought to move beyond symbol in the F.R.C. to the ultimate phase of mystical experience.

Considine's offered way to attainment and magical reanimation is directly contrasted in the novel by the disenchanted sterility of modern technological materialism and institutionalized religion, two currents against which Williams frequently directed his Romantic and esoteric theological concepts. Fleeing the house in which Considine has been shot in the head, Roger sees a car waiting with its lights on and Caithness inside. Williams transmutes this prosaic vision into a presentation of Considine's magic as an antidote to disenchantment: "This was the kind of thing that remained; the imagination of man was blown out in a moment but the light of his mechanical invention remained" (214). Discovering that Caithness has played a role in Considine's death, Roger deepens the contrast between the Romantic vision of the magus and the sterile orthodoxy represented by the vicar: "That this dreamer, this master of vision should have been destroyed by—by a traitor and a clergyman" (214).

I do not wish to take the comparison between Williams and Roger too far, but his reaction to Considine does offer us a window, albeit a murky one, into Williams's emotional and intellectual reaction to what modern occultism had to offer. He followed Waite in rejecting the self-centred approach to occultism taken by esoteric practitioners like Considine, and did not share the magus's apparent dislike of Christianity, but in Roger's attraction to Considine's imaginative credo we see a reflection of the richness Williams found in modern adaptations of kabbalistic and alchemical symbolism, as well as hints

EPILOGUE: THE COAGULATION OF BELIEF

of the ecstasy that he sought in poetry and in the ceremonial magic of the F.R.C. As we have seen, the novel directly connects Roger's experiences of mystic unity with self, world and divine to the end of desire sought within Waite's order. The achievement of this goal rested on symbolism and concepts from a number of different traditions, but Williams's fiction illustrates that modern occult materials were central to the construction of his unique, heterodox belief system, expressed through a focus on attainment in the first five novels and gathered under the umbrella of coinherence in the last two.

Whether communicating the path of Waite's Secret Tradition or his own theory of mystical interchange, Williams as fiction writer functioned as both author and prophet of his credos of union, transformation and substitution. Nurtured within the F.R.C. to take on the role of Adeptus Exaltatus, Williams seems to have remained focused on his role as tingeing stone even when, as in *Descent into Hell* and *All Hallows' Eve*, his message did not as directly reflect the F.R.C.'s initiatory process of interior transmutation and elevation of consciousness. In writing fiction he worked as a literary alchemist, exploiting the essential narrativity of esoteric knowledge as he tossed its symbols, images and concepts in the mercury of his imagination, mixing, matching, alluding, always seeking the highest degree of multivalence possible as he soaked signifiers like the Graal, the stone of Suleiman, the occultist Considine, the bestial angelical principles and the tarot trumps in symbolic elixirs coagulated from as many coinciding traditions as possible, disembedding the images, terminology and concepts of a variety of movements and philosophies to express the mystical truth he perceived to lie beneath the surface of all knowledge.

This alchemical infusion of multivalence resulted in a quality of *inventio* that Williams achieved via a cycle of influence and innovation. The imagery and thematic narratives of the novels are drawn from connections to the occult network—particularly his friendships with Waite, Lee and Nicholson—and personal experiences with modern esoteric practice, including tarot meditation, his sadomasochistic experiments, his interest in ceremonial magical devices like the Banishing Ritual, and, most centrally, his F.R.C. initiation. Drawn from life, however, his fictional manipulations of occult materials produced texts that are in themselves newly creative forms of esoteric knowledge. Williams's authorial process was a living act of formation of knowledge and belief. In the many instances in which modern esoteric phenomena informed this act, Williams produced occult fiction as a reflection of occult life. This process was reciprocal and reflexive. In inseparable relationship, narrative expresses life in Williams's fiction at the same time that life produces narrative. Fiction is produced and adjusted from memory, but it also transmutes memory. As recollections of particular F.R.C. rituals and experiences of elevated consciousness were incorporated into his novels, his fictionalized account became a part of the experience itself.

For readers of his fiction, much interpretive depth is lost without awareness of this relationship between experience and narrative. No doubt Williams hoped that his books would thrive on their own merits, both as entertaining works of fantasy and as syncretic assemblages of myth, image and principle that, in a few cases at least, might prompt the reader toward either the Burkean sublime or the "Divine Essence" which Yeats found in symbol. However, Williams's writing of life into fiction, in combination with his preference for multivalence and his appeal to esoteric knowledge, is probably at least partially responsible for the fact that his novels have never achieved broad appeal, despite the best efforts of critical studies which have attempted to bridge the interpretive gap between author and reader. The preceding chapters have followed in the footsteps of a great deal of such contextual criticism, most of it generated out of interest in his associations with the Inklings and his contributions to Christian theology. I have focused specifically on the emergence of Williams's fiction from his personal occult experiences, poking a flashlight into the more esoteric corners of the vast imagistic mansions constructed in his novels, with the ambition of providing a broadened scope of reference for any further studies that also seek to make his opaque narrative more transparent. Williams seems, as argued in Chapter Three, to have deliberately pursued opacity in order to magnify the

EPILOGUE: THE COAGULATION OF BELIEF

potential for multiple interpretations, or even to create opportunity for readers to crawl blindly into sublime ineffability. Contextual criticism such as that I have pursued in this book risks diluting this purposeful ambiguity, but I hope that by washing the mud from some of Williams's occult windows I have also contributed to emphasizing multiplicity, revealing the many dimensions of Williams's heterodoxy to future readers and critics.

It is time for Williams to be considered both as the "Third Inkling"—a valuable contributor to heterodox Christian theology—and as an important node in the network of occultist individuals, groups and texts that have played a vital role in offering alternative religious, scientific, political and social ways of thinking in modern Western culture. Williams does not seem to have considered himself as an actor in the wider occult network; his dedication was to smaller groups. His subtle references to F.R.C. rituals in his fiction—the connection between the arms of Rosamond and the High Priestess, the frequent references to the end of desire, Chloe as an echo of the Guide of Paths—indicate attempts to identify with Waite's order, and, perhaps, specifically express membership in the Holy Assembly. Yet, these affiliations link Williams to the wider occult network through the central node of A.E. Waite. Despite efforts on the part of both scholars and Waite himself to distance him from the occultist milieu of the late nineteenth and early twentieth centuries, Waite was positioned at the social and intellectual centre of the web of modern esoteric interrelations. The consanguinity of his central beliefs with those of other occultists, his sustained interaction with modern secret societies, and his emphasis on kabbalistic, Rosicrucian, alchemical, Freemasonic and tarotic knowledge, strongly indicate a close link between his Secret Tradition and the modern esoteric context from which it emerged, a relationship particularly evident in the genetic links that connect the rituals and grade structure of the F.R.C. to the Golden Dawn. In some areas, such as the theory and practice of magic, Williams developed his occult ideas independent of Waite, but the latter's influence, both textual and experiential, clearly defined his occult outlook. Williams's relationship with Waite thus supplemented his close friendships with Lee and Nicholson, connecting him to a number of other influential occultists whom Waite met, respected and was influenced by, even if he would later disavow them.

Williams is thus a node in a network of occult influence that projected from leading occult figures, including Blavatsky, Westcott, Mathers, Yeats and de Steiger, through Waite and onto the pages of his fiction. Even more significantly for the contemporary reader, his novels themselves are actors in this network, each "involved in the drama of its own making,"[22] synthesizing symbolism from a wide variety of networks and becoming, by doing so, an infinitely referential member of each, a mediator within which the translation of other network elements is enabled in the space between author and reader. In the case of the esoteric symbolism that permeates the novels, Williams's fiction granted even greater fluidity to the already adaptive symbolism of alchemy, kabbalah, magic and the tarot. Driven by interpretations generated from personal experience with this symbolism, the nodal novels of Charles Williams thus enable further translation of esoteric phenomena by readers like Mary Butts, John Starr Cooke, Paul Nagy and Gareth Knight, who have drawn on Williams's thought to create further textual actors in the occult network. Some esoteric groups have also found import in Williams's work, such as the Ancient Mystical Order Rosae Crucis, a globally significant Rosicrucian organization, which lists Williams's entire bibliography as "recommended reading" for devotees.[23] Such influence has, overall, been slight in comparison to contemporaries such as Fortune and Yeats, but regardless of their degree of impact Williams's novels show that there is much to gain by considering modern occultism as a sort of lived fiction—much to be learned about the secret ritual activity and obscure tenets of occult groups by peering through the sugges-

---

22. Howard S. Becker, Robert R. Faulkner, and Barbara Kirshenblatt-Gimblett, eds., *Art from Start to Finish: Jazz, Painting, Writing, and Other Improvisations* (Chicago: University of Chicago Press, 2006), 3, quoted in Felski, *The Limits of Critique*, 162.
23. A.M.O.R.C., "Charles Williams: The Greater Trumps," https://www.rosicrucian.org/recommended-reading-lists-charles-williams-greater-trumps.

EPILOGUE: THE COAGULATION OF BELIEF

tive veil of narrative. This is as true of Williams as it is of relationships between life and fiction found in the work of Bulwer-Lytton, Fortune, Blackwood and Crowley. Williams's novels exist in networked relationship with these figures and their texts and many more besides. Inextricably linked to his occult life, his occult fiction was borne out of his experiments with the transmutation of sexual energies, his zeal for the lush narrative and symbol of the esoteric traditions, and most of all his F.R.C. initiation. Following this descent and ascent through abyss to sublimity, he returned to the world and turned to fiction as Charles Williams, Guide of Paths.

BIBLIOGRAPHY

Andreae, Johann Valentin. *The Chemical Wedding of Christian Rosenkreutz.* Translated by Joscelyn Godwin. Grand Rapids, MI: Phanes Press, 1991.
Ashenden, Gavin. *Charles Williams: Alchemy and Integration.* Kent, OH: Kent State University Press, 2008.
Ashmole, Elias. "Prolegomena." In *Theatrum Chemicum Brittanicum.* London: Grismond, 1652.
Asprem, Egil. *Arguing with Angels: Enochian Magic and Modern Occulture.* Albany: State University of New York Press, 2012.
_____. "Contemporary Ritual Magic." In *The Occult World*, edited by Christopher H. Partridge, 382–95. Abingdon: Routledge, 2014.
_____. "Esotericism and the Scholastic Imagination: The Origins of Esoteric Practice in Christian Kataphatic Spirituality." *Correspondences* 4 (2016): 3–36.
_____. "Explaining the Esoteric Imagination: Towards a Theory of Kataphatic Practice." *Aries* 17, no. 1 (2017): 17–50.
_____. "Kabbalah Recreata." *Pomegranate: The International Journal of Pagan Studies* 9, no. 2 (2007): 132–53.
_____. "Magic Naturalized? Negotiating Science and Occult Experience in Aleister Crowley's Scientific Illuminism." *Aries* 8, no. 2 (2008): 139–65.
_____. "Patterns of Magicity: A Review of *Defining Magic: A Reader.*" *Correspondences* 3 (2015): 127–40.
_____. "Pondering Imponderables: Occultism in the Mirror of Late Classical Physics." *Aries* 11, no. 2 (2011): 129–65.
_____. *The Problem of Disenchantment: Scientific Naturalism and Esoteric Discourse, 1900–1939.* Leiden: Brill, 2014.
Atwood, Mary Anne. *A Suggestive Inquiry into the Hermetic Mystery; with a Dissertation on the More Celebrated of the Alchemical Philosophers; Being an Attempt toward the Recovery of the Ancient Experiment of Nature.* London: Trelawney Saunders, 1850.
Bacci, Roberto. "Transmutation and Homogenization of Consciousness in Italian Esotericism During the Fascist Period: Mario Manlio Rossi's *Spaccio Dei Maghi* and Julius Evola's *Maschera E Volto Dello Spiritualismo Contemporaneo.*" *Correspondences* 2, no. 2 (2014): 189–213.
Baumann, Gerd. "Grammars of Identity/Alterity: A Structural Approach." In *Grammars of Identity/Alterity: A Structural Approach*, edited by Gerd Baumann and Andre Gingrich, 18–50. New York: Berghahn Books, 2006.
Beaumont, Ernest. "Charles Williams and the Power of Eros." *The Dublin Review*, no. 479 (Spring 1959): 61–74.
Becker, Howard S., Robert R. Faulkner, and Barbara Kirshenblatt-Gimblett, eds. *Art*

from Start to Finish: Jazz, Painting, Writing, and Other Improvisations. Chicago: University of Chicago Press, 2006.

Beitchman, Philip. *Alchemy of the Word: Cabala of the Renaissance*. Albany: State University of New York Press, 1998.

Bender, C.J. "Touching the Transcendent: Rethinking Religious Experience in the Sociological Study of Religion." In *Everyday Religion: Observing Modern Religious Lives*, edited by N.T. Ammermann, 201–18. Oxford: Oxford University Press, 2007.

Berridge, E.W. (as V. H. Fra. Resurgam). "Flying Roll No. 24." In *Astral Projection, Ritual Magic, and Alchemy: Golden Dawn Material by S.L. Macgregor Mathers and Others*, edited by Francis King, 276–78. Rochester, VT: Destiny, 1987.

———. "Flying Roll No. 5: Some Thoughts on the Imagination." In *Astral Projection, Ritual Magic, and Alchemy: Golden Dawn Material by S.L. Macgregor Mathers and Others*, edited by Francis King, 47–51. Rochester, VT: Destiny, 1987.

Blavatsky, H. P. *Collected Writings, Volume VIII, 1887*. Wheaton, IL: The Theosophical Publishing House, 1966.

———. *Studies in Occultism*. London: Sphere, 1974.

Bleiler, Everett F. "Johann Valentin Andreae, Fantasist and Utopist." *Science Fiction Studies* 35, no. 1 (Mar 2009): 1–30.

Bloom, Clive. "Introduction: Death's Own Backyard." In *Gothic Horror: A Reader's Guide from Poe to King and Beyond*, edited by Clive Bloom, 1–22. London: Macmillan, 1998.

Bogdan, Henrik. "Freemasonry and Western Esotericism." In *Handbook of Freemasonry*, edited by Henrik Bogdan and Jan A.M. Snoek, 277–305. Leiden: Brill, 2014.

———. "New Perspectives on Western Esotericism." *Nova Religio: The Journal of Alternative and Emergent Religions* 13, no. 3 (2010): 97–105.

———. *Western Esotericism and Rituals of Initiation*. Albany, NY: State University of New York Press, 2007.

Bogdan, Henrik, and Martin Starr, eds. *Aleister Crowley and Western Esotericism*. Oxford: Oxford University Press, 2012.

Bosky, Bernadette. "Charles Williams: Occult Fantasies/Occult Fact." In *Modes of the Fantastic: Selected Essays from the Twelfth International Conference on the Fantastic in the Arts*, edited by Robert A. Latham and Robert A. Collins, 176–85. London: Greenwood, 1995.

———. "Even an Adept: Charles Williams and the Order of the Golden Dawn." *Mythlore* 13, no. 2 (Winter 1986): 25–34.

———. "The Inner Lives of Characters and Readers: Affective Stylistics in Charles Williams's Fiction." In *The Rhetoric of Vision: Essays on Charles Williams*, edited by Charles A. Huttar and Peter J. Schakel, 59–72. London: Associated University Presses, 1996.

Bown, Nicola, Carolyn Burdett, and Pamela Thurschwell. Introduction to *the Victorian Supernatural*, 1–19. Edited by Nicola Bown, Carolyn Burdett and Pamela Thurschwell. Cambridge: Cambridge University Press, 2004.

Budd, F.E. "English Literature and the Occult." In *A Survey of the Occult*, edited by Julian Franklyn, 84–95. London: Arthur Barker, 1935.

Bullock, Percy (as L.O.). "Flying Roll No. 27: The Principia of Theurgia or the Higher

BIBLIOGRAPHY

Magic." In *Astral Projection, Ritual Magic and Alchemy: Golden Dawn Material by S.L. Macgregor Mathers and Others*, edited by Francis King, 167–74. Rochester, VT: Destiny, 1987.

Bulwer-Lytton, Edward. *Zanoni: A Rosicrucian Tale*. 1842. Reprint, Blauvelt, NY: Rudolf Steiner, 1971.

Bulwer-Lytton, Victor. *The Life of Edward Bulwer, First Lord Lytton*. 2 vols. London: Macmillan, 1913.

Buntz, Herwig. "Alchemy III: 12th/13th–15th Century." In *Dictionary of Gnosis and Western Esotericism*, edited by Wouter J. Hanegraaff, 35–41. Leiden: Brill, 2006.

Burke, Edmund. *A Philosophical Enquiry into the Origin of Our Ideas of the Sublime and the Beautiful*. London: Dodsley, 1764.

Butler, Alison. "Arthur Edward Waite." In *The Occult World*, edited by Christopher H. Partridge, 283–87. New York: Routledge, 2015.

———. "Dion Fortune and the Society of the Inner Light." In *The Occult World*, edited by Christopher Partridge, 315–19. New York: Routledge, 2015.

———. "Magical Beginnings: The Intellectual Origins of the Victorian Occult Revival." *Limina* 9 (2003): 78–95.

———. *Victorian Occultism and the Making of Modern Magic: Invoking Tradition*. New York: Palgrave Macmillan, 2011.

Butts, Mary. *The Journals of Mary Butts*. Edited by Natalie Blondel. New Haven, CT: Yale University Press, 2002.

Byron, Glennis, and Dale Townshend, eds. *The Gothic World*. London: Routledge, 2014.

Calian, George-Florin. "*Alkimia Operativa* and *Alkimia Speculativa*: Some Modern Controversies on the Historiography of Alchemy." In *Annual of Medieval Studies at Ceu*, edited by Katalin Szende and Judith A. Rasson, 166–90. Budapest: Archaeolingua Foundation and Publishing House, 2010.

Caron, Richard. "Alchemy V: 19th–20th Century." In *Dictionary of Gnosis and Western Esotericism*, edited by Wouter J. Hanegraaff, 51–56. Leiden: Brill, 2006.

Carpenter, Humphrey. *The Inklings: C.S. Lewis, J.R R. Tolkien, Charles Williams, and Their Friends*. London: Allen and Unwin, 1978.

Carr, David. "Narrative and the Real World: An Argument for Continuity." *History and Theory* 25, no. 2 (May 1986): 117–31.

Carus, Paul. "The Oracle of Yahveh: The Urim and Thummin, the Ephod, and the Breastplate of Judgement." *The Monist* 17, no. 3 (1907): 365–88.

Cavaliero, Glen. *Charles Williams: Poet of Theology*. London: Macmillan, 1983.

———. Introduction to *Witchcraft*, by Charles Williams, vii–xviii. Wellingborough, Northamptonshire: Aquarian, 1980.

———. Review of *Alchemy and Integration*, by Gavin Ashenden. *The C.S. Lewis Chronicle* 5, no. 5 (2008): 46–51.

———. *The Supernatural and English Fiction*. Oxford: Oxford University Press, 1995.

Childs, Donald J. *T.S. Eliot: Mystic, Son and Lover*. London: Athlone Press, 1997.

Chryssides, George D. "The New Age." In *The Cambridge Companion to New Religious Movements*, edited by Olav Hammer and Mikael Rothstein, 247–62. Cambridge: Cambridge University Press, 2012.

Clukey, Amy. "Enchanting Modernism: Mary Butts, Decadence, and the Ethics of Occultism." *Modern Fiction Studies* 60, no. 1 (Spring 2014): 78–107.
Coghill, Nevill. "The Approach to English." In *Light on C.S. Lewis*, edited by Jocelyn Gibbs, 51–66. London: Geoffrey Bles, 1965.
Cohn-Sherbok, Dan, and Lavinia Cohn-Sherbok. *Jewish and Christian Mysticism: An Introduction*. New York: Continuum, 1994.
Colquhoun, Ithell. *Sword of Wisdom: Macgregor Mathers and the Golden Dawn*. New York: Putnam, 1975.
Copenhaver, Brian P. *Hermetica*. Cambridge: Cambridge University Press, 1992.
Coudert, Allison P. "Alchemy IV: 16th–18th Century." In *Dictionary of Gnosis and Western Esotericism*, edited by Wouter J. Hanegraaff, 42–51. Leiden: Brill, 2006.
_____. "Christian Kabbalah." In *Jewish Mysticism and Kabbalah: New Insights and Scholarship*, edited by Frederick E. Greenspahn, 159–74. New York: New York University Press, 2011.
Covino, William A. *Magic, Rhetoric, and Literacy: An Eccentric History of the Composing Imagination*. Albany: State University of New York Press, 1994.
Crain, Caleb. "What We're Reading: Charles Williams." *New Yorker*, 13 March 2013. http://www.newyorker.com/books/page-turner/what-were-reading-charles-williams.
Crisciani, Chiara. "The Conception of Alchemy as Expressed in the Pretiosa Margarita Novella of Petrus Bonus of Ferrara." *Ambix* 20, no. 3 (1973): 165–81.
Crowley, Aleister. *Magick in Theory and Practice*. New York: Castle, 1971.
_____. *Moonchild*. London: Sphere, 1972.
_____. *The Book of the Law: Liber Al Vel Legis*. York Beach, ME: Red Wheel/Weiser, 2009.
_____. "The Temple of Solomon the King (Book II--Continued)." *The Equinox* 1, no. 3 (March 1910): 133–280.
_____. "The Temple of Solomon the King." *The Equinox* 1, no. 5 (March 1911): 65–120.
Curtis, Jan. "Charles Williams: His Reputation in the English-Speaking World from 1917 to 1985." *Inklings-Jahrbuch* 9 (1991): 127–64.
Dan, Joseph. *Kabbalah: A Very Short Introduction*. Oxford: Oxford University Press, 2006.
Darnton, Robert. *Mesmerism and the End of Enlightenment in France*. Cambridge, MA: Harvard University Press, 1968.
Davidson, Alice E. "Language and Meaning in the Novels of Charles Williams." In *The Rhetoric of Vision: Essays on Charles Williams*, edited by Charles A. Huttar and Peter J. Schakel, 44–58. London: Associated University Presses, 1996.
Davies, R.T. "Charles Williams and Romantic Experience." *Etudes Anglaises* 8, no. 4 (Oct–Dec 1955): 289–98.
de Steiger, Isabelle. "The Hermetic Mystery 2." *The Journal of the Alchemical Society* 2, no. 7 (November 1913): 17–23.
Decker, Ronald, and Michael Dummett. *A History of the Occult Tarot, 1870–1970*. London: Duckworth, 2002.
Deveney, John Patrick. *Paschal Beverly Randolph*. Albany, NY: State University of New York Press, 1997.
_____. "Spiritualism." In *Dictionary of Gnosis and Western Esotericism*, edited by Wouter

BIBLIOGRAPHY

J. Hanegraaff, 1074–82. Leiden: Brill, 2006.

Dionysius the Aeropagite. *The Celestial and Ecclesiastical Hiearchy*. Translated by Rev. John Parker. London: Skeffington, 1984.

Dodds, David Llewellyn. *Charles Williams*. Arthurian Poets. Woodbridge, Suffolk: Boydell, 1991.

———. "Continuity and Change in the Development of Charles Williams's Poetic Style." In *The Rhetoric of Vision: Essays on Charles Williams*, edited by Charles A. Huttar and Peter J. Schakel, 192–214. Lewisburg, VA: Bucknell University Press, 1996.

———. "Review Essay: Gavin Ashenden's *Charles Williams: Alchemy and Integration*." *Charles Williams Quarterly* 126 (Spring 2008): 30–50.

Drob, Sanford L. *Kabbalistic Metaphors: Jewish Mystical Themes in Ancient and Modern Thought*. Northvale, NJ: J. Aronson, 2000.

Duriez, Colin, and David Porter. *The Inklings Handbook: A Comprehensive Guide to the Lives, Thought and Writings of C.S. Lewis, J.R.R. Tolkien, Charles Williams, Owen Barfield and Their Friends*. London: Azure, 2001.

During, Simon. *Modern Enchantments: The Cultural Power of Secular Magic*. Cambridge, MA: Harvard University Press, 2002.

Dyrendal, Asbjørn, James R. Lewis, and Jesper Aa. Petersen. *The Invention of Satanism*. New York: Oxford University Press, 2016.

Eco, Umberto. *The Limits of Interpretation*. Bloomington: Indiana University Press, 1990.

Edighoffer, Roland. "Andreae, Johann Valentin." In *Dictionary of Gnosis and Western Esotericism*, edited by Wouter J. Hanegraaff, 72–75. Leiden: Brill, 2006.

———. "Rosicrucianism II: 18th Century." In *Dictionary of Gnosis and Western Esotericism*, edited by Wouter J. Hanegraaff, 1014–17. Leiden: Brill, 2006.

Eliot, T.S. "Dante's Beatrice: Knower, Known and Knowing." *Times Literary Supplement*, 24 July 1943, 358.

———. Preface to *All Hallows' Eve*, by Charles Williams. New York: Noonday, 1948.

———. "The Significance of Charles Williams." *Listener*, 19 December 1946, 894–95.

Ellmann, Richard. *Yeats: The Man and the Masks*. New York: Norton, 1979.

Evans, Matthew. "Magnum Opus." *Lewis: Season 9*, 2015.

Faivre, Antoine. *Access to Western Esotericism*. Albany, NY: State University of New York Press, 1994.

———. *Theosophy, Imagination, Tradition: Studies in Western Esotericism*. Albany, NY: State University of New York Press, 2000.

Felski, Rita. *The Limits of Critique*. Chicago: The University of Chicago Press, 2015.

Ferguson, Christine. "Reading with the Occultists: Arthur Machen, A.E. Waite, and the Ecstasies of Popular Fiction." *Journal of Victorian Culture* (2016): 1–16.

Finlan, Stephen, and Vladimir Kharlamov. "Introduction." In *Theosis: Deification in Christian Theology*, edited by Stephen Finlan and Vladimir Kharlamov, 1–15. Cambridge: James Clarke, 2006.

Fleiger, Verlyn. "Time in the Stone of Suleiman." In *The Rhetoric of Vision: Essays on Charles Williams*, edited by Charles Adolph Huttar and Peter J. Schakel, 75–89. Lewisburg: Bucknell University Press, 1996.

BIBLIOGRAPHY

Forman, Robert K.C. *The Innate Capacity: Mysticism, Psychology and Philosophy*. New York: Oxford University Press, 1998.

Fortune, Dion. *Sane Occultism*. London: Aquarian, 1987.

———. "The Rationale of Magic." *London Forum (Incorporating The Occult Review)* 60, no. 3 (September 1934): 175–81.

———. *The Secrets of Doctor Taverner*. Wellingborough, Northamptonshire: The Aquarian Press, 1989.

Foucault, Michel. *The Order of Things*. London: Routledge, 2002.

Frater Deo in Vita Aeterna. "The Fellowship of the Rosy Cross: Its Founder and Its History." Website of the Fraternitas Rosae Crucis. http://fellowship.rosy-cross.org/history.

Frederick, Candice, and Sam McBride. *Women among the Inklings: Gender, C.S. Lewis, J.R.R. Tolkien, and Charles Williams*. London: Greenwood Press, 2001.

Gadamer, Hans-Georg. *Truth and Method*. Translated by Joel Weinsheimer and Donald G. Marshall. London: Sheed and Ward, 1999.

Galbreath, Robert. "Explaining Modern Occultism." In *The Occult in America: New Historical Perspectives*, edited by Howard Kerr and Charles L. Crow, 11–37. Chicago: University of Illinois Press, 1983.

Gauntlett, Edward. "Charles Williams and Magic." *Charles Williams Society Newsletter*, no. 106 (Spring 2003): 9–29.

———. "Charles Williams, Love & Shekinah." *Charles Williams Quarterly*, no. 126 (Spring 2008): 8–29.

Gibbons, B. J. *Spirituality and the Occult: From the Renaissance to the Modern Age*. London: Routledge, 2001.

Gikatilla, Joseph. *Gates of Light (Sha'are Orah)*. Translated by Avi Weinstein. London: Sage, 1994.

Gilbert, R. A. *A.E. Waite: A Bibliography*. Wellingborough, Northamptonshire: Aquarian Press, 1983.

———. *A. E. Waite: Magician of Many Parts*. Wellingborough: Crucible, 1987.

———. *The Golden Dawn: Twilight of the Magicians*. Wellingborough: Aquarian Press, 1983.

———. "The Masonic Career of Arthur Edward Waite." *Ars Quatuor Coronatorum* 99 (1986): 88–110.

———. "The One Thought That Was Not Untrue." In *Aleister Crowley and Western Esotericism*, edited by Henrik Bogdan and Martin Starr, 243–55. Oxford: Oxford University Press, 2012.

Gilhus, Ingvild Sælid, and Lisbeth Mikhaelsson. "Theosophy and Popular Fiction." In *Handbook of the Theosophical Current*, edited by Olav Hammer and Mikael Rothstein, 453–72. Leiden: Brill, 2013.

Gittings, Robert. "The Smell of Sulphur: 'The Lady's Not for Burning' Now." *Encounter* (Jan 1978).

Godwin, Joscelyn. *The Theosophical Enlightenment*. Albany, NY: State University of New York Press, 1994.

Goggin, Joyce. "*The Greater Trumps*: Charles Williams and the Metaphysics of Otherness." In *Tarot in Culture*, edited by Emily E. Auger, 411–38. Clifford, ON: Valleyhome, 2014.

Gorski, William T. *Yeats and Alchemy*. New York: SUNY Press, 1996.

Graf, Susan Johnston. *Talking to the Gods: Occultism in the Work of W.B. Yeats, Arthur Machen, Algernon Blackwood, and Dion Fortune*. New York: State University of New York Press, 2015.

Granholm, Kennet. *Dark Enlightenment: The Historical, Sociological, and Discursive Contexts of Contemporary Esoteric Magic*. Leiden: Brill, 2014.

———. "Locating the West: Problematizing the Western in Western Esotericism and Occultism." In *Occultism in a Global Perspective*, edited by Henrik Bogdan and Gordan Djurdjevic, 17–36. London: Acumen, 2013.

———. "Ritual Black Metal: Popular Music as Occult Mediation and Practice." *Correspondences* 1, no. 1 (2013): 5–33.

Grant, Kenneth. *Cults of the Shadow*. London: Frederick Muller, 1975.

Green, Arthur. *Introduction to the Zohar: Pritzker Edition*. Translated by Daniel C. Matt. Vol. 1. Stanford: Stanford University Press, 2004.

———. "Shekhinah, the Virgin Mary, and the Song of Songs: Reflections on a Kabbalistic Symbol in Its Historical Context." *AJS Review* 26 (2002): 1–52.

Greene, Liz. *Magi and Maggidim: The Kabbalah in British Occultism, 1860–1940*. Sophia Centre Press, 2012.

Greenwood, Susan. "Gender and Power in Magical Practices." In *Beyond New Age: Exploring Alternative Spirituality*, edited by Steven Sutcliffe and Marion Bowman, 137–54. Edinburgh: Edinburgh University Press, 2000.

Groom, Nick. *The Gothic: A Very Short Introduction*. Oxford: Oxford University Press, 2012.

Gruber, Bettina, ed. *Erfahrung und System: Mystik und Esoterik in der Literatur der Moderne*. Opladen: Verlag für Sozialwissenschaften, 1997.

Gunn, Joshua. "An Occult Poetics, or, the Secret Rhetoric of Religion." *Rhetoric Society Quarterly* 34, no. 2 (2004): 29–51.

Haage, Bernard D. "Alchemy II: Antiquity–12th Century." In *Dictionary of Gnosis and Western Esotericism*, edited by Wouter J. Hanegraaff, 16–24. Leiden: Brill, 2006.

Hadfield, Alice Mary. *An Introduction to Charles Williams*. London: Robert Hale, 1959.

———. *Charles Williams: An Exploration of His Life and Work*. Oxford: Oxford University Press, 1983.

———. "Introduction: The Writing of *Outlines of Romantic Theology*." In *Outlines of Romantic Theology*, edited by Alice M. Hadfield, vii–xiv. Berkeley, CA: Apocryphile, 2005.

Hammer, Olav. *Claiming Knowledge: Strategies of Epistemology from Theosophy to the New Age*. Leiden: Brill, 2001.

Hanegraaff, Wouter J. "Alan Moore's *Promethea*: Countercultural Gnosis and the End of the World." *Gnosis: Journal of Gnostic Studies* 1 (2016): 234–58.

———, ed. *Dictionary of Gnosis and Western Esotericism*. Leiden: Brill, 2006.

———. *Esotericism and the Academy: Rejected Knowledge in Western Culture*. Cambridge: Cambridge University Press, 2012.

BIBLIOGRAPHY

———. "Forbidden Knowledge: Anti-Esoteric Polemics and Academic Research." *Aries* 5, no. 2 (2005): 225–54.

———. Foreword to *Aleister Crowley and Western Esotericism*, edited by Henrik Bogdan and Martin Starr, vii–x. Oxford: Oxford University Press, 2012.

———. "How Magic Survived the Disenchantment of the World." *Religion* 33, no. 4 (2003): 357–80.

———. "Jewish Influneces V: Occultist Kabbalah." In *Dictionary of Gnosis and Western Esotericism*, 644–47. Leiden: Brill, 2006.

———. "Magic V: 18th–20th Century." In *Dictionary of Gnosis and Western Esotericism*, edited by Wouter J. Hanegraaff, 738–44. Leiden: Brill, 2006.

———. *New Age Religion and Western Culture: Esotericism in the Mirror of Secular Thought.* Albany, NY: State University of New York Press, 1998.

———. "Romanticism and the Esoteric Connection." In *Gnosis and Hermeticism from Antiquity to Modern Times*, edited by Roelof Van den Broek and Wouter J. Hanegraaff, 237–68. New York: State University of New York Press, 1998.

———. "The Beginnings of Occultist Kabbalah: Adolphe Franck and Eliphas Lévi." In *Kabbalah and Modernity: Interpretations, Transformations, Adaptations*, edited by Marco Pasi, Kocku von Stuckrad, and Boaz Huss, 107–28. Leiden: Brill, 2010.

———. "The Notion of 'Occult Sciences' in the Wake of the Enlightenment." In *Aufklärung Und Esoterik: Wege in Die Moderne*, edited by Monika Neugebauer-Wolk et al., 73–95. Berlin: De Gruyter, 2013.

———. "The Power of Ideas: Esotericism, Historicism, and the Limits of Discourse." *Religion* 43, no. 2 (2013): 252–73.

———. "The Trouble with Images: Anti-Image Polemics and Western Esotericism." In *Polemical Encounters: Esoteric Discourse and Its Others*, edited by Olav Hammer and Kocku von Stuckrad, 107–36. Leiden: Brill, 2007.

———. *Western Esotericism: A Guide for the Perplexed.* New York: Continuum International, 2013.

Harper, George Mills. *Yeats's Golden Dawn.* London: Macmillan, 1974.

Harrison, M. John. "M. John Harrison's Top Ten Books." *Guardian*, 28 October 2002.

Heath-Stubbs, John. *Charles Williams.* London: Longmans, 1955.

Henderson, Kerryl Lynne. "'It Is Love That I Am Seeking': Charles Williams and the Silver Stair." In *Charles Williams: A Celebration*, edited by Briane Horne, 131–52. Leominster, Herefordshire: Fowler Wright, 1995.

Heppenstall, Rayner. "Books in General." *New Statesman and Nation*, 21 May 1949, 532–34.

Higgins, Sørina. "The Matter of Logres: Arthuriana and the Inklings." In *The Inklings and King Arthur: J.R.R. Tolkien, Charles Williams, C.S. Lewis and Owen Barfield on the Matter of Britain*, edited by Sørina Higgins, 25–60. Berkeley, CA: Apocryphile, 2017.

Hillegas, Mark Robert, ed. *Shadows of Imagination: The Fantasies of C.S. Lewis, J.R.R. Tolkien, and Charles Williams.* Carbondale, IL: Southern Illinois University Press, 1979.

Hitchcock, Ethan Allen. *Remarks Upon Alchemy and the Alchemists.* Boston: Crosby, Nichols, 1857.

BIBLIOGRAPHY

Hogle, Jerrold E. "Introduction: The Gothic in Western Culture." In *The Cambridge Companion to Gothic Fiction*, edited by Jerrold E. Hogle, 1–20. Cambridge: Cambridge University Press, 2002.

Hooper, Walter, ed. *The Collected Letters of C.S. Lewis, Volume II*. New York: Harper Collins, 2004.

Howard, Thomas. *The Novels of Charles Williams*. New York: Oxford University Press, 1983.

Howe, Ellic, ed. *The Alchemist of the Golden Dawn: The Letters of the Revd W.A. Ayton to F.L. Gardner and Others, 1886–1905*. Wellingborough, Northamptonshire: Aquarian Press, 1985.

———. *The Magicians of the Golden Dawn: A Documentary History of a Magical Order 1887–1923*. Wellingborough: Aquarian, 1985.

Huss, Boaz. "The Mystification of Kabbalah and the Myth of Jewish Mysticism." *Pe'amim* 110 (2007): 9–30.

———. "Translations of the Zohar: Historical Contexts and Ideological Frameworks." *Correspondences* 4 (2016): 81–128.

Huttar, Charles A. "Arms and the Man: The Place of Beatrice in Charles Williams's Romantic Theology." In *Charles Williams: A Celebration*, edited by Brian Horne, 61–97. Leominster, Herefordshire: Gracewing, 1995.

———. Introduction to *The Rhetoric of Vision: Essays on Charles Williams*, edited by Charles A. Huttar and Peter J. Schakel, 15–24. Lewisburg: Bucknell University Press, 1996.

Idel, Moshe. *Enchanted Chains: Techniques and Rituals in Jewish Mysticism*. Los Angeles: Cherub Press, 2005.

———. *Kabbalah and Eros*. New Haven, CT: Yale University Press, 2005.

———. *New Perspectives in Kabbalah*. London: Yale University Press, 1988.

Jackson, Sharon. "Toward an Analytical and Methodological Understanding of Actor-Network Theory." *Journal of Arts and Humanities* 4, no. 2 (2015): 29–44.

James, William. *The Varieties of Religious Experience: A Study in Human Nature*. London: Longmans, Green, 1902.

Johnston Graf, Susan. "The Occult Novels of Dion Fortune." *Journal of Gender Studies* 16, no. 1 (March 2007): 47–56.

Johnston, Jay. Keynote lecture for the Sixth International Conference of the European Society for the Study of Western Esotericism: Western Esotericism and Deviance, University of Erfurt, 1-3 June 2017.

Katz, Steven T. "Mystical Speech and Mystical Meaning." In *Mysticism and Language*, edited by Steven T. Katz, 3–41. Oxford: Oxford University Press, 1992.

———, ed. *Mysticism and Language*. Oxford: Oxford University Press, 1992.

Kerr, Howard. *Mediums, and Spirit-Rappers, and Roaring Radicals*. London: University of Illinois Press, 1972.

Kilcher, Andreas. "7 Epistemological Theses." In *Hermes in the Academy: Ten Years' Study of Western Esotericism at the University of Amsterdam*, edited by Wouter J. Hanegraaff and Joyce Pijnenburg, 143–48. Amsterdam: Amsterdam University Press, 2009.

———. *Ritual Magic in England: 1887 to the Present Day*. London: Neville Spearman, 1970.

BIBLIOGRAPHY

King, Francis, ed. *Astral Projection, Ritual Magic and Alchemy: Golden Dawn Material by S. L. MacGregor Mathers and Others.* Rochester, VT: Destiny, 1987.

King, Roma A. *The Pattern in the Web: The Mythical Poetry of Charles Williams.* Kent, OH: Kent State University Press, 1990.

———. "The Occult as Rhetoric in the Poetry of Charles Williams." In *The Rhetoric of Vision: Essays on Charles Williams*, edited by Charles A. Huttar and Peter J. Schakel, 165–78. Lewisburg: Bucknell University Press, 1996.

———, ed. *To Michal from Serge: Letters from Charles Williams to His Wife, Florence, 1939–1945.* Kent and London: Kent State University Press, 2002.

Kingsford, Anna, and Edward Maitland. *The Perfect Way: Or, the Finding of Christ.* London: Watkins, 1909.

Knight, Gareth. *The Magical World of Charles Williams.* Oceanside, CA: Sun Chalice Books, 2002.

Kren, Claudia. *Alchemy in Europe: A Guide to Research.* London: Garland, 1990.

Kripal, Jeffrey J. *Mutants and Mystics: Science Fiction, Superhero Comics, and the Paranormal.* Chicago: University of Chicago Press, 2011.

Kristeva, Julia. *Powers of Horror: An Essay on Abjection.* Translated by Leon S. Roudiez. New York: Columbia University Press, 1982.

Latour, Bruno. *An Inquiry into Modes of Existence: An Anthropology of the Moderns.* Translated by Catherine Porter. Cambridge, MA: Harvard University Press, 2013.

———. *Reassembling the Social: An Introduction to Actor-Network-Theory.* Oxford: Oxford University Press, 2005.

Leavis, F.R. *The Common Pursuit.* London: Hogarth, 1952.

Leijenhorst, Cees. "Steiner, Rudolf." In *Dictionary of Gnosis and Western Esotericism*, edited by Wouter J. Hanegraaff, 1084–1091. Leiden: Brill, 2006.

Lévi, Éliphas. *Dogme Et Rituel De La Haute Magie.* 2nd ed. 2 vols. Vol. 2, *Rituel.* Paris: Germer Bailliere, 1861.

———. *The Book of Splendours.* Wellingborough, Northamptonshire: Aquarian Press, 1983.

———. *The History of Magic.* Translated by Arthur Edward Waite. London: William Rider & Son, 1922.

———. *Transcendental Magic: Its Doctrine and Ritual, Part 2: The Ritual of Transcendental Magic.* Translated by Arthur Edward Waite. London: Rider, 1896.

Lewis, C.S. "Charles Walter Stansby Williams (1886–1945): An Obituary." *Oxford Magazine* 63 (24 March 1945): 265.

Linden, Stanton J., ed. *The Alchemy Reader: From Hermes Trismegistus to Isaac Newton.* Cambridge: Cambridge University Press, 2003.

Lindop, Grevel. "Charles Williams and His Contemporaries." In *Charles Williams and His Contemporaries*, edited by Suzanne Bray and Richard Sturch, 2–17. Newcastle upon Tyne: Cambridge Scholars, 2009.

———. *Charles Williams: The Third Inkling.* Oxford: Oxford University Press, 2015.

Luhrmann, T.M. *Persuasions of the Witch's Craft: Ritual Magic and Witchcraft in Present-Day England.* London: Picador, 1989.

BIBLIOGRAPHY

Machin, James. "Towards a Golden Dawn: Esoteric Christianity and the Development of Nineteenth-Century British Occultism." *Victorian* 1, no. 1 (2013): 1–13.

Mathers, Moina (as Vestigia Nulla Retrorsum). "Know Thyself." In *Astral Projection, Ritual Magic, and Alchemy: Golden Dawn Material by S.L. MacGregor Mathers and Others*, edited by Francis King, 151–59. Rochester, VT: Destiny, 1987.

Mathers, Moina MacGregor. Preface to *Kabbala Denudata: The Kabbalah Unveiled*, by Samuel Macgregor Mathers. Blackmask Online, 2002. http://www.hermetics.org/pdf/Mathers_Kabbalah_Unveiled.pdf.

Mathers, S.L. MacGregor (as G.H. Frater D.D.C.F.). "Flying Roll No. 11: Clairvoyance." In *Astral Projection, Ritual Magic, and Alchemy: Golden Dawn Material by S.L. MacGregor Mathers and Others*, edited by Francis King, 75–83. Rochester, VT: Destiny, 1987.

———. Introduction to *The Book of Abramelin the Mage*, xv-xl. London: John M. Watkins, 1900.

———, trans. *Kabbala Denudata: The Kabbalah Unveiled*. London: Kegan, 1926.

Matt, Daniel C. Translator's introduction to *The Zohar: Pritzker Edition*, ix-xix. Stanford: Stanford University Press, 2004.

McCalla, Arthur. "Saint-Martin." In *Dictionary of Gnosis and Western Esotericism*, edited by Wouter J. Hanegraaff, 1024–31. Leiden: Brill, 2006.

McCann, Andrew. *Popular Literature, Authorship and the Occult in Late Victorian Britain*. New York: Cambridge University Press, 2014.

McCorristine, Shane. "General Introduction." In *Spiritualism, Mesmerism and the Occult, 1800–1920—Apparitions, Spectral Illusions and Hallucinations*, edited by Shane McCorristine, ix-xxvii. London: Pickering and Chatto, 2012.

McIntosh, Christopher. *Eliphas Lévi and the French Occult Revival*. London: Rider, 1975.

———. "'Fraulein Sprengel' and the Origins of the Golden Dawn: A Surprising Discovery." *Aries* 11, no. 2 (2011): 249–58.

———. "The Alchemy of the Gold- und Rosenkreuz." Paper presented at the International Conference on the History of Alchemy, University of Groningen, 17–19 April 1989.

———. *The Rose Cross and the Age of Reason: Eighteenth-Century Rosicrucianism in Central Europe and Its Relationship to the Enlightenment*. Leiden: Brill, 1992.

———. *The Rosy Cross Unveiled: The History, Mythology and Rituals of an Occult Order*. Wellingborough: Aquarian Press, 1980.

McLaren, Scott. "Hermeticism and the Metaphysics of Goodness in the Novels of Charles Williams." *Mythlore*, nos. 3–4 (2006): 5–34.

———. "A Problem of Morality: Sacramentalism in the Early Novels of Charles Williams." *Renascence* 56, no. 2 (Winter 2004): 109–24.

McLaughlin, Richard. "Chasing the Grail in England." Review of *War in Heaven*, by Charles Williams. *Saturday Review*, 1 October 1949.

———. "Drama of Belief and Unbelief." Review of *Shadows of Ecstasy*, by Charles Williams. *Saturday Review*, 23 September 1950.

Mead, G.R.S. *Fragments of a Faith Forgotten*. London: Theosophical Publishing Society, 1900.

BIBLIOGRAPHY

———. "'The Quest'—Old and New: Retrospect and Prospect." *Quest* 17, no. 3 (April 1926): 289–307.

Medcalf, Stephen. "The Athanasian Principle in Williams's Use of Images." In *The Rhetoric of Vision: Essays on Charles Williams*, edited by Charles A. Huttar and Peter J. Schakel, 27–43. London: Associated University Presses, 1996.

Mehuest, Bertrand. "Animal Magnetism/Mesmerism." In *The Dictionary of Gnosis and Western Esotericism*, edited by Wouter J. Hanegraaff, 77–82. Leiden: Brill, 2006.

Mendlesohn, Farah. *Rhetorics of Fantasy*. Middletown, CT: Wesleyan University Press, 2008.

Merkur, Daniel. "The Study of Spiritual Alchemy: Mysticism, Gold-Making, and Esoteric Hermeneutics." *Ambix* 37, no. 1 (March 1990): 35–45.

Michael, Mike. *Actor-Network Theory: Trials, Trails and Translations*. London: Sage, 2017.

Mishra, Vijay. *The Gothic Sublime*. Albany: State University of New York Press, 1994.

Moore, R. Laurence. *In Search of White Crows: Spiritualism, Parapsychology, and American Culture*. New York: Oxford University Press, 1977.

Moorman, Charles. *Arthurian Triptych: Mythic Materials in Charles Williams, C.S. Lewis, and T.S. Eliot*. Berkeley: University of California Press, 1960.

Mordecai, Huw. "Charles Williams and the Occult." In *Charles Williams: A Celebration*, edited by Brian Horne, 265–91. Leominster, Herefordshire: Fowler Wright, 1995.

Morrisson, Mark S. *Modern Alchemy: Occultism and the Emergence of Atomic Theory*. Oxford: Oxford University Press, 2007.

Murray, Alex. "'This Light Was Pale and Ghostly': Stewart Home, Horror and the Gothic Destruction of 'London'." In *London Gothic: Place, Space and the Gothic Imagination*, edited by Lawrence Phillips and Anne Witchard, 65–79. London: Continuum, 2010.

Nagy, Paul. "Charles Williams, A.E. Waite, and the Secret of *The Greater Trumps*." *Tarot Hermeneutics: Exploring how We Create Meaning with the Tarot*. http://tarothermeneutics.com/tarotliterature/chaswilliams.html.

Neilson, Keith. "Dennis Wheatley." In *Supernatural Fiction Writers*, edited by E.F. Bleiler, 623–29. New York: Charles Scribner's Sons, 1985.

Nelson, Victoria. *Gothika*. London: Harvard University Press, 2012.

———. *The Secret Life of Puppets*. Cambridge, MA: Harvard University Press, 2001.

Newman, Barbara. "Charles Williams and the Companions of the Co-Inherence." *Spiritus: A Journal of Christian Spirituality* 9, no. 1 (Spring 2009): 1–26.

Newman, William R. "Brian Vickers on Alchemy and the Occult: A Response." *Perspectives on Science* 17, no. 4 (Winter 2009): 482–506.

Newman, William R., and Anthony Grafton. "Introduction: The Problematic Status of Astrology and Alchemy in Premodern Europe." In *Secrets of Nature: Astrology and Alchemy in Early Modern Europe*, edited by William R. Newman and Anthony Grafton. Cambridge, MA: MIT Press, 2001.

Newman, William R., and Lawrence M. Principe. "Alchemy vs. Chemistry: The Etymological Origins of a Historiographic Mistake." *Early Science and Medicine* 3, no. 1 (1998): 32–65.

Noakes, Richard. "The 'World of the Infinitely Little': Connecting Physical and

BIBLIOGRAPHY

Psychical Realities Circa 1900." *Studies in History and Philosophy of Science Part A* 39, no. 3 (2008): 323–34.

Nummedal, Tara E. "Words and Works in the History of Alchemy." *Isis* 102, no. 2 (June 2011): 330–37.

O'Callaghan, Sean. "The Theosophical Christology of Alice Bailey." In *Handbook of the Theosophical Current*, edited by Olav Hammer and Mikael Rothstein, 93–112. Leiden: Brill, 2013.

Oppenheim, Janet. *The Other World: Spiritualism and Psychical Research in England, 1850–1914*. Cambridge: Cambridge University Press, 1985.

Otto, Bernd-Christian. "Historicising 'Western Learned Magic'." *Aries—Journal for the Study of Westenr Esotericism* 16 (2016): 161–240.

Otto, Bernd-Christian, and Michael Stausberg. *Defining Magic: A Reader*. Sheffield: Equinox, 2013.

Owen, Alex. *The Place of Enchantment: British Occultism and the Culture of the Modern*. London: University of Chicago Press, 2004.

Partridge, Christopher H. *The Re-Enchantment of the West: Alternative Spiritualities, Sacralization, Popular Culture, and Occulture*. 2 vols. London: T & T Clark International, 2004.

Pasi, Marco. *Aleister Crowley and the Temptation of Politics*. Durham: Acumen, 2014.

———. "The Knight of Spermatophagy: Penetrating the Mysteries of Georges Le Clément De Saint-Marq." In *Hidden Intercourse: Eros and Sexuality in the History of Western Esotericism*, edited by Wouter J. Hanegraaff and Jeffrey Kripal, 369–400. Leiden: Brill, 2008.

———. "The Modernity of Occultism." In *Hermes in the Academy: Ten Years' Study of Western Esotericism at the University of Amsterdam*, edited by Wouter J. Hanegraaff and Joyce Pijnenburg, 59–74. Amsterdam: Amsterdam University Press, 2009.

———. "Occultism." In *The Brill Dictionary of Religion*, edited by Kocku von Stuckrad, 1364–68. Leiden: Brill, 2006.

———. "Oriental Kabbalah and the Parting of East and West in the Early Theosophical Society." In *Kabbalah and Modernity: Interpretations, Transformations, Adaptations*, edited by Boaz Huss, Marco Pasi and Kocku von Stuckrad, 152–66. Leiden: Brill, 2010.

———. "The Varieties of Magical Experience: Aleister Crowley's Views on Occult Practice." *Magic, Ritual, and Witchcraft* 6, no. 2 (Winter 2011): 123–62.

Plaisance, Christopher. "Magic Made Modern?: Re-Evaluating the Novelty of the Golden Dawn's Magic." *Correspondences* 2, no. 2 (2014): 159–87.

Poller, Jake. "The Transmutations of Arthur Machen: Alchemy in 'The Great God Pan' and 'The Three Impostors'." *Literature and Theology* 29, no. 1 (2015): 18–32.

Popp-Baier, Ulrike. "Religious Experiences as Narrative: Reflections on the Advantages of a Narrative Approach." In *Religious Experience & Tradition*, edited by A. Budriunaite, 13–17. Kaunas: Vytautas Magnus University, 2012.

Portugal, Eustace. "Charles Williams." *Bookman*, March 1932, 314–15.

Principe, Lawrence M. "Alchemy I: Introduction." In *Dictionary of Gnosis and Western Esotericism*, edited by Wouter J. Hanegraaff, 12–16. Leiden: Brill, 2006.

BIBLIOGRAPHY

———. *The Aspiring Adept: Robert Boyle and His Alchemical Quest.* Princeton: Princeton University Press, 2000.

———. *The Secrets of Alchemy.* London: The University of Chicago Press, 2013.

Principe, Lawrence M., and William R. Newman. "Some Problems with the Historiography of Alchemy." In *Secrets of Nature: Astrology and Alchemy in Early Modern Europe*, edited by William R. Newman and Anthony Grafton, 385–433. Cambridge, MA: MIT Press, 2006.

Proudfoot, Wayne. *Religious Experience.* Berkeley: University of California Press, 1985.

Raine, Kathleen. *Yeats, the Tarot and the Golden Dawn.* Dublin: Dolmen Press, 1972.

Rapoport-Albert, Ada, and Theodore Kwasman. "Late Aramaic: The Literary and Linguistic Context of the Zohar." *Aramaic Studies* 4, no. 1 (2006): 5–19.

Ruska, Julius. *Tabula Smaragdina: Ein Beitrag zur Geschichte der hermetischen Literatur.* Heidelberg: Carl Winter, 1926.

Regardie, Israel. *The Complete Golden Dawn System of Magic.* 1st ed. 10 vols. Phoenix, AZ: Falcon Press, 1984.

———. *The Golden Dawn.* 4 vols. Chicago: Aries Press, 1939.

———. *The Philosopher's Stone.* London: Rider, 1938.

Reid, Sian. "As I Do Will, So Mote It Be: Magic as Metaphor in Neo-Pagan Witchcraft." *Magical Religion and Modern Witchcraft* (1996): 141–67.

Reilly, Robert James. *Romantic Religion: A Study of Owen Barfield, C.S. Lewis, Charles Williams and J.R.R. Tolkien.* Athens, GA: University of Georgia Press, 1971.

Ricoeur, Paul. "Life: A Story in Search of a Narrator." In *Reflection and Imagination: A Ricoeur Reader*, edited by Mario J. Valdes, 425-37. Toronto: Harvester Wheatsheaf, 1991.

———. "The Human Experience of Time and Narrative." In *Reflection and Imagination: A Ricoeur Reader*, edited by Mario J. Valdes. Toronto: Harvester Wheatsheaf, 1991.

Ridler, Anne. Introduction to *The Image of the City*, by Charles Williams, ix–lxxii. Berkley, CA: Apocryphile, 1958.

Ronsley, Joseph. *Yeats's Autobiography: Life as a Symbolic Pattern.* Cambridge, MA: Harvard University Press, 1968.

Roukema, Aren. "The Shadow of Anodos: Alchemical Symbolism in Phantastes." *North Wind: A Journal for George MacDonald Studies* 31 (2012): 48–63.

Florence Farr (as S.S.D.D.). "An Introduction to Alchemy and Notes." In *A Short Enquiry Concerning the Hermetic Art, by a Lover of Philalethes.* Collectanea Hermetica, 9–13. London: Theosophical Publishing Society, 1894.

Saler, Michael. "Modernity and Enchantment: A Historiographic Review." *American Historical Review* III, no. 3 (June 2006): 692–716.

———. "Rethinking Secularism: Modernity, Enchantment, and Fictionalism." 2013. http://blogs.ssrc.org/tif/2013/12/20/modernity-enchantment-and-fictionalism/.

Samuleson, David N. "Charles Williams." In *Supernatural Fiction Writers*, edited by E.F. Bleiler, 631–38. New York: Charles Scribner's Sons, 1985.

Scheper, George L. "The Cessation of Rhetoric." In *The Rhetoric of Vision: Essays on Charles Williams*, edited by Charles A. Huttar and Peter J. Schakel, 132–61. Lewisburg: Bucknell University Press, 1996.

BIBLIOGRAPHY

Scholem, Gershom. *Kabbalah*. New York: Meridian, 1990.

———. *Major Trends in Jewish Mysticism*. 3rd ed. New York: Schocken, 1974.

———. Review of *The Holy Kabbalah*, by A.E. Waite. *Orientalistische Literaturzeitung* 7 (1931): 633–38.

Shideler, Mary M. *Theology of Romantic Love: A Study in the Writings of Charles Williams*. Grand Rapids, MI: Eerdmans, 1966.

Singer, Irving. *Courtly and Romantic*. Vol. 2 of *The Nature of Love*. 3 vols. Cambridge, MA: MIT Press, 2009.

Stableford, Brian M. *Historical Dictionary of Fantasy Literature*. Lanham, MD: Scarecrow Press, 2005.

Stark, Rodney, and William Sims Bainbridge. *A Theory of Religion*. New Brunswick, NJ: Rutgers University Press, 1996.

Stevens, David. *The Gothic Tradition*. Cambridge: Cambridge University Press, 2000.

Stockhammer, Robert. "Rosicrucian Radioactivity: Alchemy around 1900." In *The Golden Egg: Alchemy in Art and Literature*, edited by Alexandra Lembert and Elmar Schenkel, 133–47. Cambridge, MA: Galda and Wilch, 2002.

Strube, Julian. "The 'Baphomet' of Eliphas Lévi: Its Meaning and Historical Context." *Correspondences* 4 (2016): 37–79.

Styers, Randall. "Magic and the Play of Power." In *Defining Magic: A Reader*, edited by Michael Stausberg and Bernd-Christian Otto, 255–62. Sheffield: Equinox, 2012.

———. *Making Magic: Religion, Magic, and Science in the Modern World*. Oxford: Oxford University Press, 2004.

Surette, Leon. *The Birth of Modernism: Ezra Pound, T.S. Eliot, W.B. Yeats, and the Occult*. Montreal: McGill-Queen's University Press, 1993.

Teeter Dobbs, Betty Jo. *The Foundations of Newton's Alchemy: Or, 'The Hunting of the Greene Lyon'*. Cambridge: Cambridge University Press, 1975.

Tilton, Hereward. "Alchymia Archetypica: Theurgy, Inner Transformation and the Historiography of Alchemy." *Quaderni di Studi Indo-Mediterranei* 5 (2012): 179–215.

———. *The Quest for the Phoenix: Spiritual Alchemy and Rosicrucianism in the Work of Count Michael Maier (1569–1622)*. Berlin: Walter de Gruyter, 2003.

Tirosh-Samuelson, Hava. "Gender in Jewish Mysticism." In *Jewish Mysticism and Kabbalah: New Insights and Scholarship*, edited by Frederick E. Greenspahn, 191–230. New York: New York University Press, 2011.

Todorov, Tzvetan. *The Fantastic: A Structural Approach to a Literary Genre*. Ithaca: Cornell University Press, 1980.

Underhill, Evelyn. *The Column of Dust*. London: Methuen, 1909.

Urang, Gunnar. *Shadows of Heaven: Religion and Fantasy in the Writing of C.S. Lewis, Charles Williams, and J.R.R. Tolkien*. Philadelphia: Pilgrim Press, 1971.

Urban, Hugh. "The Yoga of Sex: Tantra, Orientalism and Sex Magic in the Ordo Templi Orientis." In *Hidden Intercourse: Eros and Sexuality in the History of Western Esotericism*, edited by Wouter J. Hanegraaff and Jeffrey Kripal, 401–44. Leiden: Brill, 2008.

Vaughan, Thomas. "Anima Magica Abscondita: Or a Discourse of the Universal Spirit of Nature." In *The Works of Thomas Vaughan: Eugenius Philalethes*, edited by Arthur Edward Waite, 63–118. London: Theosophical Publishing House, 1919.

BIBLIOGRAPHY

Versluis, Arthur. *Magic and Mysticism: An Introduction to Western Esotericism*. Plymouth: Rowman and Littlefield, 2007.

Vickers, Brian. "The 'New Historiography' and the Limits of Alchemy." *Annals of Science* 65, no. 1 (2008): 127–56.

von Stuckrad, Kocku. *The Scientification of Religion: An Historical Study of Discursive Change, 1800–2000*. Berlin: Walter de Gruyter, 2014.

———. *Western Esotericism: A Brief History of Secret Knowledge*. London: Equinox, 2005.

Voss, Karen-Claire. "Spiritual Alchemy: Interpreting Representative Texts and Images." In *Gnosis and Hermeticism: From Antiquity to Modern Times*, edited by Roelof Van den Broek and Wouter J. Hanegraaff, 147–82. Albany, NY: State University of New York Press, 1998.

Waite, A.E. (as Grand Orient). *A Manual of Cartomancy*. 4th ed. London: William Rider and Son, 1909.

Waite, Arthur Edward. *Azoth: Or, the Star in the East*. London: The Theosophical Publishing Society, 1893.

———. *A Book of Mystery and Vision*. London: Philip Wellby, 1902.

———. "A French Method of Fortune-Telling by Cards." In *Manual of Cartomancy and Occult Divination*. London: Rider, 1912.

———. *Lives of Alchemystical Philosophers*. London: George Redway, 1888.

———. "A New Light of Mysticism." *Light* 8, no. 402 (15 September 1888): 461–62.

———. *Shadows of Life and Thought*. London: Selwyn & Blount, 1938.

———. *Studies in Mysticism and Certain Aspects of the Secret Tradition*. London: Hodder and Stoughton, 1906.

———. *The Book of Ceremonial Magic*. Forgotten Books, 2010. http://www.forgottenbooks.org/info/9781605065762.

———. "The Canon of Criticism in Respect of Alchemical Literature." *The Journal of the Alchemical Society* 1, no. 2 (February 1913): 17–32.

———. "The Ceremony of Admission to the Grade of Adeptus Exemptus, 7=4." Amsterdam: Bibliotheca Philosophica Hermetica, A.E. Waite Collection, 1916.

———. "The Ceremony of Admission to the Grade of Adeptus Major, 6=5." Amsterdam: Bibliotheca Philosophica Hermetica, A.E. Waite Collection, 1916.

———. "The Ceremony of Advancement in the Grade of Philosophus, 4=7." Amsterdam: Bibliotheca Philosophica Hermetica, A.E. Waite Collection, 1917.

———. "The Ceremony of Advancement in the Grade of Practicus, 3=8." Amsterdam: Bibliotheca Philosophica Hermetica, A.E. Waite Collection, 1916.

———. "The Ceremony of Advancement in the Grade of Theoreticus, 2=9." Amsterdam: Bibliotheca Philosophica Hermetica, A.E. Waite Collection, 1916.

———. "The Ceremony of Advancement in the Grade of Zelator, 1=10." Amsterdam: Bibliotheca Philosophica Hermetica, A.E. Waite Collection, 1916.

———. "The Ceremony of Consecration on the Threshold of Sacred Mystery for the Watchers of the Holy House." Amsterdam: Bibliotheca Philosophica Hermetica, A.E. Waite Collection, 1926.

———. "The Ceremony of Contemplation on the Further Side of the Portal Which Is

BIBLIOGRAPHY

———. 0=0 in Supernis." Amsterdam: Bibliotheca Philosophica Hermetica, A.E. Waite Collection, 1922.

———. "The Ceremony of Reception in the Portal of the Fourth Order." Amsterdam: Bibliotheca Philosophica Hermetica, A.E. Waite Collection, 1916.

———. "The Ceremony of Reception in the Portal of the Third Order, Being the Second Portal Grade." Amsterdam: Bibliotheca Philosophica Hermetica, A.E. Waite Collection, 1916.

———. "The Ceremony of Reception into the Grade of Neophyte, 0=0." Amsterdam: Bibliotheca Philosophica Hermetica, A.E. Waite Collection, 1916.

———. *The Doctrine and Literature of the Kabalah*. London: The Theosophical Publishing Society, 1902.

———. "The Great Symbols of the Tarot." *The Occult Review* 43, no. 1 (1926): 11–19.

———. *The Hidden Church of the Holy Graal*. London: Rebman, 1909.

———. *The Holy Kabbalah*. London: Williams and Norgate, 1929.

———. "The Installation of a Master of the Temple in the Worlds of Formation and Action." Amsterdam: Bibliotheca Philosophica Hermetica, A.E. Waite Collection, n.d.

———. *The Life of Louis Claude De Saint-Martin, the Unknown Philosopher, and the Substance of His Transcendental Doctrine*. London: Philip Wellby, 1901.

———. *The Pictorial Key to the Tarot; Being Fragments of a Secret Tradition under the Veil of Divination*. London: William Rider & Son, 1911.

———. "The Pontifical Ceremony of Admission to the Grade of Adeptus Minor, 5=6." Amsterdam: Bibliotheca Philosophica Hermetica, A.E. Waite Collection, 1916.

———. "The Ritual of Return in Light." Amsterdam: Bibliotheca Philosophica Hermetica, A.E. Waite Collection, 1924.

———. *The Secret Doctrine in Israel: A Study of the Zohar and Its Connections*. New York: Occult Research Press, 1913.

———. *The Secret Tradition in Alchemy: Its Development and Records*. London: Kegan Paul, Trench, Trubner, 1926.

———. *The Secret Tradition in Freemasonry*. 2 Vols. London: Rebman, 1911.

———. "Thomas Vaughan and His *Lumen De Lumine*." In *The Hermetic Papers of A.E. Waite: The Unknown Writings of a Modern Mystic*, edited by R.A. Gilbert. Wellingborough, Northamptonshire: The Aquarian Press, 1987.

———. *The Way of Divine Union*. London: William Rider and Son, 1915.

———. "What Is Alchemy?" *The Unknown World* 1, no. 1 (15 August 1894): 7–11.

Wallraven, Miriam. *Women Writers and the Occult in Literature and Culture: Female Lucifers, Priestesses, and Witches*. New York: Routledge, 2015.

Walsh, Chad. "Charles Williams' Novels and the Contemporary Mutation of Consciousness." In *Myth, Allegory and Gospel*, edited by John Marwick Montgomery, 53–77. Minneapolis, MN: Bethany Fellowship, 1974.

Webb, Eugene. "The Alchemy of Man and the Alchemy of God: The Alchemist as Cultural Symbol in Modern Thought." *Religion and Literature* 17, no. 1 (Spring 1985): 47–60.

Weber, Max. "Science as a Vocation." Translated by H.H. Gerth and C. Wright Mills. In

BIBLIOGRAPHY

Max Weber: Essays in Sociology, edited by H.H. Gerth and C. Wright Mills. New York: Oxford University Press, 1949.

Wellby, Philip S. "Arthur Edward Waite, October 2nd, 1858–May 19th, 1942: A Personal Tribute." *The Occult Review* 69, no. 3 (July 1942): 103–5.

Wendling, Susan. "'Flesh Knows What Spirit Knows': Mystical Substitution in Charles Williams' Vision of Co-Inherence." *Inklings Forever* 6 (2008).

Westcott, William Wynn [as S.A.]. "Flying Roll No. 7: Alchemy." In *Astral Projection, Ritual Magic, and Alchemy: Golden Dawn Material by S.L. Macgregor Mathers and Others*, edited by Francis King, 179–91. Rochester, VT: Destiny Books, 1987.

———. (as Frater N.O.M.). "Flying Roll No. 5: Supplementary Remarks." In *Astral Projection, Ritual Magic, and Alchemy: Golden Dawn Material by S.L. Macgregor Mathers and Others*, edited by Francis King, 51. Rochester, VT: Destiny, 1987.

———. (as Frater N.O.M.). "Flying Roll No. 19: The Aims and Means of Adeptship." In *Astral Projection, Ritual Magic, and Alchemy: Golden Dawn Material by S.L. Macgregor Mathers and Others*, edited by Francis King, 115–21. Rochester, VT: Destiny, 1987.

Willard, Thomas. "Acts of the Companions: A.E. Waite's Fellowship and the Novels of Charles Williams." In *Secret Texts: The Literature of Secret Societies*, edited by Marie Mulvey Roberts and Hugh Ormsby-Lennon, 269–302. New York: AMS Press, 1995.

Williams, Charles. "Alexander Pope." In *The Image of the City*, edited by Anne Ridler, 42–45. Berkeley: Apocryphile, 2007.

———. *All Hallows' Eve*. New York: Noonday, 1948.

———. "Blake and Wordsworth." In *The Image of the City*, edited by Anne Ridler, 59–67. Berkeley, CA: Apocryphile, 2007.

———. *Descent into Hell*. Grand Rapids, MI: William B. Eerdmans, 1979.

———. *The English Poetic Mind*. Oxford: Clarendon Press, 1932.

———. "Et in Sempiternum Pereant." *London Mercury* 33, no. 194 (December 1935): 151–58.

———. *He Came Down from Heaven*. Grand Rapids, MI: William B. Eerdmans, 1984.

———. "Introduction." In *The Letters of Evelyn Underhill*, edited by Charles Williams. London: Longmans, 1943.

———. *Many Dimensions*. Grand Rapids, MI: William B. Eerdmans, 1979.

———. *Outlines of Romantic Theology*. Grand Rapids, MI: W.B. Eerdmans, 1990.

———. *Poetry at Present*. Oxford: Clarendon Press, 1930.

———. "Sensuality and Substance." In *The Image of the City and Other Essays*, edited by Anne Ridler, 68–75. Berkeley: Apocryphile, 2007.

———. *Shadows of Ecstasy*. Grand Rapids, MI: Eerdmans, 1978.

———. *The Descent of the Dove: A Short History of the Holy Spirit in the Church*. 1939. London: Collins, 1963.

———. *The Figure of Beatrice: A Study in Dante*. New York: Noonday Press, 1961.

———. *The Forgiveness of Sins*. London: Geoffrey Bles, 1942.

———. *The Greater Trumps*. Grand Rapids, MI: William B. Eerdmans, 1978.

———. "The Index of the Body." In *The Image of the City*, edited by Anne Ridler, 80–87. Berkeley: Apocryphile, 2007.

———. *The Place of the Lion*. Grand Rapids, MI: William B. Eerdmans, 1980.

———. "The Queen's Servant." In *Taliessen through Logres, the Region of the Summer Stars and Arthurian Torso*, 160–64. Grand Rapids, MI: Eerdmans, 1976.

———. "*Time and Tide* Review of *Shakespeare and the Popular Dramatic Tradition*, by S.L. Bethell, 1944." In *The Image of the City*, edited by Anne Ridler, 37–39. Berkeley: Apocryphile, 2007.

———. *War in Heaven*. Grand Rapids, MI: William B. Eerdmans, 1980.

———. "The Way of Affirmation." In *The Image of the City*, edited by Anne Ridler, 154–58. Berkeley: Apocryphile, 2007.

———. *Witchcraft*. Wellingborough: Aquarian Press, 1980.

Williams, Charles, and Lois Lang-Sims. *Letters to Lalage: The Letters of Charles Williams to Lois Lang-Sims*. Kent, OH: Kent State University Press, 1989.

Williams, Charles, and C. S. Lewis. *Arthurian Torso, Containing the Posthumous Fragment of the Figure of Arthur*. Oxford: Oxford University Press, 1948.

Williams, Michael Allen. *Rethinking "Gnosticism": An Argument for Dismantling a Dubious Category*. Princeton: Princeton University Press, 1996.

Wilson, Leigh. *Modernism and Magic: Experiments with Spiritualism, Theosophy and the Occult*. Edinburgh: Edinburgh University Press, 2013.

Winship, George P. Jr. "The Novels of Charles Williams." In *Shadows of Imagination: The Fantasies of C.S. Lewis, J.R.R. Tolkien, and Charles Williams*, edited by Mark Robert Hillegas, 111–24. Carbondale, IL: Southern Illinois University Press, 1979.

———. "This Rough Magic: The Novels of Charles Williams." *Yale Review* 40, no. 2 (1951): 285–96.

Winter, Alison. *Mesmerized: Powers of Mind in Victorian Britain*. Chicago: University of Chicago Press, 1998.

Wolfson, Elliot R. "Murmuring Secrets: Eroticism and Esotericism in Medieval Kabbalah." In *Hidden Intercourse: Eros and Sexuality in the History of Western Esotericism*, edited by Wouter J. Hanegraaff and Jeffrey J. Kripal, 65–109. Leiden: Brill, 2008.

Wood, Juliette. "The Celtic Tarot and the Secret Tradition: A Study in Modern Legend Making." *Folklore* 109 (1998): 15–24.

Yamane, David. "Narrative and Religious Experience." *Sociology of Religion* 61, no. 2 (2000): 171–90.

Yates, Francis. *The Rosicrucian Enlightenment*. London: Routledge, 2002.

Yeats, W.B. *Autobiographies*. London: Bracken, 1995.

———. *Per Amica Silentia Lunae*. London: MacMillan, 1918.

———. "The Symbolism of Painting." In *Essays and Introductions*. New York: Macmillan, 1961.

———. *The Trembling of the Veil*. London: T. Werner Laurie, 1922.

Zaleski, Phillip, and Carol Zaleski. *The Fellowship: The Literary Lives of the Inklings*. New York: Farrar, Straus and Giroux, 2015.

Zuber, Mike A. "Spiritual Alchemy from the Age of Jacob Boehme to Mary Anne Atwood, 1600–1900." PhD diss., Universiteit van Amsterdam, 2017.

ABOUT THE AUTHOR

Aren Roukema (PhD Birkbeck; MA Amsterdam) is a Sessional Lecturer and Honorary Fellow in the English Language and Literatures Department at the University of British Columbia (UBC). He has held postdoctoral fellowships at UBC and Birkbeck, University of London and has been Editor of *Correspondences: Journal for the Study of Esotericism* since 2013. Aren works at the intersections of popular culture and heterodox religions and sciences in the Anglosphere.

www.ingramcontent.com/pod-product-compliance
Lightning Source LLC
Chambersburg PA
CBHW031845220426
43663CB00006B/503